BLOWING ON THE WIND

BLOWING
ON
THE WIND

THE NUCLEAR
TEST BAN DEBATE

1954–1960

Robert A. Divine

NEW YORK • OXFORD UNIVERSITY PRESS • 1978

Copyright © 1978 by Oxford University Press, Inc.

Library of Congress Cataloging in Publication Data

Divine, Robert A
    Blowing on the wind.

    Bibliography: p.
    Includes index.
    1. United States—Foreign relations—1953–1961.
2. Atomic weapons—Testing. 3. United States—
Politics and government—1953–1961. 4. Atomic weapons
and disarmament. I. Title.
E835.D53   327′.174′0973   77-25057
ISBN 0-19-502390-0

Printed in the United States of America

For Doug, Lisa, Richard, and Kirk

PREFACE

The fifties must seem like the distant past to a younger generation that makes "Happy Days" the nation's top-rated television program. One conjures up the images of those pleasant years when teen-agers rocked around the clock and a whole country basked under the benign, grandfatherly gaze of Dwight D. Eisenhower. From the time Ike ended the Korean War in 1953 until he left office, the nation remained at peace and enjoyed a feeling of prosperity and abundance. Frequent international crises like those in Indo-China or Suez were soon forgotten, and the domestic downturns in 1954, 1958, and 1960 failed to shake the prevailing sense of economic well-being. The hectic events that followed—political assassinations, racial conflict, student rebellion, culminating in the Vietnam fiasco and the Watergate scandal—have made the fifties seem the golden age of the recent past, the last time when life in America appeared to be normal and desirable.

Nostalgia is always a deceptive guide to the past, and in this case our sentimental view of the 1950s disguises some grim realities. The continued repression of blacks, despite the Supreme Court school desegregation decision, the violations of civil liberties symbolized by Joe McCarthy's Red Scare, the rising unemployment rates, and the slowing down of economic growth in the late 1950s were all part of the malaise that John F. Kennedy capitalized on so effectively in the 1960 campaign. But by far the gravest problem of the 1950s was one that almost no one dared confront openly—the advent of the hydrogen bomb and the attendant possibility of global destruction. Kennedy spoke of winning the missile race and recapturing world prestige; other observers talked of regaining a sense of national purpose and seeking excellence in American life; only a few scientists and intellectuals, writing in the jargon of games theory in obscure journals, dealt with the true horror of the fifties.

The new weapon, developed by both the United States and the Soviet Union and quickly integrated into their arsenals, was over a thousand times more destructive than the original atom bomb. With the new intercontinental ballistic missiles, the two super powers had the capacity to destroy each other's cities, thereby wiping out both the industrial base of each nation and a large part of the population as well. It took a long time for an incredulous public to grasp this fact—not until the strident warnings of Herman Kahn's *On Thermonuclear War,* the fallout shelter scare, and the Cuban missile crisis of the early 1960s did the American people finally comprehend the reality of nuclear catastrophe.

In the interim, they focused on the more immediate and less terrifying issue of fallout from nuclear tests. Struggling to understand the perils of the H-bomb, they seized on the potential hazard from the by-products of testing that floated back to earth in indiscriminate fashion, falling on rich and poor, strong and weak, Communist and non-Communist alike. In the pages that follow, I examine the way the American people and their leaders responded to the fallout threat. I have tried to tell the story dispassionately, with sympathy for those who felt bewildered by a new and unknown danger and with understanding for those who went to extremes in reacting to the peril. As a citizen of a nation that has yet to control the arms race it let loose on the world in 1945, I realize that I have no right to judge others for their actions. It is easy to ridicule those who participated in the fallout debate of the 1950s; I have sought instead to present the dilemma they faced and describe the way they attempted to resolve it. It is a tale without heroes or villains, and sadly, without a happy ending. But at the very least it is a story of human beings trying desperately to come to grips with the nuclear age in which we all live.

In the course of the research and writing of this book, I benefited from the help and cooperation of many individuals. I wish to thank John Wickman, Susan Jackson, and Alan Kenyon at the Dwight D. Eisenhower Library for their many courtesies. Bernice B. Nichols, curator of the Swarthmore College Peace Collection, made my visit to that excellent archive both productive and pleasant. Richard G. Hewlett, though hampered by an inflexible security system, helped me use the small amount of unclassified AEC material held by the Energy Research and Development Administration.

I am indebted to several institutions for generous funding of this project. The award of a humanities fellowship by the Rockefeller Foundation, together with a matching grant from the University of Texas Research Institute, provided me with the time free from teaching duties to complete the study. The Dora Bonham Fund of the History Department at the University of Texas helped underwrite the costs of research travel.

Finally, I am indebted to several people who gave generously of their time and advice. Rebecca Horn typed the manuscript with care and concern. Ralph Lapp made a number of useful suggestions, and Ronald Steel provided a helpful critique of a portion of the manuscript. My greatest debt is to my wife, Barbara Renick Divine. She edited the entire manuscript and gave both the criticism and the encouragement that I needed to complete it.

Austin, Texas
August 1977   R.A.D.

CONTENTS

1. BRAVO 3
2. "The Terrible Truth" 36
3. Origins of the Test Ban Debate 58
4. The 1956 Campaign 84
5. "Radiation without Representation" 113
6. "A Magic Moment" 143
7. Reversal 174
8. Moratorium 213
9. Detection 241
10. The Fallout Scare 262
11. Threshold 281
    Epilogue 315
    Appendix 325
    Notes 333
    Essay on the Sources 367
    Bibliography 372
    Index 379

BLOWING ON THE WIND

1

BRAVO

At 6:45 a.m. the morning of March 1, 1954, the Atomic Energy Commission detonated a nuclear device at the tip of Namu Island in the Bikini Atoll. Code-named BRAVO, this blast was the first shot in the CASTLE series, originally scheduled for September 1953, but delayed to permit scientists at Los Alamos to perfect a more sophisticated weapon design. For several days Air Force meteorologists charted the wind patterns at various altitudes, on the lookout for either easterly winds, which might endanger the main base at Eniwetok, or westerlies, which could threaten Marshallese inhabitants on several nearby islands. At H minus 6 hours, they forecast favorable conditions for the next day but warned of a possible shift to northwest winds above 10,000 feet 24 hours later. "The forecasts of wind aloft for BRAVO were," a later AEC report noted, "approaching the limits of human ability which the art at present allows." [1]

The huge fireball lighted the predawn skies for over a hundred miles; observers at Kwajalein, 176 miles to the south, felt the blast as buildings shook noticeably. All went well, however, until 7:07 a.m. when members of the firing party in a concrete blockhouse 20 miles from Namu reported rapidly rising radiation. By 8:00 a.m., sailors on board the CASTLE task force ships *Bairoko* and *Philip* noticed gray ash falling from the sky. The alert commanders immediately ordered all hands below decks and followed prearranged procedures to wash down and thus decontaminate their ships. The radiation readings, as high as 25 roentgens an hour on the *Bairoko,* soon fell below dangerous levels. The Marshallese on the nearby islands of Rongerik, Rongelap, Ailinginae, and Utirik were not so fortunate. At Rongerik, amphibious aircraft evacuated 28 Americans from a weather and observation station on March 2, but the Navy was unable to remove 64 natives until the next day, more than 48 hours after the nuclear blast. By March 5, American ships had evacuated 236 natives from the four islands to hospitals at Kwajalein, where they received expert medical care. They had been exposed to between 14 and 175 roentgens (200 roentgens was normally considered the minimum fatal dose), and though none died, nearly all suffered painful radiation burns, loss of hair, and dangerous lowering of their blood counts. The 28 Americans from Rongerik received much lower doses, and after careful examination at Tripler Army Hospital in Honolulu they all returned to duty.[2]

Meanwhile, unknown to American officials, a small Japanese fishing boat, the *Fukuryu Maru,* had been casting its nets for tuna some 85 miles to the east of Bikini on the morning of March 1. Aware of an American notice not to enter an area of some 50,000 square miles around Eniwetok during the CASTLE test series, Captain Hisakichi Tsutsui and Fishing Master Yoshio Misaki had carefully kept their boat, the *Lucky Dragon* in translation, outside the danger zone. They knew they were not far from Bikini, but since no bomb tests had been held there following the 1946 CROSSROADS series, they felt no concern. While most of the crew were eating breakfast, one seaman, Shinzo Suzuki, went on deck to check the nets and while staring at the overcast sky, he was startled to see a dazzling light in the west gradually change from a yellow-white to red and then to flaming orange. He raced back to the cabin to announce, "The sun rises in the west." His shipmates feared that Suzuki

4

had seen a "pika-don," the Japanese word for an atomic explosion, but the absence of any sign of a mushroom against the clouds on the horizon reassured them. Within a few minutes they felt the shock wave from BRAVO, but after a brief moment of panic, they went back to work on their nets. Then about two hours later a slight drizzle began to fall, and with it a coating of sandy white ash. They brushed off the silvery flakes and continued to work and at the end of the day hosed down the ship to remove the last remnants of "the white sand from heaven." Disturbed by the day's unusual events, and disappointed by their meager catch of tuna, they decided to return to Japan, still unaware that they had been exposed to a dangerous dose of radiation.[3]

I

The American people had first learned of the forthcoming CASTLE series on January 8, 1954, when the Atomic Energy Commission announced that it would conduct "weapons tests of all categories" in the Pacific sometime in the spring. The AEC made no mention of a hydrogen bomb explosion, but knowledgeable observers speculated that the tests would include a thermonuclear bomb dropped from a plane. The government had never released any information about MIKE, the first H-bomb test at Eniwetok held on November 1, 1952, but rumors spread that the device used then had blown a hole a mile wide and 175 feet deep in the ocean floor. On the eve of BRAVO, *Newsweek* anticipated that by the end of the week, "man may have discovered that he now had the power to destroy mankind."[4]

The preparations for CASTLE had begun in January 1954, when Task Force 7 moved thousands of servicemen, technicians, and scientists to Eniwetok. The AEC had scheduled seven nuclear shots from March 1 through April 22—six large hydrogen detonations and one smaller atomic blast. The experience with MIKE in 1952 convinced the AEC that Eniwetok was too small for hydrogen explosions, so the six thermonuclear tests were scheduled for Bikini, vacant since the 1946 atomic tests, with the single atomic shot to be held on Eniwetok. The government announced the coordinates of the 50,000 square mile restricted area and warned all shipping to stay out. The AEC rejected the suggestion of one of its members that the United Nations be asked to send an observer to witness the tests; CASTLE was to be conducted in secret. AEC Chairman Lewis L. Strauss did invite President Eisenhower to fly out to observe one of the shots, but Ike declined, writing casually on Strauss's memo, "Don't believe I can do it." [5]

On March 1, a few hours after BRAVO, the AEC issued a terse announcement in Washington stating that "Joint Task Force SEVEN had detonated an atomic device" in the Marshall Islands. There were no details on the size or nature of the explosion and commentators were left to wonder whether the United States had tested an atomic or a hydrogen bomb. The AEC had planned to make no further announcement until it completed the CASTLE series, but the fallout which forced the evacuation of the exposed Americans and Marshallese made it impossible to keep BRAVO secret. When a letter from a serviceman with Task Force 7 appeared in a Cincinnati newspaper on March 11, the AEC broke its silence with a brief, five-sentence communiqué announcing that 28 Americans and 236 residents of the Marshall Islands had been exposed to radiation during "a routine atomic test." "There were no burns," the AEC stated. "All are reported well. After completion of the atomic tests, they will be returned to their homes." [6]

The nation seemed to take the news calmly, though demands for more information soon developed. The *New York Times* explained to its readers that the radiation exposure probably came from "a 'fall-out' of radioactive waste and activated moisture from a cloud drifting from the explosion," and then added that "exposure to mild radiation is not necessarily dangerous." Two members of the Congressional Joint Committee on Atomic Energy, Representative Chet Holifield of California and Senator John Pastore of Rhode Island, admitted that while the test was larger than expected, the radiation problem stemmed from an unexpected wind shift. Other members of Congress were less complacent. Representative James Van Zandt of Pennsylvania told reporters that the test destroyed an area 12 miles in diameter, while Representative Carl Durham of North Carolina, ranking Democrat on the Joint Committee, said, "it is such a horrible thing, it's best to tell the world about it." Republican Dewey Short of Missouri drew an even more pessimistic conclusion. "H-weapons are getting so big that if they get much bigger," he commented, "we won't be able to test them."[7]

Panic over fallout first broke out in Japan with the return of the *Lucky Dragon* on March 14. By the time the tuna boat docked in its home harbor of Yaizu, 120 miles from Tokyo, nearly all the crew had come down with nausea, fever, bleeding gums, and other classic symptoms of radiation poisoning. Within two days, doctors from Tokyo had made the obvious diagnosis and Japanese newspapers carried huge headlines announcing that the 23 seamen had been stricken by the American atomic test. Japanese authorities moved quickly, hospitalizing several of the crew members and destroying 800 pounds of their tuna catch. But the people of Japan, remembering Hiroshima and Nagasaki, refused to be reassured so easily. A tuna scare swept over the islands as people boycotted fish markets and finally forced the government to use Geiger counters to inspect all fish offered for sale. Anti-Americanism flared up, despite a statement of sympathy over "this regrettable accident" from the American ambassador and offers of medical help for the victims by the American doctors at the U.S.-financed atomic bomb casualty hospital in Hiroshima. The Japanese government demanded that the United States conduct a formal inquiry, and left-wing student groups mounted violent anti-American protests in the streets.[8]

The alarm felt by the Japanese soon spread to the United

States. American newspapers gave front-page coverage to the tuna scare and *Life* magazine ran a feature story on the fate of the *Lucky Dragon*. The *New York Times* reported on March 21 that the AEC had quietly set up a network of atmospheric monitoring stations to detect radiation in the air after high readings caused by tests in Nevada in 1953. Less than a week later, the AEC admitted that the level of radiation in the air over the United States had increased since the BRAVO shot, but added that it was still "far below levels which could be harmful in any way to human beings, animals, or crops." Meanwhile, Representative W. Sterling Cole, Republican of New York and Chairman of the Joint Committee on Atomic Energy, announced plans for a congressional investigation of BRAVO and the failure of the AEC to take proper precautions against radioactive fallout.[9]

Predictably, reporters now turned to President Eisenhower for an explanation. At the presidential news conference on March 24, a reporter asked Ike about the "uranium curtain of secrecy" which shrouded all AEC activities. The President, following the advice given him beforehand by press secretary James Hagerty, replied that as soon as AEC Chairman Strauss returned from a fact-finding trip to the Pacific test grounds, he would arrange for him to meet with the reporters and give them a full explanation of the BRAVO accident. When TV newsman George Herman pressed for some immediate comment on the fallout danger, Eisenhower ignored Hagerty's advice and answered: "It is quite clear that this time something must have happened that we have never experienced before, and must have surprised and astonished the scientists."

The press had a field day with the President's admission. Reporters speculated that the H-bomb test had gotten out of hand and probed every possible Washington source for comment. Secretary of Defense Charles Wilson obliged them by calling BRAVO "unbelievable," and Representative Chet Holifield delighted reporters by saying that the blast was so great "that you might say it was out of control."[10]

A worried nation and an equally concerned President waited for Strauss to return from the Pacific. On Friday, March 26, he cabled Eisenhower, "Second test this morning. Hope report to you Tuesday." The papers for March 30 carried front-page stories on the second blast, a hydrogen explosion considerably smaller than BRAVO that went off on March 26 without any fallout incident. But the brief and uninformative AEC announcement gave no details and thus only heightened the suspense.

Lewis Strauss arrived in Washington on schedule and went immediately to the White House to report to the President. After listening to the AEC chairman, Ike conferred with Hagerty on the best way to have Strauss reassure the American people. After debating several possibilities, Hagerty and Strauss decided that the AEC chairman would attend the President's news conference the following day, March 31, and read a prepared statement "setting at ease fears that bombs had gotten out of control." Hagerty then tipped off wire-service reporters to the forthcoming report: at last the American people would recive an authoritative account of the tragic BRAVO episode.[11]

II

When Lewis Strauss walked into the Indian Treaty Room in the old War-State-Navy building at the side of Dwight D. Eisenhower on the morning of March 31, he was marking the climax of a long climb from obscurity. Born in Virginia, Strauss started out at 16 as a traveling salesman for a shoe company. By the time he was 20, he had become Herbert Hoover's right-hand man in the World War I Food Relief Administration, accompanying his chief to Paris during the peace conference. There he met investment banker Mortimer Schiff of Kuhn, Loeb and Company, who offered him a job. He married the daughter of a senior partner in Kuhn, Loeb in 1923 and five years later, at the age of 33, he had become a full partner himself. He had been a member of the naval reserve since 1925, and during the defense emergency in 1941 he entered active service as a Lieutenant Commander. He quickly caught the eye of James Forrestal, the future Secretary of the Navy, worked as his special assistant throughout the war, and left the Navy in 1945 with the rank of Rear Admiral, a title that he treasured even more than his reputation as a successful Wall Street banker. President Truman appointed him to a five-year term on the newly-created Atomic Energy Commission in 1946 and then after a brief return to banking in the early 1950s, Strauss became chairman of the AEC under Eisenhower in 1953.

Strauss had both the virtues and the faults of a self-made man. Opponents were quick to note his arrogance and his refusal to heed the advice of others. Experience had given him unshakeable confidence in his own ability and judgment; he rarely doubted the wisdom of his decisions. He held his convictions strongly, and none more than his distaste for Communism which he had imbibed from his lifelong idol, Herbert Hoover. In the depths of the depression, he had refused to let Kuhn, Loeb import gold from England because he suspected it came from Soviet mines.

His great love was science. First exposed to physics in high school, he regretted his inability to pursue scientific study in college, but he made up for this lapse by becoming a patron of science in the 1930s. The death of his mother from cancer in 1935 led him to give large sums to medical research, but he never lost his original attraction to physics. He became an admirer of Ernest O. Lawrence, the Berkeley Nobel laureate, helping to fund his cyclotron, and in 1939 Strauss contributed to the then esoteric research on uranium fission conducted by Leo Szilard and Enrico Fermi at Columbia University. In his first stint with the AEC, he single-handedly forced the Commission to begin a program of long-range detection that discovered the first Soviet atomic blast in 1949 and he engaged in a bitter duel with Chairman David Lilienthal over the hydrogen bomb, finally securing support from Congress and scientists like Ernest Lawrence to overcome the majority on the Commission that opposed its construction.

His friends saw a very different man, warm, intensely loyal and, above all, a dedicated humanitarian. His outward coolness, they claimed, was really only shyness; his owlish appearance and lack of formal education made him unduly sensitive to criticism. Behind his immaculate clothes and gentle, Old World manners, he viewed the world compassionately, giving large sums not only for research but to help the refugees from fascist tyranny in the 1930s. He was, wrote one neutral observer, the prototype of Western man: "optimistic, shrewd in business dealings, inquisitive about natural science, humanistic, basically religious."

Eisenhower clearly agreed with this estimate. Despite the fact that Strauss had worked for Robert Taft in 1952, the new President not only chose the Admiral, as he liked to be called, to head the AEC, but gave him the additional title of special adviser to the President on atomic energy. This dual position gave Strauss direct, personal access to Eisenhower and with it enormous power and responsibility. After his swearing-in ceremony in July 1953, Strauss recalled, Ike took him aside and told him, "my chief concern and your first assignment is to find some new approach to the *dis*arming of atomic energy." Strauss used the power to dominate the AEC, forcing several dissident members to resign and becoming the Commission's sole spokesman; he never gave any sign of suffering pangs of guilt over the responsibility for overseeing the nation's nuclear arsenal. "The atom is amoral," he explained to one questioner. "The only thing that makes it immoral is man."[12]

In some ways, Lewis Strauss reminds one of John Adams—pompous, shrewd, patriotic but often mean, petty and unpredictable. James Hagerty commented in his diary that on April 2, 1954, the Admiral told him, in strictest confidence, that the *Lucky Dragon* was not a Japanese fishing boat at all—it was a "Red spy outfit" snooping on the American nuclear tests. A few days later, Strauss repeated this comment to Hagerty and then added, "If I were the Reds, I would fill the oceans all over the world with radio-active fish. It would be so easy to do!" As Benjamin Franklin once wrote of Adams, "He means well for his country, is always an honest man, often a wise one, but sometimes, and in some things, absolutely out of his senses."[13]

Strauss was careful to avoid any mention of Red ships or radioactive fish when he got up to read his prepared statement to reporters at the end of Eisenhower's March 31st news conference. It was Strauss's first press conference since taking office nine months earlier, and he was ill-at-ease as he began reading the mimeographed text. The words, if not the manner of delivery, were designed to reassure an anxious nation. BRAVO, Strauss declared, was never out of control. It was larger than expected, he admitted, but the main difficulty was the sudden and unexpected shift in the wind. He stressed the speed and efficiency with which Task Force 7 had removed the 28 Americans and 236 Marshallese, the skilled medical care they had received, and the excellent condition of all who had been exposed. As for the 23 Japanese fishermen, it was regrettable that they had ignored the AEC warning and had been exposed as a result of their "inadvertent trespass," but reports on their condition suggested that they, too, would quickly recover. Strauss dismissed rumors of contaminated fish in the Pacific as unfounded, denied that any "fall-out radioactivity" was moving on ocean currents toward Japan, and belittled reports of a slight rise in background radiation in the continental United States by noting that it was "far below the levels which could be harmful in any way to human beings, animals, or crops." The radioactivity from the tests would quickly disappear, he concluded, but the military gains for the United States would be enduring. The nation should rejoice that the tests more than fulfilled the expectations of the scientists and that "enormous potential has been added to our military posture by what we have learned."[14]

Strauss would have been well-advised to stop with this persuasive statement. But when reporters asked him to respond to a few questions, he consented. Most dealt with issues he had touched on already, and Strauss simply elaborated on his earlier remarks. Then Richard Wilson of Cowles Publications asked him how large and how powerful an H-bomb might be. Strauss replied:

> **A.** Well, the nature of an H-bomb, Mr. Wilson, is that, in effect, it can be made to be as large as you wish, as large as the military requirement demands, that is to say, an H-bomb can be made as—large enough to take out a city.
> (A chorus of "What?")
> To take out a city, to destroy a city.
> **Q.** How big a city?
> **A.** Any city.
> **Q.** Any city, New York?
> **A.** The metropolitan area, yes.

Realizing belatedly the impact of what he had said,* the Admiral quickly cut off the questioning. On the way back to the White House, a restrained Eisenhower remarked, "Lewis, I wouldn't have answered that one that way."[15]

The President was right. The next day, the *New York Times* headline read, "H-BOMB CAN WIPE OUT ANY CITY." In the ensuing article, there was scarcely any mention of the BRAVO fallout or its Pacific victims. Instead the press concentrated on the far more frightening thought of single H-bombs destroying whole cities, while civil defense experts suddenly enjoyed a new vogue. In his own backhand way, Lewis Strauss had quieted the nation's concern over fallout by raising the spectre of nuclear holocaust. Who could worry about the fate of some Japanese fishermen or Marshallese natives in the Pacific when New York, Washington, Chicago, and other urban centers faced possible obliteration? Thanks to Strauss, BRAVO had touched off a long overdue public discussion of the horrors of the hydrogen bomb.[16]

---

* Strauss later noted in the official AEC transcript of the press conference that he had meant "put out of commission," not "to destroy."

III

The idea of a hydrogen bomb dates back to the wartime Manhattan Project, and its fulfillment was testimony to the brilliance and persistence of one man—Edward Teller. When the Los Alamos laboratory was first established in 1943 to design the atomic bomb, the physicists led by Robert Oppenheimer were certain that the fission of either uranium-235 or plutonium atoms would lead to a tremendous release of energy. Their chief problem was to design a bomb that would safely contain the potential power until it was detonated. Teller, a Hungarian physicist who had fled to the United States in the 1930s and had been recruited by Oppenheimer to work at Los Alamos, realized that a far more awesome weapon could be developed by the process of fusion—joining together isotypes of hydrogen to form helium. Enormous heat would be required to sustain such fusion, but a successful atomic bomb would create the necessary temperature, in excess of 100,000,000 degrees Fahrenheit. Teller tried to persuade Oppenheimer and others to pursue his concept, but they concentrated on perfecting the atomic weapon, letting him conduct his theoretical studies but refusing to engage in the massive research program he envisaged.

After the war, Teller continued to press for a hydrogen bomb, but neither the government nor his fellow scientists would support his ambitious program. Teller, a brooding man with dark, luxuriant eyebrows, a fierce will, and a deep, doomsday voice, refused to give up. In part he was driven by an insatiable scientific curiosity, but he also was motivated by a deep hatred of the Soviet Union. Born in Hungary of a Jewish family, he had studied in Germany and then come to the United States to escape Hitler's persecution. He always remembered Russian oppression of Hungary. As early as the Battle of Stalingrad in 1942, he began warning his wartime associates, one recalled later, "that victory would make Soviet Russia an even greater menace to democracy than Nazi Germany."[17]

The first Russian atomic bomb, detected in 1949, gave Teller his opportunity. He joined with Ernest Lawrence to lobby for a crash program to build what contemporaries called the Super, a hydrogen bomb that would use an atomic bomb as the trigger. Oppenheimer, Lilienthal, and a majority of the scientists advising the AEC opposed such an effort on technical as well as moral grounds. Oppenheimer pointed out that an attempt to build the Super would handicap America's atomic program—the manufacture of one kilogram of tritium, the isotope of hydrogen Teller planned to use, required 80 kilograms of plutonium, the main ingredient of the fission bomb. With support from the Joint Committee on Atomic Energy, Teller finally overcame Oppenheimer's objections. On January 31, 1950, President Truman authorized work to begin on the Super, and six months later, as many scientists had feared, the White House ordered a crash program to produce tritium for the new project.[18]

The technical difficulties proved far greater than the political ones. For the next year, Teller worked with mathematicians at Los Alamos on complex equations in an effort to achieve a theoretical breakthrough. Early in 1951, following an approach suggested by Stanislaus Ulam, he tried a new idea. Frederic de Hoffmann did the laborious calculations by hand, confirmed later by John von Neumann's ENIAC computer. The new calculations seemed promising, but Teller waited for the outcome of Operation GREENHOUSE, an AEC atomic test in the Pacific that proved the principle of thermonuclear burning. "Without such a test," Teller wrote later, "no one of us could have had the confidence to proceed further. . . ." With proof that an atomic bomb would sustain fusion, Teller was ready to reveal his new discovery at a two-day meeting at the Institute for Advanced Study in Princeton attended by all five AEC members and such noted scientists as Robert Oppenheimer, Hans Bethe, and Enrico Fermi. Once he described his breakthrough, which is still classified, all opposition to the H-bomb vanished. Bethe called his idea "a stroke of genius," and even Oppenheimer concurred, saying that if Teller had put forth this concept earlier, he would never have opposed Super.[19]

The next step was a full-scale test of a hydrogen explosion. While Teller and his associates worked on the design, President Truman appointed a five-member committee which included Oppenheimer, Vannevar Bush, head of the wartime science program, and CIA chief Allen Dulles, to advise him on American disarmament policy. When Bush learned of the forthcoming thermonuclear test, he proposed canceling it and instead making an overture to the Soviet Union to prohibit all hydrogen detonations. Arguing that any violation would be easy to detect, Bush claimed that this would be the last chance to spare the world the agony of thermonuclear weapons. In particular, he objected to the scheduled date for the test, November 1, 1952, just three days before the presidential election. After a brief hesitation, Truman ordered the test to proceed when he learned that weather conditions would force a six-month delay if the shot did not take place by early November.[20]

The MIKE test on November 1, 1952, was the world's first thermonuclear explosion, but the United States did not yet have the hydrogen bomb. Using liquid tritium and deuterium, isotypes of hydrogen that had to be refrigerated to incredibly low temperatures, the device was larger than a two-story house and weighed some 65 tons. The resulting blast, estimated in the range of 10 megatons, was almost 1000 times more powerful than the bomb dropped on Hiroshima. Unknown to the American people, who were simply told that the AEC had successfully fired a hydrogen device in the Pacific, MIKE obliterated the entire island of Elugelab, over a mile in diameter, leaving behind a huge crater in the ocean floor.[21]

Nine months later, on August 12, 1953, American officials detected the first Soviet hydrogen explosion. President Eisenhower soon informed the American people of this fact, warning that the Russians now possessed "the capability of atomic attack upon us, and such capability will increase with the passage of time." What neither Eisenhower nor Strauss revealed, however, was that the Russian device had used dry hydrogen isotopes that did not require unwieldy refrigeration. The Soviets now appeared not only to have caught up with American nuclear technology but to have moved closer than the United States to a deliverable hydrogen bomb.[22]

The importance of BRAVO to American scientists and to the Eisenhower administration was that it, too, was a dry bomb. Apparently Teller and his associates had discovered that lithium-6 deuteride, a stable chemical formed from lithium-6 and detuterium, each easily produced in existing AEC separation plants, released the precious tritium when touched off by a fission explosion. The American bomb was thus a fission-fusion reaction: a small atomic bomb served as the trigger, creating the heat to transform the lithium-6 deuteride into tritium and begin a self-generating fusion explosion. Unlike the Russian device, which yielded less than one megaton of energy, the American bomb tested at Bikini on March 1, 1954, gave off 15 megatons.[23]

The implications for national security were staggering. Public estimates of the atomic stockpiles of the two super powers at the end of 1953 indicated that the United States possessed between three and four thousand nuclear weapons, compared to three to four hundred for Russia. Physicist Ralph Lapp estimated in 1954 that the American stockpile amounted to about 500 megatons; a few American H-bombs would soon double the power of the American deterrent, but the Russians could quickly match that destructive force with their own thermonuclear weapons. Moreover, Lapp warned, there was no theoretical limit to the size of H-bombs, though he did think that after 50 megatons the point of diminishing returns was reached. Even more ominous, both sides were working on intercontinental ballistic missiles and it would be only a few years before they had perfected both the missiles and the small hydrogen warheads that would usher in a new age of pushbutton war in which an entire city could be destroyed in minutes. Such was the new reality suddenly confronting the American people in the aftermath of BRAVO. It is little wonder that they proved unable to absorb and react to it in 1954.[24]

IV

The public debate touched off by the BRAVO fallout and the Strauss bombshell began in late March. In the United States, the first reactions were shock and disbelief. "What is *fantastic*," a *Newsweek* reader in Illinois wrote to the editor, "is that it could have been allowed to happen." The *New Republic* took issue with the size of the H-bomb. Pointing out that a 5 megaton bomb would be large enough to destroy Moscow, the editors asked, "what military justification is there for a 12 megaton bomb?" Many observers objected to the secrecy surrounding the tests and demanded that the AEC inform the American people of the nuclear facts of life and death. The *Nation* called for pause in testing to permit some "hard political thinking." "One or two more explosions like this," the editorial warned, "and we might not be able to think." The normally staid *Scientific American* concluded, "Just as war is too important to be left to the generals, so the Thermonuclear Bomb had become too big to be entrusted any longer to the executive sessions of rulers in Washington."[25]

The most widespread reaction was a call to stop all tests permanently. In a letter to the editors of the *New York Times* on March 25, Margaret Casanova of Hamden, Connecticut, demanded the cessation of testing, writing, "We have stepped over the boundary line of human decency already." Three days later, Lewis Mumford, the well-known writer on technology, repeated this plea in a letter to the *Times*. "Let us cease all further experiments with even more horrifying weapons of destruction," Mumford proposed, "lest our own self-induced fears further upset our mental balance." Mumford's letter attracted national attention as magazines as far apart ideologically as *Time* and the *Nation* reprinted it. By April, the White

House was receiving more than 100 letters, telegrams, and post cards a day protesting continued nuclear tests. "Dear Mr. President," read many identical cards illustrated with a mushroom cloud, "There must be a world-wide ban on the H-bomb!" Suspecting a Communist plot, presidential aides forwarded such cards to the F.B.I., but they could not dismiss the protests so easily. Letters calling for an end to testing from such respectable people as Hank Brennan, a *Time* editor, and Arthur Compton, a noted scientist who had recommended going ahead with the H-bomb in 1950, testified to the broad range of American opinion that was outraged by BRAVO.[26]

Not all Americans agreed with the protestors. The editors of the *New York Times* reminded Mumford that "It is the business of science to enter the unknown." Ernest Lindley urged the readers of *Newsweek* to ignore the "thoughtless clamor for an end to atomic experiments" and pointed out that only "a fool-proof system of international inspection" would permit the United States to stop its tests. The Cold War provided the simplest rebuttal. Max Ascoli, the editor of the liberal but fiercely anti-Soviet *Reporter* magazine, commented that "it is difficult to see how anybody who is not a Communist agent can object to our manufacturing H-bombs and then testing them." "The heart of the conspiracy against humanity is not in the Atomic Energy Commission," wrote a New York resident to the *Times*, "it is in the Kremlin, and the danger to civilization is not a tritium atom but a totalitarian monolith." *Time* magazine agreed, pointing out that the Communists "conduct their experiments in aggression not on remote Pacific Ocean atolls" but upon the masses of Europe and Asia. "Not tuna, but men and women by the millions, were deliberately killed or contaminated by terror in the Communist experimental aggression in Estonia, Poland, Greece, China, Malaya, Indo-China," concluded the Luce publication in the most astonishing non-sequitur of the entire fallout debate.[27]

Abroad the outcry against the American nuclear tests was even louder than the domestic furor, with fewer voices raised in counterpoint. Asians were naturally most concerned, aware as they were that so far the only victims of America's nuclear bombs were the inhabitants of Hiroshima and Nagasaki, the Marshallese islanders, and the Japanese fishermen. Prime Minister Jawaharlal Nehru of India made the most eloquent and influential statements. "These experiments show man is unleashing power which can ultimately get out of his control," Nehru said on March 28, and then three days later, after pointing out the proximity of Asia to the Pacific test grounds, he asked rhetorically, "How can we be sure that our children may not go gradually blind or contract some internal disease?" In a formal address to the Indian Parliament on April 2, Nehru called for an immediate "standstill agreement" by the United States and Russia to prohibit nuclear tests while the United Nations worked out a comprehensive disarmament agreement. Expressing sympathy for the exposed Japanese seamen, the Prime Minister closed by saying, "It is of great concern to us that Asia and her peoples appear to be always nearer these occurrences and experiments and their fearsome consequences, actual or potential."[28]

Other Indian leaders echoed Nehru's sentiments in private conversations with Americans. J. J. Singh, the ambassador to the United States, pointed out to David Lilienthal that American nuclear policy "made people in Asia feel that we did not value colored people's lives as we did white people's." The Indian finance minister put it more succinctly to *New York Times* correspondent Cyrus Sulzberger when he explained Indian resentment over American tests: "Too many people live in this part of the world." The only Asian to come to the defense of the United States was Japanese foreign minister Katsuo Okazaki who felt that Russia should also be asked to halt its nuclear tests, explaining that "we cannot ask America alone to stop the experiments." Aware of the prevailing Asian sentiment, Henry Cabot Lodge, U.S. ambassador to the United Nations, used great care in replying to Nehru's call for a standstill in testing.

Avoiding a direct refusal, Lodge simply said that the Prime Minister's suggestion "is entitled to respectful attention." [29]

In Europe, two men with worldwide influence voiced deep concern over thermonuclear testing. Dr. Albert Schweitzer, the famed musician, philosopher, and physician, called upon scientists everywhere to speak out against these "horrible explosions." "Only they have the authority to state that we can no longer take on ourselves the responsibility for these experiments;" he declared, "only they can say it." On Easter Sunday, April 19, 1954, Pope Pius XII devoted most of his message to the radiation hazards of the hydrogen bomb. Warning that man now had the capability of "polluting in a lasting manner the atmosphere, the land, and also the oceans," the Pope called for efforts to banish nuclear war without making any specific reference to tests themselves. [30]

The most heated debate broke out in England. In late March the Labor Party introduced a resolution in Parliament asking the Government to seek a summit meeting with the Soviet leadership to arrange for the suspension of all testing. Many Conservatives showed sympathy for this proposal, and even the staid *London Times* endorsed it. Prime Minister Winston Churchill tried desperately to rally supporters to the Government's side by terming the American H-bomb the best deterrent to World War III. But Churchill, old and weary, fared poorly in the ensuing debate and was finally forced to admit that the United States had failed to give Britain any advance information about the nature and power of the H-bomb. Only when 104 Laborites signed a petition calling for surrendering control of all nuclear weapons to the UN and for an immediate ban on H-bomb tests did the Conservative majority finally vote down the original resolution. In the process, however, Churchill promised to seek a summit conference on nuclear weapons in the near future. [31]

The worldwide furor over the H-bomb reached a peak in April when the Eisenhower administration made public the first pictures and details on Operation IVY, the 1952 series which featured the 10 megaton MIKE shot. This decision had been reached at a meeting of the National Security Council in mid-March, after BRAVO but before the Strauss press conference. The President announced plans for release of a 27½ minute film of IVY on March 26, and press secretary James Hagerty made elaborate arrangements for advance press briefings and photo deliveries with the strict injunction that the media wait until April 7 before using any of this material.

". . . All hell broke loose last night and this AM over H-bomb release," Hagerty wrote in his diary on April 1. Drew Pearson had violated the agreement and published the details on March 31, forcing the *New York Times* and other newspapers to follow suit the next day.[32]

Television stations and news magazines had to wait for the April 7 deadline, but the impact of their visual presentation was far greater than that of the newspaper accounts. The black-and-white AEC film, shown on national television on prime time, contained shots of the task force deploying in the Pacific, the erection of test towers on the sandy, coral islands of Eniwetok Atoll, and close-ups of the huge MIKE device on Elugelab. Then came the explosion which wiped out the island. "The camera showed the mushroom cloud," reported *Time*, "rising through menacing black skies like a great, poisonous-looking gob of whipped cream." A week later the AEC released even more impressive color photos which *Life* magazine featured in a four-page spread with the caption, "The Awesome Fireball." Fearful of negative reactions abroad, the National Security Council restricted overseas distribution to the single black-and-white film. But there was no way to halt the export of magazines and periodicals with the vivid evidence of America's first thermonuclear explosion. The genie had escaped from the bottle—all the Eisenhower administration could do now was try to reassure a frightened world that the danger could be contained.[33]

V

". . . The American people, and more particularly other people throughout the world," Joint Committee Chairman Sterling Cole wrote to the President on April 5, "have been struck with terror by the horrible implications of nuclear weapon development—and I think with much justification." Cole went on to urge Eisenhower to announce that the United States would neither build nor test any weapons larger than those it already possessed. Eisenhower had already been thinking along the same lines. On April 5, preparing for a televised speech to the nation that evening designed to ease public fears of Communism, economic recession, and thermonuclear weapons, the President called Lewis Strauss to ask if it would be accurate for him to tell the nation that the administration had no plans to make H-bombs on a "bigger and more destructive scale." After checking with the Joint Chiefs of Staff, Strauss reported back that the military thought it would be "appropriate" for the President to state that the existing bombs were "of the size required by our war plans and that we do not propose, under present circumstances, to test larger and yet ever larger weapons."[34]

The President, however, decided not to include any reference to the size of future nuclear weapons. Instead he told the American people that hydrogen bombs were not "a great threat to us." The certainty of American nuclear retaliation would prevent the Russians from attacking, though he added that "since insanity still exists, I will again say there is still an element in that threat that we must calculate very coldly and very carefully." Aware that these words provided little reassurance about the dangers of fallout, the President told James Hagerty on April 6 that he wanted to reveal at his press conference the next day his decision not to experiment with larger weapons. Apparently tipped off by Hagerty, Merriman Smith of the Associated Press opened the questioning on April 7 by asking Eisenhower whether the United States planned to build "bigger and bigger H-bombs?" "We know of no military requirement that could lead us into the production of a bigger bomb than has already been produced," the President responded. When reporter May Craig asked what the U.S. would do if the Russians built still larger bombs, Eisenhower explained that there was no advantage in building an H-bomb beyond a certain explosive limit.[35]

While the President made these reassuring statements publicly, Secretary of State John Foster Dulles took a quite different line in private talks with NATO diplomats. Warned by the American ambassador to France that public opinion in Western Europe was "now bitterly demanding the cessation of tests," Dulles arranged to meet secretly with the NATO foreign ministers on April 23. Nuclear weapons, he told them, were the only way the United States could defend Western Europe against superior Soviet conventional forces. In case of attack, he explained, the United States "must be free to use atomic weapons against appropriate elements of the enemy's military power." Restating his belief in massive retaliation as the only way to restrain Russia, Dulles warned against any form of unilateral disarmament by saying, "Self-imposed military inferiority is an invitation rather than a deterrent to war." The foreign ministers listened intently ("You could have heard a pin drop as the Secretary talked," an aide commented), and then indicated their acquiescence, if not agreement, by their ensuing silence.[36]

Back in Washington, however, Eisenhower decided to order an interdepartmental study of the test ban concept. AEC commissioner Thomas Murray, a holdover Truman appointee, had first suggested an international moratorium on testing to the President in early February, before BRAVO. On Strauss's advice, Ike had rebuffed Murray, telling him that such a move would depend on Soviet cooperation "and experience has not provided any encouragement for that degree of reliance." After a more thorough examination of this idea in the spring, administration officials decided that any short-run propaganda advantage from an American-sponsored test ban would be more than offset by the damage it would do to the nation's nuclear technology. In late June, Eisenhower accepted their recommendation, agreeing that a test ban ran contrary to the national interest.[37]

Meanwhile the CASTLE series continued in the Pacific. The AEC announced the third shot on April 7, but made no further public statement until mid-May, when it abruptly noted that the series had ended and stated cryptically, "The tests were successful in the development of thermonuclear weapons." In fact, there were a total of six hydrogen blasts: BRAVO and two others over 10 megatons, a May 5 shot of almost 7 megatons, one designed by Teller's new Livermore Laboratory that almost fizzled, and the final blast of slightly under 2 megatons on May 14. BRAVO was not only the largest explosion in the CASTLE series; it has proven to be the biggest bomb the United States ever detonated, validating Eisenhower's promise not to build larger and larger weapons. The other shots were undoubtedly designed to test various explosive configurations for the Atlas intercontinental ballistic missle, already under construction as part of the crash program begun in February.[38]

The American people, unaware of the full significance of CASTLE, soon began to lose interest in the hydrogen bomb debate. "I took one look at the bomb pictures today in the paper," commented a San Francisco bootblack on April 3. "I'm not scared but I don't want to see any more of them." A more sophisticated commentator observed, "People have reached the saturation point and can't grasp the enormity of this bomb's potential compared with its predecessors." A Gallup poll taken in mid-April seemed to back up this assessment. Asked what chance they thought there was that their city would be attacked with a hydrogen bomb, 39 per cent responded "not much chance," 24 per cent "fair chance," and 33 per cent "good chance." It is worth noting, however, that for inhabitants of cities over 500,000 in size, 54 per cent thought there was a "good chance" of such an attack. On the broader question of whether they thought H-bombs would be used in case of a war with Russia, 63 per cent said yes and only 26 per cent no.

The most interesting response that Gallup received came to the question of whether the H-bomb had made another world war more or less likely. A surprising 54 per cent answered less likely, only 20 per cent said more likely, with 15 per cent thinking it made no difference and 11 per cent expressing no opinion. It is difficult to know whether the majority in this case was expressing genuine optimism over the bomb or merely reflecting a blind hope that a weapon so destructive would make war unthinkable. Claims like the one in *Newsweek* to the effect that if you lived in a major city, "the odds against your survival in an H-bomb war would be about a million to one," suggest that many Americans may have reacted simply by trying to ignore a danger they could neither comprehend nor control. They placed their faith in the government, as revealed in a Gallup poll in which 71 per cent opposed the unilateral suspension of nuclear tests, and hoped for the best.[39]

Events in the spring of 1954 helped the people bury their fears of the H-bomb. The Army-McCarthy hearings which had begun in March dominated the newspapers in April; every day, fascinated viewers watched this drama unfold on their television screens. Abroad, the Viet Minh siege of Dien Bien Phu and the desperate French bid for survival in Indo-China drew attention as the Eisenhower administration struggled with the question of extending last-minute aid. Later in April, the revelations of the AEC hearings which resulted in stripping Robert Oppenheimer of his government security clearance led to passionate outcries from many American scientists and an intense debate over the 1950 decision to build the H-bomb which focused attention away from the issues of testing and fallout. By May the American people were so absorbed in the new chapter in American racial relations begun by the Supreme Court school desegregation decision that they appeared to have forgotten about the hydrogen bomb and its awful implications.[40] BRAVO had set a pattern which would appear again and again in the fifties—sudden interest in nuclear tests, intense debate and public discussion, and then the equally abrupt dropping of the issue.

VI

The Marshallese and Japanese victims of BRAVO could not escape its consequences so easily. On April 24, 1954, eleven spokesmen for the more than 11,000 inhabitants of the Marshall Islands sent a softly-worded petition to the United Nations, which had ultimate jurisdiction over the Pacific Trust Territory administered by the United States. In this document, they complained about the burns, nausea, and loss of hair of their fellow islanders who were exposed to BRAVO's fallout and the removal of so many people from Eniwetok, Bikini, Kwajalein, and other islands used for bomb tests. "Land means a great deal to the Marshallese," they explained. "Take away their land and their spirits go also." Though the petitioners spoke well of American guardianship in general, they asked that all bomb tests "be immediately ceased," but if they had to be held in the future, that "all possible precautionary measures" be taken. Two weeks later, Ambassador Lodge expressed American sorrow over the injuries, promised continued medical care and a monetary indemnity to the victims, but refused to make any guarantees for the future.[41]

In July, a full-dress debate took place before the UN Trusteeship Council on the issue of American nuclear tests within the trust territory. Under the trusteeship agreement of 1947, the United States governed the area and could close it for strategic reasons, but once a year it had to submit a report on the welfare of the nearly 60,000 inhabitants of the Marshall, Caroline, and Mariana islands. The Trusteeship Council usually received the reports without comment, but in 1954 the Soviet Union and India offered resolutions condemning the American nuclear tests. The Russians wanted to ban all tests inside the trust territory permanently; the Indians wanted tests suspended in this region pending a ruling on their legality by the International Court of Justice. Mason Sears, the American delegate to the Trusteeship Council, accused the Russians of trying to wring a propaganda advantage out of the plight of the Marshall islanders. He promised that, in the future, precautions would be taken to prevent fallout accidents but he insisted that the U.S. would continue its tests "so long as the Communists continue theirs." In a clever move, the United States brought Dwight Heine, a Marshallese school teacher who had been educated in Hawaii on a government scholarship and who had also served as an American military interpreter, to speak for the islanders. Heine repeated the statements made in the April petition, which he had helped draft, but he accepted the inevitability of future tests and asked only that the United States exercise greater care in conducting them. "The H-bomb is a 'super-fire-cracker,'" he declared, "which needs 'super safety rules' in its handling." [42]

The Trusteeship Council, dominated by countries friendly to the United States, turned down both the Indian and Russian resolutions. Then the delegates approved a British–French–Belgian motion that expressed regret at the suffering of the Marshall islanders and asked only that the United States take proper precautions in future tests. The vote on this resolution was 9 to 3, with Syria joining India and Russia in opposition. Most observers interpreted this action as an implicit endorsement of the American right to continue testing in the Pacific Trust Territory, though there was negative reaction. The *New Republic* praised India's Krishna Menon for his contention that no nation had the right to poison the world's atmosphere, while Emanuel Margolis argued in the *Yale Law Journal* that the Pacific tests violated the historic principle of freedom of the seas. "The conclusion seems inescapable," Margolis wrote: "the laws of humanity suggest and the law of nation requires immediate and permanent cessation of the thermonuclear experiments in the vast expanse of the Marshall Islands proving grounds."[43]

The United States government ignored these criticisms and instead devoted considerable effort to reassuring the world that the Marshallese had suffered no lasting injury from the fallout. In the UN debates, both Lodge and Sears claimed that the islanders had fully recovered from their injuries. In its semi-annual report on July 30, 1954, the AEC repeated this assertion, stating, "The medical observations to date indicate that there is no reason to expect any permanent after effects on the general health of these people." Nearly a year later, however, a Navy doctor who had treated the victims reported to the American Medical Association that the injuries had in fact been much more serious than the AEC had admitted at the time. Most of the Marshallese had experienced only skin lesions and loss of hair, conditions which cleared up in a few months, but the 64 people on Rongelap, who had been exposed to 175 roentgens, developed serious blood disorders. Their white cell counts fell to 50 per cent of normal in some cases, and several of the children nearly died. All eventually recovered, but American doctors were keeping a close check on the survivors, who had been moved to the island of Majuro in the southern Marshalls. By the end of 1955, there was as yet no sign of long-term damage, such as leukemia or genetic defects.[44]

In Japan, the BRAVO fallout led to even greater controversy. Seven of the *Lucky Dragon* crewmen remained hospitalized through the end of April 1954, and Japanese officials refused to permit American doctors to examine them. John M. Allison, the American ambassador, again called the incident "unfortunate and regrettable," promised a financial indemnity to the fishermen, and offered medical assistance which the Japanese finally accepted on April 30. By the end of May, the condition of the seven seamen improved as their damaged bone marrow began to produce more white blood corpuscles. The tuna scare also eased in July when the Japanese government released a report by a scientific survey team that assured the people that both the waters around Bikini and the fish caught there were free of radioactivity.[45]

The situation suddenly worsened toward the end of the summer, however, when two of the fishermen suffered relapses. Japanese doctors became alarmed at finding traces of strontium-90 in the bones of the victims. A product of fission not found in nature, strontium-90 has a chemical nature similar to calcium and lodges in the bone where it gives off radiation that can cause cancer. In early September, Aikichi Kuboyama, a 39-year-old radioman from the *Lucky Dragon,* lay near death. Again Japanese officials refused to let American doctors examine him, and when Kuboyama finally died on September 24, the people of Japan mourned him as the world's first H-bomb casualty. While Ambassador Allison expressed his government's "extreme sorrow and regret," angry demonstrators paraded outside the American embassy in Tokyo carrying signs demanding an end to U.S. nuclear tests in the Pacific.[46]

An ugly dispute soon arose over Kuboyama's death. The Japanese government listed the cause as "radiation sickness," citing an autopsy which an American doctor had observed. But when other American experts suggested that jaundice, possibly caused by improper blood tranfusions rather than by radiation exposure, had in fact caused Kuboyama to die, anti-American sentiment swept over Japan. Despite repeated denials from Japanese doctors, who pointed out that the autopsy revealed the presence of radioactive elements in Kuboyama's liver and bone marrow, officials of the AEC and the Defense Department continued to assert that Kuboyama was not a victim of American nuclear fallout.[47]

Fortunately, the Eisenhower administration moved quickly to make amends. Ambassador Allison, who was negotiating on the amount of indemnity to be paid to Japan, handed Kuboyama's widow a check for one million yen (about $2,800) immediately, thereby acknowledging American responsibility for his death. Two months later, Prime Minister Yoshida capped a visit to the

United States by coupling a statement of his concern over H-bomb tests with an admission of their necessity. President Eisenhower reciprocated by expressing American regret over the exposure of the 23 seamen and the death of Kuboyama. Allison finally reached a settlement with the Japanese foreign minister on January 4, 1955. The United States agreed to pay two million dollars as compensation for the loss of Japanese life and property occasioned by the fallout from American nuclear tests. Recalling this episode years later, Allison commented, "I am inclined to believe that I should have made an apology at the very beginning." Such a statement, Allison explained, would have horrified the AEC as an admission of American guilt, but it would have gone far towards easing understandable Japanese sensitivity.[48] It is hard to disagree with Allison. The AEC did not intentionally dust the Marshall islanders and the Japanese fishermen with fallout, but the Commission must bear the blame for failing to admit full responsibility for the accident and for trying to disguise the true extent of the damage.

VII

Worldwide concern over fallout increased again in the fall of 1954 as a result of Kuboyama's death and news of a Soviet nuclear test. The first report on a Russian detonation came from Japan, where scientists relied on long-range instruments to detect the telltale change in the atmospheric pressure and the subsequent increase in background radiation. The Soviet government announced this test in late September but gave no information about the size or nature of the explosion. A month later the AEC confirmed the Russian shot and tried to play down the fallout aspect. "As is generally the case with nuclear detonations," the AEC commented, "these tests have resulted in some widespread fall-out of radioactive material, but insignificantly in the United States."[49]

Europeans reacted most strongly to the revived fallout peril.

Winston Churchill created a sensation in England when he warned the House of Commons that an "undue number" of nuclear explosions might damage the earth's atmosphere for the next 5000 years. Churchill's statement was apparently based on a misunderstanding of fallout data the U.S. had given him, but public opinion in Europe accepted his forecast as an authoritative warning. Charles-Noel Martin, a physicist, gave an even more alarming report on the possible consequences of thermonuclear explosions in a paper he delivered in December to the French Academy of Sciences. Martin speculated that as few as ten H-bombs could change the weather by blotting out the sun and might cause an appreciable rise in radiation levels which in turn could lead to dangerous genetic effects. Despite the lack of any specific evidence, Martin's paper, along with Churchill's warning, led to a growing resentment in Europe over nuclear weapons. American commentators worried about "grave political and strategic repercussions" from this anti-bomb sentiment and voiced suspicion that Moscow was "slowly and successfully mobilizing international opinion" as a way to halt the scientific progress upon which "the safeguarding of democracy may ultimately depend."[50]

In the United States, scientists began to voice equally disturbing doubts about bomb tests. In the November issue of the *Bulletin of the Atomic Scientists,* physicist Ralph E. Lapp gave the American people the first detailed description of fallout and its perils. Lapp, a free-lance writer and consultant who had worked on the Manhattan Project, made a crucial distinction between local and global fallout. The atomic bomb had produced only local fallout, that is, a scattering of radioactive fission products, in the area devastated by the bomb's heat and blast effects. The hydrogen bomb, however, had created not only the local fallout, which had dusted the Marshall islanders and the Japanese seamen, but global fallout, radioactive particles that had escaped into the stratosphere and then gradually fell back to earth in rainfall. Though Lapp focused his attention on the danger of local fallout in case of nuclear war, warning that 50 superbombs could envelope the entire northeastern United States "in a serious to lethal radioactive fog," his remarks about global fallout had equally frightening implications. The bomb tests produced forms of radiation that circled the globe and returned to the ground thousands of miles from the point of the explosion.[51]

One of the world's foremost geneticists, Professor A.H. Sturtevant of the California Institute of Technology, spelled out the possible effects of this slight addition to natural radiation from bomb tests. Experiments with fruit flies and mice, Sturtevant explained, proved that radiation caused genetic mutations which "seriously affect the efficiency of individuals in later generations," giving rise to birth defects, physical deformities, and early death. Based on the assumption that in humans 1 roentgen would cause an undesirable mutation in the sex cells of 1 out of every 10,000 persons exposed, Sturtevant calculated that BRAVO alone, by subjecting the American people to a minute .0035r, would lead to the birth of 70 infants with defective genes. Worldwide, he calculated the genetic cost of BRAVO at 1800 children. "And every new bomb exploded," he concluded, ". . . will result in an increase in this ultimate harvest of defective individuals."[52]

The AEC responded quickly in an effort to reassure the American people. Dr. Willard Libby, a newly-appointed member of the AEC who had won international acclaim as a chemist for discovering how to use radioactive carbon-14 to date ancient rocks, confirmed Lapp's analysis of local and global fallout and even admitted that "the most frightening and insidious characteristic of radioactivity" was its invisible nature. But in a speech to a conference of the nation's mayors in December 1954, Libby minimized the impact of global fallout on human beings. The amount of radioactivity that fell back to earth, he pointed out, was only a fraction of the radiation man was normally exposed to in nature. "Generally speaking," Libby concluded, "there is no immediate hazard to the civilian population in this type of fallout."

Dr. John C. Bugher, chief of the AEC's Division of Biology and Medicine, gave a stronger rebuttal in a speech to industrial health specialists in September. He admitted that studies of the survivors of Nagasaki and Hiroshima had revealed a higher rate of leukemia than normal and had shown a slight "statistical shortening of life expectancy." But these effects came from local fallout. In regard to the danger of cancer from global fallout, Bugher estimated that "the amount of such material now present over the United States would have to be increased by the order of 1 million times before an increased frequency of bone sarcoma from this cause could be recognized." He was equally disdainful of Sturtevant's predictions of the genetic consequences of global fallout, advising his listeners to ignore wild speculation based on unfounded assumptions. "Such distortions of emphasis," he argued, "are comparable to contending that meteors from outer space are a major threat to safety on our highways and threaten the survival of all motorists."[53]

In the light of these conflicting claims and denials, it was difficult for the average citizen to comprehend the extent of this new danger he faced. Many Americans, however, began to realize that the Marshall islanders and the Japanese fishermen were not the only victims of BRAVO. At the very least, people wanted to know more about the effects of testing on the environment. Warning that "no one yet knows just how much radiation a human being can take" without jeopardizing his offspring, *Newsweek* declared, "The question, 'how dangerous is fallout,' is potentially the most dangerous gap in modern man's scientific knowledge." *Time* agreed, commenting that without additional information, it would be impossible to estimate "how many H-explosions (in tests or in war) would be necessary to do damage to the whole earth." Eugene Rabinowich, the editor of the *Bulletin of the Atomic Scientists*, blamed the AEC for its excessive secrecy about a problem which "may end in a slow but irreparable decay of the human race." "Mankind as a whole has the right to all information which may help to evaluate the possible long-range hereditary effects of the use of atomic energy in peace and war," he insisted.[54]

By the end of 1954, a growing feeling of pessimism pervaded both the scientific and public discussion. In a rare television interview, Robert Oppenheimer summed up the fears of many when he said of the perils of radioactivity, "You can certainly destroy enough of humanity so that only the greatest act of faith can persuade you that what's left is human." Ralph Lapp pinpointed the reason why so many people dreaded radiation. It "cannot be felt and possesses all the terror of the unknown," he explained. "It is something which evokes revulsion and helplessness—like a bubonic plague." E. B. White spoke for millions of laymen when he reminded the scientists of the danger of poisoning the earth. "There is not a single scheme of mouse or man, of man or nation, that doesn't depend for its success on the existence of a friendly atmosphere, one that will support life," he wrote in the *New Yorker*. "Without a benign habitat, everything loses its point. . . ."

BRAVO had thus touched a deep and sensitive nerve, giving rise to fear which bordered on terror. For a while, people could forget the ominous particles that drifted silently through the stratosphere and fell slowly back to earth with each rainfall. But eventually they had to face the danger which the H-bomb had brought to the world. "The question for the Administration is whether to meet the fears of people throughout the world with silence or with fact and reason," the editors of the *New Republic* pointed out.[55] Neither the President nor the AEC could delay much longer a full disclosure of the fallout peril.

"THE TERRIBLE TRUTH"

The Eisenhower administration debated the wisdom of a full public disclosure of the fallout peril throughout the fall of 1954 and the early winter of 1955. The AEC, surprisingly, favored a report to the American people. The military at first objected, but after a special interagency task force recommended a policy of disclosure to the National Security Council, the Pentagon acquiesced. The AEC completed its fallout statement by late November only to face opposition from the State Department. Secretary Dulles feared that revelations of the extent of fallout from H-bombs would interfere with his delicate negotiations to persuade the NATO countries to accept a rearmed West Germany as a member of the Western alliance. Chairman Strauss agreed to withhold the report pending the completion of the NATO arrangements, but he warned President Eisenhower on December 10, 1954, about leaks to the press of information which was "being treated in a sensational manner." Upon Dulles's return from Europe, Strauss concluded, "we should release the information we have now evaluated and which it is desirable for the public to know. . . ."[1]

When Dulles continued to assert that the report would "adversely affect certain international situations," Strauss received strong support from Val Peterson, the Federal Civil Defense Administrator. Peterson had first learned the details of the fallout peril at an AEC briefing on July 8, and, recognizing its importance for civil defense planning, he pushed hard for disclosure. In a conference with state and city officials on December 27, he spoke guardedly of the danger in case of nuclear war, warning that "there is no farmer or rancher who may not be right in the middle of the fallout," but he could not be more specific. Finally, on January 28, 1955, Peterson informed the Civil Defense Advisory Council, made up of 3 governors, 3 mayors, and 6 private citizens, of the details contained in the still undisclosed AEC report. They joined him in urging the President to override the State Department and release the report immediately.[2]

The debate within the administration reached its climax in early February. Strauss and Peterson presented their arguments to the National Security Council, and Eisenhower finally told them to consult with public relations experts on how best to inform the people. Last minute objections from the deputy director of the Bureau of the Budget, who feared that "one certain consequence will be an increased demand for the banning of atomic weapons," and from William Robinson, the president of Coca-Cola, Inc., whom Ike considered the "best public relations man" in the country, led to further delay. Robinson argued that the report would create an adverse reaction abroad, and when reporters asked Eisenhower about the danger of fallout from H-bombs on February 9, he replied in vague terms, saying only that "There are certain radioactive effects that in the immediate vicinity can be very, very bad, indeed, as we well know." Later that day, however, after the AEC had made a few changes in the report to satisfy Robinson and Dulles, the President told Strauss to "go ahead" with publication.[3]

The administration had waited too long. On February 10, both the *Bulletin of the Atomic Scientists* and the *New Republic* published a long article by Ralph Lapp describing in detail the fallout pattern from BRAVO. Using data from a speech that AEC Commissioner Willard Libby had made on December 2, 1954, Lapp estimated that the debris from the March 1 shot covered an elliptical area nearly 200 miles long and 50 miles wide, some 8,000 square miles in all. If such a bomb fell on Washington, a deadly cloud of radioactivity would cover the entire state of Maryland, killing far more people than those who would perish from the initial heat and blast. Commenting on the frightening implications for civil defense, Lapp called on the AEC to "release authentic data" that would provide "a basis for strengthening our national security." The press quickly seized on the article to chastise the AEC, incorrectly putting the blame on Strauss rather than Dulles, and to echo Lapp's demand for more information. "Disclosure and discussion are needed to reduce the disasters of warfare," commented Michael Straight in the *New Republic,* "and to reawaken concern in the alternatives to war."[4]

I

The AEC report, finally released to the public on February 15, 1955, confirmed Lapp's analysis of the dangers of fallout. Distinguishing between local and global fallout, the report described the debris from BRAVO as covering a cigar-shaped area extending 220 miles in length and 40 miles at its widest. If such a bomb were dropped on a city, the AEC admitted, half the population living up to 160 miles downwind from the explosion would be killed. All but ignoring the bulk of the report, which dealt with global fallout, the press played up these sensational local effects. "Drifting down from the sky," proclaimed *Newsweek,* "the ash will poison everything it touches within a cigar-shaped area of 7,000 square miles. It can threaten all life in a state the size of New Jersey." *Time* calculated that if an H-bomb hit Cleveland, the fallout, carried on the normal northwesterly winds, would doom everyone in Pittsburgh, 100 miles away, and might even threaten the population of Washington.

The news magazine noted the AEC advice that such simple measures as washing off the deadly dust and taking shelter in basements would greatly reduce the casualties, but they still found the danger alarming. "Even without exaggeration the story was fantastic," commented *Time,* while *Newsweek* labeled the AEC report as "the terrible truth."[5]

The main body of the report, however, dealt with global effects from testing rather than the immediate hazards from nuclear war. In sober terms, the AEC described strontium-90 as the most dangerous long-term byproduct of nuclear explosions. Its half-life of 28 years (the time it takes for 50 per cent of a given amount of Sr^{90} to dissipate) created a serious problem, the AEC stated, especially since the substance, with its similarity to calcium, could enter the food chain through uptake from the soil by plants and eventually become lodged in human bone. "The amount of radiostrontium now present in the soil as a result of all nuclear explosions to date would have to be increased many thousand times before any effect on humans would be noticeable," the report reassured the public. Because its radioactivity was so weak, the AEC observed, Sr^{90} did not pose any genetic danger. Other global fallout substances did have the power to cause mutations, but the total exposure to date was only 0.1r, or about 1/100th of the average radiation exposure an individual received from natural causes during his or her reproductive lifetime. "It is about the same as the exposure received from one chest X-ray," the report pointed out.

In commenting on these hazards, the AEC argued that while testing created risks both to human health and genetic well-being, they were minute compared to the advantages gained for "the security of the nation and of the free world." The danger was no greater than that involved in manufacturing conventional explosives or "in transporting inflammable substances such as oil or gasoline on our streets and highways." The AEC promised to take every possible precaution in conducting future tests and concluded by reaffirming, "None of the extensive data collected from all tests shows that residual radioactivity is being concentrated in dangerous amounts anywhere in the world outside the testing areas."[6]

The administration tried hard to reinforce the matter-of-fact tone of the AEC report. In a statement accompanying the release on February 15, James Hagerty said that the President hoped that the new information would quiet the speculation, "much of it exaggerated," over fallout and spur public support for civil defense. Lewis Strauss also issued a separate statement in which he tried to minimize the danger. He pointed out that the radioactivity from most fallout disappeared within a few hours; he denied that American nuclear tests had created "any serious public hazard" and he played down the genetic risk, though he admitted the evidence on this point was too slight to permit "an incontrovertible forecast." Whatever the danger from testing, he concluded, until there was a workable international agreement on disarmament, "the study and evaluation of the effects of weapons which might be used against us and the improvement of our means of self-defense are a paramount duty of our Government."[7]

The public response was mixed, with major attention focused on the civil defense implications. On February 22, Senator Estes Kefauver of Tennessee held a hearing before his Armed Services subcommittee at which he and Senator Stuart Symington of Missouri criticized the AEC for the long delay in releasing the fallout report. Ralph Lapp made the same charge in a follow-up article in the *Bulletin of the Atomic Scientists*. The physicist accused the administration of keeping "secret the facts about fallout—a superbomb effect of life-and-death importance to millions of Americans." He also found the report incomplete, asking why the AEC ignored such issues as the lingering nature of local fallout and the danger from inhaling fallout particles. Other commentators, however, came to the defense of the administration by restating the national security argument. "The U.S. realizes the consequences of atomic and hydrogen war," argued the editors of *Time*, "but until there is sensible and secure international control, it intends to go on improving nuclear weapons and trying to establish defenses against them."[8]

Only a few people spoke out on the issue of global fallout. The *New York Times* called for "more research and study" on the problem "of continued release of small but abnormal amounts of radioactivity into the atmosphere." Linus Pauling, a Nobel laureate in biochemistry from Cal Tech, startled a television audience by warning that global radiation might cause cancer. "Leukemia is one of the great dangers," Pauling said in an NBC interview, claiming that the fallout dose might be just enough to trigger this dread disease in susceptible victims. Val Peterson added a new element of danger when he told a "Meet the Press" panel that the next development could be a cobalt bomb that would have a doomsday effect. By placing a wrapping of cobalt around an H-bomb, Peterson explained, scientists could create enough radioactivity to "drift around and around the world and kill everybody." Peterson hastened to add that no one would be foolish enough to use such a suicidal weapon, but the editors of the *New Republic* were impressed enough to label 1955 not just "Year 9 of the Atomic Age" but "Year 1 of something far worse."

Worried by such alarming statements, President Eisenhower tried to reassure the nation. The purpose of the AEC report, he pointed out at a news conference, was to give people information about fallout which they could use to protect themselves in case of nuclear attack. Disturbed by the scare stories that resulted, Ike commented wryly on the human tendency to recoil in horror from nuclear realities and then added, "You have to look facts in the face, but you have to have the stamina to do it without just going hysterical."[9]

A decision the President had made months earlier, however, heightened the growing public concern. On February 13, two days before the AEC report was released, Lewis Strauss announced the beginning of Operation TEACUP, a series of small atomic blasts at the government's proving grounds near Frenchman's Flat, Nevada. The bombs to be tested, Chairman

41

Strauss explained, would be small weapons under 50 kilotons designed for battlefield use. The AEC would take every possible precaution to prevent radioactive fallout, but the tests were vital to national security and could not be canceled. "The consequences of any other course," Strauss declared, "would imperil our liberty, even our existence."

Adverse weather conditions, which threatened to shower nearby Nevada communities with fallout, forced a three-day postponement of the first shot. Finally, on February 18, an Air Force plane dropped an atomic bomb which exploded about 1000 feet from the ground, creating what newsmen called an "unspectacular" blast which could still be heard 30 miles away. On February 23, Strauss reported to the President that the first two shots had been successful and then invited Eisenhower to attend the next test, saying "it would be most helpful to morale if he did." The President wisely declined.[10]

A week later, TEACUP began to cause public concern. On March 1, a security guard ventured into the danger area at Frenchman's Flat and received heavy, though not fatal, radiation exposure. Four days later, Chicago reported radioactive rain resulting from the March 1 test which led to the highest Geiger counts the city had ever recorded. By March 10, the Weather Bureau was reporting a huge radioactive cloud stretching for nearly 1000 miles over the United States from Nebraska to New Jersey. The cloud passed over New York, making the city's air four times as radioactive as usual, but AEC scientists assured skeptical New Yorkers that there was no danger to health. In Colorado, two university scientists warned on March 12 that the Nevada tests had polluted the state's atmosphere to a dangerous degree. Quigg Newton, the mayor of Denver, quickly disputed this claim, while the state's governor, Ed C. Johnson, called for the arrest of the offending professors. The two scientists stood their ground, however, telling the press that there was no "safe" level of radioactivity and warning of such possible consequences as lung cancer, leukemia, and the birth of deformed children.[11]

Public concern, at times bordering on panic, began to develop by mid-March. In southern California, close to the test site, supermarkets started selling Survival Food Kits costing $5.40 and consisting of enough supplies to feed four people for three days. "We've gone far enough in testing those atom bombs," commented a Los Angeles beautician. "It's making a nervous wreck of me and lots of my customers." "Isn't it high time that bomb-testing be dispensed with," wrote one *Newsweek* reader, who warned about the "indirect annihilation of the human race" through "the slow process of food contamination." Another writer commented sardonically, "Why not an X-bomb, which could blow up all scientists of the world before they have a chance to blow us up?" Yet despite these fears, few Americans bothered to study the information the government had released. A Gallup poll taken in early March showed that only 17 per cent of those asked could explain correctly what was meant by fallout; 9 per cent gave confused answers and a staggering 74 per cent simply did not know. *Newsweek* had the most convincing explanation. "The whole idea of atomic war was so horrible," the editors wrote about the people's reaction, "they just declined to think about it. Lacking facts, they invented fiction."[12]

II

Throughout the spring of 1955, the Atomic Energy Commission conducted an intensive public relations campaign designed to convince the American people that the fear of fallout was groundless. The editors of the conservative *U.S. News and World Report* cooperated with AEC officials in a six-page article entitled "The Facts about A-bomb 'Fall-out': Not a Word of Truth in Scare Stories over Tests." Charging unnamed people with deliberately generating "fear of A-bomb tests among Americans," the editors interviewed government leaders and scientists to set the record straight. Debunking reports of radioactive clouds crossing the United States, the article cited experts who stated that the highest fallout from the Nevada tests was just 0.2r, a "tiny amount" that exposed an individual to less radioactivity than "wearing a luminous-dial wrist watch." The editors admitted that strontium-90 could be dangerous in large quantities, but so far, according to AEC spokesmen, the amount of Sr^{90} in the air was only .001 of the permissible dose. "Tests indicate that an H-bomb explosion could be conducted every week for an indefinite period without raising the level of this substance to dangerous heights," the article stated. As for the genetic danger, the evidence was ambiguous. Citing experiments with fruit flies that showed radiation producing a hardier breed, the *U.S. News* claimed that "some experts believe that mutations usually work out in the end to improve species." Fallout from a nuclear war would be dangerous, the article concluded, but tests did not produce enough radiation to be "hazardous either to people now, to future generations, to food crops, or even the weather." [13]

The congressional Joint Committee on Atomic Energy held a hearing on April 15 that gave AEC spokesmen an even better forum for rebutting their critics. Chairman Clinton Anderson of New Mexico opened the session by affirming his belief that nuclear tests were "vital to the security of the free world." Leaving no doubt about the purpose of the hearing, Anderson stated the need to clear up "public misapprehension and unwarranted concern" about the Nevada tests. The witnesses, all from the AEC, quickly obliged him.

Lewis Strauss led off by denying reports of damage to American health. "So far as we are aware," he said, "no civilian has ever been injured as a result of these tests." Fallout in most cities "has barely added to the level of nature's background radiation," Strauss continued. Willard Libby followed him with detailed figures on natural radiation, leading committee member Carl Hinshaw of California to conclude that "the amount of increased radiation due to the atomic tests is almost undetectable."

Dr. Merril Eisenbud, manager of the AEC's New York

operations office, described the system used to monitor the fallout of strontium-90 nationwide. As of September 1954, the level of Sr^{90} in the soil was approximately 1 millicurie per square mile, only 1/1000th of the permissible amount. He admitted that "no risk is ever absolutely zero," but he argued that the danger from this minute deposit of Sr^{90} was "very, very small." Dr. John Bugher, chief of the division of biology and medicine, backed him up by pointing out that this amount was only 0.2 per cent of natural radioactivity. Asked to estimate the effect of this level on human health, Dr. Bugher replied that it would have to be raised "between 100,000 and a million times" before "we could expect to detect any change in human pathology and disease due to the isotope."

The AEC witnesses were equally sanguine about the genetic effects. Strauss admitted that additional study was needed to determine precisely the impact of radiation on heredity, but he called the likelihood of the Nevada tests producing defective genes "remote." Dr. E.L. Green, an Ohio State University geneticist under contract to the AEC, agreed, calling the chance of test-induced mutations showing up in future generations "unlikely."

The most striking testimony came from meteorologists who denied charges that nuclear tests changed the world's weather. Every year people complained that atomic tests produced abnormal heat and cold, prolonged drought, and an increase in tornados, explained Dr. Harry Wexler of the U.S. Weather Bureau. Citing evidence compiled by his associates, Wexler said that there was no direct association between nuclear explosions and weather conditions. Dr. John Von Neumann, an AEC Commissioner and famed mathematician, did speculate that the dust clouds from H-bomb tests could conceivably block solar heating and thus reduce world temperatures. But he quickly noted that it would take more than one hundred H-bomb blasts to equal the power of the volcano Krakatoa, whose eruption in the nineteenth century did lower temperatures slightly over the earth for three years.

45

Lewis Strauss summed up the AEC's position at the end of his statement to the Joint Committee. Testing was not dangerous, he reiterated, except possibly in its genetic effects, and the Commission was spending over $1.5 million each year to subsidize basic research to clear up this point. The vital consideration, he reminded the Committee, was the imperative necessity of testing to maintain the American lead over the Soviet Union in nuclear technology. "The weapons which we test are essential to our national security and that of the free world;" Strauss argued, "they have been and may well continue to be a deterrent to devastating war." [14]

Even while Strauss spoke, the TEACUP tests continued in the Nevada desert. By early May, there had been twelve detonations, nearly all of small, tactical bombs with several involving army units stationed only 3000 yards from ground zero to show how these nuclear weapons could be used in warfare. The climax came on May 15 when the AEC set off a 40-kiloton bomb over a mock city which reporters dubbed "Doomstown." The blast, felt in Las Vegas 75 miles away, leveled brick-and-frame houses, leaving only a precast concrete home standing. Officials estimated that all the inhabitants of "Doomstown" would have perished from either the shock wave or radiation. Civil Defense observers concluded that the only way to survive nuclear war was to "dig in or get out," but military commentators were more favorably impressed by the lessons of TEACUP. "Not only does the U.S. have the edge in strategic air," concluded a writer in *Time,* "but it now has a family of weapons that renders U.S. conventional forces more powerful than those of any enemy." The hydrogen age had truly arrived; a 40-kiloton bomb was now considered to be a "conventional" weapon ready for use in any future war. [15]

It was left to Lewis Strauss to make the final comment on TEACUP. In a speech to the American Medical Association's convention in Atlantic City on June 6, he accused those who claimed nuclear tests poisoned the atmosphere or produced "future generations of monsters" of committing "an act of irre-

46

sponsibility." Using a now familiar analogy, he asserted that all the nuclear explosions to date had not increased the earth's radioactivity more than the equivalent of a single chest X-ray. Given the presence of H-bombs in the arsenals of those "who are hostile to Western ideals of freedom and human dignity," he argued, "we have no choice but to perfect, test and produce nuclear weapons." The only solace, the Admiral concluded, was that continued American strategic superiority "may very well be the main deterrent to a third and infinitely more terrible world war." [16] In other words, the hazards of fallout from testing were minute compared to the suffering the world was being spared by America's advancing technology.

III

While the AEC tried to quiet public fears over fallout, a far-reaching debate broke out within the scientific community. Aware of their responsibility to inform the American people about this complex and technical issue, scientists began to speak out on the potential danger of fallout. Those who hoped the discussion would lead to a clear and rational analysis were doomed to disappointment. The participants revealed many of the same biases and emotions that ran through the dialogue between the AEC and its critics. Given the lack of precise data and laboratory evidence, the scientists ultimately rested their judgments on deeply-held political beliefs and moral values.

Japanese scientists provided the crucial evidence that led their American counterparts to comprehend the true magnitude of the fallout problem. Ralph Lapp and others in the United States had been puzzled by the large amounts of radioactivity produced by BRAVO. They knew that a pure fusion explosion would release very little radiation; strontium-90 and the other radioactive substances found in fallout were fission products. They theorized that the BRAVO fallout came from the atomic bomb trigger of what they conceived to be a fission-fusion weapon, but they kept wondering why a small atomic bomb would produce so much radiation. Mituo Taketani, an eminent physicist at Tokyo University, gave them the answer when he revealed that the radioactive ash on the *Lucky Dragon* contained traces of uranium-237, an isotope which could only come from normal uranium, U^{238}, rather than U^{235}, the rare form used in the atomic bomb. The only possible explanation was that BRAVO had been a fission-fusion-fission bomb; that is, an atomic trigger to provide the initial heat by fission, a layer of lithium deuteride to produce hydrogen fusion, and then a wrapper of common uranium that would fission under the impact of a thermonuclear explosion.

Rumors about such a weapon led Garnett Horner of the *Washington Star* to ask President Eisenhower on March 16 if BRAVO had actually been "a super-H-bomb with a jacket of natural state uranium?" If so, Horner continued, just what were the implications of this "so-called bargain basement U-bomb?" In a reply deleted from the published press conference transcript, the President said, "I don't think I should attempt to answer it." The question, he added, was technical in nature, and while he could give "a fairly accurate answer," he would prefer to have Admiral Strauss give out whatever information the AEC considered to be "in the public domain."

The Admiral remained silent, but *Time* and *Newsweek* carried stories the next week giving a detailed description of what they termed the "U-bomb." Both news magazines stressed the cheapness of ordinary uranium to point out that the new weapon was both inexpensive to produce and virtually limitless in destructive power. Simply by adding more and more U^{238} to the bomb's casing, the United States could build bombs of incredible force. Because the weapon relied primarily on fission, the resulting radioactivity would be enormous, possibly even greater than Peterson's hypothetical cobalt bomb. The U-bombs, the magazines concluded, added little to American security. Their use in a nuclear war threatened to create enough fallout to destroy the attacker as well as his victim and they were so easy and cheap to produce that Russia would soon have them in profusion.[17]

Scientists immediately began to comment about the nature and implications of the super bomb. Ralph Lapp alluded to its three-stage character in scientific articles and in testimony before a congressional committee, but it was British physicist J. Rotblat who gave the fullest analysis in an article in the May 1955 issue of the *Bulletin of the Atomic Scientists*. In terms a layman could understand, Rotblat explained the advantages of using ordinary uranium. Not only was it much cheaper than U^{235}; it provided far more power than the thermonuclear reaction of lithium deuteride. "The energy released per fission is thus 20–40 times greater than per fusion," Rotblat wrote. He calculated that the fission of U^{238} supplied 80 per cent of the super bomb's power and accounted for nearly all the resulting fallout. Ignoring local effects, Rotblat concentrated on the global consequences of sending massive amounts of fission products into the atmosphere. A few tests might not do much damage to man's genes, he observed, but the detonation of as many as 75 H-bombs could double the natural level of radiation and lead to a disastrous increase in human mutations. Mankind's very future was at stake, Rotblat claimed, warning that "there is something particularly sinister about a bomb which is so designed as to poison the whole world with radioactivity."[18]

Willard Libby confirmed Rotblat's analysis of the bomb's composition in a little-noted speech on June 3, but the AEC Commissioner drew very different conclusions. Speaking to a University of Chicago alumni group, Libby described a superbomb that released 10 megatons of fission energy and contaminated 100,000 square miles with radioactive fallout. While he spoke in highly technical terms and avoided any direct reference to the weapon's configuration, scientists quickly realized that only a fission-fusion-fission bomb with an outer layer of U^{238} could produce these results. Reporters who listened to the speech, however, did not make this deduction, and as a result the press only mentioned Libby's reassuring conclusion that tests of such bombs "do not constitute any real hazard to immediate health." The strontium-90 level would have to increase 10,000-fold to cause bone cancer, the genetic danger was less from fallout than from natural background radiation, industrial workers in atomic plants were safely exposed to 15,000 times more radiation than the public received from bomb tests—these familiar arguments led journalists to conclude that Libby's speech was just one more salvo in the AEC's public relations campaign.

Worried scientists spent more than a week patiently educating members of the Washington press corps on the true significance of Libby's words. Finally, on June 12, the *New York Times* printed a front-page story by Anthony Leviero pointing out that the AEC Commissioner had indicated that the H-bomb "can be made with the cheapest atomic explosives in virtually limitless size." The next day the *Washington Post* and the *Christian Science Monitor* carried similar stories on what one commentator called "probably the most important event of our times." Starting with Libby's statement that a 10 megaton H-bomb would contaminate 100,000 square miles, reporters speculated on the huge area that a bomb several times larger would cover with its deadly fallout. Such talk finally led a Massachusetts resident to suggest a new word to the editors of the *New York Times*—"vivacide"—to signify the death of all life on earth.[19]

Just how dangerous was the fallout from the three-stage H-bomb? Scientists wrestled with this difficult question throughout 1955, trying to avoid both the exaggerated public fears and the soothing AEC assurances. They quickly ruled out the doomsday notion. Physicists discounted any chance of nuclear bombs touching off an uncontrollable chain reaction that would consume the entire earth; biologists were equally sure that even the fallout from an all-out nuclear war would not in itself destroy mankind. Instead they focused on two lesser, but nonetheless serious, issues: the somatic danger to present human health and the genetic risk to future generations.

The lack of medical evidence about the impact of low-level radiation on the body made scientists very cautious and thus limited this aspect of the debate. Studies of the survivors of Hiroshima and Nagasaki provided the best information. Researchers at Tufts Medical School reported that the incidence of leukemia was 600 times the normal rate among those who recovered from radiation exposure at Hiroshima. The small number of cases, only 44 out of the 31,000 studied, however, made it difficult to apply this data to global fallout. Aware that repeated small exposures could have very different effects, scientists agreed tentatively that fallout might lead to a slight increase in leukemia in the world's population. Evidence both from the Japanese experience and laboratory experiments with mice showed that radiation exposure could also lead to a lessening of life expectancy, probably on the order of only a few days or weeks at the most. The experts could not account for this "radiation senility," nor could they be sure it would result from the very low levels of global fallout.[20]

Biologists were much more certain that fallout created a genetic danger for the human race. Professor C.H. Waddington, a Scottish geneticist, summed up the prevailing consensus when he wrote that "any atomic explosion which produces an increase in radioactivity, however small, in regions inhabited by man will add something to humanity's store of newly mutated and most harmful genes." The disagreement came over the extent of the danger. Some experts, such as Alfred H. Sturtevant of Cal Tech, estimated that 1800 of the 90 million children born in the world in 1954 possessed genetic defects caused by bomb radiation. Norman J. Birrell, a Canadian zoologist, worried more about the long-term consequences. Admitting that the additional mutations "would not spell the doom of humanity," he nevertheless predicted a decline in human vitality which would persist for "the next few hundred thousand years" until all the degenerate individuals were weeded out by the evolutionary process. Waddington felt that the genetic risks were far less drastic, but he urged his colleagues to calculate

51

them more precisely "so that we can decide how far we shall go in running up biological debts which our descendants will have to pay."[21]

These pessimistic assessments did not go unchallenged. Dr. Shields Warren, a Boston physician and former director of the AEC's division of biology and medicine, argued that the genetic danger from testing was "so slight in relation to other risks as to be disregarded." Six distinguished scientists who served on an AEC advisory committee agreed, estimating that the defective individuals produced by bomb radiation would number only in the hundreds. ". . . The few radiation-induced defectives will not change measurably the number of about 40,000 defectives" born each year in the United States, they concluded. Herman M. Slatis, writing in *Science,* felt that these mutations were so small that they "might go almost unnoticed." But he quickly reminded his readers of "the basic fact . . . that any irradiation is bad," and warned that society should be protected against any general increase in the mutation rate.[22]

The most authoritative statement came from Hermann J. Muller of Indiana University, who had won the Nobel prize in 1946 for demonstrating that X-rays could produce mutations in fruit flies. Muller had left the United States in 1933 to work at the Institute of Genetics in Russia but he returned in 1937 after breaking with the Soviets over their insistence that acquired characteristics could be inherited. Regarded as the world's leading expert on radiation-induced genetic effects, Muller gave his views on fallout in a speech to the National Academy of Sciences in Washington on April 25, 1955.

Muller began his address by denouncing the statements on both sides of the debate "as special pleadings, dictated by ulterior motives." Radiation does cause mutations in direct proportion to the exposure, he affirmed, and nearly all such mutations are harmful. But he then stressed the minute number of genetic effects caused by bomb tests compared to the "natural mutations already present." He argued that the "tens of thousands" of test-induced changes would "be completely lost to sight" in the billions of individual Americans in the next 20 generations. A single medical X-ray, he warned, would do greater genetic damage to an individual than all the bombs exploded so far. Muller still did not deny the unfortunate consequences of testing, but he balanced them against the ruthless nature of Soviet totalitarianism to conclude that tests "are at the present stage necessary to prevent our being put at a military disadvantage." Like Strauss, Muller placed the defense of freedom above the real but limited dangers from nuclear experimentation.[23]

Despite Muller's reassuring views, the AEC stupidly blacklisted him from an international conference he was scheduled to address in Geneva in the summer of 1955. Lewis Strauss later apologized publicly, but the damage had been done. The *Bulletin of the Atomic Scientists* published Muller's prepared remarks in November, and it was clear that the geneticist had begun to change his mind about the dangers from testing. In the new paper, he emphasized the cumulative impact of every mutation on future generations, terming each such change "a postponed disaster." "Thus the genetic damage," he asserted, ". . . is seen to be far greater than the damage to the exposed individual himself." Citing the survivors of Horoshima and Nagasaki, Muller explained that it would take several generations for the hereditary changes to show up and predicted that the victims' descendants would have "twice as many ills of genetic origin as we have." He made no reference to bomb tests in these remarks, but he closed by warning people to guard against "the dangerous fallacy that what cannot be seen or felt need not be bothered with."[24]

By the fall of 1955, most geneticists seemed to be in agreement with Muller's modified view. The danger of harmful mutations from bomb testing was slight for any single individual, but the cumulative impact on the human race was likely to be larger than anyone would welcome. Geneticists felt their responsibility was to guard what Muller termed man's "most valuable irretrievable possession." Whatever military imperatives called for bomb tests today had to be balanced off against the cost to those yet unborn. Danish biologist Mogens Westergaard stated the situation most eloquently when he wrote: [25]

> Unfortunately, . . . we have reached a stage where human mistakes can have a more disastrous effect than ever before in our history—because such mistakes may drastically change the course of man's biological evolution.

IV

Scientists failed to arrive at a clear consensus in 1955, but a majority seemed to believe that the dangers to human life from testing were slight. John Cockcroft, a respected English physicist, conducted a thorough study of the level of radioactivity from bomb tests in Britain. In a widely cited report in *Nature,* the leading British scientific publication, Cockcroft concluded that the tests had increased the normal background radiation by only about 1 per cent, a rise "so low that it should not cause any anxiety." Three American scientists carried out a similar survey in the United States and reported their results in the June issue of the *Bulletin of the Atomic Scientists.* Their study showed that testing so far was likely to cause about 20,000 mutations and shorten life expectancy by 2 or 3 days. They viewed these findings as more disturbing than the AEC would admit but not as critical as alarmists claimed. "Each citizen will have to come to his own conclusions," they wrote, "based upon his own assessment of the relative evil of 20,000 mutations as compared with the information derived from a series of bomb tests." [26]

Most scientists appeared to agree with Hermann Muller that testing was vital to national security. L.W. Nordheim, a Duke University physicist, pointed to both the original atomic bomb test at Alamagordo in 1945 and to BRAVO as cases where the experts had been surprised by the power of the resulting blasts. "The distance from the concepts and theoretical calculations to the incredibly complex phenomena that take place in a nuclear explosion," he explained, "is so great that one cannot be sure of one's ground without actual experiments." Dr. Howard L. Andrews, head of the radiobiology section of the National Cancer Institute, agreed. In a speech to the Washington Academy of Medicine on May 13, 1955, Andrews warned against "the hysterical banning of all nuclear experiments" and called the development of nuclear weapons "an essential part of our defense effort." But Andrews did insist that all such tests be conducted with utmost care to "minimize radiological hazards;" the nation could not permit the test sites to be used as "mere playgrounds for the amusement of bomb-happy scientists."

The favorite argument of those who defended nuclear tests was to portray them as the only alternative to all-out war. Sometimes they did this by asserting that the casualties from testing were minute when compared to the deaths and suffering that would result from a full-scale nuclear attack. "We must . . . take the calculated risk of some radiation injury now in order that we prevent annihilation later," claimed Dr. Andrews. Even as concerned a scientist as Ralph Lapp dismissed the global fallout risk from testing as "of minor importance" as compared to the danger from local radiation in the aftermath of a nuclear war. The assumption seemed to be that tests magically warded off the ultimate catastrophe; that the world faced a choice of evils and the only rational alternative was testing. Professor Nordheim made this point when he declared that the "objective of our policy must be peace without appeasement." The controversy over testing, he continued, served only to obscure "the real problem" of nuclear war "by sidetracking the attention of the world."[27]

There was only one proposition which was universally affirmed—the need for more information on the effects of radiation on human life. Scientists of all persuasions joined together to advocate further research to provide the data they needed to assess the risks involved in testing.

The Federation of American Scientists, representing the most politically-active and socially-concerned members of the profession, called on the United Nations to create a commission of inquiry. In a statement released on March 6, 1955, the Federation suggested that such a commission, made up of scientists from around the world, could collect data and evaluate "the biological and genetic effects of radiation on human beings." This study could lead to agreement on a threshold, a specific limit on the amount of radiation mankind could tolerate, and could perhaps culminate in the UN setting a quota on the number of tests each nation would be allowed to conduct annually. Carefully avoiding any call for a test ban, the Federation statement stressed the danger humanity faced from fallout and urged a truly international quest for knowledge and control.[28]

More conservative members of the scientific establishment displayed similar concerns. The Council of the American Association for the Advancement of Science proposed a committee to study radiation hazards in December 1954. Before that effort materialized, however, the National Academy of Sciences, a quasi-governmental body of some 500 of the nation's senior scientists, revealed plans for its own comprehensive study. The Academy's announcement was the result of an initiative by the trustees of the Rockefeller Foundation. On February 23, Dean Rusk, president of the Foundation, had written to Eisenhower suggesting that the National Academy of Sciences undertake a study of radiation effects "with particular attention to the possible danger to the genetic heritage of man." Rusk added that the Rockefeller trustees wanted to fund the project. Despite objections from Lewis Strauss, who argued that the AEC was already spending $3 million in radiation research, the President responded favorably. On April 8, Detlev W. Bronk, president of the National Academy, announced the appointment of a committee of eminent scientists to study the fallout problem and report its findings to the Academy.

Most scientists applauded the creation of the new committee, though one noted that its membership included several experts who had been associated with the AEC. The nationalistic nature of the Academy's study led to a more serious objection. In contrast to the Federation of American Scientists' proposal, the Academy's committee reflected a purely American viewpoint, and in light of the close ties of both the Rockefeller Foundation and the National Academy to the Eisenhower Administration, few expected a report recommending an end to nuclear testing.[29]

The *New York Times* summed up the reactions of many Americans. The editors expressed the widely held Cold War belief that we could not "afford to discontinue our tests of improved atomic bombs," but at the same time they worried about "adding to the background of feeble radiation to which life has been exposed for millions of years." The *Times* felt the National Academy's study would provide the clarification that everyone wanted and hoped it would establish agreement on a threshold "that may not be crossed without imperiling mankind."

In Paris, Robert Oppenheimer, once a national hero for his role in developing the atomic bomb and now an outcast, commented on the scientists' dilemma. Asked by an interviewer about the danger of bomb tests, Oppenheimer pointed to the amazing gap in the knowledge of experts, especially on the effects on heredity. "Physicists don't know," he said. "Specialists in genetics don't know. Nobody knows, and we must take account of this ignorance."[30]

ORIGINS
OF THE
TEST BAN DEBATE

The controversy among scientists was accompanied by an equally significant debate among political leaders over ways to curb the arms race and spare the world the devastation of nuclear war. On February 17, 1955, two days after the AEC published its report on fallout, Prime Minister Winston Churchill announced that Britain had discovered the secret of the H-bomb and would proceed to build its own thermonuclear weapons. The 80-year-old Churchill defended this decision in a two-day debate in the House of Commons in early March. In somber tones, the Prime Minister declared that with the new weapon "the entire foundation of human affairs was revolutionized and mankind placed in a situation both measureless and laden with doom." The only salvation, he continued, lay in deterrence. With the awesome hydrogen bomb in their arsenals, none of the major powers would dare resort to war. "Then it may be that we shall by a process of sublime irony have reached a stage in this story where safety will be the sturdy child of terror," Churchill predicted, "and survival the twin brother of annihilation."

The Labor Party challenged this concept of defense through deterrence, but in late March Parliament voted to support the

British government's H-bomb program. The Laborites voted to make opposition to nuclear testing a major issue in the forthcoming elections in which foreign secretary Anthony Eden sought to succeed the retiring Churchill as prime minister. Eden led the Conservatives to victory at the polls in May, but in the process he was forced to commit his government to the goal of seeking new international efforts at nuclear disarmament. Thus America's principal European ally joined the ranks of those calling for negotiations to control the arms race.[1]

Other voices soon joined in. In his Easter message to the world, Pope Pius XII dwelt on the dangers fallout posed for mankind. Citing "the horrors of monstrous offspring," the Pontiff warned that nuclear tests were doing unknown damage to "that mysterious something which is deep down in every living thing." The leaders of the newly-emerging nations in Asia and Africa, meeting in April at Bandung in Indonesia, expressed concern over the exposure of their peoples to bomb radiation. At the opening of the conference, both India's Nehru and Indonesia's Sukarno called on the nuclear powers to end their tests. Pro-Western spokesmen in the third world finally succeeded in inserting a provision for international inspection in the Bandung Conference's resolution that demanded "the prohibition of the production, experimentation and use of nuclear and thermonuclear weapons of war." Pending the negotiation of such a ban, the Bandung delegates appealed to the United States and Russia "to suspend experiments for such weapons."[2]

The growing world pressure for nuclear restraint led the United States to reconsider its traditional position on nuclear disarmament. Since 1946, when Bernard Baruch presented the original American proposal to the United Nations, the U.S. insisted that a foolproof system of inspection and control had to be established before any actual reduction in nuclear arms could take place. The Soviet Union, on the other hand, advocated the immediate outlawing of nuclear weapons without any safeguards, thereby creating an impasse which had doomed the Baruch plan and all subsequent disarmament discussions in the UN. The advent of the hydrogen bomb had produced a new effort at negotiation in a five-member United Nations subcommittee consisting of representatives from the United States, Great Britain, France, Canada, and the Soviet Union. This disarmament subcommittee met for six weeks in London during the spring of 1954 and adjourned without making any significant progress. In the fall of 1954, however, the Soviets indicated for the first time a willingness to discuss an international arms control agency with powers of inspection, thus giving rise to hopes for a possible breakthrough at the subcommittee's next session, scheduled to take place in London in the spring of 1955.[3]

The first sign of a new American initiative on disarmament came on March 19, 1955, when President Eisenhower appointed Harold Stassen to the newly-created position of special assistant to the President on disarmament. Stassen had long been active in American politics, emerging as a Republican presidential hopeful after serving as Governor of Minnesota and a member of the American delegation to the San Francisco conference which founded the United Nations. In 1948, he lost out to Thomas Dewey in the race for the GOP nomination, but four years later he backed Eisenhower and as a reward was appointed chief of the Foreign Operations Administration. Known both for his boundless energy and limitless ambition, Stassen was determined to use his new White House post to rescue disarmament policy from its low priority status within the State Department. He would hold cabinet rank and report directly to the President, but at the same time he had to contend with Secretary of State John Foster Dulles, who jealously guarded his control over all aspects of American foreign policy. In appointing Stassen as his personal adviser, Eisenhower apparently hoped to broaden the range of choices in disarmament policy, but at the same time he ensured a bitter contest between two strong-minded men.

Stassen, dubbed "Secretary of Peace" by the press, moved

with his characteristic zest to carry out Eisenhower's mandate. Charged with formulating a unified disarmament policy out of the conflicting ideas of the Pentagon, State Department, and AEC, Stassen drew upon all these agencies, as well as the CIA, in organizing his staff. In addition, he formed eight special task forces, each chaired by a distinguished private citizen, to review all aspects of the arms race. In his first report to the President on May 26, 1955, Stassen concluded that the traditional American goal of eliminating all nuclear weapons was no longer feasible; instead, he recommended the more modest aim of arms control, seeking by various measures to regulate the weapons race. Inspection would be central to any agreement, and highest priority was put on guarding against a surprise nuclear attack.[4]

Stassen and his aides gave careful consideration to the idea of a test ban as part of an arms control plan. The initial suggestions for a ban, notably by Nehru in 1954, had grown out of the fear of radioactive fallout. David R. Inglis, a physicist at Argonne National Laboratory (a cooperative venture run by several midwestern universities and funded by the AEC), offered a different rationale in a series of magazine articles in late 1954 and early 1955. Noting that all previous disarmament efforts had broken down over inspection, especially over Russian refusal to permit foreign supervisors into their territory, Inglis pointed out that a test ban did not require such on-site control. Instruments located outside a nation's borders could detect nuclear explosions at long-range, he argued, and thus an agreement to suspend testing would be virtually self-enforcing. He admitted that a test ban would not be disarmament, since the superpowers would continue to possess the dread weapons, but "it would slow down the rate of development of new techniques of offense and allow the techniques of defense to come closer to catching up." The greatest advantage of a test ban, according to Inglis, was as a first step, a way to break the stalemate and with hope move the nuclear powers toward agreement on more significant disarmament measures. It would also serve, he contended, to prevent the spread of nuclear weapons to other nations; no one could develop an H-bomb without testing it first.

Inglis made a persuasive case for halting nuclear tests without getting enmeshed in the scientists' radiation debate. His proposal, by avoiding any surrender of national sovereignty, was far more realistic than plans that called for the destruction of existing nuclear arsenals. His ideas appealed to those who feared the proliferation of nuclear weapons as well as to others who worried most about the need to move the United States and the Soviet Union off dead center on disarmament. Liberal columnist I. F. Stone summed up the reactions of many to Inglis's suggestion when he wrote, "As a first step away from mutual destruction, no more tests." [5]

President Eisenhower, however, did not agree. When asked by a reporter on February 23, 1955, if the administration had given any thought to a test ban, the President said it had been studied and rejected. Eisenhower indicated that he was far more interested in a comprehensive disarmament proposal than a piecemeal approach. ". . . I see nothing to be gained," he declared, "by pretending to take little bits of items of that kind and deal with them separately." Stassen concurred. After a full interdepartmental study, he advised the President that "a moratorium on H-bomb testing would not be in the interest of the U.S. and should not be agreed to except as a part of a comprehensive disarmament agreement."

After rejecting the test ban concept, Stassen came up with the idea of mutual aerial inspection as the best way to break the disarmament deadlock. When President Eisenhower met with Nikita Khrushchev and Nikolai Bulganin at the Geneva summit conference in August 1955, he surprised them with the "open skies" proposal that Stassen, with the help of Nelson Rockefeller, had devised. Stressing the strong American concern over surprise attack, Eisenhower suggested that the two superpowers exchange blueprints of their major military installations and permit each nation to inspect the other's terrain from the air. The Russian leaders reacted coolly, and though the U.S. continued to advocate variations of the "open skies" plan, it never fulfilled the hopes of Eisenhower and Stassen as the catalyst for a comprehensive agreement on arms control.[6]

I

The Eisenhower administration decided to work through the United Nations to ease worldwide fears over radioactive fallout. Influenced both by the Federation of American Scientists' call for a UN radiation study and by a resolution to the same effect by Senator Frederick C. Payne of Maine, the State Department authorized Ambassador Henry Cabot Lodge to bring up the subject. Lodge first revealed the new American initiative at a meeting in San Francisco on June 21 to commemorate the founding of the United Nations. Noting the concern many world leaders had expressed over fallout, Lodge suggested that the UN gather all available scientific evidence on the effects of radiation on mankind. Lodge was sure that properly conducted nuclear tests did not threaten human health, and he believed that the collected data "could set at rest unjustified fears, combat sensational distortion in the light of truth, and lead to humanity's learning how to deal best with the problems of atomic radiation." A month later, Lodge formally requested that this proposal be placed on the agenda for the fall General Assembly meeting. When that body convened in New York on September 22, Secretary of State Dulles urged the delegates to vote for the study Lodge had proposed. Dulles stressed again the American belief that there was no danger from "properly safeguarded nuclear testing," but he felt that the UN should enlighten the world on "a subject of such transcendent concern."[7]

While the United States sought a UN study to alleviate anxiety, other nations tried to broaden the American proposal to include sensitive political aspects. Thus India wanted a committee that would not only collect data but make recommendations to restrict radiation, and the Soviet Union proposed adding a test ban to the resolution. James J. Wadsworth, the American representative to the General Assembly, fought hard against these suggestions. He objected strenuously to the Soviet test ban idea, repeating the familiar American argument that carefully conducted tests did not "constitute a threat to human health." He insisted that a UN committee could not make binding evaluations of radiation danger; "every nation must come to its own conclusion—each nation must satisfy itself on this problem," he contended. Pointing to the rumors and scare stories about fallout, he stressed the single goal of gathering and disseminating all the available data on radioactivity. ". . . We want the facts," he declared, and "we must let the facts speak for themselves."

The General Assembly's Political Committee began considering the American resolution for an 11-member committee on November 1. Challenged by both India and Russia, who wanted to add several neutralist and communist nations to the body, including mainland China, Wadsworth finally accepted a compromise amendment to include four additional countries, Argentina, Belgium, Egypt, and Mexico. After rejecting a Soviet motion to suspend all nuclear tests indefinitely by a vote of 36 to 17, the Political Committee approved the amended American resolution unanimously. In early December, the full General Assembly rejected amendments offered again by India and Russia and then approved the creation of the new committee.[8]

The United Nations Scientific Committee on Radiation was charged with collecting all available data on the effects of "ionizing radiation upon man and his environment." Each year it was to make progress reports, but the full study was not due until July 1, 1958. Made up of scientists from 15 nations, the committee had no power to set radiation standards nor to make recommendations in regard to nuclear testing. As the United States had intended, it was a reporting agency, designed solely, as Wadsworth noted, to "define precisely the present exposure of the population of the world to ionizing radiation." American officials viewed it as a concession to world opinion, one that would not interfere with continued nuclear testing and would postpone further consideration of radiological hazards for two and a half years. The appointment of Dr. Shields Warren of Boston to serve as the American delegate on the scientific committee reflected the same motivation. Dr. Warren, a former AEC official, viewed fallout as harmless and could be counted on to uphold the American contention that properly conducted bomb tests offered no danger to mankind.[9]

II

A new series of Soviet nuclear tests in the last half of 1955 frustrated American hopes for allaying public concern over fallout. The AEC announced the first Russian shot on August 4 without elaborating on its nature. The Soviets kept silent when the United States reported additional Russian tests on September 24 and November 10. The only test the Kremlin acknowledged was a huge hydrogen explosion on November 22. Nikita Khrushchev, traveling in India with Marshall Bulganin, boasted that the Soviet Union had detonated "the most powerful" H-bomb ever, estimating it to be "equal to several megatons of conventional explosives." Western observers calculated the size at between 2 and 4 megatons, far smaller than BRAVO, but they were impressed by the fact that the Russians had dropped this bomb from a plane rather than firing it from a tower. Russia now clearly had a deliverable H-bomb.

The huge air-burst on November 22 created an enormous amount of fallout. Within three days, several Japanese cities reported radioactive rain, and by the end of November most of Europe was experiencing increased atmospheric radiation. Even the United States witnessed a sharp rise, but rather than blaming the Russians for menacing human health, the AEC issued a reassuring statement that fallout radioactivity "has been far below levels that would be hazardous to the health of exposed persons."[10]

The Soviets responded by renewing their call for a test ban. They had first suggested such a step on May 10 during the 5-nation disarmament subcommittee talks in London. After a long delay, Secretary of State Dulles had replied on November 11 by insisting that any such proposal would have to include "proper safeguards," such as inspection by an international agency, before it could be considered. The new Soviet offer for a reciprocal suspension of nuclear tests, made on November 28, led to a prompt, if ambiguous, American response. Secretary Dulles told a press conference on November 29 that the United States had studied the "complex" issue of a test ban for many months and had not yet found "a formula" which would be "both dependable and in the interests of the United States." He promised only to give the matter further study and consideration.[11]

Nuclear testing could not be dismissed so easily. On December 13, Khrushchev and Bulganin capped off their trip to India by issuing a communiqué with Prime Minister Nehru calling for an "unconditional prohibition of the production, use and experimentation of nuclear and thermonuclear weapons." American officials, noting the absence of any inspection features, treated this statement as propaganda, but they were more disturbed by Pope Pius's Christmas Eve message. Unlike the joint Indian-Soviet communiqué, the Pope's statement linked a test ban with agreements both to eliminate nuclear weapons and to provide effective international supervision. Recalling his previous concern over radiation hazards, the Pontiff called his three-part plan for nuclear disarmament "an obligation in conscience" for nations and their leaders.

American officials became alarmed by the growing worldwide demand for a test ban. They resented the fact that the Russians escaped criticism for their fallout by the clever propaganda ploy of advocating suspension just after completing their own test series. Moreover, the Pentagon feared that the Soviets were now ahead of the United States in weapons technology, not just in testing a bomb dropped from a plane, but in perfecting nuclear warheads for future ballistic missiles. If the United States were to agree to a test ban, even one like the Pope's with adequate safeguards, the nation's security might well be jeopardized.[12]

With these considerations in mind, Dulles once again defined the American position on nuclear testing in a press conference on January 11, 1956. When a reporter asked if he had found the formula he was looking for in November, Dulles replied that the government had not discovered "any basis which would seem to warrant us in suspending bomb tests." "We feel it imperative to keep to the forefront of scientific knowledge in that field," the Secretary emphasized. He pointed out that Harold Stassen was working on a general international disarmament proposal and he said that a test ban would have to wait until a comprehensive plan "with proper inspection safeguards" could be formulated.[13]

The creation of a disarmament subcommittee by the Senate Foreign Relations Committee in January provided a new forum for discussion of a test ban. Chaired by Hubert Humphrey of Minnesota, a liberal Democrat with a reputation in the 1950s as a staunch Cold Warrior, the disarmament subcommittee consisted of six members from the Foreign Relations Committee, four senators from the Armed Services Committee, and two more from the Joint Committee on Atomic Energy. The subcommittee, split evenly between Republicans and Democrats, held a series of twelve hearings over the next year which began in obscurity but gained increasing public attention. As the hearings continued, Humphrey moderated his earlier hawkish position and emerged as the leading Democratic spokesman for arms control.

Harold Stassen led off for the administration at the first hearing on January 25. After surveying the many facets of disarmament, Stassen dealt with testing as only a symptom of a greater evil, "the arms competition rooted in international tensions and the problem of war itself." He termed weapons tests "essential" for national security and argued that the Soviets were exploiting the testing issue for propaganda purposes. Secretary Dulles made the same points in the second hearing, on Feburary 29, and laid special emphasis on the need for "a system of inspection so thoroughgoing and comprehensive that it will exclude for practical purposes a sudden surprise attack of devastating magnitude." He spoke of the need to balance the risk of nuclear war against the hazards of testing and expressed a hope that in the future the United States could find a way to curb the arms race. But for the present, he placed his faith in the continued development of America's nuclear stockpile. Admiral Strauss made the strongest case for testing in his testimony on March 7. Past experiments, he pointed out, had helped the AEC develop a wide variety of atomic and hydrogen bombs, and "further tests will result in the perfection of still more precise weapons."

In the course of these hearings, Chairman Humphrey and Senator John Pastore, a member of the Joint Committee on Atomic Energy, brought up the crucial issue of detection. Commenting on the supposed self-enforcing nature of a test ban, Pastore asked Stassen if we could not tell "every time the Russians have an explosion?" "We can tell the big ones under usual circumstances," Stassen replied, "but you can't necessarily tell every one." When Humphrey raised the same point with Dulles, the secretary of state refused to respond, saying the issue of detection at long range involved "a number of elements of uncertainty." Pressed by the senator, Dulles finally took refuge by saying an answer would require "classified information." Strauss was even less helpful, telling Humphrey that he could not discuss detection in an open hearing. These replies, though unresponsive, did call into question one of the most appealing features of a test ban—the idea that it could be enforced without an elaborate inspection system.[14]

While the Senate hearings continued in Washington, Harold Stassen left for London to attend the spring meeting of the five-nation disarmament subcommittee. His major proposal was a variation of "open skies"—a suggestion that the United States and Russia take the first step toward disarmament by making small areas of their territory accessible to inspection. The Soviets countered with a plan for the gradual reduction of conventional forces coupled with a ban on all nuclear tests. Although the Russian offer was unacceptable, since it failed to include any inspection procedures, some observers thought it marked a significant breakthrough—for the first time, the Soviets showed a willingness to discuss general disarmament without insisting on a total prohibition on all nuclear weapons. England, France, and Canada tried to secure agreement for a compromise plan that included the reduction of both nuclear and conventional forces, limitations on nuclear testing, and a stringent provision for international supervision. The talks ended in the usual deadlock, however, when neither of the superpowers would yield. The Americans kept claiming that the Russians wanted disarmament without inspection; the Soviets denounced the United States for demanding inspection without disarmament.[15]

Stassen reported on the impasse to the Humphrey subcommittee on June 7. The United States, he said, was willing to discuss a test ban as part of a comprehensive disarmament arrangement, but not as "an isolated advance agreement." Nuclear research and development was the "lifeblood" of America's military strength, Stassen told the senators, and thus, "it is essential that the United States continue exploration and testing in the field of thermonuclear weapons." Privately, Stassen was not so sure. In a meeting with his eight task forces on May 29, he had expressed considerable interest in negotiating a separate test ban. His civilian advisers, however, especially physicists Ernest Lawrence and Edward Teller, had objected strongly, and Stassen had dropped the idea.[16]

Within the State Department, there was no dissent. Ambassador James Wadsworth spelled out the American position on a test ban in a speech to the UN's General Assembly on July 13, 1956. Replying to India's Krishna Menon, who had proposed suspending all tests, Wadsworth contended that "properly conducted nuclear tests" did not constitute a hazard to human health. "Limitation on the testing of nuclear weapons is logical, enforceable, and sound from a security standpoint," he concluded, "only as an integral part of a disarmament program in which we have agreed to limit the nuclear threat itself." Thus despite growing world pressure, the Eisenhower administration had not changed its mind. Nuclear testing must continue until the nations of the world had reached agreement on a comprehensive and workable disarmament treaty, one with an effective system of enforcement.[17]

III

Two Democrats challenged the administration's rigid stand on nuclear testing. The first was Thomas Murray, the lone Truman appointee on the AEC, who played gadfly to Lewis Strauss. Unhappy with the Admiral's penchant for secrecy in atomic matters, Murray made his dissent public in a widely-noted speech in New York City on November 17, 1955. The maverick AEC commissioner began by confirming that the American H-bomb was a fission-fusion-fission weapon that depended largely on uranium-238 for its destructive power. He stressed the awesome nature of the super bomb and warned that its radioactive fallout "could be catastrophic." "A sufficiently large number of such explosions would render the earth uninhabitable to man," he declared. "This is plain fact." He went on to describe the perils of strontium-90, claiming that it could cause bone tumors. There was a limit to how much of this poisonous substance man could safely tolerate, he asserted. "Beyond that limit danger lies, and even death."

Murray's solution to the nuclear dilemma was to convene an "Atomic Summit" at the Pacific proving grounds to observe America's next thermonuclear blast. He would invite several thousand people to form "an audience representative of all the peoples of the world" to learn firsthand of the true horror of the H-bomb. Once people realized that "man now has the power to put an end to his own history," Murray concluded, they would join together to demand complete disarmament.

Although Murray's speech attracted considerable attention, his fellow AEC commissioners quickly scotched the proposal for a public nuclear test. Undaunted, Murray began to develop another idea which he advocated both inside the AEC and in secret testimony to the Joint Committee on Atomic Energy. Appalled by the destructive force of H-bombs, he suggested that the United States rely instead on tactical atomic bombs for its defense. The military already possessed enough super bombs to use against Soviet cities; what the United States needed was a diversified arsenal of smaller nuclear weapons for use in limited wars. When neither the AEC nor the Joint Committee paid any attention to his idea, however, Murray decided it was time to take his case to the public again.[18]

On April 12, 1956, he once more attracted national attention. Testifying at an open hearing of the Humphrey disarmament subcommittee, Murray pleaded for what he termed "rational nuclear armament." Claiming that it made no sense to develop and test bigger and bigger H-bombs, he suggested that the United States unilaterally forego any further tests of H-bombs in the megaton range. His proposals included a limit on the number of H-bombs in the U.S. stockpile, a moratorium on H-bomb tests, and a sharp increase in both the testing and production of tactical atomic weapons. Pressed by senators who accused him of advocating unilateral disarmament, Murray carefully explained that his goal was simply to achieve a balanced nuclear arsenal as "a deterrent to war." He was not concerned about the fallout from testing H-bombs, nor did he care whether or not the Russians would also give up thermonuclear tests. All he wanted to do, he kept saying, was to concentrate on developing "such weapons as are demonstrably useful for the purpose of actual warfare."[19]

Nine days later, a better-known Democrat joined Murray in his call for ending H-bomb tests. Adlai Stevenson, defeated by Eisenhower in 1952 when he ran as a reluctant candidate, had decided in 1956 that he wanted to be president. Disillusioned with Ike's lack of leadership, he announced his candidacy in late 1955 and soon found himself locked in a hectic primary fight with Senator Estes Kefauver of Tennessee. On April 21, Stevenson took time out from the primaries to speak on international issues to the American Society of Newspaper Editors. After accusing the Eisenhower administration of coming "dangerously close" to losing the Cold War, Stevenson proposed giving "prompt and earnest consideration to stopping further tests of the hydrogen bomb." He mentioned Murray's testimony to the disarmament subcommittee and made the same point, finding little "sense in multiplying and enlarging weapons of a destructive power already incomprehensible."

On the surface there seemed to be much in common between the appeals by Stevenson and Murray. Both men wanted the United States to stop tests of H-bombs even without an international agreement, and both ignored the issue of fallout in stating their views. But their objectives were very different. Murray was primarily concerned with increasing the nation's reliance on tactical weapons and preparing for limited wars; Stevenson's goal was to recapture "the moral initiative" in the world. Worried over criticism of the United States by the people of Asia and Africa, Stevenson wanted to impress mankind with America's peaceful forbearance. For Stevenson, a unilateral test suspension was "a step which would reflect our determination never to plunge the world into nuclear holocaust, a step which would affirm our purpose to act with humility and a decent concern for world opinion."[20]

The press reacted cautiously to Stevenson's H-bomb proposal. *Time* noted that it was a "perilous issue" for a layman to discuss, and Walter Lippmann wondered what experts had helped the candidate draft his speech. Stevenson reacted angrily to Lippmann's column, informing him in a personal letter that he had spent "two or three days" taken out from the campaign to write the text himself. "Permit me to at least claim the poor thing as my own and no one else's—in whole or in part!" Stevenson commented.[21]

On April 24, three days after making the test suspension speech, Stevenson repeated his suggestion in a statement criticizing the administration for being "dangerously dilatory" in the race with the Russians to develop intercontinental ballistic missiles. President Eisenhower, who had refrained from commenting on Stevenson's speech, quickly seized on the inconsistency of his opponent's position at a press conference on April 25. "It is a little bit of a paradox to urge that we work just as hard as we know how on the guided missile and that we stop all research on the hydrogen bomb, because one without the other is rather useless," the President told reporters. "So I think research without tests is perfectly useless, a waste of money." The AEC would proceed with nuclear tests, the President added, not to develop a more destructive bomb but instead to perfect it for a variety of military uses.[22]

Stevenson realized that he had been placed on the defensive. In a letter to Arthur Schlesinger, he expressed confidence that he was "on the right track on the hydrogen bomb," but he admitted he did not have it "properly put forward yet." He finally replied to Eisenhower on May 4. Insisting that "the H-bomb and the guided missile are entirely different," Stevenson argued that he wanted the ICBM developed while pressing toward "complete control of thermonuclear power and its use for peaceful purposes only." If it turned out that the ICBM was useless without a hydrogen warhead, then "there is all the more reason for trying to control thermonuclear weapons development at once." In a note to adviser Benjamin V. Cohen two days later, Stevenson confessed that he was tired of being "badgered about the H-bomb business" and asked Cohen to send along any suggestions he might have to clarify the issue. "There is much confusion, evidently, about the missile and the bomb," Stevenson added. The confusion seemed to be in Stevenson's mind; by this time, he may have wished that he had never brought such a complicated issue into the political arena.[23]

Support for a ban on hydrogen bomb testing surfaced at a Senate disarmament subcommittee hearing on June 8. Chairman Humphrey, the only committee member in attendance, heard representatives of scientific and pacifist groups testify in favor of the Murray and Stevenson proposals. Charles C. Price, a University of Pennsylvania chemist speaking for the Federation of American Scientists, advocated a ban on "any further nuclear weapons tests" as a "preliminary step" toward universal disarmament. Similar pleas came from witnesses representing the American Friends Service Committee, the Church of the Brethren, and the Women's International League for Peace and Freedom. They cited the danger from fallout, the need to give the United Nations control over all armaments, and the importance of appealing "to the morality and conscience of so much of the rest of the human race."[24]

The *Bulletin of the Atomic Scientists* supported the call for a test ban in its June issue. David Inglis contributed an article in which he argued that a test ban, which he termed "self-enforcing," would both prevent the spread of nuclear weapons to other nations and slow down the existing arms race between the United States and Russia. He called Stevenson "inconsistent" for urging continued missile development and said it was imperative to couple a prohibition on ICBM tests with an H-bomb moratorium. In an accompanying editorial, Eugene Rabinowich endorsed Inglis's views and censured Stevenson for suggesting unilateral action. The only way to stop testing, the editor insisted, was by an agreement with Russia. Above all, the United States must move quickly, before the advent of ICBM's and a new era of pushbutton war. A negotiated test ban, Rabinowich concluded, was "literally the last opportunity to avoid an irrevocable deadlock of mutual terror. It is, in fact, *now* or *never*."[25]

Most Americans, however, failed to share Rabinowich's sense of urgency. Newspapers and magazines soon lost interest in the controversy over a test ban. "The general public," commented a sympathetic *New Republic* on the reaction to Stevenson's speech, "has responded with colossal indifference." The old pattern of sudden public concern and then a return to the prevailing apathy had asserted itself again. The American people, unable to face the true horror of the hydrogen bomb, preferred to ignore it despite the occasional warnings of men like Murray and Stevenson. Radiation was the one aspect that touched a sensitive nerve; the fear of fallout, of what I. F. Stone called "the radioactive dusts" that fall "gently and impartially as the rain," was alone capable of arousing the American people. Until they tapped this emotional issue, the advocates of a test ban were doomed to frustration.[26]

IV

Despite the criticism, the United States continued its program of thermonuclear testing in the spring of 1956. On February 22, the AEC announced Operation REDWING, a series of more than a dozen nuclear explosions at the proving grounds in the Pacific. Four days later Lewis Strauss explained that the tests would include both atomic and hydrogen bombs and that the major goal would be to perfect defensive weapons designed to repel enemy air and missile attacks against the United States. Strauss claimed that the fallout hazard had been "greatly exaggerated." There was some danger to human health, he admitted, but "it is a calculated risk that we must take in order that our freedom be preserved."[27]

Protests quickly developed. The Japanese Diet requested that the United States cancel the tests. India registered formal objections with the United Nations Trusteeship Council, and the Soviet Union claimed that the American tests, which it termed "intolerable," violated the UN Charter. At home, a New York resident appealed to the President to call off REDWING, writing that "every time an explosion occurs we are very possibly sealing the doom of humanity on earth." A group of Chicago clergymen and pacifists, including Catholic Bishop Bernard J. Sheil, petitioned Eisenhower in March, asking him to postpone the tests while seeking an agreement with Russia to end all such experiments.[28]

The administration politely but firmly rejected these requests. The State Department informed the Trusteeship Council that the United States would take "all feasible precautions" to avoid fallout and told the Japanese government that the tests were necessary "to defend the free world." There was no health hazard, White House spokesmen assured concerned Americans, citing the February 15, 1955, AEC report to the effect that fallout was no more dangerous to the individual than a single chest X-ray. They explained that the President himself had made the decision to proceed "after careful and comprehensive studies were made that convinced him that there was no practical alternative."[29]

When the Soviet Union began a secret test series of its own in March, the administration debated whether to inform the American people. Chairman Strauss made a brief announcement of the first Russian test on March 21, but a week later he asked the President's permission to keep silent about a second Russian shot which the AEC estimated at between 10 and 20 megatons. Eisenhower consulted Stassen, who recommended a "routine" announcement, which Strauss dutifully made on April 2.

There was also considerable discussion over whether to invite American newsmen and foreign observers to witness RED-WING. The State Department was opposed, with Under Secretary Herbert Hoover, Jr., arguing that "every bit of emphasis and publicity on tests brings closer the time when we will be faced with the necessity of discontinuing them. . . ." Strauss favored the idea, and the President finally compromised. At a news conference on April 4, he announced that a group of 15 American journalists and civil defense officials would be invited to observe REDWING. There would be no foreign representatives in the delegation. When a reporter asked Eisenhower if he planned to go himself, the President said no. "I believe it is not essential that I go," he explained, "because the reports are very detailed." He favored the peaceful uses of atomic energy and did not want to "use the Presidency to publicize the other . . . very necessary parts of it."[30]

As the date for the tests approached, pacifist groups continued to protest. The Women's International League for Peace and Freedom called on Ike to cancel REDWING on April 21, claiming this would have a "tremendous moral effect" on world opinion. Clarence Pickett sent a telegram to the White House on May 4 on behalf of the American Friends Service Committee. Pointing out that the United States had already exploded 65 nuclear weapons, he said the world was convinced of their "terrible destructive power." Lewis Strauss dismissed these objections as "propaganda" by "some intelligent and patriotic persons who are unfamiliar with the facts." White House aides replied more calmly, saying simply that the government had taken "elaborate precautions . . . to prevent hazards from the tests."[31]

REDWING began on May 5 with an unannounced H-bomb shot that yielded less than a megaton. Bad weather and unpredictable winds forced a 13-day postponement in the first test to be observed by the 15 reporters and civil defense officials. Finally on May 21, an Air Force plane released a hydrogen bomb over Namu Island at Bikini. It exploded with a force of 10 megatons at a height of 15,000 feet, creating a huge fireball some four miles in diameter. The winds blew the fallout from America's first air-burst H-bomb to the north, far from any inhabited islands. To the relief of AEC officials, there was no repetition of the BRAVO accident, though they finally admitted in June that a navigational error had caused the pilot to miss the intended target by four miles. The President announced the successful test at his news conference on May 23, taking pride in the AEC's report of greatly-reduced fallout.

Military analysts dwelt on a point Eisenhower had not made—the United States had finally matched the Soviet Union in testing an H-bomb delivered from an airplane.[32]

V

The National Academy of Sciences issued its long-awaited report on radiation hazards on June 12. For over a year, six committees composed of the nation's leading experts had studied the impact of all forms of radiation—natural, medical and dental X-rays, and fallout from bomb tests. Their findings were generally reassuring. The individual committees saw little cause for concern about the effect of fallout on the weather, the oceans, or the world's food supply. The scientists concluded that the bomb tests had not raised worldwide radiation to dangerous levels; in their opinion, X-rays were a greater source of danger. In only two areas, genetic effects and the uptake of strontium-90, did the report mention any long-term problems.

Attention centered on the statement by the genetics committee. Chaired by Warren Weaver of the Rockefeller Foundation and including scientists of such diverse viewpoints as H. J. Muller and Shields Warren, this group warned that all radiation was undesirable since it caused harmful mutations. Since there was no threshold below which radiation did not cause genetic damage, the report stated, "the concept of a *safe* rate of radiation simply does not make sense." The committee estimated that the real danger would come from exposure to enough radiation to double the natural mutation rate, a figure they estimated at between 30 and 80 roentgens. Concentrating on the exposure of the reproductive organs during the first 30 years of life, the committee calculated that natural radiation contributed 4.3r over this period, medical and dental X-rays 3.0r, and fallout from bomb tests only between 0.02 and 0.5r. They recommended a limit of 10r exposure to individuals in their first 30 years and suggested that the greatest danger came from overuse of X-rays. Noting that radiation from bomb testing had led "to considerably less irradiation of the population than have the medical uses," the geneticists nevertheless cautioned against any increase in exposure from any source, including fallout from nuclear tests.

The committee on pathological effects reported that it could find no evidence that low-level radiation endangered human health, "although a theoretical minor shortening of life span could not be ruled out." Only large-scale radiation, on the order of 50r or more, caused such problems as skin lesions, lowered blood counts, and leukemia. As long as human exposure was kept below the level of 10r over a thirty-year period, as the geneticists recommended, there would be no likely health hazard. The one exception, the report pointed out, would be widespread contamination from strontium-90. This substance, with its global dispersion in the stratosphere, its long half-life of 28 years, and its characteristic of concentrating in human bone, might prove troublesome in the future. The report concluded, however, that existing levels could lead to the uptake of only 0.2r in an individual's lifetime, a thousand times below the permissible dose.[33]

In a remarkable coincidence, a similar report by the British Medical Research Council appeared the same day, June 12. The English researchers confirmed the American findings, concluding that there was virtually no pathological danger from fallout and dismissing the genetic risk as "negligible." Like the American scientists, the British saw greater danger in medical X-rays and found no reason to recommend a halt to bomb tests. They also felt uneasy about Sr^{90} and called for greater research on this problem.[34]

Lewis Strauss was delighted with the National Academy of Science report. He issued a public statement praising the National Academy for performing "a public service of major importance." In a note to the President, he warned Ike to disregard "misleading headlines" in the press which played up the possible genetic danger. "These findings," Strauss told Eisenhower, "support the public statment which I made in February of last year."

Most observers agreed with the Admiral's assessment. A delighted *U.S. News and World Report* told its readers that "despite the scare headlines," fallout "isn't a big danger after all." Citing the National Academy report, the editors pointed out that the "average person receives 30 times as much radiation from medical X-rays as from fall-out." The editors of *Science* found both the British and the American reports reassuring, stating the long-term genetic danger and the risks in strontium-90 "must be balanced against the needs for defense. . . ." On the basis of the National Academy report, *Time* concluded that fallout "would do no appreciable harm unless the tempo of bomb testing is increased many times over." [35]

Uncertainty about strontium-90, however, led to continuing debate within the scientific community over the fallout problem. Willard Libby provided the most detailed information about this mysterious substance in speeches and articles in scientific journals. The Sr^{90} produced by H-bombs, he pointed out, rose into the stratosphere where he calculated it took about ten years before it all fell back to earth. Washed out of the atmosphere by rainfall, the strontium-90 stayed in the top two-or-three inches of the soil. Absorbed by plants and grasses, it entered the human food chain from the milk of cows and then settled, like calcium, in the bones. At each level, there was a gradual filtering out of Sr^{90}, so that the amount finally deposited in the body was minute. There was no genetic hazard, Libby contended, since the beta radiation from Sr^{90} in the bones was too weak to reach the reproductive organs. Indeed, Libby was so certain that Sr^{90} did not pose any danger that he told one audience that "it is possible to say unequivocally that nuclear weapons tests as carried out at the present time do not constitute a health hazard to the human population insofar as radiostrontium is concerned." [36]

Ralph Lapp disagreed strongly with Libby. In speeches and

articles, Lapp kept pointing to the long life of strontium-90 to warn that it might cause bone cancer 50 years after the last nuclear test. In a speech in New Jersey only a few days after the National Academy's report, Lapp predicted that if bomb tests continued at double the present rate until 1962, they would produce enough Sr^{90} to expose the entire world population to the maximum permissible dose. Disputing the AEC's claim that the current level was only $1/1000$th of the amount considered dangerous, he estimated that the atmosphere already contained 15 per cent of the total that the world could safely absorb. As if to underscore Lapp's contention that constant exposure to small amounts of radiation could endanger human health, the AEC reported in July the death of a scientist who had worked at its Brookhaven National Laboratory from 1946 to 1948. An autopsy revealed that his bones contained 1000 times the maximum safe radiation level.[37]

The public showed much greater interest in the startling testimony of General James M. Gavin to a congressional committee that was released on June 28. Describing the likely consequences of a nuclear attack on Russia, General Gavin estimated there would be "several hundred million deaths . . . depending upon which way the wind blew." Asked to clarify his statement, Gavin said that if it was blowing from the northwest, most of the casualties would be Russian, but if the wind came from the southeast, many people in Western Europe would die from the fallout. Another Pentagon spokesman commented privately that if the wind were "unfavorable," the death toll could run as high as 500 million and include nearly half the population of the British Isles. Compared to this awesome fallout effect, the potential danger of strontium-90 from nuclear testing seemed quite remote to the average American.[38]

VI

REDWING continued in the Pacific through June and into July. The AEC made no announcement of additional tests after the

shot of May 21, but Japanese scientists used long-distance monitoring devices to report one additional test in May, two more in
June, and the last five in the series in July. Presumably most
were H-bomb blasts in the megaton range; Japanese sources
claimed that eight of the ten tests involved thermonuclear
weapons.

Admiral Strauss issued the only official statement about the
tests on July 19, following a trip to the Pacific proving grounds.
Recalling that President had expressed the hope at his April 25
news conference that REDWING would lead to bombs with
much reduced fallout, Strauss claimed that the AEC had fulfilled this objective. The bombs tested in the Pacific, Strauss announced, had achieved "maximum effect in the immediate area
of a target with minimum widespread fall out hazard." As a
result, the AEC was convinced that hydrogen bombs could be
used in warfare without inflicting massive deaths from fallout.
"Thus the current series of tests," Strauss concluded, "has produced much of importance not only from a military point of
view but from a humanitarian standpoint."[39]

Commentators were quick to point out the techniques that
the AEC had probably used to perfect a "clean" bomb. Detonating an H-bomb in the air would reduce fallout substantially by cutting down on the amount of radioactive debris
sucked up from the ground. Removing the outer layer of U^{238},
and thus reducing the bomb to a simple fission-fusion one,
would also greatly lessen the resulting radioactivity. But there
was a limit to how far the AEC could go in cleaning up the H-
bomb; the atomic trigger, with its resulting fission products,
was still essential to produce the thermonuclear explosion.

Critics quickly jumped on Strauss for claiming that the AEC
had perfected a "humanitarian" weapon. The *New Republic* accused him of trying to overcome "the radiation jitters" touched
off by the National Academy report and the Gavin testimony,
calling his July 19 statement "a sedative to calm public nerves."
Eugene Rabinowich accused the Admiral of inviting "misin-
terpretation," since there was no way to guarantee that the Rus-

sians would remove the outer layer of U^{238} and thus reduce the fallout of weapons they might use against the United States. Ralph Lapp thought that the opposite was more likely the case. Since both the cheapness and the great power of the H-bomb come from its fission of U^{238}, he thought the Russians would probably increase the outer casing of ordinary uranium to produce a truly terrifying weapon. "War is a dirty business," he explained. "Science has not succeeded in making it any cleaner. Part of the madness of our time is that adult men can use a word like humanitarian to describe an H-bomb."[40]

Admiral Strauss may have gone too far when he boasted of the relative cleanliness of the newest American H-bombs. But in stressing the search for a weapon with greatly reduced fallout, he found a rationale for nuclear testing that the AEC could exploit in the continuing public debate over a test ban.

THE 1956
CAMPAIGN

In the summer of 1956, politics once again occupied center stage in American life. After defeating Tennessee Senator Estes Kefauver in the California primary, Adlai Stevenson moved steadily toward the Democratic nomination, finally winning it on the first ballot at his party's convention in Chicago. When Stevenson permitted the delegates to choose his running mate, a wild scramble ensued before Kefauver narrowly defeated Senator John F. Kennedy of Massachusetts for the vice-presidential nomination. On the Republican side, Dwight Eisenhower, who had suffered a heart attack in September 1955, announced on February 29 that he felt he had fully recovered and would run for a second term. The only suspense involved Vice President Richard M. Nixon. At first Eisenhower said that he would leave the choice of his running mate to the GOP convention, but he finally gave the nod to Nixon in April. Harold Stassen led a belated attempt to drop the vice president from the ticket only to have the Republican delegates make Nixon their unanimous choice in August.

Few expected the issue of nuclear testing to arise during the fall campaign. Stevenson had made no further mention of a test ban after his April speech; the Democratic platform called only for "a comprehensive survey of radiation hazards from bomb tests." Advisers urged the Democratic challenger to focus on such topics as the President's health, Nixon's character, and the lack of vigorous White House leadership in domestic affairs. The Republicans, who could boast that Eisenhower had ended the Korean War six months after taking office, planned to deflect any attacks on the administration's foreign policy by playing up the fact that they had kept the nation at peace. Suez seemed to be the only international issue the Democrats were likely to exploit; Egypt's Gamal Nasser had seized the canal in July, touching off a crisis that Dulles was trying desperately to contain.[1]

The unexpected Soviet resumption of nuclear testing on August 24 led to an important change in administration policy. Instead of playing down the Russian shots, as they had in the past, Eisenhower and Strauss decided to publicize them in an effort to discredit the Kremlin's advocacy of a test ban. On August 26, the White House released a statement by Strauss announcing the August 24th blast and comparing the publicity given to American tests with the secrecy of the Russian ones. "The Soviet Union has never given the world any assurances with respect to the way in which it conducts nuclear-weapons tests," Strauss noted. The President reported a second Soviet detonation at his news conference on August 31, commenting that it was "notable" that the Russians did not inform the world of their experiments. After a third Soviet test on September 2, Secretary of the Army Wilber M. Brucker contrasted the clandestine nature of the Russian shots with the "open and above board policy of announcing well in advance our tests of nuclear weapons."[2]

The Soviet Union responded with a renewed call for an international test ban agreement. Claiming that their tests took place at high altitudes and caused little fallout, the Russian leaders said that they were ready to stop testing as soon as the United States halted its experiments. Marshall Bulganin, the Soviet premier, made a formal proposal to this effect in a letter to President Eisenhower on September 11 which the White House made public three days later. Calling for a halt to both atomic and hydrogen bomb tests, Bulganin claimed that such a move would be "the first important step toward the unconditional prohibition of these types of mass destruction weapons." On the all-important point of inspection, the Soviet leader dismissed the need for any supervision with the assertion that "the present state of science and engineering" made it possible to detect any violation at long range.[3]

Instead of rejecting the Soviet proposal immediately, the President authorized the National Security Council to restudy the whole question of a test ban. Eisenhower had long been uneasy about the wisdom of testing H-bombs and his doubts had grown stronger by 1956. On August 30, he reminded Strauss that he had told him "several times about my hope that the need for atomic tests would gradually lift and possibly soon disappear." He went on to inform the AEC chairman that Isadore Rabi, a Columbia University physicist whom Ike respected greatly, shared "such a belief." At the same time, Harold Stassen was pressing again for an American initiative on the test ban issue, and this time Secretary of State Dulles, worried over the success of Russian propaganda abroad, began to side with him against the continued objections of the AEC and the Pentagon. The Bulganin proposal was thus ensured of full and careful consideration within the National Security Council; for the first time since BRAVO, the Eisenhower administration appeared ready to reverse its stand on nuclear testing.[4]

I

Apparently unaware of the debate within the administration, Adlai Stevenson suddenly injected the test ban issue into the campaign in the course of a speech on foreign policy on September 5. Addressing the American Legion's annual convention in Los Angeles, the Democratic candidate spent most of his time rebutting Republican claims to a monopoly on the peace issue. Then he made two proposals of his own—a suggestion that the draft be ended in the near future and a renewal of his April proposal "to halt further testing of large nuclear devices, conditional upon adherence by the other atomic powers to a similar policy." Stevenson did not elaborate on his test ban proposal, except to note that other nations had indicated "their willingness to limit such tests," and in the furor over the draft statement, many newspapers ignored this part of this speech.

It was Vice President Nixon's rebuttal the next day that called attention to Stevenson's renewed plea for a test ban. Speaking to the same audience, Nixon praised Eisenhower as a "symbol of peace" to the world and labeled Stevenson's call for a halt to nuclear tests "not only naive but dangerous to our national security." "To have taken such action," Nixon continued, "would have been like telling police officials that they should discard their weapons provided the lawbreakers would offer to throw away their machine-guns. . . ."[5]

The issue then seemed to die out. Stevenson made no further reference to a test ban for the next two weeks and the national press ignored the proposal, except for the *New Republic,* which praised it routinely. The only significant comment came from AEC Commissioner Thomas Murray, who restated his call for a ban on all tests over one megaton and a corresponding increase in both the testing and development of smaller H-bombs for tactical use. Taking a position midway between Stevenson and the Eisenhower administration, Murray deplored "campaign talk" about a problem which he felt required "rational public argument conducted with utmost seriousness on the highest possible level."[6]

Dwight Eisenhower did not believe it was possible to discuss such a complex issue in a political campaign. Accordingly, he devoted most of his first major campaign speech, broadcast to the nation over radio and television on September 19, to a sober review of the world situation. Stressing his administration's success in maintaining peace, the President referred only briefly to Stevenson's test ban proposal, saying, "We cannot prove wise and strong by any such simple device as suspending, unilaterally, our H-bomb tests." He dismissed his opponent's suggestion as a "theatrical national gesture," and asserted that he favored "explicit and supervised international agreements" as the only sound way to achieve arms control.

Thoroughly angered by Ike's remarks, Stevenson hastily prepared a reply in a speech given at Silver Spring, Maryland, the next day. Like the President, he spent most of his time on other foreign policy issues, but he did not deny that he was advocating unilateral nuclear disarmament. His proposition, Stevenson maintained, was for the United States to "take the lead in promoting curtailment by all nations of hydrogen-bomb tests." [7]

Despite these heated exchanges, a nuclear test ban was not yet a major campaign issue. Each candidate had only mentioned the subject in passing. The President, convinced that testing was a dangerous subject that could easily be distorted in political debate, preferred to leave it alone. Stevenson's advisers, aware of the respect that Eisenhower's national security views commanded, suggested the Democratic candidate avoid challenging the popular general in his own field of expertise. But Stevenson felt a strong moral commitment to speak out on an issue which he believed went to the very heart of the Cold War. Ignoring the professional politicians, as well as the cynics who accused him of exploiting public fears to win votes, he proceeded to make the test ban a central theme of his campaign. [8]

Stevenson renewed the attack on the administration's policy in Minneapolis on September 29. Criticizing Eisenhower for refusing to debate his test ban proposal, the challenger called nuclear disarmament "the first order of business in the world today." Once again he advocated test suspension as the best way to "get off the dead center of disarmament." If we stopped testing and the Russians did not, Stevenson argued, then "at least the world will know we tried." For the first time in the campaign, Stevenson gave a second reason for halting nuclear tests—"the danger of poisoning the atmosphere." Claiming that "the actual survival of the human race itself" was involved, he declared that scientists believed that "radioactive fallout may do genetic damage with effects on unborn children which they are unable to estimate."[9]

The Republicans responded with a fierce counterattack. While the President maintained his silence on this issue, GOP spokesmen lashed out at Stevenson for endangering American security with his irresponsible charges. Thomas Dewey, the unsuccessful Republican candidate in 1944 and 1948, warned that Stevenson's H-bomb proposal "would result in stripping the free world of its best defense—our leadership in the field of atomic energy." The Russians could not be trusted to follow our lead if we stopped testing, Dewey told a national television audience, and then warned against trading the mature judgment of Dwight Eisenhower for "an impulsive, ill-informed man in the White House." "One act of weakness, one act based on misinformation," Dewey concluded, "could plunge this world into another war." A Republican "truth squad" led by Senator Karl Mundt followed Stevenson around the country pointing out that the *Daily Worker* endorsed his test ban proposal. Senator William Knowland told a Baltimore audience that the Russians would never agree to proper safeguards and without such measures a test ban was "meaningless"; Attorney General Herbert Brownell warned in New York that Stevenson's test ban would "bring joy to the hearts of those who expect to wipe out the free nations one by one."[10]

Vice President Richard Nixon wove all these themes together in his assaults on Stevenson's H-bomb ideas. He variously accused the Democratic candidate of advocating "catastrophic nonsense," of displaying "appallingly naive judgment" in calling for a ban when the Russians were stepping up their tests, and of resorting to "shotgun attacks on the policies of a President who is a symbol of peace throughout the world." Nixon delivered his most scathing attack in Philadelphia on October 3. Claiming that Stevenson's proposal raised "grave doubts" about his ability to conduct foreign policy, Nixon compared a test ban without inspection to "playing Russian roulette but with only the Russians knowing which chamber had the fatal bullet in it."[11]

To Stevenson's deep embarrassment, even former President Harry Truman joined in the criticism. Asked by a reporter in Detroit on October 6 to comment on the Democratic candidate's test ban idea, Truman replied, "we should retain our advantage and if that means testing bombs, well okay." Stating that he agreed with Ike that test suspension would weaken "our power to guard the peace," Truman expressed doubt that the Russians would ever agree to adequate supervision. White House press secretary James Hagerty immediately issued a statement saying, "Mr. Truman is on our side" in the test ban debate, while disarmament adviser Harold Stassen pointed out that he did not know of "any responsible Democrat" who had supported Stevenson's proposal. Truman tried to undo the damage by saying, "I'm in back of Adlai," but he added that "we can't possibly quit [testing] til this Russian business is under control."[12]

President Eisenhower, who regretted these partisan attacks, finally spoke out on the test ban issue at his press conference on October 5. The real problem with suspension, he explained, was that it took "months and months" to prepare for nuclear tests. One party could thus use a moratorium to make secret preparations for resumption. Then even though their violation would be discovered, "they could make tremendous advances where we would be standing still." Given this opportunity for a head start, the President concluded, "I think it would be foolish for us to make any such unilateral announcement."

The next day the White House released a long statement detailing the administration's objections to a unilateral test ban. The President pointed out how vital nuclear weapons were to offset superior Communist manpower, stressed the need to continue testing to reduce fallout from H-bombs, and reiterated the argument that a violator could use the suspension period to prepare "elaborate tests" that could reduce or even wipe out "our present commanding lead in the field of nuclear weapons." Eisenhower's greatest concern, however, was his fear that political discussion of such a proposal could "lead only to confusion at home and misunderstanding abroad." Ignoring the fact that the Republicans themselves were responsible for much of the partisan distortion, Ike declared, "This specific matter is manifestly not a subject for detailed public discussion—for obvious security reasons." [13]

At this point, rumors began to appear in the press that the National Security Council had recommended a test ban to Eisenhower and that the President had rejected the proposal after Stevenson advocated it publicly. To rebut the insinuation that Eisenhower's stand was politically motivated, the Pentagon leaked information to reporters indicating that a test ban would undermine national security. Both the United States and Russia, according to these sources, were on the verge of perfecting nuclear warheads for ICBMs and for experimental anti-missile missiles. Tests were essential to explore these breakthroughs; a moratorium in which the U.S. stopped testing while the Russians secretly completed preparations and then violated an agreement might well upset the delicate balance of nuclear power in the world.

A reporter raised this issue at the President's news conference on October 11. Citing "widely circulated" accounts that both Stevenson's draft and H-bomb proposals had been designed to preempt similar initiatives by the administration, the questioner asked Eisenhower to comment. Growing red in the face, the President repeated his concern about discussing sensitive national security issues in a political campaign. He firmly denied any plans within his administration to "eliminate the draft," but he made no similar disclaimer on the test ban proposal. Instead he simply cut off all further discussion by stating, "Now, I tell you frankly, I have said my last words on these subjects." [14]

With the records of the National Security Council still tightly sealed, there is no way to know whether the President had indeed rejected a test ban recommendation, and if he had, whether political or security factors played the decisive role. But there can be no doubt that Eisenhower deeply resented Stevenson for bringing such a sensitive topic into the political arena. "The issue of American policy on nuclear testing, resting as it did on scientific as well as security considerations," he wrote in his memoirs, "was scarcely a subject to be debated in a political campaign." He felt that the H-bomb raised questions that transcended a presidential election. "My God, we have to simply figure a way out of this situation," he told an aide on October 12, referring to the dilemmas posed by the arms race. "There's just no point in talking about 'winning' a nuclear war."

But despite Eisenhower's personal distaste for Stevenson's test ban proposal, it was enhancing his chances for reelection. Stevenson, lacking access to classified nuclear data, seemed unable to persuade the American people that his idea was sound. His own vagueness contributed to public distrust. Beginning with a call for a unilateral suspension in April, he had added the condition that other nations follow our lead in September, but he had never made clear whether the ban would apply only to large H-bombs, as Murray proposed, or include all nuclear tests, nor had he ever spelled out any details for inspection and supervision. Even his rationale was unclear. The main advantage seemed to be that a test ban would break the disarmament deadlock and lead to more significant steps, but in a speech in Minneapolis he had touched on another aspect, the idea that tests themselves poisoned the atmosphere and thus had to be stopped to protect human health. As a result, GOP spokesmen had found it easy to ridicule his ideas and portray him as both dangerous and irresponsible. Trying desperately to mount an attack against a popular incumbent, Stevenson had succeeded only in placing himself on the defensive.[15]

II

Stung by the Republican rebuttals, Stevenson remained silent on the test ban issue during the first week of October. The professional politicians continued to advise him to turn to other subjects, but he was encouraged by expressions of support from such leading scientists as Ralph Lapp, Charles Price of the Federation of American Scientists, and Laurence H. Snyder, president-elect of the American Association for the Advancement of Science. Most of all, Stevenson resented Eisenhower's statement that he had spoken his "last words" on nuclear testing. Convinced that not to "tell the people the truth" would be worse than losing the election, he decided to state the case for a test ban once more on a trip to the West Coast.[16]

In a speech in Seattle on October 9, Stevenson dealt at length with atomic energy. Expressing astonishment at the sneers and ridicule, as well as the distortions, the Republicans had heaped on his test ban proposal, the Democratic candidate promised to continue suggesting ways "to save man from the greatest horror his ingenuity has ever devised." He would gladly defer to someone else's ideas, but he refused to accept "the apparent Administration position that we are powerless to do anything to stop this headlong race for extinction." The audience greeted his words with loud cheers, and when he repeated this theme at Portland, Oregon, and Oakland, California, the response was even more favorable. After his Oakland address, reported Harrison Salisbury in the *New York Times,* his listeners gave him "the biggest and longest spontaneous demonstration he has had at any time on any issue since the start of the campaign."

Encouraged, Stevenson played up his proposal for a test ban in speeches at Long Beach and San Diego. He hammered hard at the President for his refusal to debate the issue. "I say that there can be no 'last word' on this fateful subject until mankind is freed of the menace of incineration," Stevenson declared. With the cheers of the audience ringing in his ears, he announced that he would devote an entire televised address on Monday, October 15, to nuclear testing, entitled his speech, "The Greatest Menace the World Has Ever Known."[17]

For the first time, the Democratic candidate's campaign seemed to gather momentum. The professional advisers, sensing that he had struck a popular chord, stopped their protests.

Senator Clinton Anderson, the Democratic chairman of the Joint Committee on Atomic Energy, qualified his earlier opposition to a test ban. Rebutting a White House press release, Anderson stated that he now favored an immediate halt to tests of all bombs over one megaton. "Mr. Stevenson has offered a new and constructive approach on controlling H-bomb tests," the senator declared, "and I wholeheartedly support it." Anderson, who still had private reservations, was apparently trying to maneuver Stevenson into accepting Thomas Murray's proposal for a ban restricted to large H-bomb blasts.

Stevenson returned to his farm in Illinois to prepare for the forthcoming televised speech. Taking time out to answer his mail, he told correspondents that he was confident that he was doing the right thing. "I am sure I am on sound ground here and that the administration is unspeakably culpable in its failure to do anything whatever about the most terrible thing on earth," he wrote to an English friend. Answering a Texan who objected to his position, Stevenson assured him that the U.S. could continue to prepare for tests in case of a Russian violation of a test ban. "Meanwhile," he pointed out, "we would gain an incalculable political and moral advantage throughout the world." Sending a copy of this letter to Senator Lyndon Johnson, Stevenson complained that his remarks on nuclear tests had been "quite deliberately distorted."

He spent most of the weekend working on the text of his address with Harrison Brown, a Cal Tech geochemist who had first urged him to tackle the test ban issue. He finally persuaded both Clinton Anderson and Stuart Symington, the Senate's leading Democratic expert on defense, to appear with him in the Chicago studio where the telecast would originate. Both men spent the time before the program trying to get Stevenson to tone down his remarks, but the candidate was adamant. The two senators finally agreed to give their own views separately during the last five minutes of air time.[18]

Stevenson began his remarks with a somber warning that the nuclear arms race "threatens mankind with stark, merciless, bleak catastrophe." He admitted that the Soviets had blocked all efforts at disarmament, but nevertheless he felt the United States had to keep trying to break the stalemate. He offered four reasons for a halt to testing. First, the United States already possessed bombs large enough to destroy entire cities; there was no need to develop bigger ones. A second advantage lay in the fact that a test ban did not require inspection, since any violation could be easily detected. "You can't hide the explosion any more than you can hide an earthquake," he argued. In the third place, a prohibition on testing would halt the spread of nuclear weapons to other countries, and thus would help prevent "a maniac, another Hitler" from possessing the H-bomb. Finally, Stevenson contended that a test ban would spare the world the hazards of radioactive fallout, especially strontium-90, which he called "the most dreadful poison in the world." Denying that he was an "alarmist," he admitted that scientists were not sure how dangerous the threat of fallout was, but "they know the threat will increase if we go on testing." The only sensible course, he concluded, was "to stop the testing as soon as possible."

Despite this warning about fallout, Stevenson laid the greatest stress on disarmament. Pointing out that both Britain and Russia had expressed a willingness to stop testing, he asked, "What are we waiting for?" He promised that if he were elected, he would immediately call an international conference to work out a test ban agreement. He did not favor unilateral disarmament, nor did he see any danger from an international agreement, claiming we would continue research and development during a moratorium and could resume testing within 8 weeks of a Soviet violation. Finally, he could not understand "the President's desire to end this discussion which so keenly concerns all mankind." Saying that this was one subject upon which there never could be "any last word," he appealed for the United States to take the initiative "for the rescue of man from the elemental fire which we have kindled. . . . We must regain the moral respect we once had and which our stubborn, self-righteous rigidity has nearly lost."[19]

In the few minutes that remained after Stevenson spoke, the

two Democratic senators endorsed his views. Anderson saw the test ban as a way to achieve "disarmament by obsolescence," with the dread weapons gradually becoming out-of-date, while Symington, after spending most of his time attacking Eisenhower's failure to develop long-range missiles, stated his belief that "the search for peace will start with the end of H-bomb testing."[20]

Stevenson was delighted with the reaction to his speech. Thousands of telegrams arrived at his headquarters, and a number of prominent scientists, led by Dr. Henry Smyth of the Institute for Advanced Study at Princeton, a former member of the AEC and author of the authoritative Smyth Report on the atomic bomb, voiced their approval for the test ban proposal. Party leaders rallied behind Stevenson, with such influential senators as Mike Mansfield and Albert Gore giving public endorsements. The *Nation* praised the test ban, claiming that "Mr. Stevenson has struck pay dirt." The *Reporter* dismissed administration objections as reflecting a "Pentagon-knows-best" attitude, while editor Max Ascoli wrote that Stevenson's proposal "magnificently espoused the cause of American initiative in world affairs."[21]

There was also considerable dissent. Such influential columnists as Arthur Krock and Ernest K. Lindley were distressed by Stevenson's assumption that inspection was not needed to police a test ban. They both warned that the Soviets would not hesitate to cheat and endorsed the administration's insistence on adequate safeguards for the supervision of any test ban agreement. The editors of the *New York Times* agreed. "We are confident that as between Mr. Stevenson's proposals and President Eisenhower's 'safety first' procedure," they wrote, "American opinion will sustain the President." *Time* suspected that Stevenson was simply looking for votes and warned that the H-bomb was too serious a matter to be decided "by nothing more than the appeal of a political candidate in search of an issue." Despite his public position, Clinton Anderson shared this reservation. ". . . My chief quarrel with Stevenson's position," he wrote in his memoirs, "was simply that I deemed it inappropriate for a presidential campaign. It was too difficult for the public to grasp in all its subtleties."[22]

Despite this criticism, many Republican leaders began to worry that Stevenson had succeeded in taking the peace issue away from the President. Senator Ralph Flanders informed White House Chief-of-Staff Sherman Adams on October 16 that he thought Stevenson had made a legitimate proposal which the administration ought to pursue. "I suggest that serious work along this line be undertaken and publicized," Flanders urged, "otherwise, the Administration remains at both a political and moral disadvantage." Dulles was skeptical, but James Hagerty and Sherman Adams felt that Eisenhower should respond to Stevenson's speech. The President concurred, directing Hagerty to have the AEC, the Pentagon, and the State Department prepare a statement detailing the various efforts the administration had made to curb the arms race since 1953.

While Eisenhower embarked on a speaking tour of the West, his principal national security advisers met in Washington to discuss the proposed statement. Admiral Strauss, Secretary of Defense Charles E. Wilson, disarmament adviser Stassen, and Secretary of State Dulles broke down the assignment into several parts, with each man responsible for a portion. Dulles, who disapproved of the idea, offered a long memorandum rebutting Stevenson's proposal. Tests, the Dulles memorandum argued, were necessary to perfect smaller weapons and reduce fallout. If a test ban had been adopted in April when Stevenson first suggested it, the United States would have been deprived of the valuable military information from Operation RED-WING. Dulles was even more contemptuous of the radiation hazard. "From a health standpoint," he wrote, "there is greater danger from wearing a wrist watch with a luminous dial."[23]

The President rejected the secretary's proposed reply and instead instructed his advisers to continue working on a comprehensive statement of the administration's disarmament position. Meanwhile, he ignored Stevenson's call for a test ban in his own campaign speeches, preferring to point instead to his many contributions to world peace, ranging from the Korean armistice to the open skies proposal. Reaching the West Coast on October 18, Eisenhower finally replied to Stevenson obliquely by telling a Portland audience that in foreign affairs they had to choose between "hard sense and experience versus pie-in-the-sky promises and wishful thinking." At Los Angeles the next day, the President coupled Stevenson's test ban proposal with his earlier call for an end to the draft. Without mentioning his opponent by name, Eisenhower referred scornfully to those who "tell us that peace can be guarded—and our nation secured—by a strange new formula. It is this: simultaneously to stop our military draft and to abandon testing of our most advanced military weapons." Pointing out that there was no cheap or easy way to achieve peace, the President concluded, "I do not believe that any political campaign justifies the declaration of a moratorium on ordinary common sense."[24]

III

The Soviet Union destroyed whatever political advantage Stevenson had gained from his stand on nuclear testing. On October 19, the State Department released the text of a letter to the President from Marshall Bulganin in which the Russian leader renewed his September 11 offer for a ban on all atomic and hydrogen tests. Calling such an agreement "the first step toward the solution of the problem of atomic weapons," Bulganin noted with approval that "certain prominent public figures in the United States" were advocating a similar procedure. Inspection was not necessary, the Soviet leader pointed out, since "in the present state of scientific knowledge," it was impossible to detonate a nuclear explosion secretly.

When the White House released the text of Bulganin's letter the next day, the press interpreted it as blatant interference in the American presidential election. Press secretary James

Hagerty did nothing to discourage this assessment. He labeled the letter "a propaganda exercise," and when a reporter asked if this meant the Soviets had endorsed Stevenson, Hagerty smiled broadly as he replied, "no comment." Caught by surprise, the Democrats tried to make the best of a difficult situation. Vice-presidential candidate Estes Kefauver told a California audience that a test ban was "necessary to the very survival of the world," while Governor Averell Harriman of New York claimed that Bulganin's letter showed that Stevenson's proposal had "caught the imagination of the world." From Chicago, Stevenson issued a statement on October 21 condemning the administration for dismissing the Russian offer "out of hand" and called upon the President to give "serious consideration" to a proposal that contained the "possibility for reducing tension and the danger of war—most of all nuclear war." [25]

In his formal reply to Bulganin, released later on October 21, Eisenhower denounced the Soviet leader in scathing terms. He pointed out that the United States insisted that any test ban must include "systems of inspection and control, both of which your Government has steadfastly refused to accept." The President particularly resented the veiled reference to Stevenson, claiming that it "constitutes an interference by a foreign nation in our internal affairs." This message, which the *New York Times* called "one of the most strongly worded diplomatic communications in recent years," made no concession to the Russians on the test ban issue. Eisenhower promised only to continue working for genuine disarmament and to close "no doors which might open a secure way to serve humanity." [26]

Placed on the defensive again, Stevenson released another statement the next day expressing his own resentment over the nature and timing of the Soviet offer. But he insisted that the "real issue is not Mr. Bulganin's manners or Russian views about American politics. The real issue," Stevenson contended, "is what we are going to do to save the world from hydrogen disaster."

There was no way, however, that Stevenson could escape the

damage the Soviets had inflicted on his candidacy. "Though the Democratic nominee had been looking everywhere for support for his H-bomb proposals," James Reston commented wryly, "Moscow was the one place he wanted to keep quiet." The party professionals who had warned Stevenson not to challenge Eisenhower on national security had been proven correct. As *Newsweek* pointed out, Bulganin had transformed the test ban "into a political kiss of death with an electorate hugely mistrustful of Russia's intentions."[27]

Republican orators made the most of their new opportunity. William Knowland of California, the Senate minority leader, sent a telegram to Stevenson on October 21 asking him to denounce Premier Bulganin for "unwarranted interference . . . in our free American elections." When the Democratic candidate failed to reply, Knowland sent a second telegram calling on Stevenson to repudiate both Bulganin's meddling and his proposal "to stop tests without the safeguarding inspection." Thomas Dewey made more pointed attacks in a California speech in which he accused Stevenson of walking into a "Communist mousetrap" and making "the most dangerous proposal ever made by any American in our lifetime." As usual, Richard Nixon delivered the most savage verbal assaults, describing Stevenson as being a "clay pigeon" for Soviet sharpshooters, comparing him to Neville Chamberlain betraying Czechoslovakia at Munich, and accusing him of playing a "cruel hoax" on the American people by trying to capitalize on their fear of nuclear weapons. The test ban proposal, the vice president told a San Diego audience, was "the height of irresponsibility and absurdity" and proved that "the Stevenson leadership would increase the chances of war."[28]

President Eisenhower regretted these rhetorical excesses. When Secretary Dulles talked with him about the forthcoming administration statement on nuclear testing, the President said that he wanted the document "to be so factual as to be uninteresting." He cautioned Dulles against any personal criticisms and against any rigid language that would "publicly tie his hands so that in the future [he could] do nothing." Instead the President wanted to inform the American people of the many efforts he had made in the past to achieve nuclear disarmament and of the dangers from an unsupervised test ban.

The six-page paper released the next day under the President's signature stressed the importance of proper safeguards in any effective disarmament agreement. In sober, responsible language, the statement insisted that "the critical issue is not a matter of testing nuclear weapons—but of preventing their use in nuclear war." The administration denied that a test ban could be self-enforcing, claiming that "in view of the vast Soviet land-mass," it would be impossible to detect all nuclear explosions the Russians might conduct. The statement also denied that the fallout from testing was dangerous, citing the National Academy of Science report to assert that this radioactivity was far less than people received "from medical X-rays or natural sources in a lifetime." The real danger would come from Soviet violations of a test ban which could wipe out or even reverse "our present commanding lead in nuclear weapons." Testing, the statement concluded, had to be continued to protect national security. At the same time, the administration promised to work for genuine disarmament complete with "sound safeguards and controls."[29]

The White House released two additional documents designed to bolster the administration's position. The first, a memorandum on weapons tests and peaceful uses of the atom, revealed that the United States had taken the initiative in proposing the "atoms-for peace" program for sharing atomic energy to produce electric power with other nations while the Soviets had concentrated solely on perfecting nuclear weapons. The second document listed the various disarmament proposals made by the United States, from the Baruch plan in 1946 through "open skies" in 1955. The failure to achieve nuclear disarmament was placed on the Russian refusal to accept any form of on-site inspection.

The President summed up his views on the test ban issue in

the course of a major campaign speech at Madison Square Garden on October 25. He accused the Democrats of advocating "disarmament without inspection," and warned that such a policy could lead only to war. True peace, he asserted, depended on "the most advanced military weapons." The real challenge before the world was not the testing of nuclear weapons but "making impossible their use in any nuclear war." Reminding his listeners of his first-hand experience with the horrors of war, he dedicated himself to the relentless pursuit of peace. "In this mission," he concluded, "we shall never rest—nor ever retreat."[30]

Despite his own obvious distaste for the test ban as a political issue, Eisenhower had exploited it brilliantly. On one level, he had permitted his subordinates to use Bulganin's unwelcome support of Stevenson's proposal to portray the Democratic candidate as a Communist dupe, a man who could not be trusted to stand up to the Russians in the Cold War. At the same time, the President himself had taken the high road, confining his objections to the test ban to national security considerations. Given Eisenhower's status as the man most responsible for victory in World War II, it is not surprising that Stevenson's quixotic effort to challenge him on the most important defense issue of all backfired. The wonder is that it came so close to succeeding. Had Bulganin not interfered so clumsily in the presidential campaign, the momentum Stevenson picked up with his October 15 test ban speech might have enabled him to transform a runaway Republican election into a close race.

IV

Political discussion of a test ban was bound to renew the fallout debate among scientists; a Willard Libby speech once again served as the point of departure. Addressing the American Association for the Advancement of Science at the dedication of their new headquarters building in Washington on October 12, the AEC commissioner startled his audience by minimizing the danger of strontium-90 to man. Citing new evidence, Libby claimed that less than 30 per cent of the Sr^{90} in the topsoil found its way into human bones, instead of the earlier estimate of 70 per cent. The amount of strontium-90 in the stratosphere, which Libby calculated to be 24 megatons, had not increased despite the additional 6 megatons deposited by American and Soviet tests in 1956. Fallout and the natural decay of Sr^{90} had led to an equilibrium. More important, Libby contended that the amount of strontium-90 entering the bodies of American children would stabilize at no more than one one-hundredth of the maximum permissible concentration. Thus he concluded that "the body burden to be anticipated 15 years from now probably will be substantially the same as it is today."[31]

Skeptical scientists quickly challenged Libby's reassuring remarks. The Federation of American Scientists issued a report by its radiation hazards committee charging that the AEC commissioner had mistakenly assumed that fallout came back to earth uniformly. Contending that the rate was much heavier in some parts of the world, the FAS committee claimed that some human beings had already reached the danger point from strontium-90 fallout. Dr. William Neumann, a biochemist at the University of Rochester, stressed the fact that when radioactive debris entered the stratosphere, there was no way to protect people from its effects. Once we reach that "point of no return," Neumann warned, then "we are simply out of luck." Charles I. Campbell, writing in *Science,* pointed out that Libby's figures were based on the assumption that there would be no further tests. If testing continued, Campbell argued, within 35 years mankind would be exposed to 10 times the current levels of Sr^{90}, thereby endangering the health of children who absorbed far more Sr^{90} in their growing bones than did adults.

The question of a safe level of strontium-90 became an issue in itself. On November 3, the Stevenson campaign released a letter from Dr. Evarts A. Graham, a famous St. Louis cancer surgeon, claiming that the maximum permissible concentration

(MPC) cited by Libby was 10 times too high. Instead of using the MPC for industrial workers, Graham argued, the AEC should set the limits for the general population at one-tenth that level. Using this standard, Graham claimed that Libby's figures showed that children would be exposed to at least 10 per cent of the MPC from the milk they drank, thereby creating "a public health problem of serious magnitude." Replies from the AEC showed only that there was no agreement among scientists on either a safe or desirable level for Sr^{90} fallout. Given this impasse, many sympathized with the view of a layman, E. B. White, who wrote, "The correct amount of strontium with which to impregnate the topsoil is *no* strontium."[32]

Inevitably, the debate over fallout led many prominent scientists to take political stands on the test ban proposal. A group of 10 faculty members at Cal Tech began the process on October 14 by endorsing Stevenson's proposal, calling it "a useful way to get the [disarmament] negotiations out of the deadlock stage." Other professors eagerly proclaimed their support for Stevenson's test ban: 11 physicists from Columbia University on October 16, 24 Washington University of St. Louis scientists on October 17, 37 faculty members from the City College of New York on October 18, 73 scientists from the Argonne National Laboratory on October 21, and finally 13 from Yale on November 3 who declared that continued testing would mean releasing "uncontrollable forces that can annihilate us and our foes alike." Such distinguished figures as H. J. Muller, Bentley Glass, and Nobel laureate Carl D. Anderson lent their prestige to the Democratic candidate, as did the Federation of American Scientists, in calling for an end to all tests of large nuclear weapons on October 24. The most disturbing statement came from Dr. William G. Cahan, a cancer specialist, who explained in a letter to the *New York Times* that "the addition of even the smallest amount of radiation to the many causes of cancer which are still unknown . . . may be enough to tip the scales."[33]

104

AEC Chairman Lewis Strauss quickly took charge of the administration's rebuttal. On October 16, the Admiral released a telegram from Dr. Shields Warren of Boston describing the deposit of Sr^{90} in human bone from fallout as a "minute fraction" of the permissible level. National security, not radioactivity, should determine bomb testing, Warren argued. "To permit us to fall behind [the] Russians is disastrous; to wait for them to catch up to us is stupid." Strauss made the same points himself in a speech at Battle Creek, Michigan, on October 19. National security, he contended, required continued testing to perfect new weapons; the 1956 Pacific tests had helped the U.S. develop an anti-missile warhead. The AEC chairman dismissed charges of fallout "poisoning" the atmosphere as "lurid" stories originated by "Soviet propagandists." Radioactivity was only "a vague, unproven danger to generations yet unborn," according to Strauss, compared to "the more immediate and infinitely greater dangers of defeat and perhaps of obliteration at the hands of an enemy who possesses nuclear weapons of mass destruction."[34]

Robert Cutler, the President's national security adviser, joined with Strauss in soliciting support from other segments of the scientific community. He brought 12 distinguished scientists to Washington on October 19, arranged for them to meet personally with Eisenhower, and then helped them draft a reply to Stevenson's October 15 speech. In their statement, released by the White House on October 21, the scientists expressed their regret over "the injection into a political campaign of statements and conclusions which extend beyond the limits of existing scientific evidence."

Just before the election, two more well-known scientists, Ernest O. Lawrence and Edward Teller, spoke out strongly in favor of continued testing. Terming the danger from fallout as "insignificant," the two physicists disputed Stevenson's claim that a test ban would be self-enforcing by arguing that "not all atmospheric tests can be detected with instruments." They rested their case, however, on the contention that testing was essential for weapons development. "We are never sure a device will work until it is tested," Lawrence and Teller asserted; "and we cannot take a new forward step until we know that our last idea works."[35]

The conflicting statements from scientists bewildered the public. The concerned citizen did not know whom to believe, the distinguished professor who said that strontium-90 threatened human life or the equally distinguished scientist who said the fallout danger was remote compared to the risk of nuclear war. The problem was the matter of degree. Test ban advocates always stressed the great potential hazard from fallout over a long period of time; their opponents minimized the danger by pointing to similar or greater risks that people routinely accepted, such as luminous wristwatches and medical X-rays. Instead of enlightening the electorate with their arguments, commented Eugene Rabinowich sadly, the experts had "merely served to discredit scientists as (relatively) objective advisers of public opinion." Science and politics, he concluded, simply did not mix.[36]

V

Neither the standoff among scientists nor the Bulganin letter deterred Stevenson. In a speech to 18,000 cheering supporters in New York's Madison Square Garden on October 23 he restated his conviction that a ban on nuclear tests was the key to peace. Such a step would advance "the health of the world," he asserted, without weakening American security. ". . . The transcending question before humanity," Stevenson declared, "is whether there will be any tomorrow at all." Three days later, he told an Illinois audience that unless steps were taken soon to control the arms race, the next development would be a cobalt bomb. Calling such a step "madness," the Democratic candidate pleaded for a halt to "this policy of trying to preserve the peace by a preponderance of terror." The consequences for mankind, he prophesied, could only be "bone cancer, deformed children, sterility."

Stung by the administration's October 24 statement on nuclear testing, Stevenson replied with a position paper of his own at the end of the month. The President, Stevenson charged, was "insensitive to the danger of radioactive fallout; he cited studies by the Federation of American Scientists that showed dangerously high levels of strontium-90 in some regions of the world. The Republicans had deliberately distorted his proposal, the candidate charged. "I repeat again for the dozenth time that I have never proposed the prohibition of tests of other than large H-bombs." He closed by quoting Albert Einstein's statement that whatever the outcome of World War III, he was certain that World War IV would be fought with "sticks and stones," to reiterate his belief that "the modern technology of war is putting humanity back on the road to the cave."[37]

It is difficult to gauge the public response to Stevenson's appeal. His mail increased sharply after the October 15th speech calling for a test ban, with nearly all the correspondents expressing their support. The letters, averaging 1000 a day, came from the affluent suburbs of northern cities, and most of the writers were professional people—doctors, lawyers, professors, and scientists. The President's mail reflected the same trend. Nine out of ten people writing the White House on testing in October urged the President to change his stand. "For humanity's sake," wrote one Massachusetts woman, "I beg that you will lead and in every possible way encourage free and open debate leading to the ending of H-bomb tests." Correspondents described the scientists advising the President as "Frankensteins" and called the testing policy "un-Christian, un-American, un-humanitarian." Many of the writers were Republicans who expressed a fear that nuclear tests poisoned the air, injured their children's health, and threatened the lives of those yet unborn. They echoed Stevenson's concern that the arms race could end only in disaster, "in a wiped-out civilization," in the words of one Bostonian or with what a Michigan resident described as "the destruction of nations and the annihilation of mankind." [38]

Yet for all their eloquence, these citizens do not appear to have been expressing the sentiments of the majority of the American people. When the Gallup poll in late October asked people whether the United States should "call off hydrogen bomb tests for the present," 56 per cent said no, only 24 per cent replied yes, and 20 per cent expressed no opinion. The *Newsweek* network of political reporters in 50 states confirmed that a majority of the people opposed Stevenson's stand on testing. These journalists estimated that the general public was against a test ban by margins of from 2-1 to 3-1, with only the scientists evenly divided. Instead of gaining support from his gamble, the Democratic candidate appeared to be losing undecided voters. Undoubtedly he did make some converts among the Republican upper middle class, but the mass of the American people preferred to trust the President on the complex and frightening issue of nuclear testing. [39]

Two dramatic episodes at the very climax of the campaign made the question academic. On October 29, the Suez crisis broke with the Israeli attack into the Sinai and the subsequent Anglo-French invasion of Egypt. The President immediately canceled all political speeches to concentrate on the danger abroad. Then on November 4, the Soviet Union invaded Hungary and brutally suppressed an insurrection by brave but hopelessly outmanned "freedom fighters." In the face of these twin international crises, the American people rallied behind Eisenhower, grateful to have such an experienced leader to support. Stevenson's slim chance for victory vanished as Republican orators pointed to Hungary as proof of the folly of trusting the Russians. Belittling Stevenson's test ban proposal as naive, Thomas Dewey declared that the fate of the "freedom fighters" revealed that "a Russian promise is an invitation to national suicide." The *New York Times* summed up the prevailing view when it editorialized that after Suez and Hungary, "it is not conceivable that a United States Administration would weaken its arsenal, or, if it did, that the American people would support the action."[40]

VI

The American people reelected Dwight D. Eisenhower by an overwhelming margin on November 6, 1956. Improving notably on his 1952 performance, the President swept 41 states and received nearly 58 per cent of the popular vote. Nearly all the pundits attributed his victory to the twin GOP boasts of peace and prosperity; ending the Korean War and presiding over an era of abundance were the achievements for which the people rewarded the popular President. Ironically the very threats to peace in Hungary and the Middle East at the campaign's climax simply increased Eisenhower's appeal to the electorate and turned a substantial lead into a near landslide.

The issue of nuclear testing did not play a major role in the outcome. Though one commentator felt it cost Stevenson as many as 3 million votes, most believed that it merely reinforced a commitment to the President on the part of those who planned to support him anyway. The experts who had warned Stevenson not to challenge Eisenhower on a national security issue were right; the test ban failed to convert many Republicans or attract many independent voters. Stevenson, however, was not sorry that he had advocated the test ban. During the campaign, he told *Newsweek*, "There are more important things than winning elections." Afterwards, he confided to admirers his conviction that "I was right on the H-bomb," and expressed his belief that his views "ultimately must prevail." He had raised the issue out of genuine concern, not political expediency, and his only regret was that Eisenhower had dismissed his proposal with "discourteous arrogance."[41]

There was no doubt about Stevenson's sincerity, but one could question the way he handled the issue. From the outset,

Stevenson failed to present a precise and clear proposition. He wavered between the idea of halting all nuclear tests and simply banning large H-bomb experiments. He never came to grips with the inspection problem, claiming that a ban would be self-enforcing despite administration arguments to the contrary. Above all, he did not indicate whether he favored a unilateral moratorium, with the United States free to resume testing if the Soviets failed to stop, or an international agreement with some of the safeguards that the administration advocated. This vagueness made it easy for the Republicans to distort his views and difficult for voters to grasp them.

Even his admirers in the scientific community ultimately became critical of Stevenson's test ban rhetoric. Such men as Eugene Rabinowich and David Inglis felt that the overpowering reason for a test ban was to break the disarmament stalemate and pave the way for meaningful arms control measures. Yet instead of stressing this first step concept, Stevenson relied more and more on the radiation peril, playing on the emotions of the electorate by repeated references to poisoned air, deformed children, and rising cancer rates. As scientists, they realized how tenuous the evidence was concerning fallout hazards; as concerned citizens, they believed that the future of mankind was at stake in the arms race. Thus their gratitude to Stevenson for raising the issue was tempered by a sadness that he had permitted a "simplified" fallout argument to receive "more emphasis and public attention" than the potential benefits of nuclear disarmament.[42]

Even more important is the question of whether Stevenson actually advanced the test ban cause by involving it in partisan politics. Some evidence suggests that he may have blocked an administration initiative to seek a negotiated test ban with the Soviet Union. Late in the campaign, four Democratic senators, led by Clinton Anderson, sent a telegram to the White House demanding to know if the National Security Council had recommended such a step in September. In public statements, they insinuated that Eisenhower had rejected this proposal only after Stevenson had raised the test ban in the campaign. On November 1, James Hagerty issued a reply in which he said that the President had never altered his basic view that any international agreement on nuclear weapons must include "proper safeguards." This oblique answer avoided any reference to the National Security Council and thus left open the possibility that this body had indeed recommended a test ban to the President in September.[43]

After the election, Stevenson renewed the claim that the NSC had voted unanimously in mid-September to seek a test ban only to have this recommendation "set aside for obviously political reasons." When this charge was brought to Eisenhower's attention at a news conference in January, 1957, the President avoided a direct answer. Instead he said that he never revealed NSC recommendations, adding, "I make the decisions, and there is no use trying to put any responsibility on the National Security Council—it's mine."

It is quite likely that the NSC did recommend that the United States explore the possibility of a test ban agreement with Russia in September 1956. Moreover, it is reasonable to suppose that Eisenhower was at first favorably inclined toward such a step. In 1959, he told a group of advisers that "three or four years ago," in the words of his listeners, "he had the idea of stopping atmospheric tests. He encountered enormous resistance and found very little support initially." By September 1956 that opposition, from the AEC and the Pentagon, had weakened and the time seemed opportune to approach the Soviets. At that moment, Stevenson brought the issue into the presidential campaign and made a diplomatic initiative impossible. Such an explanation, while speculative, does account for Eisenhower's utter disgust with Stevenson for raising the issue and his subsequent refusal to debate its merits publicly.[44]

Thus the Democratic challenger may well have snuffed out a promising attempt to achieve a test ban in 1956. Despite his idealism and sincerity, Stevenson politicized a delicate diplomatic issue and thereby ensured administration opposition. Yet in the long run, his eloquent advocacy brought the test ban out of obscurity and into the forefront of public discussion. It was now on the national agenda and could no longer be ignored. Given the apathy of the American people toward nuclear disarmament, Stevenson had performed a remarkable feat of public education.

CHAPTER

5

"RADIATION
WITHOUT
REPRESENTATION"

With the election safely over, the Eisenhower administration reviewed its stand on nuclear testing. The result was a five-point disarmament program which Ambassador Henry Cabot Lodge presented to the United Nations General Assembly on January 14, 1957. The heart of the plan, as Lodge outlined it, was a call for an end to the production of nuclear weapons under strict international supervision. Once this ambitious goal had been achieved, Lodge continued, the United States would be willing to negotiate a treaty to eliminate "all nuclear test explosions." In addition, the American proposal included reductions in conventional forces, registration of all intercontinental ballistic missile tests, and a variation on "open skies."

Although billed as a new departure, the comprehensive plan simply restated the traditional American insistence on placing a priority on halting the manufacture of nuclear weapons. For the first time, the United States was willing to include a future test ban in the package, but the insistence that the Soviets first agree to international inspectors guaranteeing a halt in arms production virtually ensured its rejection. Most observers had seen the test ban as a way to loosen the disarmament logjam. The Eisenhower administration was now proposing just the op-

113

posite—holding out a test ban as a reward for Russian agreement on complete nuclear disarmament.

In an effort to placate world opinion, the United States did offer to negotiate an interim agreement requiring that all nuclear tests be announced in advance and permitting limited international observation. Norway, upset by heavy radioactive fallout from the autumn Soviet tests, had proposed such a plan in November 1956. The Russians, however, countered with a resolution calling for the immediate cessation of all testing. Once it was clear that there was no easy compromise available, the General Assembly voted unanimously to refer all proposals to the five-nation disarmament subcommittee which was due to resume its deliberations in London in mid-March.[1]

Growing world concern over testing made it necessary for the United States and Great Britain to coordinate their policies. When President Eisenhower flew to Bermuda in March to meet with Prime Minister Harold Macmillan, who succeeded Anthony Eden after the Suez fiasco, the two leaders devoted considerable time to the test ban issue. With Britain planning to test its first H-bomb in May, Macmillan wanted to be certain that Eisenhower was not going to change American policy. The President reassured the Prime Minister, and in their final communiqué, they stated their agreement that "continued nuclear testing is required, certainly for the present." They minimized the danger from fallout and promised "to conduct nuclear tests only in such manner as will keep world radiation from rising to more than a small fraction of the levels that might be hazardous." Then, in an attempt to outmaneuver the Russians, Eisenhower and Macmillan renewed the American offer to register all tests in advance with the UN and permit limited observation if the Soviets would do likewise.

The Bermuda conference indicated that American resistance to a test ban was as great as ever. Publicly John Foster Dulles tried to paint the registration proposal as one of "the first steps down a new path," but privately he told members of Congress that the Bermuda joint communiqué on testing "was largely psychological in purpose." The Eisenhower administration apparently hoped that promises to conduct tests carefully, to announce them publicly, and to let selected international officials observe them would counter growing demands for an end to testing.[2]

An abrupt change in Harold Stassen's position in the Eisenhower administration on the eve of the London disarmament talks revealed that Dulles's uncompromising views still determined American policy. Since appointing Stassen as disarmament adviser in 1955, the President had tried to mediate the sharp differences between the two strong-minded men. In December 1956, Eisenhower informed Dulles that he had been "brutally frank" in telling Stassen that he could no longer challenge the Secretary of State's primacy in the disarmament field. The President, who regarded Stassen as "head and shoulders above most people in government," hesitated to take drastic action, but finally on March 1 he announced that henceforth Stassen would report to him through the State Department. The press immediately labeled the shift a demotion and concluded that Dulles would now prevent Stassen from expressing his views directly to the President.[3]

Stassen still retained the title of disarmament adviser, and he headed the American delegation to the five-nation subcommittee talks in London that began on March 15. After a month of futile negotiation, Stassen returned to the United States to confer with Dulles and Eisenhower. The Secretary praised his new subordinate for making "a serious effort to reach an initial partial agreement," but warned that progress could only come slowly. The President was equally guarded after a private meeting with Stassen at his Augusta retreat. Advances in the disarmament field, he commented, were "likely to come by steps carefully measured and carefully taken."

As Stassen returned to London to continue the negotiations, Dulles summed up the administration's attitude at a press conference on April 23. Asked if it would be possible to achieve a test ban separately from a comprehensive disarmament agreement, Dulles replied that while nothing was "impossible," he felt that such a separation would be "rather difficult." He went on to minimize the health dangers from fallout and to assert that the administration did not feel that "the risks of continued testing are sufficiently great so that we should take great risks in another direction." The only hope he held out to test ban advocates was the willingness to reconsider "in the light, perhaps, of further scientific information than is now available." For the moment, at least, the administration appeared to be unyielding in its commitment to a policy of conducting nuclear tests which it felt were vital to American security.[4]

I

Public concern over the fallout danger did not end with the presidential election. At hearings held by Senator Humphrey's disarmament subcommittee in December 1956 and January 1957 witnesses continued to voice their fears. A St. Louis housewife described the radioactivity from tests as "a worldwide consumer problem" as she declared that people were "faced with the contamination of milk, cheese and vegetables." Another witness warned scientists that America's children could not be used as "white mice or guinea pigs . . . to find out how much strontium-90 the human body can tolerate." Warren Weaver, who chaired the genetics committee for the National Academy of Sciences report on radiation hazards, reminded the subcommittee that even the present low level of 0.1r from testing meant 6,000 additional damaged children. He felt that national security needs justified the risk, but he added, "I do not think it is fair to anybody to say that fallout is harmless. It is not harmless." Senator Humphrey agreed. While he was not sure how dangerous fallout was, he believed it raised a vital issue that involved "the whole mental, physical, and social health of the American people and the people of the world."[5]

The Atomic Energy Commission tried hard to remove these lingering fears about fallout. Merril Eisenbud, manager of the

AEC's New York office, who was in charge of the agency's radiation monitoring system, spoke out repeatedly. In a Washington speech on November 15, 1956, Eisenbud stated that all the nuclear tests conducted so far had raised the level of strontium-90 in the human body only slightly, at most not more than 7 per cent above natural background radiation. Eisenbud was more particular in remarks at a New York symposium in February, 1957. He estimated that a child born in 1956 would receive a maximum uptake of 2.3r of Sr^{90} over the next 70 years from existing test fallout. If tests continued, the maximum would still be no more than 5r, compared to a lifetime exposure of from 7 to 23r from natural sources. Since man had adapted to the continuous radiation from cosmic rays and the earth's crust, Eisenbud argued, the small increase from bomb testing posed no serious threat to human existence.[6]

A trio of Columbia University scientists, headed by J. Laurence Kulp, provided the first reliable data on the amount of strontium-90 absorbed by humans. In a study funded by the AEC, the three researchers analyzed more than 1500 bones from around the world to determine their Sr^{90} content. Their findings were reassuring. The bones, all dating from 1955, showed that the human uptake of strontium-90 averaged only 0.12 micromicrocuries per gram of calcium, or 1/10,000th of the maximum permissible concentration. This incredibly low figure, one-millionth of one-millionth of a curie, indicated that the body discriminated quite effectively against strontium-90 in the digestive process. Kulp and his coworkers did find, however, that the uptake in children, whose bones were still being formed, was much higher, sometimes three or four times the concentration in adults. From the available evidence, they concluded not only that the present danger was "very small," but that by 1970 the uptake of Sr^{90} would still be less than 2 micromicrocuries.

These findings attracted nationwide attention. The *New York Times* featured them in a front-page story that said the Kulp report indicated that testing could continue at the present rate without endangering human life. William Laurence, the *Times'* science reporter, called the results "heartening," and claimed they proved that Stevenson's charges in the recent campaign were unfounded. Ralph Lapp, however, dissented. In a letter to *Science,* he pointed out that the three researchers had based their conclusions on insufficient evidence. Citing the absence of any bones of infants, he warned that those born after the 1954 BRAVO shot might well experience far higher concentrations of Sr^{90}. Lapp also disputed the future projections, arguing that continued testing could lead to a much more dangerous level of strontium-90 in the human body.[7]

Despite the new evidence, scientists were still divided over the possible danger of strontium-90. The problem stemmed from the lack of hard evidence; most experts felt that they simply could not make a firm judgment on the skimpy available data. Many hoped that the UN Scientific Committee on the Effects of Atomic Radiation would come forth with an authoritative answer. But this body, which held meetings in New York in 1956 and Geneva in 1957, was still collecting information and was not due to issue its report until the summer of 1958. Meanwhile, a bewildered public tried to accept the reassuring AEC statements while wondering about the validity of more disturbing estimates from skeptical scientists.[8]

II

In the spring of 1957, the nuclear powers went ahead with plans for testing in defiance of world opinion. On January 24, the AEC announced a new series of atomic tests scheduled for the Nevada proving grounds in late spring and early summer. Chairman Strauss had proposed the tests to Eisenhower on December 21, 1956, claiming that they were necessary to perfect "air defense and anti-submarine warheads." After conferring with Dulles, the President gave his approval on the understanding that all the tests would be held in Nevada and that fallout would be kept to a minimum. The AEC dubbed the series PLUMBOB, explaining to the public that most of the shots would be fired from balloons moored to the ground. In this way, the explosions would take place at altitudes high enough to avoid sucking up surface debris and thereby avoid heavy local fallout.[9]

Despite the fact that the PLUMBOB tests would be confined to the continental United States, the Japanese government protested vigorously. In diplomatic notes on March 20 and April 29, Tokyo asked the Eisenhower administration to cancel the tests and join in an international moratorium with the Soviet Union and Great Britain. Dulles replied that the United States could not abandon its tests "without adequate safeguards" and could not rely upon "the good intentions of certain nations who, by the record of past action, do not warrant such reliance." He promised the Japanese that the American tests would be low-yield ones which "will be conducted in such a manner as not to result in any significant addition to radiation levels throughout the world."

PLUMBOB, delayed nearly two weeks by the weather, finally began on May 28 at Frenchman's Flat. In the next six weeks, the AEC detonated 6 atomic weapons ranging in size from a few kilotons up to a large, 80-kiloton bomb. American commentators speculated that the tests were designed to perfect tactical weapons, anti-missile missile warheads, and a relatively clean atomic trigger for the nation's H-bombs. Most of the shots were fired from platforms on the moored balloons at altitudes of 600 feet or more. Very little fallout resulted, and consequently the world press, realizing that only H-bomb explosions caused global fallout, virtually ignored PLUMBOB.[10]

A new round of Soviet tests attracted far more attention. After detonating four explosions in August and September, the Russians spaced out additional shots in November 1956 and January and March 1957. Then in April they conducted five tests within a two-week period, creating heavy fallout that circled the globe. The Japanese experienced radioactive rain and snow as Geiger counters measured levels higher than those following the 1954 BRAVO test. The government sent loud-speaker trucks into city streets to warn people to wash off all fresh fruits and vegetables and to boil drinking water. Hostile groups paraded outside the Russian embassy and Japanese officials sent a formal protest to the Soviet Union. The Kremlin ignored the uproar. Instead of apologizing, Nikita Khrushchev told journalists that Soviet scientists had perfected an H-bomb too powerful to test, one that "could melt the Arctic icecap and send oceans spilling all over the world." [11]

Britain's announcement in January of plans to test her first H-bomb at Christmas Island in the central Pacific provoked the greatest outcry. The Hawaiian legislature passed a resolution protesting "the inherent danger" to its citizens from the proposed British test and the islands' delegate to Congress complained to the White House of "possible danger to the people of Hawaii." The AEC opposed making any formal objections for fear of jeopardizing future American tests in the Pacific. Secretary Dulles explained to a press conference that British plans to detonate their bomb at a high altitude would prevent any fallout danger to Hawaii.

The Japanese felt differently. Prime Minister Nobusuke Kishi sent a formal protest to London, warning that the Christmas Island test would endanger the Japanese fishing industry. When the British government politely turned down the Japanese request to cancel the test, Kishi sent a prominent Japanese Christian educator to England to plead for reconsideration. Pacifist groups in Japan, meanwhile, began publicizing a plan to send a "suicide sitdown fleet" to the Christmas Island area to demonstrate their opposition to the forthcoming test.

The insensitivity of the three nuclear powers created a growing feeling of indignation throughout the world. Each country justified its tests on grounds of national security, but none would admit any responsibility for exposing all mankind to the resulting fallout and its unknown perils. With the Japanese leading the way, the people of the world began to demand a halt to nuclear testing. "Not since Hiroshima," commented *Newsweek*, "had such a bitter and fateful debate raged over the building, testing, and ultimate use of the A-bomb—and its vastly more destructive offspring, the H-bomb. Governments, scientists, military men, just plain citizens—all were caught up in the controversy."[12]

The most eloquent appeal to man's conscience came from Lambaréné in French Equatorial Africa. In late 1956, Norman Cousins, the editor of the *Saturday Review*, had gone there to ask Dr. Albert Schweitzer to speak out against the nuclear tests. Schweitzer, the world-famous musician, philosopher, and theologian, usually avoided attempts to use his name to promote causes, but he listened intently as Cousins explained his belief that "there was no one in the world whose voice would have greater carrying power than his own." The doctor revealed that he had been following the test ban controversy closely and that he felt passionately that fallout threatened human life. After several days of reflection, Schweitzer told Cousins that he would speak out. "All peoples are involved," he said, "therefore the matter transcends the military interests of the testing nations. It is clearly in the human interest that the tests be stopped."[13]

Schweitzer decided to make his appeal to the Norwegian committee which had awarded him the Nobel Peace Prize in 1952. The 82-year-old philosopher completed his statement in early April and sent it to the committee's chairman, Uunar John, who read it to the world on Radio Oslo on April 24, 1957.

Entitling his remarks, "Peace or Atomic War" Schweitzer focused his attention on the danger that nuclear fallout posed for human life. He singled out strontium-90 for special emphasis, describing the way it moved from the soil to grass, through a cow's stomach into milk, and finally entered the bones of growing children. The amount was small, he admitted, but he noted, "What the radiation lacks in strength is compensated for by time. It works day and night without interruption." He also

121

cited the genetic danger to warn that bomb explosions could lead to "a catastrophe that must be prevented under every circumstance." Global fallout, he concluded, was "an astounding event in the history of the earth and of the human race," one that people had to understand and to act against quickly. "The end of further experiments with atom bombs," Schweitzer prophesied, "would be like the early sun rays of hope which suffering humanity is longing for."

Fifty nations received Schweitzer's words as spoken by Uunar John, but not a single American radio station carried them. The *New York Times* printed a front-page story, but most American newspapers and magazines ignored the appeal; Cousins's *Saturday Review* was the only popular periodical that published the full text. Indeed, Schweitzer's statement might have gone virtually unnoticed in the United States had not Willard Libby decided to give an official reply.[14]

The AEC Commissioner's rebuttal took the form of an eight-page public letter. While Libby voiced his great respect for the philosopher, he contended that Schweitzer's appeal was not based "on the latest scientific information on radioactive fallout." The carefully-compiled AEC records showed that human exposures "are very much smaller than those which would be required to produce observable effects in the population." There was a slight risk, Libby admitted, but it was "extremely small compared with other risks which persons everywhere take as a normal part of their lives." He discussed the danger from strontium-90 and the long-term genetic hazards at length, concluding that both were less damaging to man than natural background radiation. Risk, he explained, was an essential part of modern life, the price we paid for "our pleasures, our comforts, and our material progress." It would be far more dangerous to run "the terrible risk of abandoning the defense effort which is so essential under present conditions to the survival of the Free World . . ."

Libby's reply led to a lively debate. Both *Time* magazine and the *New York Times* found his words persuasive, showing that there was no real cause for alarm as Schweitzer believed. But Harrison Brown challenged Libby's definition of a small risk in a *Saturday Review* article. "When we say that the leukemia rate is increased by only 0.5 per cent," Brown argued, "the number appears small. But when we say that 10,000 *individuals* are killed each year, . . . the number suddenly seems very large." Eugene Rabinowich objected to comparing fallout to risks people took voluntarily, such as medical X-rays or airplane travel. Fallout is the product of "deliberate government action," he contended; moreover, we inflict this radiation "on the whole population of the world—and not only on our own people, or our own allies, or our potential enemies." The editor of the *Bulletin of the Atomic Scientists* agreed that Schweitzer's data was unverified and exaggerated, but his words expressed a moral truth that transcended scientific evidence. People responded to Schweitzer's appeal, Rabinowich explained, because it was based "on a sound and highly rational desire of mankind to reverse the trend which brings it closer every day to a suicidal situation."[15]

By the end of April, world attention focused on the forthcoming British H-bomb test on Christmas Island. The Labor Party decided to challenge the government's decision in Parliament, offering a resolution to postpone the shot pending a new effort at an international test ban agreement. In the debate that ensued, Laborites stressed the health issue, warning of "the dangers to humanity" from bomb fallout. A report issued in mid-April by the British Atomic Scientists Association proved embarrassing to the government's case. Claiming that even very low doses of radiation could cause leukemia and bone cancer, the report estimated that 1000 people would die for every megaton of explosive power released in the Christmas Island test. In the United States, chemist Linus Pauling repeated this estimate and went further, asserting that previous bomb blasts had doomed 10,000 people to die from leukemia. The percentage of the world's population affected by fallout was small, Pauling declared, but the absolute number was "large enough to anyone interested in human suffering to be concerned about it."

These claims led to near hysteria in Great Britain. Pacifists staged parades and demonstrations that attracted mass support; petitions demanding an end to testing and even a total ban on nuclear weapons began to appear. Bertrand Russell spoke for millions of Britons when he called for a test ban, saying, "I do not wish to be an accomplice in a vast atrocity which threatens the world with overwhelming disaster." Prime Minister Harold Macmillan was startled by the depth of feeling revealed by the protests, commenting later, "I began to realize how profound and how widespread was the concern, and how easily it could be exploited." The most sensational proposal came from Harold Steele, a 63-year-old chicken farmer, who announced plans to sail alone to Christmas Island and perish in the bomb blast. "I willingly sacrifice myself," he declared, "to prove to the world the horror of this devilish thing." [16]

The British government stood firm in the midst of the outcry. In Parliament, Conservative Party spokesmen accused the Laborites of talking "unmitigated nonsense," and hinted darkly of a Communist conspiracy. Lord Cherwell, Churchill's science adviser in World War II, told the House of Lords that fallout posed no danger to the world's population, terming the protesters "hysterical people." An eminent American scientist, Ernest O. Lawrence, backed the government's stand. In London as an adviser to Harold Stassen at the UN disarmament subcommittee meeting, Lawrence dismissed the talk of leukemia and bone cancer as a "lot of nonsense." "No one is going to be hurt by these tests . . . ," Lawrence asserted; "the radiation is so infinitesimal afterward that there can't possibly be any ill effects." In early May, Parliament sustained the government's position by a vote of 309 to 258.

As the date of the Christmas Island test drew near, foreign governments registered their objections. Japanese Prime Minister Kishi's special envoy spent several weeks in unsuccessful talks with British diplomats. The West German *Bundestag* passed a resolution calling on the United States, the Soviet Union, and Great Britain to halt all tests by international agreement. The Soviets, who had just completed their own test series, now joined the ranks of those demanding a ban. The Russian delegate at the London disarmament talks proposed an agreement to stop testing without any inspection safeguards, and on May 10 the Supreme Soviet offered to stop all future Russian tests if the United States and Britain would also desist.

The British ignored these entreaties. On May 15, a Vickers Valiant jet bomber dropped England's first H-bomb over Christmas Island. It exploded at a height of 3 miles, filling the sky with its huge fireball but creating very little fallout. The next day Harold Macmillan informed Parliament that Britain had now entered the select circle of full-fledged nuclear powers; for a nation still recovering from the humiliation of Suez, it was a proud moment. The British H-bomb, Macmillan stressed, had produced an "almost negligible" amount of fallout.

The British tested two more H-bombs at Christmas Island, one on May 31 and another on June 20. Harold Steele failed to complete his rendezvous with death, arriving in the Pacific after the tests had been completed. "I'm greatly disappointed," he told reporters, "This trip has cost me my entire life savings." The worldwide indignation began to fade as the British bombs proved relatively clean, adding only slightly to the stratosphere's inventory of strontium-90. But Harold Macmillan realized that the controversy had only just begun. Fallout, he told a colleague, would be "the grappling point" in politics for some time to come. "After all, it presents many features useful to the agitator," he pointed out. "It had an appeal for the mother, the prospective mother, the grandmother, and all the rest, and every kind of exaggeration or mis-statement is permissible."[17]

III

The Schweitzer appeal and the furor over the British H-bomb test led Linus Pauling to call upon American scientists to speak out on the test ban issue. Pauling, born in Oregon in 1901, had spent his entire career at Cal Tech, earning his Ph.D. there in chemistry in 1925 and eventually heading the division of chemistry and chemical engineering. A brilliant research scientist, he had won a Nobel Prize in 1954 for his book, *The Nature of the Chemical Bond*. He was no stranger to political controversy. In the early Cold War years, he had criticized the containment policy and had joined several organizations dominated by Communists. The House Un-American Activities Committee had accused him in 1951 of following "a pattern of loyalty to the Communist cause," and Senator Joseph McCarthy called him "a hidden Communist." Refused a passport on three separate occasions, Pauling had consistently denied membership in the Communist Party, but he never recanted his left-wing views.

Many scientists admired Pauling's independence and personal courage, but few regarded him as a responsible spokesman for the scientific community. He was too opinionated, too dogmatic, too controversial. A man of supreme self-confidence, noted one commentator, from the time he was a young man Pauling "was aware of his powers and knew where he wanted to go." He was a brilliant speaker, delighting college audiences with his wit, his personal commitment, and his unqualified absolutes. In the test ban movement, he finally discovered a cause to which he could devote his great energy and intelligence; he resigned his administrative posts at Cal Tech and enlisted in the crusade which would ultimately bring him the Nobel Peace Prize.[18]

On May 15, 1957, the same day as the first Christmas Island test, Pauling spoke to an honors day assembly at Washington University in St. Louis. Citing Schweitzer's appeal, he dealt at length with the test ban issue, describing his own position as stemming from "humanitarian" rather than scientific concerns. "I believe that no human being should be sacrificed to a project," he declared; "and in particular I believe that no human being should be sacrificed to the project of perfecting nuclear weapons that could kill hundreds of millions of human beings, could devastate this beautiful world in which we live."

The audience reacted so favorably, giving Pauling prolonged applause and a standing ovation, that he decided to go ahead with an idea he had mentioned to several friends the day before. He would frame a petition by American scientists appealing for an international agreement to halt all nuclear tests. Two Washington University professors, biologist Barry Commoner and physicist Edward U. Condon, helped him draft the petition and circulate it among faculty members across the nation. Beginning with a nucleus of 27 signatures, including those of noted geneticist H. J. Muller and Laurence H. Snyder, president of the AAAS, nearly 2000 scientists signed Pauling's petition by June 1. Two days later, he released it to the press and sent a copy to the White House.[19]

The petition called for an international agreement to halt nuclear testing as soon as possible. Moderate in tone, it cited the fallout danger without making any specific claims that tests caused bone cancer or leukemia. Instead, the petition referred in general terms to "damage to the health of human beings" and the possibility that bomb radiation could cause "an increase in the number of seriously defective children." An end to testing, the scientists claimed, would help break the disarmament stalemate and prevent the spread of nuclear weapons to other nations. For all these reasons, the appeal concluded, "We deem it imperative that immediate action be taken to effect an international agreement to stop the testing of all nuclear weapons."

Many distinguished scientists signed the Pauling petition. In addition to Muller and Snyder, more than 50 members of the National Academy of Sciences were represented. Biologists predominated, contributing 32 per cent of the signatures, compared to 17 per cent for physicists, 15 per cent for biochemists and 14 per cent for chemists. A *U.S. News* analysis showed, however, that only half the signers were listed in *American Men of Science,* the profession's authoritative directory. Most of the rest were graduate students, fellowship holders, and laboratory technicians. Moreover, the editors pointed out, the men most knowledgeable on atomic issues, the physicists, were very lightly represented. Out of 77 members of the physics department at the University of California at Berkeley, for example, only 3 had signed the petition.

A majority of the nation's leading scientists did not sign Pauling's petition. Some may not have had the opportunity, but many deliberately refused. Professor Joel H. Hildebrand, chairman of the chemistry department at Berkeley, refused on patriotic grounds. Accusing Pauling of intruding into "the realm of international diplomacy where a scientist possesses no peculiar knowledge or wisdom," Hildebrand placed national security above whatever risks testing involved. "Freedom was won for us by men who valued it above life," he argued; "we should preserve it even at the cost of lives." One of Pauling's colleagues at Cal Tech, George Beadle, chairman of the biology department, felt that those speaking in the name of science "ought to confine their public statements to their own fields." Scientists had the right of all citizens to give their views on public issues, Beadle added, but they should "make it clear that they are speaking not as experts but are expressing private opinions." [20]

Pauling ignored his critics. Instead he made increasingly extreme claims about the effect of testing on human health. In an ABC television interview, he estimated that fallout would lead to 200,000 defective children over the next 20 generations. He also contended that radiation from bomb tests shortened life expectancy. He calculated that each roentgen of exposure hastened an individual's death by two weeks; continued bomb testing, Pauling asserted, would mean that one million people would lose from 5 to 10 years of their normal life expectancy.

The controversy Pauling had generated died down in mid-June, but the scientific community remained divided. Many observers agreed with the *New Republic*'s comment that the resort to polemics had confused rather than clarified the issues. "The debate is not enlightening," the editors wrote, "because it is an argument, principally, between two groups of extreme partisans, both guilty of asserting scientific claims unconfirmed by the evidence." Above all, the conflicting views expressed by Pauling and his critics disturbed the American people. They wanted clear answers. Was fallout dangerous or not? Should the United States continue testing? Could they trust the reassuring report by the National Academy of Sciences? Aware of this prevalent public concern, Congress stepped in to try to compel the scientists to come forth with a satisfactory explanation of the radiation problem.[21]

IV

The Joint Committee on Atomic Energy had begun a staff study on fallout in the summer of 1956. In March 1957, the committee announced plans to invite the nation's leading scientists to give testimony before a special subcommittee on radiation. The chairman of this body, Congressman Chet Holifield, a liberal Democrat from California, worked with staff members to ensure that the hearings would deal with every aspect of the radiation problem. They prepared a detailed outline and asked the 50 witnesses invited to testify to confine their remarks to specific, assigned topics. Instead of the usual rambling committee hearing, Holifield hoped to preside over a scientific seminar which would present the American public with all the known facts on fallout.

The subcommittee hearings on radiation began on May 27, 1957, and ran for eight days. Held in the ornate Senate Caucus Room, the site of the famous Army-McCarthy hearings three years earlier, they were well-attended. Reporters from twelve foreign countries joined a large American press corps that followed the scientific testimony carefully and tried to translate it into layman's language for their readers. More than forty witnesses appeared; many were AEC employees, but several academic scientists known to be critical of the government's nuclear policies were also included. Chairman Holifield stressed at the outset the subcommittee's determination to lay out the facts rather than to substantiate predetermined conclusions. His goal, he stated, was "to delineate those areas where we have knowledge from those where we have little or no knowledge, with a view to determining the areas of research which need more intensive effort." The other committee members, including Representative Sterling Cole of New York and Senator Henry Jackson of Washington, remained relatively silent during the proceedings. Senator Clinton Anderson of the Joint committee, who was not on the subcommittee, attended the hearings and played gadfly.[22]

The first few witnesses were Atomic Energy Commission officials who sketched out the broad outlines of the radiation problem. Their candor was refreshing. Dr. Charles L. Dunham, head of the division of biology and medicine, stated forthrightly that radiation was dangerous, commenting that "any quantity of radioactive fallout is undesirable." The real question, he argued, was to weigh the radiation hazard against the "positive benefits of nuclear energy." Dr. Alvin C. Graves, who supervised testing for the AEC, startled the subcommittee by stating that a truly clean H-bomb was technically impossible. The necessity for an atomic trigger, he explained, meant that some fallout would always result; at best, you could reduce the amount of fission to make a relatively clean weapon.

Graves gave the subcommittee members the clearest explanation of fallout. When a neutron hit the uranium-235 in a fission explosion, it transformed it into U-236, an unstable element that quickly split into other isotopes. The fission products that resulted varied widely; 1 time in 20, strontium-90 was the end product. Thus on the average, 5 per cent of the bomb's fallout consisted of strontium-90, a substance not found in nature. Sr^{90} emitted beta particles, weak radiation which penetrated only a few inches into surrounding tissue. For this reason, the strontium-90 which lodged in human bone, while it had a long half-life of 28 years, posed no genetic problem; the radiation might eventually cause bone cancer or leukemia, but it would not affect the reproductive organs. Another fission product, cesium-137, present in about 7 per cent of fallout, sent out the more deadly gamma rays that could reach the human gonads and cause harmful mutations. Cesium-137 had a shorter half-life and stayed in the human body for a relatively short time, but while present it posed a grave genetic danger.[23]

Most of the testimony that followed centered on strontium-90. AEC witnesses admitted for the first time that they had been aware of this potential hazard before the BRAVO shot. In July 1953, the AEC had held a conference at the RAND Corporation think-tank at Santa Monica at which scientists had discussed the possible danger from Sr^{90} fallout. As a result, the Commission created Project Sunshine to collect samples of fallout from across the world and measure the strontium-90 content. The designers of Project Sunshine, which Willard Libby supervised, arbitrarily set 100 micromicrocuries of Sr^{90} per gram of calcium as the maximum permissible concentration, and dubbed this new measurement a Sunshine Unit. Thus hiding behind misleading nomenclature, the AEC began monitoring the strontium-90 fallout long before the American public was aware of this new danger.[24]

Another administration witness, Lester Machta of the Weather Bureau, described how the Sr^{90} fallout returned to earth. Thrown into the stratosphere by the force of the nuclear explosion, the fission products slowly seeped back into the troposphere, the layer of the earth's atmosphere extending up to about 40,000 feet, and then fell quickly to the ground, usually mixed with rain or snow. Contrary to what was previously thought, Machta explained, the fallout pattern was not uniform. New evidence indicated that far more strontium-90 entered the troposphere in more northerly latitudes, where the jet stream assisted the exchange, than in equatorial regions. Machta said the data was incomplete, but he estimated that twice the normal level of fallout occurred between 25 and 60 degrees north latitude, the band of heaviest population in the

United States and Europe. Merril Eisenbud, in charge of the Project Sunshine monitoring network, confirmed Machta's findings, but Willard Libby refused to agree. With his theory of uniform global fallout under attack, the AEC commissioner claimed that the heavier deposits were due to local fallout that never escaped from the troposphere and were blown by prevailing winds and rainfall patterns into the north temperate zone. Clinton Anderson pointed out that whatever the cause, the higher concentration of Sr^{90} in some areas exposed the people of those regions to much greater danger.[25]

Other witnesses described what happened to the Sr^{90} after it reached the earth. Eisenbud explained how it entered the food cycle through milk, and even though the human body discriminated heavily in favor of calcium, small amounts built up in the skeleton, particularly in growing children. Estimating that in addition to the 1 million curies of strontium-90 fallout already on the ground, another 2.4 million would eventually fall from the stratosphere from bombs already tested, he predicted that by 1970 children in the United States would have between 4 and 6 Sunshine Units in their bones. Given the MPC of 100 Sunshine Units, Eisenbud saw no cause for alarm, stating, "I personally am not apprehensive as to the long-range hazards." Senator Anderson, however, was not so sure. Comparing the Sr^{90} in the stratosphere to "a bank account up in the sky sending down a little all the time," he wondered what would happen if we kept making heavy deposits from continued nuclear testing.

Dr. Laurence Kulp, the Columbia University scientist in charge of the AEC-financed study of the Sr^{90} content in human bones, tried to reassure the senator. He stated that the current levels of strontium-90 in the skeleton were too small to cause any concern, and he predicted that even continued testing over the next 5 years would not raise the levels to more than 8 Sunshine Units for adults or 24 for children, compared to the MPC of 100 units. Dr. William F. Neumann of the University of Rochester School of Medicine disagreed. He admitted that the present level of Sr^{90} in human bone was "quite low," but said he would "part company" from Kulp on future predictions. In order to keep Senator Anderson's bank account balanced, he calculated, the nuclear powers would have to limit their tests each year to a total of 2.2 megatons of fission. Since BRAVO alone released 10 megatons of fission products, Neumann pointed out, the United States, the Soviet Union and Great Britain would have to exercise great restraint. "The number of megatons that can be exploded is so small," he concluded, "some kind of international control of the production and release of fission products is inevitable."

Other scientists found Neumann's figures misleading, but they were intrigued with his idea of a limit on testing megatonnage. Dr. Wright Langham of the AEC's Los Alamos laboratory suggested a maximum of 10 megatons a year for all tests, arguing that this amount would keep the Sr^{90} well below the MPC. Eisenbud and Kulp agreed that more than 10 megatons a year would create a future Sr^{90} fallout hazard and thus backed Neumann's concept of an international agreement to limit the size and number of nuclear tests.[26]

No such consensus emerged over the most crucial issue debated at the hearings—whether or not a threshold existed below which radiation did not cause bone cancer or leukemia. Professor Edward P. Lewis of Cal Tech presented the case against a threshold. He cited a recent article he had published in *Science* in which he examined data from three groups of human beings exposed to radiation—the survivors of Hiroshima and Nagasaki, patients treated with heavy doses of X-rays, and radiologists who received repeated exposure owing to their occupation. In all three cases, Lewis found a heavy incidence of leukemia, directly proportional to the degree of radiation exposure. Thus he argued that there was no safe level of radiation; each exposure, no matter how slight, had a cumulative effect, increasing the individual's chances of developing cancer. Applying this linear theory to fallout, Lewis estimated that the very small dose each American received annually,

0.001r, would cause an additional 1000 leukemia deaths each year.

Several other scientists supported Lewis's position. Dr. Walter Selove, a University of Pennsylvania physicist who spoke for the Federation of American Scientists, claimed that there was no such thing as a "permissible" level of fallout. The slightest additional radiation could "harm a considerable number of individuals," he warned, and radiation levels approaching the current MPC might mean the deaths of millions. Dr. W. L. Russell of Oak Ridge and Dr. Hardin Jones of the University of California's Radiation Laboratory presented evidence from experiments with mice that showed that radiation led to dramatic shortening of their life span, ranging from 19 to 112 days of the normal 800-day life expectancy. Although these experiments were conducted at relatively high radiation levels, in excess of 100r, both researchers believed that the resulting shortening of life was directly proportional to the dose at any level. Translated into human terms, Russell calculated that each exposure of 1r lopped 20 days off an individual's life.[27]

Dr. Shields Warren led a heated rebuttal to the linearity theory by radiologists. Warren asserted that there was a threshold below which radiation did not damage human health, citing the existence of background radiation in nature throughout man's history many times greater than fallout exposure. Warren read a statement from Dr. Jacob Furth, president of the American Association for Cancer Research, terming the argument that there was no threshold for inducing cancer "pure speculation not backed by data." Other witnesses pointed to the lack of evidence on low-level radiation effects; one scientist testified that experience with radium indicated that a skeletal content of at least 2 microcuries, the equivalent of 2000 Sunshine Units, was required to cause a bone tumor. These radiologists admitted that the evidence favoring a threshold was sketchy, but they were convinced it existed.

In a roundtable discussion near the end of the hearings, Lewis and Warren failed to resolve the threshold issue. Both men admitted that the data on human exposure to very low level radiation was too meager to prove either theory. The most Warren would concede was that linearity was "a possibility," but not "a reasonable probability." Lewis seized on this concession to argue that even the remote chance that all radiation exposure endangered human health should lead the government to try to prevent all future fallout. Dr. Ernest Pollard of Yale agreed. He was unsure about the validity of the linear theory, but until scientific evidence clearly established the existence of a threshold, he believed it was safer to assume all radiation hazardous.[28]

The geneticists, on the other hand, were unanimous in declaring that fallout caused dangerous mutations in direct proportion to human exposure. There was no genetic threshold, declared Professor James F. Crow of the University of Wisconsin, adding, "This means that there is no such thing as a safe dose of radiation to the population." He conceded that the genetic damage from present fallout levels was slight. Estimating the 30-year reproductive lifetime exposure to be 0.1r, he told the subcommittee that this would lead to an increase of only 0.2 per cent in the rate of birth defects. Projected for the 2 million children likely to be born to American parents over the next few years, however, Crow estimated an additional 8,000 infants with gross defects, 20,000 stillbirths, and 40,000 embryonic deaths, with still heavier genetic casualties in subsequent generations. He stated that while this hereditary damage would be only "a very small fraction of the total human death, disease and misery," he felt that "even one unnecessary individual tragedy is too many . . . unless it offers some compensating benefit for mankind."

Other witnesses confirmed Crow's statement. Bentley Glass of John Hopkins made the same points and suggested that the NAS report, which he had helped write, was too optimistic on the genetic danger from fallout. The only consolation he offered was to exonerate strontium-90, pointing out that its beta radiation did not effect the reproductive organs. H. J. Muller revealed that he had changed his mind completely about the genetic impact of testing. Warning that the nuclear explosions had already doomed millions yet unborn to birth defects, he called continued testing "a monstrous mistake of policy for both sides." Professor A. H. Sturtevant, one of the first geneticists to speak out against fallout, expressed his disagreement with the AEC's claim that testing involved a necessary risk, comparable to wearing a wristwatch with a radium dial. The difference, Sturtevant explained, was that the individual had no freedom of choice with bomb testing—each explosion exposed every person in the world to genetic damage. It was up to the government, he argued, to explain the benefits that balanced off this hazard. "It seems reasonable to ask for as detailed and objective a statement of the reasons for continued testing as is consistent with security considerations," he concluded.[29]

Willard Libby and other scientists who spoke for the AEC replied by comparing the slight risk from fallout to the grave danger of nuclear war. Asserting that we take risks "every minute" of our lives, whether driving on the highway, swimming at the beach, or breathing the air in industrial centers, Libby said that fallout was infinitely preferable to "the risk of annihilation" which could result "if we surrendered the weapons which are so essential to our freedom and our actual survival." Shields Warren said it would be "inexcusable for us to jeopardize our own safety and that of the rest of the free world" simply to end fallout, while Laurence Kulp described the radiation from testing as "trivial" compared to the "continued hazard of nuclear warfare." Ralph Lapp gave the administration spokesmen strong support when he estimated that a nuclear attack on the United States would not only kill 80 million Americans outright, but also lead ultimately to 272 million genetic casualties over the next few generations.

Senator Anderson, bothered by Libby's vague references to national security, asked the AEC Commissioner to document his position. Libby responded with a written statement explaining that the United States was in a period of "radical transition" in its weapons program, changing over from bombs delivered by aircraft to warheads aboard rocket-powered missiles. Each new missile, he explained, requires a new warhead, and each warhead must be tested. "To cut off testing, therefore, means the cutting off of the introduction of improved nuclear-weapons systems," he argued. He could not give specific details without violating security, he explained; the subcommittee would have to accept his word that nuclear tests were vital "for the survival of our Nation and that of the free world." Disturbed when Clinton Anderson continued to probe on this point, Senator Henry Jackson came to the administration's defense. What it all came down to, he asserted, was balancing "a danger of an undetermined nature" against the risk of "total hydrogen catastrophe to all free nations."[30]

The hearings ended on June 7 without arriving at any consensus on the fallout danger. The proceedings, commented the *New York Times,* "have been marked by scientific uncertainty and conflict over what fall-out radiation would do to present and future generations." In the absence of firm data on the effects of low-level radiation, the experts could not agree whether there was a threshold below which fallout did not injure human health. Although the genticists agreed that even the slightest amounts of radiation caused harmful mutations, they were unsure of the cumulative impact of testing on succeeding generations. And despite general agreement that current levels of Sr^{90} were not dangerous, the forecasts for the future varied widely.

The hearings did serve, however, to shake confidence in the AEC's assertion that fallout posed no problem for the American people. The uncertainty revealed at the hearings suggested that the administration had not been leveling with the public. The disclosure that fallout was much heavier in the north temperate zone, the agreement that tests should be limited to no more than 10 megatons a year, and the statement that a clean H-bomb was technically impossible all contradicted previous

AEC pronouncements. In a speech on the floor of the House on June 28, Chairman Chet Holifield scored the administration for failing to inform the American people of the true nature of the fallout danger. "We are now dealing with a global health problem," Holifield concluded.[31]

Nearly everyone agreed that ignorance and secrecy were the crux of the problem. Ralph Lapp urged the AEC to be more open with the American people and to release all available information to the press. He and other witnesses stressed the need for more intensive research to clear up such issues as the existence of a threshold and future levels of strontium-90 from continued testing. Dr. Alan T. Waterman of the National Science Foundation explained that the fear of the unknown was what made fallout such a frightening problem for the average American. "When one realizes a danger he has no control over, and knows nothing about," he argued, "to him it is a big danger. . . ."

Even more serious than the lack of data, however, was the inherent difficulty in interpreting and understanding the various risks involved. "Perhaps the most striking thing about fall-out fever is the question of *statistical death*," noted one writer. "What is the morality of statistical death?" How was the average American to balance off a slight increase in the cancer rate or a rise in the number of defective children in future generations against the peril of falling behind Russia in the arms race? "We must face again," commented Eric Sevareid, "the Solomon question of whether, as a civilized people, we shall take a present security risk upon ourselves in the name of our descendants." In light of the evidence presented at the hearings, the burden of proof was now on the administration. The government would have to show how the potentially serious hazards from fallout could be justified in the name of national security. Nuclear tests could no longer be taken for granted; the AEC would have to prove that they were a necessary evil.[32]

V

The radiation debate, touched off by Schweitzer's appeal, the Christmas Island tests, and Pauling's petition and culminating in the Holifield subcommittee hearings, led to a sharp change in public attitudes in the spring of 1957. When the Gallup poll asked in April if the United States should cease testing if all other nations did so, 63 per cent said yes, 28 per cent no, and 8 per cent gave no opinion. Only six months earlier, 56 per cent of those Gallup asked had opposed a test ban. The percentage who knew what fallout was had risen to 28 per cent, compared to 17 per cent in 1955. More than half of this knowledgeable group believed that there was "real danger" from test fallout, and 69 per cent favored a multilateral agreement to halt nuclear testing. In letters to magazine editors, individuals revealed that fear of fallout was behind their opposition to testing. "Once upon a time, war affected only those in the line of fire," wrote a *Newsweek* reader; "now it reaches into the third and fourth generation." One woman explained to Norman Cousins that she felt guilty "because, at first unknowingly but later knowingly, I have been feeding my children food of dubious purity."[33]

The White House mail reflected the changing sentiment. In May and June, letters, telegrams, and petitions calling for a halt to testing came pouring in from religious and pacifist groups as well as from ordinary citizens. Many were friendly in tone, such as the one that called on the administration to "go the second mile" in reaching agreement with the Russians on a test ban. "If we can make one small beginning," the writer argued, "perhaps we can turn the tide of the world back toward sanity and peaceful living." But some were bitter. One elderly Californian suggested that the President vacation with his grandchildren at the Nevada Proving Grounds so that "you may all have the advantages of this healthful spot. In our family," the writer added, "an eight-year-old child is slowly dying of leukemia."[34]

Calls for an end to testing began to be heard with increasing

139

frequency. Norman Cousins urged the United States to stop unilaterally, convinced that "world public opinion will compel all other nations to do likewise." Max Ascoli argued the same way in the *Reporter,* calling nuclear tests "acts of hostility against mankind." The Federation of American Scientists took a more moderate stand by advocating a halt to all tests above 100 kilotons. In Congress, Representative Charles Porter of Oregon proposed a test ban conditioned on similar restraint by the other nuclear powers and Montanan Mike Mansfield made a Senate speech to the same effect. Warning that the world was reaching a "saturation point" from fallout, he asserted that "a multilateral ban on nuclear tests is an essential first step if mankind is to survive."[35]

Advocates of testing tried hard to counter the growing public shift toward cessation. Administration spokesmen continued to belittle fallout as too negligible to threaten the health of American citizens. Lewis Strauss told a congressional committee that a luminous watch dial gave off more radioactivity than "all that received from the accumulated fallout to date." Secretary of Defense Charles E. Wilson claimed that cigarette smoking was much more dangerous than fallout, while Willard Libby said that an individual was more likely to be hit by lightening than to suffer any injury from fallout. According to Libby, moving from sea level to a higher altitude exposed a person to more additional radiation than the radioactivity from bomb tests.[36]

The argument that the danger of nuclear war far outweighed the risks from testing came up again and again. The *New York Times* felt that tests were necessary to develop improved weapons "to keep us out of an all-out nuclear war." "Indeed their discontinuance or curtailment," the editors wrote, "would then be a real disservice to present and future generations." Former President Harry Truman agreed. In a newspaper article in May, Truman called the fallout "a small sacrifice" compared to "the infintely greater evil of the use of nuclear bombs in war." He asked the American people "not to be panicked by the Soviet campaign of fear" which was "intended primarily to cripple the defense of the West." In the form letter that he sent to those who wrote the White House objecting to testing, Lewis Strauss contrasted the small risk of fallout with "the infinite human devastation that would result from the massive use of nuclear weapons in warfare."[37]

To the dismay of test ban advocates, both the administration and its supporters began to suggest that the protesters were following the Communist party line. Eisenhower opened up this line of attack at a press conference on June 5 when he commented that the call for test cessation "looks like almost an organized affair." Pressed by reporters to explain what he meant, the President said he had simply noted "there does seem to be some organization" behind the protests. "I didn't say a wicked organization," Ike added. The *U.S. News* had no doubt about what organization the President had in mind, calling the anti-test movement "Communist-inspired." In Congress, Representative Francis Walter of Pennsylvania pointed to Linus Pauling's long association with Communist-front groups to accuse him of spreading Soviet propaganda; Representative Lawrence H. Smith of Wisconsin singled out Norman Cousins for serving as a dupe of the Communists in enlisting Schweitzer in the test ban cause. Claiming that "the Communist conspiracy" was stirring up "a national hysteria," Smith appealed to the American people not to "let the superficial, disputed fear of radioactivity blind us to the greatest threat of all—atheistic Communism."[38]

The charge that the test ban movement was nothing more than Communist propaganda went far wide of the mark. Nearly all observers agreed that there was a deep and increasing fear of radiation spreading across the world. Eric Sevareid pointed out that while much of the concern might be ill-founded, it was nevertheless genuine. So far Russia had manipulated opinion cleverly, despite its own frequent tests, by proposing an immediate end to testing; it was time, he suggested, for the administration to call Moscow's bluff.

Other observers felt that whatever the true facts about radiation, it would be best to err on the side of safety. "The world has suddenly become a small sphere—too restricted in surface area for the 'safe' testing of super-bombs," wrote Ralph Lapp and Jack Schubert. "It is apparent that the atomic dice are loaded," editorialized George DuShane in *Science.* "The percentages are against us and we ought not play unless we must to assure other victories." Until there was proof to the contrary, argued the *New Republic,* "the only safe hypothesis on which to base policy is . . . that every bomb test creates additional radio-poisons which will kill a certain number of people."[39]

The most persuasive argument of all dealt with the world-wide impact of fallout. Whatever national advantages that might accrue to the United States from testing, warned Eugene Rabinowich, had to be weighed against the hazards to all mankind. "Whether this danger is great or small," he contended, "the most important thing is that it is *universal* and *compulsory.*" It was misleading to say that Russia and America were testing, pointed out Japanese physicist Mitsuo Taketani. "They are conducting nuclear bomb and weapons maneuvers," Taketani charged. "The whole population of the world is being used as guinea pigs." Americans might be willing to run the risk of leukemia and bone cancer, but the rest of mankind had no choice. They were innocent bystanders in what the *New Republic* called an era of "radiation without representation."[40]

"A MAGIC
MOMENT"

The outcry over radiation led to a reconsideration of American policy on nuclear testing in the spring of 1957. President Eisenhower, disturbed by the fallout problem, began to place greater weight on the need to reassure world opinion than on the military's pleas for continued testing. Harold Stassen pressed hard for a reversal in administration policy while Secretary of State Dulles, aware of potential Soviet propaganda victories, moderated his earlier opposition to a test ban and took a more neutral position. This shift left Lewis Strauss and the military and civilian leaders in the Pentagon as the only ones firmly opposed to any agreement with the Soviets to halt nuclear tests.

The first sign of a possible breakthrough came during a 10-day recess in the London disarmament talks in May. The usual deadlock had developed at the five-nation subcommittee meetings, which had begun in mid-March. Harold Stassen presented the American package, which called for an agreement to halt the production of all nuclear weapons as a precondition to a test ban; Valerian Zorin, the Russian negotiator, responded with an appeal for an immediate and unconditional halt to tests, without any inspection. Despite the unacceptable Soviet proposal, Stassen returned to the United States convinced that the Russians genuinely wanted to end nuclear testing. He suggested that the United States at least consider viewing a test ban as a possible "first step" toward nuclear disarmament. When this proposal began to receive favorable comment, Admiral Arthur Radford, chairman of the Joint Chiefs of Staff, responded by declaring, "We cannot trust the Russians on this or anything. The Communists have broken their word with every country with which they ever had an agreement."[1]

President Eisenhower was furious with Radford. In his press conference on May 22, Ike expressed his hope that the London talks would achieve progress and cautioned Americans against being either "recalcitrant" or "picayunish" in their approach to arms control. "We ought to have an open mind and make it possible for others, if they are reasonable, logical men," the President continued, "to meet us halfway so we can make these agreements." In a letter to Representative Sterling Cole a few days later, Eisenhower again expressed his concern over nuclear testing, saying that he had repeatedly insisted to Strauss that it be held "to the absolute minimum." Some tests were necessary, Ike admitted, but he hoped the London talks would lead to "some form of limitation." "I do want to assure you that my position is far from being inflexible—has indeed been a constant effort to find a way out of what has for so many years seemed an impasse," the President concluded. Sherman Adams recalled later how determined Eisenhower was in 1957 to break the disarmament deadlock. He said the President told him, after a stormy scene with Strauss and Radford: "Something had got to be done. . . . This is a question of survival and we must put our minds at it until we can find some way of making progress."[2]

The debate over disarmament policy reached a climax at a White House meeting on Saturday, May 25. For more than two hours, Stassen, Dulles, Radford, Strauss, deputy secretary of defense Donald Quarles, and national security adviser Robert Cutler discussed the wisdom of entering into a temporary test ban agreement with the Russians as a first step toward a more comprehensive arms control settlement. The President finally decided to go ahead with a new proposal, though he modified several of Stassen's suggestions in order to placate Strauss and Radford. Stassen was to return to London with a written "talking paper" which would offer the Soviets a brief suspension in testing in return for future limitations on nuclear weapons production. The new offer was tentative in nature and Eisenhower carefully instructed Stassen to secure approval from the NATO allies before presenting it to the Russians.

After the meeting ended, Secretary of State Dulles announced to the press that the President had authorized a significant shift in American policy, although he did not disclose the actual contents of the new proposal. The immediate public reaction was favorable; even *Time,* normally skeptical of Russian intentions, agreed that "the first reversal in the eleven-year-old East-West armaments race might be in sight." At a press conference on June 5, the President cautioned against excessive optimism. He stressed the military's belief that testing was necessary to perfect new weapons designed to defend the nation against attack and he said that only an ironclad disarmament agreement, one that "would forever ban the use of these weapons in war," could permit the United States to give up testing permanently. But pending that ultimate goal, he was willing to proceed on a "step-by-step basis." Despite these reservations, it appeared that for the first time the Eisenhower administration was ready to forego its earlier insistence on a total disarmament package and seek a first-step agreement involving some form of limitation on nuclear tests.[3]

In his eagerness to implement this new policy, Stassen almost brought about its premature death. Returning to London in late May, he revealed the proposal to British and French diplomats. But before their governments could express their views, he outlined the plan to Zorin and tactlessly gave the Russian negotiator a written copy of the proposal. When the British and French leaders protested to the President, an embarrassed Eisenhower apologized and permitted Dulles to order Stassen

back to Washington for a private reprimand. Harold Macmillan found the new proposal distasteful, since it would freeze
the British nuclear stockpile at a very low level; the French
liked it even less, since they were still striving to develop nuclear weapons of their own. Neither ally, however, could object
publicly in the face of mounting demands for test cessation
from their own countrymen.

The Russians sought to profit from the divisions within the
western camp. On June 14, Zorin startled his fellow negotiators
by announcing that the Soviet Union was giving up its demand
for a complete test ban in favor of "a two or three year moratorium." Moreover, the Russian delegate stated that his government was now willing to accept a system of international control, with monitoring posts on British, American, and Soviet
soil. For the first time since nuclear disarmament talks had
begun in 1946, the Russians seemed willing to accept the key
American demand for on-site inspection.[4]

While the State Department and Pentagon looked for catches
in the Russian proposal, Eisenhower greeted it as a "hopeful"
sign. In a press conference on June 19, he told a reporter that
his opposition to a permanent test ban in any agreement short
of full disarmament did not apply to Zorin's new offer. "I
would be perfectly delighted to make some satisfactory arrangement for temporary suspension of tests," the President
answered. Although Eisenhower quickly added that such a
moratorium would be conditional on progress toward a more
comprehensive settlement, he expressed confidence that a test
suspension could pave the way to genuine disarmament. He
admitted under questioning that a temporary halt in testing
would mark a major shift in American policy. A few hours later
press secretary James Hagerty issued a statement stating that
Ike had "not intended" to suggest that American policy on testing had changed. The press, however, quickly concluded that
the President had instructed Stassen to agree to a brief test suspension, probably on the order of less than a year. The White
House meeting of May 25, Zorin's test suspension proposal,

and Eisenhower's willingness to embrace a step-by-step approach all indicated that the United States had abandoned its opposition to a test ban in an effort to break the disarmament deadlock.[5]

I

Edward Teller found the direction of administration policy alarming. An intense, brooding man, the Hungarian-born scientist combined a deep distrust for the Russians with an abiding faith in the deterrent power of U.S. nuclear weapons. Known to the American people as the father of the H-bomb, a label he tried to shrug off but which he nevertheless took great pride in, Teller had left the University of Chicago in 1953 to join Ernest O. Lawrence at Berkeley. The two men had fought together to secure approval for the H-bomb in 1950 and they had later persuaded the AEC to create the Livermore Radiation Laboratory at the University of California to share the task of weapons-design with Los Alamos. For the next several years, Teller worked on the development of new types of nuclear bombs and warheads while he continued to preach the doctrine of peace through atomic power. He had no qualms about his work and he never shared the moral adversion to the H-bomb of many of his colleagues. "To my mind," he wrote in 1957, "the distinction between a nuclear weapon and a conventional weapon is the distinction between an effective weapon and an outmoded weapon."

Teller was a restless man who was constantly spinning off new ideas and theories. He left the details to others as he jumped from concept to concept. A childhood injury in which he lost part of his foot kept him from engaging in sports, but his competitive spirit found an outlet in chess and poker. A cartoonist's delight with his thick, bushy eyebrows, he had an animated face and he enchanted audiences with his deep voice and lively gestures. He led such a hectic life that Enrico Fermi once said to him, "In my acquaintance, you are the only monomaniac with several manias." He loved nothing better than a fight, and he now decided it was time to use his influence to prevent a reversal of American policy on nuclear testing.[6]

On June 20, 1957, Teller, accompanied by Ernest Lawrence and by Mark Mills of the Livermore Laboratory, appeared before the military applications subcommittee of the Joint Committee on Atomic Energy at the request of Senator Henry Jackson. Although the closed hearing was supposed to deal with ICBM warhead design, Teller suddenly changed the subject. Noting that the AEC had reduced fallout by 90 per cent in the most recent nuclear tests, Teller claimed that a test ban would prevent American scientists from achieving their goal of a completely clean bomb. Lawrence and Mills backed up their colleague, stating that the Livermore Laboratory had now perfected bombs that were 96 per cent free of radioactivity. Impressed by this testimony, Senator Jackson arranged for the three scientists to speak to the full Joint Committee and then told the press that they contended it would be "a crime against humanity" for the United States to stop testing before a clean bomb was developed.

Representative Sterling Cole shared Jackson's enthusiasm. He called the White House and arranged for the three Californians to meet with the President personally. Teller, Lawrence, and Mills postponed their return to the West Coast, stayed in Washington over the weekend, and then went with Lewis Strauss to give their views to Eisenhower in a 40-minute meeting on June 24.[7]

Chairman Strauss introduced the three scientists to the President and reviewed the progress the AEC had been making in reducing fallout from America's nuclear weapons. Ernest Lawrence then explained that his colleagues were developing the technology to "make virtually clean weapons, not only in the megaton range but all the way down to small kiloton weapons." Repeating the phrase he had used to the Joint Committee, the Nobel laureate argued that it would a "crime against humanity" not to do so. Edward Teller then went into detail, estimating that within six or seven years his laboratory should be able to perfect weapons that would not create any fallout beyond the area of initial blast. Not only would this relatively clean weapon be useful in limited wars, permitting American troops to employ it on the battlefield, but it would also allow the use of atomic explosives for such peaceful purposes as dredging harbors, blasting out canals, and releasing underground minerals. Further testing, however, was essential to confirm theoretical calculations and ensure continued progress.

The President expressed great interest in these remarks, but he reminded the scientists of the "extremely difficult world opinion situation" he faced. ". . . He did not think that the United States could permit itself," read the official minutes of the meeting, "to be 'crucified on a cross of atoms,' so to speak." Not only did the administration have to contend with "intense Soviet propaganda," but there was also "an actual division of American opinion . . . as to the harmful effects of testing."

The scientists replied that a test ban would be unwise for yet another reason. Their experiments had convinced them, Mills argued, that it would be relatively easy for a nation to evade a test ban by conducting secret nuclear explosions. Teller voiced his belief that it would be impossible to police such an agreement "with certainty." Strauss then suggested that the President reassure world opinion by inviting the United Nations to send observers to witness the next American test series. Eisenhower liked this idea and indicated that he would bring it up at his next press conference. At the same time, he would inform the world that American tests were designed "to clean up weapons and thus protect civilians in event of war."

As the scientists prepared to leave, the President asked them if it would be possible to share the secret of clean bombs with the "other fellow." The implication was clear—it would be far better to have the Russians attack the United States with clean rather than dirty bombs in case of nuclear war. The scientists, shocked at the idea of giving technology to the Soviets, replied that it would be impossible to separate out other "technological advances of great value" which they wanted to keep secret. Teller added that the Russians might gain a great advantage over the United States if they perfected clean bombs through continued testing while the United States stopped out of respect for world opinion. Then, as a wry afterthought, he commented that it would always be possible to make clean bombs dirty, if the military so desired, by using certain "additive materials." [8]

The meeting with Teller and his colleagues left a deep impression on Eisenhower. The next day he told Dulles that they had assured him that with continued testing they could develop clean weapons in 4 to 5 years. The President also repeated the scientists' argument that tests could be hidden, telling the secretary that "they feel we are playing with fire [in] suggesting [the] banning of tests." The secretary also met with the three scientists, but he was apparently more skeptical of their claims. In a note to Eisenhower the next day, he warned him not to "indicate reversing position on suspension" at his next news conference. [9]

The President followed Dulles's advice when he met with the press on June 26. Calling testing "one of the most complicated subjects that the Government has to deal with," he reaffirmed his commitment to test suspension as part of a broader disarmament agreement with the Soviets. Then he began to recount his meeting with Teller, Lawrence, and Mills. With growing enthusiasm he repeated their statement that present American bombs were 96 per cent free of fallout, and said that they had told him that continued testing for 4 or 5 years would result in "an absolutely clean bomb." Such a weapon would destroy only by blast and heat, the President explained, adding that there would "be no fallout to injure any civilian or any innocent bystanders."

Ike's sweeping statement caught the press by surprise. Members of the Joint Committee were puzzled. Teller, Lawrence, and Mills had told them that it would take 6 to 7 years to perfect a virtually clean weapon; the President had both shortened the time required and transformed the bomb into an "absolutely" clean one. Diligent reporters talked to scientists, who expressed considerable skepticism over the President's claims. The experts kept insisting that although it might prove possible to remove most of the fallout, some radioactive debris from the atomic-bomb trigger was inevitable in any feasible H-bomb. By the end of the week, *Newsweek* commented, "what an 'absolutely clean' H-bomb might be remained a mystery to most scientists and congressmen, as well as to the public."[10]

For the most part, reactions to the clean bomb statement were predictable. Those who favored continued testing hailed this new development as a clinching argument. Sterling Cole declared that "humanity, decency and conscience demand" that the United States perfect the clean H-bomb; the *New York Times* predicted that "the 96 per cent clean bomb would become a telling political weapon" that would redress "the entire world balance of power;" *U.S. News* stated confidently that whatever "slight hazard" testing posed to human health "is now almost entirely eliminated." Critics of testing were outraged. To call a bomb "clean" that can "put the match to man's cities," charged Norman Cousins, is to indulge in "the language of madmen." Regardless of the degree of fallout, David Inglis argued, the H-bomb "means carnage such as man has never known, obliteration of the institutions on which civilization depends." "Is it 'cleaner' to be vaporized by H-bomb blast than to be poisoned by H-bomb fallout?" asked the editors of the *New Republic*. They saw no difference and contended that "Strauss and his technicians" were simply pleading "for a continuation of the arms race."

Nikita Khrushchev tried to take advantage of the uproar. Traveling in Czechoslovakia, the Soviet leader expressed surprise that Eisenhower would say such "a stupid thing." "How can you have a clean bomb to do dirty things?" he asked. James Hagerty quickly replied for the President, calling Khrushchev's comment, "rather amazing." "The avoidance of mass human destruction in an atomic war is and always has been a prime objective of President Eisenhower," Hagerty declared.[11]

Eisenhower ignored the controversy. At his news conference

in July 3, he announced his intention of inviting foreign observers to future American tests to "see just exactly how much radio fallout there is from those bombs." "We are trying to make small bombs, clean bombs," the President insisted. But even friendly columnists were not so sure. Ernest Lindley, usually supportive of the administration, felt that the clean bomb argument was purely a debating tactic, a good propaganda ploy to justify tests that were really designed to perfect more advanced weapons for the Pentagon. James Reston was equally skeptical, suggesting that the President had been taken in by the reputations and expertise of Lawrence and Teller. What Eisenhower needed, he argued, was a special science adviser to sift out the various technical issues and give the President a balanced and independent judgment. "An increasing number of the major foreign-policy issues facing the nation," Reston contended, "are now, at bottom, scientific and technological issues on which the President must be guided by scientists and technicians who themselves are deeply divided." [12]

Reston had pinpointed Eisenhower's dilemma. Faced with complex scientific issues, Ike was the prisoner of his technical consultants on such issues as testing and fallout. As long as Strauss kept the President from consulting with a broad spectrum of the scientific community and confined his contacts to men like Lawrence and Teller, the administration's policy was unlikely to change. Eisenhower clearly wanted to respond to growing international demands for a test ban, but his own style of governing frustrated his best intentions.

II

While the clean bomb issue stalled Stassen's push for test suspension, John Foster Dulles moved to regain control over administration disarmament policy. Aware of the need to deal with the worldwide concern over fallout without sacrificing American security, the secretary sought to tie any temporary test ban to a broader agreement restricting the production of nuclear weapons. If the Russians were only bluffing on a test ban, he could expose their insincerity by negotiating in good faith; if they genuinely wanted a halt to testing, then he could achieve the long-desired first step toward nuclear disarmament.

Dulles carried out his delicate diplomacy in a series of maneuvers in the summer of 1957. First, he called a press conference on June 25 to clarify Eisenhower's statement of June 19 in which the President apparently accepted test suspension without insisting on a Russian agreement to halt weapons production. The United States, Dulles explained, was willing to agree to a temporary test moratorium in return for Soviet agreement on a future cutoff in weapons manufacture. On July 3, Dulles permitted Stassen to make a formal proposal to this effect at the London subcommittee talks. The American negotiator offered a ten-month suspension in testing. During this interval, the nuclear powers were to complete the details of an adequate inspection system and reach agreement on a future halt to the production of nuclear weapons. At the end of the ten-month period, the United States would be willing to extend the moratorium if progress were made on the inspection system and the cutoff agreement.[13]

Neither the Soviet Union nor Great Britain found the new formula attractive. Valerian Zorin countered with the earlier Soviet demand for a 2- to 3-year test suspension under some vague form of international supervision but without any mention of a curb on weapons manufacture. Given the intense public pressure for a test ban in England, the British government had no choice but to agree to the American proposal. But privately Prime Minister Macmillan expressed his distaste for a plan that would halt the build-up of the meager British stockpile of atomic and hydrogen bombs. In describing the problem to his cabinet, he referred to "the terrible dilemma in which we find ourselves, between the Scylla of test suspension and the Charybdis of 'cut-off' of fissile material."[14]

The Secretary of State ignored the British and Soviet reservations in recounting the advantages of his proposal for the United States. In a nationwide radio and television address on July 22, Dulles stressed the necessity of preventing a nuclear war which "could threaten life anywhere on the globe." Total nuclear disarmament was impossible, he agreed, but safety lay in a step-by-step program to bring the arms race back under control. The goals he outlined included an open skies aerial inspection plan to guard against surprise attack and a future cutoff in weapons production to keep the existing stockpiles from mounting. The ten-month test suspension was the first vital step, he explained, since it would give the superpowers time to develop a monitoring system that could detect "significant nuclear tests and make evasion a highly risky business." Even this modest achievement, however, would not be easy. Effective enforcement of a test ban would require on-site inspection, with all the complications that entailed.

Throughout his remarks, Dulles walked a tightrope between satisfying American security needs and pleasing world opinion. He tried to reassure Americans about the lack of danger in a temporary test ban, saying that such a brief suspension "would not dislocate our existing scientific staffs." Since ten months was presumably the normal hiatus between American test series, there would be no sacrifice of national security. At the same time, if the Soviets did not accept American terms, the United States would continue with its planned program of tests to perfect the next generation of nuclear weapons. He hoped, nonetheless, that the negotiations would succeed and make it possible "to go further." "The risks of seeking to move forward," he concluded, "are far less than the risks of being frightened into immobility. . . . The whole world faces a grim future if the war threat is not brought under some international control."[15]

However persuasive Dulles's rhetoric may have been at home, it failed to convince the Russians. Even though the secretary went to London to take personal charge of the talks in late July, the Soviets refused to agree to the American terms for a test suspension. After his return to the United States, he and President Eisenhower decided to make a final offer, one designed to force either successful negotiations or an outright refusal by the Russians.

The President announced the new American proposal at a press conference on August 21. In an effort to achieve a "first-step disarmament program," Eisenhower stated, he had authorized Dulles to make a "significant change" in the July 3 plan. "We will be willing," the President declared, ". . . to include a suspension of testing of nuclear weapons for a period up to two years under certain conditions and safeguards." As Stassen presented the proposal in London, the United States would extend the initial suspension to 12 months, and then pledge to renew it for a second year if progress was achieved on both an adequate inspection system and an agreement to halt weapons production.

By offering to extend the test suspension to 2 years, the United States had come close to matching the Soviet demand for a 2- to 3-year moratorium. But the insistence on a reciprocal Russian agreement on a halt in weapons production doomed this proposal. The Russians clearly wanted to use the pressure of world opinion to force the United States to accept a ban on testing; for them, test suspension was an end in itself, not a first step toward comprehensive nuclear disarmament.[16]

Dulles had suspected that the Russians were bluffing all along, and when Zorin flatly rejected the final American proposal on August 27, he was prepared to take solace with a propaganda victory. The next day President Eisenhower issued a new plea for Russian acceptance, saying an outright rejection would be "tragic" in its impact on world peace. "Such a Soviet attitude," the President warned, "would condemn humanity to an indefinite future of immeasurable danger."

On August 29, the United States joined with England and France in offering a comprehensive disarmament package that contained the two-year test suspension, along with open skies, a cutoff on nuclear weapons production and other features known to be unacceptable to the Soviet Union. Dulles and Eisenhower simply wanted the American plan on the record in its entirety. When the expected Soviet rejection came in early September, the disarmament subcommittee adjourned without setting a place or time for its next session. The first serious attempt to negotiate a test ban had failed.[17]

All that remained was the inevitable appeal to world opinion. When the UN General Assembly opened in New York later in September, Dulles and Ambassador Lodge both were on hand to explain America's position. The secretary told the delegates that the United States wanted genuine disarmament, but in light of Soviet intransigence as revealed in London, it had no choice but to continue testing in order to develop weapons with greatly reduced fallout. He promised that American nuclear experiments would be conducted without "raising whatsoever the levels of radioactivity in the world" and expressed the hope that the "sweeping, almost contemptuous Soviet rejection" of the American suspension offer was not fatal.

Lodge echoed his superior. Testing, he told the General Assembly's Disarmament Commission on September 30, was only "the top of the iceberg that bears testimony to the dangerous mass below." The real danger was nuclear war, and in light of that reality, "we must ensure that we are free to continue the development and research of which testing is an integral part."

President Eisenhower made the same explanation to Japanese Prime Minister Nobusuke Kishi, who had again called for an end to nuclear tests. The United States was on the verge of perfecting "important defensive uses of nuclear weapons, particularly against missiles, submarines and aircraft," the President replied. He could suspend tests only if the Russians agreed to stop producing additional nuclear weapons. Until that time, he must reluctantly go ahead with experiments vital to the security of the entire free world. Like Dulles, he promised only to "keep world radiation from rising to more than a small fraction of the levels which might be hazardous."[18]

What had gone wrong? In the spring, rising world opinion

had seemed so strong that most observers had expected the United States and the Soviet Union to agree on some form of test limitation. Schweitzer's appeal had stirred the imagination of millions; Pauling's petition had shown a growing revolt among scientists. Norman Cousins felt that there had been "a magic moment last spring when . . . the administration was within an inch of calling off tests." Cold War tensions, however, had proved too strong to be overcome so easily. Russian stubbornness, together with Teller's last minute raising of the clean bomb issue, had swept away the false euphoria. With each superpower fearful that the other might reap an unknown advantage from a test ban, both exploited the disarmament negotiations for propaganda purposes. Once again political innovation had failed to rise to the level of technological achievement.[19]

III

The breakdown in the London disarmament talks was accompanied by a sharp increase in nuclear testing. On August 22, the Soviets began a new series with a shot in the megaton range at their Siberian proving ground. Four more occurred in September and October, with one described by the Soviets as a "mighty hydrogen warhead of a new design." The sixth and final blast in the Russian series took place on December 28. The British conducted three atomic tests at the Maralinga range in Australia in the early fall and a final H-bomb shot at Christmas Island on November 8. Meanwhile, the United States continued the PLUMBOB series begun in late May. By the time of the last shot on October 7, the AEC had conducted twenty-four atomic tests ranging from a few kilotons up to one of 40 kilotons, the largest yet detonated in the continental United States. Thirteen had been fired from balloons, nine from high towers, one in the air from an Air Force Genie rocket, and one 800 feet below the ground.[20]

The underground shot, code-named RANIER, attracted the

most attention. Suggested to Teller originally by geophysicist David T. Griggs, RANIER was designed primarily to demonstrate how nuclear tests could be conducted without fallout. The AEC chose a mountain at its Frenchman's Flat proving ground composed of soft, volcanic tuff. Technicians drilled a tunnel some 2000 feet into the mountain's side, circling it back for the last 400 feet to form a spiral for the actual detonation site. On September 19, with observers as close as 2½ miles away, the 1.7 kiloton underground bomb exploded uneventfully. The blast vaporized the volcanic rock to form a chamber 110 feet in diameter but did not break through to the earth's crust above, which moved a bare six inches.

The AEC was delighted with the results of RANIER. The volcanic tuff absorbed all the bomb's radioactivity. Commenting on an analysis of the atmosphere right after the blast, an enthusiastic Willard Libby reported: "Not even krypton showed up, and, for goodness sake, if the krypton doesn't get out, the thing is really sealed gas tight." The advantages were obvious— if world opinion forced the United States to stop testing in the atmosphere, RANIER showed how the AEC could still verify its nuclear advances.

But the underground test raised a new problem which was not fully appreciated at the time. The great attractiveness of a test ban was the ease of detection; aerial sampling of radioactive debris and other scientific techniques could reveal an atmospheric explosion at great distances. But the only way to detect an underground blast was by seismograph, and the initial readings on RANIER were inconclusive. Despite advance notice from the AEC, many reporting stations in the United States failed to register the shock waves, while others found it difficult to distinguish RANIER's seismographic tracings from those of a minor earthquake that occurred about 50 minutes later. Whatever benefits underground testing could bestow on a world troubled by fallout were more than offset by this new complication.[21]

The Eisenhower administration, meanwhile, planned to go

ahead with a new series of H-bomb tests in 1958. On August 2, Admiral Strauss had formally requested the President's assent for HARDTACK, a program of twenty-five thermonuclear experiments in the Pacific to begin the following May. Calling HARDTACK "critical" for American weapons development, Strauss listed a series of objectives which included high-altitude shots to perfect an anti-missile missile, "exploratory firings" to enhance the development of clean bombs, and "proof tests of warheads" for the new intercontinental ballistic missiles. The President reluctantly gave his approval. He asked Strauss to restrict the number of tests to those "absolutely necessary," and he insisted that the Admiral clear any public announcement of HARDTACK with him personally.

Strauss submitted a draft statement to the President on September 12, and three days later the White House issued a carefully-worded announcement of HARDTACK. The United States had repeatedly offered to suspend testing, the statement declared. In view of the Russian rejection, the administration had no choice but to proceed with a process that was "essential to the defense of the United States and of the free world." Every effort would be made to hold fallout to a minimum, the world was told, and the tests themselves should achieve progress toward the goal of relatively clean nuclear weapons. Recalling Eisenhower's earlier promise, the statement added that an appropriate United Nations agency would be invited to send observers to witness one of the HARDTACK shots.[22]

This announcement underlined the harsh realities of the nuclear dilemma. In spite of growing world concern over fallout and the increasing demand for a test ban, the three nuclear powers had detonated 42 bombs in 1957, compared to 19 in the previous year. This doubling of the rate of testing might be explained on the grounds that the superpowers were trying to complete as many experiments as possible before a test ban was finally negotiated. But such an optimistic conclusion ignored the fact that the United States, which had contributed 24 of the 42 blasts in 1957, was planning at least 25 thermonuclear tests in the coming year. Nuclear testing had obviously survived its first major challenge, and there was still no end in sight.[23]

IV

The protests against nuclear testing continued despite the bleak outlook. Pacifists, viewing the tests as the most vulnerable part of the war system they opposed, began a new round of activity. Such traditional groups as the American Friends Service Committee and the Women's International League for Peace and Freedom circulated petitions in the summer of 1957 calling on the United States to cease all H-bomb tests. "All mankind bears the intolerable burden of the arms race, the dangers of radioactive fallout and the threat of catastrophic war," declared a document signed by 10,000 California Quakers. More radical pacifists favored direct action. On August 6, 1957, the 12th anniversary of Hiroshima, 30 members of a group calling itself Non-Violent Action Against Nuclear Weapons demonstrated outside the gates of the AEC proving ground in Nevada. When 11 pacifists tried to enter the Frenchman's Flat reservation, they were arrested and given suspended sentences for trespassing.

Other religious groups joined in the demand for a test ban. The world Council of Churches commemorated the Hiroshima anniversary by asking the three nuclear powers to reach agreement to suspend all future tests. This body suggested that if international action proved impossible, individual Christians should urge their governments to act unilaterally "in the hope that others will do the same, a new confidence will be born, and foundations laid for reliable agreements." The Lutheran World Federation adopted a similar resolution at a meeting in Minneapolis in late August, calling particularly on the United States to take the lead by suspending tests for at least a few months. Later in the year, an interdenominational group of clergymen, including A. J. Muste, a leading Christian pacifist, Harry Emerson Fosdick, and Martin Luther King, Jr., sent a telegram to Eisenhower pleading for an American test moratorium that would place a moral obligation on the British and the Soviets to "do the same."[24]

A distinguished group of scientists arrived at a different assessment of the nuclear peril facing the world. Acting on the urging of Bertrand Russell and financed by millionaire American industrialist Cyrus Eaton, 24 eminent men of science from ten countries on both sides of the Iron Curtain met at Pugwash, Nova Scotia, from July 6 to July 11. Their final report revealed a remarkable consensus. They noted the danger from fallout, calculating that the present level would lead to roughly a 1 per cent increase both in cancer deaths and genetic mutations. Such hazards were small, however, compared with others which man faced from natural causes. The real peril, they warned, came not from fallout but from the risk of all-out nuclear war. "The principal objective of all nations," read the Pugwash statement, "must be the aboliton of war and the threat of war hanging over mankind."

Two of those attending explained how they had arrived at this conclusion. Eugene Rabinowich argued that a test ban represented a "simplistic" approach to the complex disarmament problem. It might be a step toward peace, but at best it "would produce no more than a temporary (and objectively unfounded) relaxation of the fear of war." An Austrian physicist, Hans Thirring, went further in minimizing the testing issue. Claiming that at most only 100,000 people would die from fallout, he argued that this sacrifice would not be "in vain," if "we succeed in healing mankind of the childhood disease of waging wars."[25]

A widely-read novel reinforced the scientists' warning that nuclear war, not testing, posed the gravest danger to the world. In the summer of 1957, William Morrow published Nevil Shute's *On the Beach,* the story of how the fallout from a nuclear war fought in 1961 gradually wiped out the entire population of the globe. Shute focused on an American submarine commander who sought refuge in Australia from the deadly radiation created by 4700 cobalt bombs that had fallen in the northern hemisphere. After a visit to the lifeless Puget Sound area, the hero returned to Melbourne to wait for death with his Australian girl friend. When she asked him why they would perish, he replied, "It's the winds. It's mighty difficult to dodge what's carried on the wind. You just can't do it." Shute let an Australian scientist explain how nuclear weapons got out of control. "The trouble is," he said, "the damn things got too cheap."

On the Beach had a remarkable appeal to the American people. The publisher sold almost 100,000 copies in the first six weeks as the novel quickly displaced *Peyton Place* from the top spot on the best seller lists. Some forty newspapers with a total circulation of 8 million began serializing the book in September; for many, it was the first time they had ever carried installments of a novel. Reviewers recognized that Shute had written a potboiler that stretched available scientific evidence beyond the limits of credibility, yet they dealt with his work sympathetically. In the *New Republic,* Robert Estabrook compared it favorably to *Uncle Tom's Cabin,* calling it an "evangelical" book designed to arouse people from their apathy. S.L.A. Marshall found it "more revealing than the whole library of scientific literature intended to cry warning," while the reviewer for the *Bulletin of the Atomic Scientists* praised Shute for bringing home to people "the horror of nuclear war which the public may not be able to articulate."[26]

More than any of the protests in 1957, *On the Beach* revealed the real anxiety of the American people over fallout. It was not the tests, with their possible long-term poisoning of the atmosphere and genetic damage to future generations that troubled most citizens. Nor was it just the blast and heat from nuclear weapons that would instantaneously kill millions of people near the point of impact. Rather it was the dread of lingering fallout after a nuclear attack, the clouds of deadly radioactivity that would last for weeks and possibly months, inflicting a slow but certain death on those who survived the initial assault. By focusing on this secret horror, Shute had touched a sensitive nerve and revealed the surrogate nature of the fallout issue. Unable to cope with the possibility that their whole way of life would perish under a rain of white ash, the American people tried to pretend that the fallout from tests was the only peril they need worry about. Once they could exorcize this devil through a test ban, then they could relax. But *On the Beach,* however exaggerated its scientific assumptions, made even this pretense untenable.

In a curious way, the impact of the novel fitted in with the AEC's continuing effort to reassure the American people that the fallout peril was overstated. In the form letter he used to respond to test ban advocates, Lewis Strauss reiterated that the risk of testing was "very small" compared to the "risk of catastrophe which might result from a surrender of our leadership in nuclear armament." The true danger facing all Americans, he stressed, was "the infinite devastation that would result from the massive use of nuclear weapons in warfare."

The Atomic Energy Commission tried to alleviate public concern in a variety of ways. In October, its Advisory Committee on Biology and Medicine issued a report justifying testing as "a military necessity." The fallout danger, the scientists said, was "well within tolerable limits." They forecast only an additional 196 deaths from leukemia in the United States each year from test radiation, no more than 800 more defective births annually, and at most only a few days, if any, decrease in life expectancy. In December, Willard Libby announced that the United States had joined with Russia in a joint program to sample strontium-90 levels in the soil of the two nations. The AEC commissioner had further reassuring news. His agency, Libby reported, was studying the use of special fertilizers designed to neutralize radioactive fallout in the soil and was investigating the possibility of anti-radiation pills to use in case of nuclear attack. The pills would contain a heavy dose of calcium that hopefully would lessen the body's uptake of strontium-90 from food contaminated by fallout.[27]

Yet even the AEC could not entirely ignore or minimize the danger that radiation posed to mankind. On December 10, the agency announced new safety standards for those working in the atomic industry. Following recommendations made by the National Committee on Radiation Standards, the AEC cut the maximum exposure for an atomic worker by two-thirds, from 15r a year to 5r. The original industrial safety level had been set in 1935 at 0.5r a week, and then lowered to 0.3r a week in 1946. Under the new standards, a worker would be allowed an average exposure of less than 0.1r a week. Worried about the long-term effect of radiation on the reproductive organs, the AEC regulations set the average exposure at 5r a year, over a long period of time, with no more than 15r permitted in any single year. In addition, the AEC recommended that the population exposure be limited to one-tenth the level of those employed in atomic industries, or an average of 0.5r a year. Even though this proposed maximum was far above the current fallout level of an estimated 0.1r a year, the government's new figures were hardly encouraging. In its 1956 report, the National Academy of Sciences had recommended a total 30-year exposure of 10r. If fallout should reach the population maximum of 0.5r a year regularly, it would mean that an individual would be exposed to 15r during his reproductive lifetime from testing alone, not including medical and dental x-rays or natural background radiation.[28]

In spite of these potentially dangerous statistics, the administration continued to play down the world radiation hazard. When a Czech delegate proposed that the United Nations hold an international scientific conference to discuss the fallout hazard, American representative James Wadsworth opposed the resolution. Defending American testing as an obligation imposed by necessity in "a world where experience shows that weakness invites aggression," he insisted that tests were "only a minor source of the ionizing radiation which is harmful to human beings." He suggested that instead of calling a conference, the General Assembly wait for the report of the UN scientific committee, due in July 1958. After a brief debate, the Assembly voted unanimously to follow this course, asking only that the scientists try to speed up their study. Once again the United States was procrastinating. By the time the scientists reported in the summer of 1958, the AEC should have completed the HARDTACK nuclear tests in the Pacific and, with a new harvest of technical knowledge, the administration might then be more receptive to world opinion.[29]

V

The gravest weakness of the test ban movement in America lay in its fragmentation. In the summer of 1957, small groups with such exotic names as the Society to Abolish Nuclear Explosions and the Committee for 10,000 Babies were springing up in California. The need for a central organization led to the founding of the National Committee for a Sane Nuclear Policy in the fall of 1957. SANE, as the new group came to be known, grew out of meetings by concerned citizens in New York and Philadelphia in the spring. The prime movers were Norman Cousins, publisher of the *Saturday Review* and long-time champion of the United World Federalists, and Clarence Pickett, the elderly executive secretary of the American Friends Service Committee. Preliminary talks in Philadelphia in May led to a decision to call an organizing meeting for the proposed group in New York. The founders all agreed that the focus should be on "the moral issue of stopping nuclear bomb tests."

Some 27 individuals met at the Overseas Press Club in New York City on June 21 to form a steering committee for the new organization. Attempting to broaden their membership beyond the original group of one-worlders and Quakers, they were pleased to have such pillars of the establishment as former AEC Commissioner Gordon Dean and General Electric Board Chairman Charles E. Wilson in attendance, along with Graham DuShane, the editor of *Science,* and Norman Thomas, the veteran socialist leader. E.B. Lewis of Cal Tech spoke to the parti-

165

cipants, propounding his belief that even small amounts of fallout could cause cancer; another scientist, William Neumann of the University of Rochester, described the problem facing the group as "a mixture of science, morality and politics." Before breaking up, those present agreed to meet again in the fall, asking Homer Jack, a Chicago Unitarian minister, to serve as interim director and issue a weekly newsletter to prospective members.[30]

The organizers of SANE faced a series of difficult problems. One was money. The Friends Committee on National Legislation supplied small sums for the newsletter, while Norman Cousins spent more than $1000 of his personal funds. Eventually, Lenore Marshall, a wealthy New Yorker, became the group's sustaining patron, but SANE never escapecd the shaky financing which plagued its early days. A name became a second consideration. Erich Fromm, a prominent psychologist and author of *Escape from Freedom,* suggested that the new organization emphasize the insanity of unchecked nuclear testing. Admitting that it was "pathological" for people to be afraid when there was nothing to fear, he told Pickett that the lack of fear over the current arms race was even worse, calling it "a symptom of a kind of schizophrenic indifference . . . which is so characteristic of our age." Heeding his suggestion that they advocate a return to sanity, the organizers finally settled on the title, The National Committee for a Sane Nuclear Policy.

The final issue was how SANE could best influence national policy. Some members wanted a broad attack on the whole problem of disarmament; others preferred a quiet approach to policy-makers, following the model of the Council on Foreign Relations. Catherine Cory, a West Coast organizer for the Friends Committee on National Legislation, struck the note that prevailed. "Ending bomb tests is the issue," she wrote to Cousins and Pickett. The man on the street "becomes paralyzed at the complexities of 'general disarmament,' " she warned. But in calling for an end to bomb tests, she continued, "at last we have an issue that the average Joe understands." The majority accepted this analysis and decided to begin with a full-page newspaper advertisement stressing the fallout hazard. More conservative participants like Dean and Wilson, viewing such a campaign as quixotic and woolly-minded, dropped out of SANE.[31]

"WE ARE FACING A DANGER UNLIKE ANY DANGER THAT HAS EVER EXISTED," read the banner headline in the SANE advertisement that appeared in the *New York Times* on November 15. The copy, written in almost apocalyptical language, went on to tell Americans that "the sovereignty of the human community" transcended the narrower interest of "groups, tribes or nations." "In that community, man has natural rights. He has the right to live and to grow, to breathe unpoisoned air, to work on uncontaminated soil." At the end, the ad stated that while a halt to testing would not in itself abolish the perils of the arm race, it would "eliminate at least one real and specific danger." Readers who agreed were asked to send donations to SANE and to urge President Eisenhower to propose that the UN enforce a worldwide suspension of testing.[32]

The sponsors signing this call to arms leaned heavily toward the liberal side of the political spectrum. They included clergymen Harry Emerson Fosdick and Paul Tillich, scholars Lewis Mumford, James Shotwell, and Pitirim A. Sorokin, novelists James Jones and John Hersey, and such diverse public figures as Eleanor Roosevelt, Norman Thomas, and Cleveland Amory. Equally significant were those who declined to be listed. Neither Gordon Dean nor Charles E. Wilson appeared on the list, and one businessman who did, Harry H. Bullis, chairman of the board of General Mills, insisted that his name be removed. Other non-signers included Hermann J. Muller, Chester Bowles, Bentley Glass, Graham DuShane, Hans Bethe, and Max Ascoli. Their reasons for refusing varied, but Eugene Rabinowich summed up the attitudes of many when he objected to such emotional phrases as "poisoned air" and "uncon-

167

taminated soil." While such qualitative language was "colorful," he felt that most scientists believed their task was to "help replace qualitative attitudes by quantitative judgments."

The advertisement drew mixed reactions from the public. Critics complained that it was too one-sided. One ardent Cold Warrior stressed its similarity in wording and tone to Communist propaganda, while a more moderate correspondent noted that it ignored the fact that fallout hazards were "negligible by comparison with the tragedy of nuclear war." Ernest Dichter, a pioneer in motivational advertising, warned that SANE's scare tactics were likely to boomerang, "driving people toward escapism instead of toward action." He suggested that a more positive approach was necessary to overcome the public's fatalism.[33]

But the ad did seem to reach the "average Joe" that Catherine Cory had talked about. Within three weeks, the New York office had received favorable responses from 1700 people and donations totaling nearly $10,000. Typical was the reaction of a Denver resident who sent in a check for $2 with the words, "This is THE idea I have been waiting for." Encouraged by this outpouring SANE began forming local committees in cities across the nation, with each one sponsoring similar advertisements in regional newspapers. The response to these appeals was more limited, but by mid-1958 SANE had chapters operating in 130 localities with a total membership of nearly 25,000.

At the very least, SANE had discovered that many Americans shared its founders' concern over the fallout issue. The pacifist cause, which had suffered from attrition during the intense years of the Cold War, now began to develop new strength. SANE, as its Washington lobbyist later explained, had helped reveal the existence of "a vacuum in the American peace movement." Norman Cousins and Clarence Pickett helped bring together advocates of world government, Quakers, and liberal idealists with a host of middle-class Americans aroused by the presence of strontium-90 in their milk. Traditional internationalists and foreign policy experts remained skeptical of such a direct approach to a complex issue. Their disapproval proved far less damaging, however, than the march of technology, for the Soviet launching of Sputnik on October 4, 1957, created a new obstacle that greatly dimmed the chances of SANE to influence national policy.[34]

VI

The Russian achievement in sending the first artificial satellite into orbit caught Americans by surprise. They had been looking forward to a similar feat by the highly-publicized American Vanguard program; now suddenly the Soviet Union appeared to have passed the United States in the crucial area of space technology.

The initial reaction was a curious mixture of admiration and fear. Nearly all the journals hailed the Russians for taking mankind's first step toward what *Newsweek* termed "the conquest of outer space." *Time* grudgingly admitted that it was "a milestone in history." Scientists particularly rejoiced in what they considered to be a remarkable technical feat. But as the *Nation* noted, "the old Cold War fixation" quickly returned. *Newsweek* referred to the peril of success "by the controlled scientists of a despotic state;" *Time* spoke ominously of "a Communist achievement with serious implications for the West." Even the *Bulletin of the Atomic Scientists* expressed regret that "one faction of mankind has increased its power to coerce the others."[35]

The most significant outcome of Sputnik was to convince a majority of Americans that their nation had fallen behind in the all-important missile race. Experts in rocketry had already warned the country of this possibility, and in late August the Soviets had boasted of the first successful test of their ICBM. Though some greeted this report skeptically, the press reported that in June, and again in September, the Atlas missile, America's entry into the ICBM race, had exploded in flight. The Soviet satellite proved that the Russians had perfected rocket boosters large enough to power an intercontinental missile thousands of miles across the earth's surface. Lyndon B. Johnson, the Senate majority leader, summed up the prevailing consensus on October 18 when he declared, "we must assume that the Soviet Union can produce any bomb, any rocket, any weapon that we can produce."

The administration tried hard to reassure a worried public. Clarence Randall, special adviser to the President on foreign trade, called Sputnik, "a silly bauble," while outgoing Secretary of Defense Charles E. Wilson dismissed it as "a neat scientific trick." Eisenhower told the nation that despite Sputnik, the United States was still ahead in the missile race and that no crash program was called for. At the same time, he expressed disgust with scientists who joined with Democratic politicians in denouncing the administration for letting the Soviets overtake our lead in technology. On November 25, he told Strauss he was "distressed" by Edward Teller's remark that Sputnik was a greater defeat for the United States than Pearl Harbor.[36]

The President turned for help to the Science Advisory Committee in the Office of Defense Mobilization. In a meeting in mid-October, these scientists, who included Hans Bethe of Cornell, Isidor Rabi of Columbia, and James J. Killian, the president of MIT, discussed the broader implications of Sputnik for American society and politics. Rabi argued forcefully that the President needed "an outstanding full-time scientific adviser" on the White House staff. Killian agreed, and also suggested the creation of a small committee of scientists on the model of the Council of Economic Advisers.

Eisenhower liked the idea of a science adviser from the start, and after discussing it with Sherman Adams and Robert Cutler, he asked Killian to take on the assignment. When he accepted, the President scheduled an address to the nation on November 7. He described the new arrangement, praising Killian as a man of sound judgment who could give him the technical advice he so clearly needed. At the same time, Eisenhower sought to calm the post-Sputnik panic. He boasted of American progress toward achieving virtually clean H-bombs and declared that the United States was well ahead of the Russians in nuclear technology, "both in quantity and in quality." "We intend to stay ahead," the President added. He admitted that the outlook was not quite so rosy in the missile race, but he promised a renewed effort to regain the lead.

Killian appeared to be an ideal choice for the new post. Though not a research scientist, he was an able administrator who enjoyed the confidence of the American scientific community. A graduate of MIT, he had served as an administrative assistant to Karl Compton and then succeeded him as president of MIT in 1948. He was no stranger to Washington, earlier serving on the Office of Defense Mobilization's advisory board and chairing the President's Board of Consultants on Foreign Intelligence Activities. A southerner by birth, Killian spoke with a soft drawl that masked a steely resolve and a tough intellect. Described by one observer as "disarmingly pleasant," he had many friends and surprisingly few enemies among the nation's leading scientists.[37]

At Killian's request, the President transferred the Science Advisory Committee from the Office of Defense Mobilization and reorganized it as the President's Science Advisory Committee (PSAC), a White House agency to be headed by Killian. The revised board retained such distinguished members as Hans Bethe and Isidor Rabi, but Killian added a number of prominent scientists who had never before served as government consultants. Despite this new blood, some critics pointed to the fact that nearly half the members were administrators rather than researchers, and that physical scientists far outnumbered the biologists. Yet under Killian's guidance, PSAC became an effective voice for the American scientific community, allowing the ideas of academic scientists to compete with the more parochial and defense-oriented views of Pentagon and AEC officials. Men like Bethe and Rabi would now have a chance to balance the views of a Teller or a Lawrence at the White House level. For the first time since the fallout debate began, the President had access to a broad spectrum of scientific opinion.[38]

The creation of PSAC, however, failed to halt the growing sense of national peril in the aftermath of Sputnik. In early November, after the Societs sent up a second satellite carrying a dog, the press became frantic. "For the first time in its history," declared *Newsweek,* "the Western world finds itself mortally in danger from the East." Foreign policy experts proved no less extreme in their assessment. On November 7, the Gaither committee submitted a very pessimistic report to the National Security Council. Appointed by the President to advise on national defense, this group of businessmen and academic specialists, headed by H. Rowan Gaither, Jr., of the Ford Foundation, forecast Soviet strategic superiority over the United States by 1960. Their remedy was a crash program in missiles and a massive civil defense effort to cut estimated American casualties from 120 to 55 million in the event of a Soviet nuclear attack. Eisenhower was appalled at these recommendations, particularly at the projected costs, which ranged up to $48 billion, and he ordered the Gaither report to be shelved.

The President relied instead on Killian and his committee to expedite the lagging American missile program. A new Secretary of Defense, Neil H. McElroy, took over from Charles E. Wilson, and gradually a mood of grim determination replaced the post-Sputnik uproar. Eisenhower's own refusal to be panicked served as a steadying influence, as did the display of bipartisan support shown by the Democratic leaders in Congress, Lyndon Johnson and Sam Rayburn. "Not since World War II had there been such unity of purpose in the West," *Newsweek* reported in mid-November. "Democrats and Republicans alike . . . found themselves in complete agreement on the necessity of surpassing the Russians in the field of science and technology." [39]

Admirable as the new mood of national dedication was, it further dampened the prospects for a nuclear test ban. With the entire country bent on overtaking the presumed Russian lead in strategic striking power, no one wanted to risk a moratorium on weapons development. Eugene Rabinowich, always skeptical of the easy optimism that infected the test ban cause, warned that Sputnik meant that it was no longer feasible to talk of suspending testing. Instead, the United States had to move ahead quickly to perfect a new generation of missile warheads and try to develop an anti-missile missile. Until that was done, Rabinowich contended, the most one could hope for would be "an internationally agreed 'ceiling' on the annual release of radioactivity into the atmosphere." He regretted that the nation's scientists would have to surrender their quest for a test ban, which had become "a symbolic act, signifying abhorrence of atomic war," but scientists above all had to face reality. ". . . The call for cessation of weapons tests has lost its rational justification—at least, for some time to come," he concluded.[40]

Rabinowich was right. Sputnik had ended the first phase of the quest for a test ban. As the American people and their leaders agreed on the need to regain the strategic lead from the Russians, they were deaf to pleas for a halt to testing. Yet the fear of radiation that had manifested itself in 1957 through the Holifield subcommittee hearings, the Pauling petition, and the formation of SANE suggested that the setback was only temporary. Once the nation recovered its balance, the realization that fallout created a potential hazard to human life was certain to lead to new demands that the United States take the lead in ending this dangerous experimentation.

CHAPTER

7

REVERSAL

In the fall of 1957, the Soviet Union sought to capitalize on Sputnik by taking the offensive on disarmament negotiations. The first move came at the United Nations, where the Russian delegate proposed on October 28 that the five-member disarmament subcommittee be scrapped. To replace this western-dominated group, the Soviets suggested that the UN Disarmament Commission be expanded from the eleven members of the Security Council to include all 84 nations of the world organization. The United States opposed this resolution, fearful that such a large body would serve only as a forum for Soviet propaganda attacks. Instead, Ambassador Lodge proposed increasing the Disarmament Commission to 25 members, but still leaving the actual negotiation to the five-nation subcommittee. The General Assembly finally voted to accept the American plan, but it was a meaningless victory for the United States. The Soviets simply announced that they would boycott all future meetings of the subcommittee and its parent Disarmament Commission until the Communist bloc achieved equal representation.[1]

Nikita Khrushchev made a second attempt to outflank the United States on arms control in late 1957. On December 10, he had Premier Nikolai Bulganin, who was purely a figure-head, send a letter to President Eisenhower calling for a summit conference in early 1958. The 15-page message reiterated previous Soviet positions on disarmament and ended with a new proposal—a pledge by the United States, the Soviet Union, and Great Britain to refrain from all nuclear tests for the next 2 or 3 years beginning on January 1, 1958

The Bulganin letter came at a sensitive time for the Eisenhower administration. Just two weeks earlier, the President had suffered a slight stroke that left him with an awkward speech impairment. At first aides feared Ike would have to cancel a trip to a NATO conference in mid-December, but the President recovered quickly and went ahead with the journey. Eisenhower and his advisers firmly opposed the unsupervised test ban Bulganin suggested, but they wished to delay a reply until they had consulted with the NATO allies. Though both Britain and France favored a summit meeting, their leaders were adamantly against a test ban. Britain wanted to test new additions to its small nuclear stockpile in 1958, and France was determined to perfect an atomic bomb and detonate it in the Sahara by the year's end. At the conclusion of the NATO conference on December 19, the Western allies compromised with a proposal asking the Soviets for disarmament talks on the foreign ministers' level.[2]

After his return to the United States, the President continued to delay sending a reply to Bulganin. He recognized that the Soviets were winning the propaganda battle for world opinion; on December 10, Prime Minister Nehru of India had hailed Bulganin's call for a three-nation test suspension and had urged the President to agree to such a moratorium. Eisenhower told the Indian leader on December 15 that while he, too, favored an end to testing, American security required that such a step be accompanied by a ban on the production of nuclear weapons. This response, restating as it did the traditional American refusal to separate testing from actual disarmament, failed to stem the growing world belief that the

United States was blocking a sincere Russian attempt to end the dangerous nuclear experiments.

President Eisenhower finally replied to the Kremlin on January 12, 1958. He expressed a willingness to meet with Bulganin and Khrushchev at the summit, but only after the substantive issues had been discussed and refined by meetings at the ambassadorial and foreign minister level. The United States, he declared, could not agree to the proposed uninspected test ban. Instead, he repeated the August 29 offer of a test suspension linked to a cutoff in future nuclear weapons production. In addition, he suggested that technical experts from the United States and the Soviet Union begin meeting immediately to work on the details of inspection systems for both test cessation and a weapons curb.

The Soviets found the President's reply unacceptable. Bulganin sent a second letter on February 1 proposing that the leaders meet soon and make the Soviet request for a test ban the first item on their agenda. In a series of diplomatic notes, the State Department kept pointing out that a summit could only be held if substantial agreement were achieved at a lower level. In an *aide memoire* handed to the Soviet ambassador in Washington on March 6, Secretary Dulles affirmed his belief that if "a meeting of Heads of Government" were to take place, "it will be held not as a spectacle, not to reaffirm generalities, but to take serious decisions which will lead to an international atmosphere of cooperation and goodwill." [3]

These diplomatic exchanges, despite their carefully-contrived pleasantries, revealed a fundamental divergence between the two superpowers. The Soviets, aware of the enormous advantage they had gained from Sputnik, hoped to pressure the United States into agreeing to an immediate test ban with no strings attached. The Eisenhower administration, on the other hand, sought to delay any agreement to suspend testing until it had duplicated the Soviet feat in space, narrowed the apparent gap in the missile race, and tested the next generation of nuclear warheads. Aware of the need to placate world opinion, Eisenhower and Dulles were playing for time while they searched for a way to slow down the arms race without jeopardizing the nation's security.

I

The new Soviet initiatives paralleled a growing rift within the Eisenhower administration. Harold Stassen, long restive over Dulles's refusal to consider a more flexible policy on testing, decided to challenge the secretary openly. In late December, he submitted a proposal to break open the American disarament package and seek a first step agreement with the Russians limited solely to a test ban. Stassen, convinced that the United States ought to test out Soviet sincerity in bilateral talks, proposed a two-year suspension of testing that would be enforced by an international team of supervisors. Unlike earlier American proposals, Stassen's plan gave up the insistence on a cutoff in the manufacture of nuclear weapons.

Eisenhower ordered a thorough study of the new proposal. A five-member panel of the President's Science Advisory Committee turned in a careful analysis to the full National Security Council, which discussed it at length on January 6. To the surprise of some members, strong support for Stassen's proposal came from such unexpected sources as UN Ambassador Lodge and Treasury Secretary Robert Anderson. Stassen, who had the reputation of being "a terrific presenter," bolstered his case with an array of charts and graphs. Dulles remained silent, letting Secretary of Defense Neil McElroy and General Nathan Twining, chairman of the Joint Chiefs of Staff, oppose the plan on military grounds. Lewis Strauss joined in the opposition, and after a lengthy discussion, the President reluctantly agreed to table Stassen's proposal. For the time being, at least, the administration would continue to insist on linking a test ban to a cutoff in weapons production.[4]

Stassen realized that his defeat meant the end of his tenure as special assistant to the President. Frustrated by Dulles's unrelenting opposition, he began to consider leaving the administration to run for the GOP nomination for governor of Pennsylvania. The President finally called him in for a long conference on February 7, asking him to resign as disarmament adviser and take another position within the administration. Stassen opted for a new career in politics, announcing on February 15 that he was leaving the White House staff to enter the governor's race in Pennsylvania. A week later, the State Department announced that James Wadsworth, the deputy ambassador to the UN, would take over Stassen's duties as the American representative in all future disarmament negotiations. While Wadsworth would also participate in forming policy, he remained under State Department control and did not serve as the President's special disarmament adviser.

The departure of Harold Stassen marked the end of a difficult three-year assignment. Boxed in by Dulles and Strauss, he had nevertheless succeeded in raising alternative disarmament policies at the White House level and had forced Eisenhower to look more broadly at the international implications of nuclear testing. He had been unable to persuade the President to pursue separate test ban negotiations, but by the time Stassen left the White House, Eisenhower had moved far toward acceptance of his views. Indeed, one likely reason for his removal in early 1958 was to make a shift to a more flexible policy feasible. The President could not side with Stassen against 'Dulles without humiliating his Secretary of State; with Stassen gone, it would be far easier for Eisenhower to persuade Dulles it was time to negotiate seriously with the Russians for a test ban agreement.[5]

II

While the internal debate went on within the Eisenhower administration, Senator Hubert Humphrey emerged as the leading congressional advocate of a more flexible policy. On November 4, 1957, he sent a telegram to the President urging him to split apart the August 29 disarmament proposal. Claiming that a test ban with international inspection would be a significant first step toward disarmament, Humphrey proposed a two-year suspension without any mention of a corresponding weapons cutoff. The President sent back a perfunctory reply, simply saying that he and his advisers were reviewing the whole issue of arms control.

In early 1958, SANE approached the Senator with a draft resolution calling for a moratorium on testing under international supervision. In a conference in Washington on January 11, a SANE delegation asked Humphrey to help them find a Senator to introduce the resolution in Congress. Though Humphrey said he favored a resolution "broad enough to gain support and meet the objection that 'you can't trust the Russians,' " he backed away from the role of sponsor. Two weeks later, he told SANE that he would hold a new round of hearings on the test ban issue designed to attract national attention. In addition, he planned to give a major speech on disarmament in the Senate on February 4. Pleased by this cooperation, the leaders of SANE made plans to publicize the senator's speech as widely as possible.[6]

In his address to the Senate on February 4, which ran over 70 pages, Humphrey again urged the administration to break apart its comprehensive arms control package. He warned that the constant American rejection of Soviet proposals created a bad impression on the world, allowing the Soviets to "score . . . many propaganda victories." A first-step agreement on a specific issue would have a positive effect on opinion abroad and lead to more substantial achievements in future negotiations. "To me," Humphrey argued, "it would be significant to obtain an agreement on suspension of nuclear tests with an adequate system of inspection and detection." The Senator accepted the administration's contention that the U.S. was ahead of the Soviet Union in nuclear technology; the best way to preserve that lead would be to freeze weapons development with a test ban.

SANE went all-out in praise of Humphrey's speech. Trevor Thomas, the executive director, sent telegrams to 55 local chapters asking them to solicit at least 25 individual letters to Congress endorsing the senator's remarks. Thomas shared his enthusiasm with his correspondents, telling one that Humphrey's speech was "a revolutionary political development" that "must not be allowed to die." A letter to the *Times* signed by New York City SANE members, including Erich Fromm and Norman Thomas, called attention to the Senate address and urged prompt action to implement it. A test ban, they wrote, would be "the one most obvious step toward halting a world competition in destructiveness which can have only one end." [7]

On February 28, Senator Humphrey began a new series of hearings before his subcommittee on disarmament. Harold Stassen was the first witness. The former presidential disarmament adviser spelled out in detail a four-point plan for a trial test ban agreement with Russia. Though Stassen carefully refused to say whether this was the same proposal he had suggested to Eisenhower, it followed the same line of thinking. The plan proposed the creation of a United Nations supervisory agency, an inspection system consisting of 12 posts in Russia and the United States, a 2-year suspension of all weapons tests, and continuing negotiations for further disarmament measures.

Under intense questioning by members of the subcommittee, Stassen defended his plan as both workable and desirable. He explained that inspection stations equipped with proper scientific instruments could "make it as certain as anything on earth can be certain" that all tests would be detected. Citing the RANIER underground test in 1957, he explained that seismographs could pinpoint suspicious subsurface events and an inspection team could then check out the site to distinguish between an earthquake and a nuclear explosion. He told Senator Pastore that he believed such an agreement could be negotiated within six months, compared to the years that would be required for the administration's comprehensive disarmament package. When Senator Saltonstall expressed concern that a halt in testing would jeopardize American security, Stassen replied that there was no safety in "an all-out arms race." ". . . The best approach for security and peace," he argued, "is to begin to open up on both sides to inspection and begin to get control of these weapons."

Throughout the hearing, Stassen stressed the need to educate the people, the Congress, and the administration on the need to bring the arms race under control. Though he refused to give any details of his experience as a presidential adviser, he admitted that he had met with strong resistance from the Pentagon and the AEC. Always the optimist, Stassen expressed his hope that "as this issue is focused on around the world, the Atomic Energy Commission would find that it was a wise first step to take." Above all, Stassen insisted that the test ban would not weaken national security. "It does not take away a single bomb, a single plane, a single missile or a single gun," he declared, "and we must remain very powerful." [8]

The administration leaders realized that Humphrey and Stassen were trying to build up irresistible public pressure for a separate test ban agreement. The President still had his doubts. On February 5, the day after Humphrey's Senate speech, Eisenhower told Dulles that the outcry for a test ban was isolated, consisting only of "Humphrey and a few more shouting." He told the secretary that our ties to our allies, who were still developing their own nuclear weapons, prevented us from considering such a step. Dulles was not so sure, "advising that he would not place our entire argument against banning of tests solely on our allies."

Eisenhower ignored this counsel. On February 26, he told his news conference that the "great difficulty" with the Stassen proposal was its effect on the NATO allies. They were "in different states of producing the weapons that require testing," the President explained, and thus were opposed to a test ban at this time. But the very fact that Eisenhower tried to put the onus on England and France suggested that he was not strongly opposed to a test ban. He had repeatedly made clear his own personal distaste for testing in memoranda to Strauss, and alert reporters now sensed that the President was ready to consider a further shift in American policy. The *New York Times* reported on February 25 that the administration was considering a separate test ban negotiation. The White House ignored the report, but speculation over an impending change in disarmament policy continued. At the very least, Humphrey and Stassen had succeeded in making a separate test ban agreement a viable option in 1958.[9]

III

In the scientific community, the debate over fallout reached a new intensity in the early months of 1958. Two distinguished scientists, Linus Pauling and Edward Teller, emerged as the chief spokesmen for the contending viewpoints. In books and magazine articles and on television, these antagonists presented their views dogmatically, each refusing to concede any possibility of truth or justice to his opponent. If the clash of ideas served mainly to confirm previously-formed opinion, at least the dialogue forced the American people to grapple with the thorny issues of radiation and disarmament.

Pauling made the first move. On January 13, 1958, he presented UN Secretary-General Dag Hammarskjold with a copy of his 1957 petition that had been signed by 9235 scientists from around the world. Initially seeking only American signers, Pauling had agreed to circulate his petition abroad in response to frequent requests in the summer of 1957. The wording was the same, citing the hazard of radiation in calling for an international test ban agreement. The new signatures included those of 37 Nobel laureates as well as 36 Fellows of the Royal Society of London and 216 members of the Soviet Academy of Sciences.

Teller responded with an article in *Life* entitled "The Compelling Need for Nuclear Tests." With a caption on the magazine's cover reading, "Dr. Teller Refutes 9,000 Scientists," he took issue with the petition's assertion that nuclear experiments threatened human health. "Such tests," Teller asserted, "do not seriously endanger either present or future generations." He went on to express his distrust of the Russians and argue that continued testing would benefit mankind by leading to a clean bomb.[10]

The two scientists had an opportunity to debate their differences personally on a San Francisco educational television program. For an hour they traded barbs. Speaking in his high-pitched voice, Pauling warned that "the man who gives the order to test a superbomb is dooming 15,000 children to a defective life." Responding in heavily-accented tones, Teller claimed that a test ban would enable the Soviets to carry on secret experiments which would undermine American security. Edward R. Murrow tried to repeat this exchange before a national audience on "See It Now," but Teller begged off. Murrow replaced him with Willard Libby, who admitted that fallout was increasing in the United States but still claimed that it was "a risk that we can and should tolerate." Pauling reiterated his dire prophecies, claiming that existing fallout would mean that "about 1,000,000 persons" would die from leukemia alone. At the end of the telecast, Murrow intoned: "There *is* danger in the continued testing of nuclear weapons. Scientists disagree only as to the degree and depth of the danger."[11]

Teller and Pauling spelled out their differences most clearly in books that appeared in 1958. Collaborating with RAND scientist Albert Latter, Teller published *Our Nuclear Future* early in the year. In this volume, the authors combined a careful summary of nuclear physics with an impassioned plea for continued bomb testing. Pauling's book, *No More War!,* came out in the summer. Described by one reviewer as "a tract for the times," the volume repeated Pauling's warnings about the fallout peril and concluded with a plea for world government. Determined to reach the American people with his message, Pauling gave away over 1500 copies of his book to influential individuals, including every member of Congress.[12]

Though Teller and Pauling dominated the ensuing debate because of their powerful personalities, many others participated. Harrison Brown of Cal Tech, Hans Bethe of Cornell, and Jay Orear of Columbia all joined Pauling in arguing for a test ban; Lewis Strauss and Willard Libby helped Teller in stating the case for continued testing. Three issues gradually emerged in this discussion. The first was the familiar dispute over the potential danger of radiation. Secondly, the two sides opened up a new argument on detection, disagreeing on the possibility of distinguishing between underground tests and earthquakes. Finally, they clashed over the transcendent question of whether a test ban would promote or injure the national interest.

IV

There had been some significant advances in scientific knowledge about fallout since the 1957 congressional hearings. In February 1958, Laurence Kulp and his associates at Columbia published a second report on the strontium-90 content of human bones. Their findings were not reassuring. The three scientists reported that the level of Sr^{90} had increased by one-third from June 1956 to June 1957. Moreover, the amount found in children was far higher than in adults, ranging up to ten times as much. Kulp and his colleagues did not express any great alarm at their conclusions, forecasting that even with continued testing, the level of strontium-90 in children by the 1970s would be no higher than 21 micromicrocuries, or about one-fifth the MPC. Other observers pointed out, however, that if testing did continue unabated, by the end of the century the level of Sr^{90} in human bones would be dangerous.[13]

An AEC report in April caused even greater concern. Heavy fallout from Soviet tests, the agency announced, had led to a sharp increase in radiation levels in the northern United States. In New York City, the Sr^{90} readings had doubled, making it "one of the hottest spots in the world." Even this increase, the AEC argued, was not dangerous, since it would not lead to exposure of more than 5 per cent of the MPC. Another government report confirmed the uneven fallout pattern. Much more Sr^{90} reached the ground north of a line between Denver and Philadelphia, with New York City receiving more than twice as much as Miami. Despite the AEC assurances, citizens in northern cities felt uneasy; the Minneapolis *Star* began printing the daily radiation count as part of its weather summary.[14]

Most scientists were still uncertain of the degree of danger fallout posed for mankind. The *Bulletin of the Atomic Scientists* devoted an entire issue to the subject in January, 1958. In calm, restrained prose, the various authors spoke of the potential dangers, but pointed out that the lack of precise data prevented them from reaching any firm judgments. The genetic hazard was clearest, commented James Crow, but fallout contributed "only a small fraction to the natural irradiations." The evidence on somatic effects was much more tenuous. Heavy doses of radiation did cause leukemia and bone cancer, but there simply was no way to prove whether small exposures had a similar effect. The argument over whether a threshold existed below which radiation was harmless could not be resolved with the existing evidence, reported William Neumann. "There simply are not enough data on which to speculate intelligently." The essence of the problem, concluded the editors of the symposium, lay in what factor observers chose to stress—the quite small part of the world's population that was probably affected by radiation, or the relatively large numbers of individuals who made up even the tiniest fraction of all mankind.[15]

Linus Pauling insisted that it was the total number that counted. In his speaking and writing, the Cal Tech biochemist extrapolated from the meager data available to calculate the total casualties from each bomb test. Arguing that the fallout from BRAVO had exposed individuals to one-tenth of the background radiation, he estimated that this one experiment alone would ultimately lead to the birth of 15,000 defective children. He found the somatic danger even greater. Using the figures supplied by Kulp for the level of strontium-90 in human bone, Pauling concluded that the present rate of testing would cause an additional 8000 deaths a year from leukemia, 1600 more from bone cancer, and 90,000 from the shortening of life expectancy. "At the present time," Pauling argued, "there is nobody in the world who can deny that there exists a real possibility that the lives of 100,000 people now living are sacrificed by each bomb test. . . ." The villain was strontium-90, which Pauling termed "a terrible poison" that did not exist in nature. "One teaspoonful of this poison," he warned, "distributed equally among all the people in the world, would kill all of them within a few years."

In the spring of 1958, Pauling came forth with a new danger from testing that no one else had mentioned—carbon-14. The neutrons released in bomb tests created a 10 per cent increase in the amount of C^{14}. Even though carbon-14 emitted very little radiation, its extremely long half-life of over 5,000 years created a serious genetic hazard. According to Pauling, over the next 300 generations, the release of C^{14} from bombs already tested would cause at least one million defective births. On this basis, he concluded that carbon-14 was "a greater menace to the human race than the shorter-lived radioactive elements."[16]

In contrast, it was difficult to believe that Edward Teller was discussing the same phenomenon as Pauling. In his book and the *Life* magazine article, Teller minimized both the genetic and somatic effects of fallout. He admitted there was some impact on heredity, but it was so slight that it would "increase the chance of mutations by only a very small amount." The effect on human health was much more dubious. "We do not know that a single person will die permaturely from diseases of blood and bone," he told a congressional committee. He took particular issue with the argument that fallout radiation shortened normal life expectancy. Claiming that smoking one pack of cigarettes a day could shorten a person's life by nine years and being 10 per cent overweight could reduce it by one and a half years, Teller asserted that "world-wide fallout is as dangerous as being an ounce overweight or smoking one cigarette every two months."

Teller's favorite argument was to cite the increased exposure to natural radiation at higher altitudes to show that small increases did not affect human health. The inhabitants of Tibet and Peru, exposed to far higher radiation than that from bomb fallout, had experienced no grave genetic defects over the centuries, he argued. Studies of the leukemia rates in Denver, San Francisco, and New Orleans showed that the two sea-level cities had a higher incidence of the disease than Denver with its much greater radiation from cosmic rays. Teller did admit that fallout might cause a slight increase in bone cancer and leukemia, but in the long run no one would be aware of this effect. In the next 30 years, he pointed out, some 6 million people in the world would die of these diseases. It was possible that 10,000 more would succumb from fallout, but Teller concluded, "Statistical methods are not able to find the difference between 6,000,000 and 6,010,000."[17]

Several other scientists joined with Teller in rebutting Pauling's carbon-14 claims. Willard Libby, the world's leading authority on C^{14}, contended that most of the radiocarbon from bomb tests ended up in the world's oceans and thus could not cause human mutations. Laurence Kulp and his associates at Columbia charged that Pauling had magnified the amount of carbon-14 produced by bomb tests by a factor of 50. The effect on heredity would be minimal, they claimed, amounting to less than 0.1 per cent of the natural radiation level. In a letter to the *New York Times,* Kulp and his colleagues concluded, "Exaggerated statements by respected scientists only add to the public's confusion and do not contribute to the solution of this problem." Ralph Lapp, though sympathetic to Pauling's crusade, agreed with this assessment. In a letter to Norman Cousins, he warned "that friend Pauling got off base in discussing the C^{14} hazard."[18]

V

The question of whether or not underground nuclear tests could be detected led to an equally sharp disagreement among scientists. After the September 1957 RANIER shot had proved it was possible to hold underground tests, the administration realized that their detection was crucial to the consideration of a test ban. Experience had shown that it was possible to monitor blasts in the atmosphere even at great distances. The same techniques would not work for shots below the surface, however. The President's Science Advisory Committee discussed this issue and recommended in early 1958 that an Ad Hoc Working Group be created to study the RANIER data and make recommendations. Hans Bethe, the distinguished Cornell physicist, headed the panel, which consisted of representatives from the AEC, the Defense Department, the CIA, and the PSAC.[19]

While the Bethe panel conducted its study, the AEC touched off a public furor in early March by announcing that RANIER had not been detected by seismic stations more than 250 miles away from the Nevada test site. Journalist I. F. Stone, recalling reports that stations thousands of miles away recorded tremors from RANIER, checked with the Coast and Geodetic Survey, which confirmed that its station in College, Alaska, 2300 miles distant, had detected the seismic waves from the underground blast. Stone reported this information to Senator Humphrey, who accused the AEC of distorting scientific evidence "to prove a political point." Willard Libby sent a letter to Humphrey calling the earlier AEC statement an "inadvertent" mistake and apologizing on behalf of the agency. At a brief hearing held by the Joint Committee on Atomic Energy, Libby repeated this explanation, saying the AEC had been guilty of a bureaucratic mix-up.[20]

Senator Humphrey used this incident to focus the hearings of his disarmament subcommittee on the detection issue. The subcommittee heard first from Jay Orear, a young physics professor from Columbia University who had recently completed an analysis of detection techniques for a larger study of disarmament problems. Orear argued persuasively that underground tests could be identified with a proper inspection system. Then on April 17, Hans Bethe confirmed this view in secret testimony before the subcommittee which was later released after heavy censorship.

Orear and Bethe explained to the senators that there were four ways to detect nuclear explosions. The most effective technique for atmospheric tests involved sensitive microbarometers, which recorded the acoustic waves created by bomb blasts. In addition, electromagnetic instruments that measured light waves and actual samples of radioactive dust collected by aircraft could be used to confirm explosions in the atmosphere. But the only way to record underground nuclear shots was by seismograph, and this method posed the difficult problem of distinguishing between such blasts and earthquakes.

The critical factor, according to both Orear and Bethe, was the first motion recorded by the seismograph. In the case of an explosion, which sent shock waves outward in all directions, the first motion was always upward, or positive. But in earthquakes, which involved lateral movement in the earth's crust, some of the waves were positive and others negative, or downward, depending on the direction of the instrument from the occurrence. To distinguish between a nuclear blast and an earthquake, the experts contended, it was necessary to have a network of seismographs so that you would have readings in all four quadrants around a suspicious event. If all the readings were positive, then you could be sure it was an explosion; if some were negative, you could then be certain it was an earthquake.

Orear and Bethe both advocated a network of seismic stations in both the United States and Russia that would monitor all seismic events. Orear suggested 25 such inspection posts in Russia and 7 in the United States; the censors deleted the exact number Bethe recommended. Inspection teams would examine the seismic records for each underground disturbance. Both men felt that the instruments alone would be sufficient to distinguish between earthquakes and explosions down to 4.5 on the Richter scale, which meant that all nuclear shots above 2 kilotons would be automatically detected. For disturbances that registered below 4.5 on the Richter scale (RANIER, at 1.7 kilotons, had measured 4.2), inspectors would conduct an on-site examination to determine if the cause had been an earthquake or a nuclear blast. Orear believed that a geologist could quickly tell from examining the earth's surface whether a blast had been detonated below ground; Bethe argued that the presence of roads and other signs of human activity would point to the likelihood of an underground test.

The two witnesses differed slightly in their estimates of how effective such a seismic detection system would be. Orear was the more positive, scoffing at the idea of the Russians holding secret tests underground. He said that it was "questionable whether you are going to use nuclear explosions for a hand grenade," and again, that an undetected test would be little larger than "a firecracker." The only weapons the Russians could test secretly, he argued, would be "within an order of magnitude of conventional weapons." Bethe admitted that the seismic system would "never give you 100 percent proof," but he felt that on-site detection would make it very difficult for the Russians to conduct secret tests underground. He did acknowledge, however, that there were at least 2500 earthquakes a year equivalent to a 1 kiloton explosion and that a certain fraction would require on-site inspection. The Russians might succeed in getting away with one or two isolated tests, but they could never conduct a whole series without being caught. Given the American lead in nuclear technology, Bethe thought a test ban, with a thorough inspection system, was well worth the risk.[21]

Edward Teller disagreed strongly. In testimony to the Humphrey subcommittee, as well as in his television appearances and writing, the nation's foremost advocate of testing argued that the Russians would find a way to conduct secret underground tests. "Hiding tests means organized lying," he explained, "and organized lying is something . . . which can be safely practiced in Russia." He refused to specify exactly how the Russians would evade an inspection system, taking refuge in the obvious need to keep such speculation classified. But he insisted that it would not be difficult. "In the contest between the bootlegger and the police," he asserted, "the bootlegger has a great advantage." The Russians, he kept insisting, could not be trusted; "I am virtually certain that they will find methods to cheat," he declared on "Meet the Press." Teller was especially indignant at Orear's claim that small tests would be useless for weapons development. He called this a "flagrant misstatement" and stated flatly that small tests "can improve one's big weapons."

Willard Libby deviated slightly from Teller's hard line in his testimony before the Humphrey subcommittee. He agreed that it would be difficult to develop a foolproof inspection system, but he admitted that such perfection was not really necessary. A feasible control network would need only to be effective enough to make the chances of being caught very high. "So I mean test inspection, though difficult, may be practical," he explained. But Libby was skeptical of on-site inspection as a way to distinguish between an earthquake and a nuclear explosion. He told the Senate subcommittee that it took four months to find the radioactivity released below ground by RANIER, despite the fact that the AEC knew the exact location of the blast. RANIER had left no telltale traces on the earth's surface. "If you were not watching at the instant the bomb went off," Libby stated, "you would not have known there had been a bomb fired under it."[22]

In the minds of the senators, the testimony of Teller and Libby more than offset the optimistic views of Orear and Bethe. They wanted a foolproof inspection system, since anything less would mean putting trust in Russia's good faith. Senator Alexander Wiley, a Republican from Wisconsin, expressed his distrust of the Soviets and added, "if you make an agreement and you do not keep your own powder dry, you may have another Pearl Harbor." Senator Stuart Symington agreed with Wiley. "If you made one more mistake of that character," he warned, "you would never have a chance to make another."[23]

VI

Radiation and detection were subordinate to the main issue in the continuing debate among scientists—the wisdom of a test ban itself. Teller and Libby repeated the familiar arguments in favor of testing. National security required that the United States develop new weapons—warheads for the next generation of missiles and small, tactical bombs for battlefield use. In view of the Soviet advantage in conventional forces, the United States had to maintain its strategic advantage. "We can stay ahead only by moving ahead," Teller declared. He also stressed the need to complete the quest for the elusive clean bomb. "We must have the clean weapons to save the innocent bystander, to save our allies," Teller argued. "By trying to be supercautious now, we may unnecessarily sacrifice millions of human lives in a dirty nuclear war later." Libby made the same point, but he also stressed the need to harness nuclear explosions for peaceful purposes, such as excavating harbors, generating heat, and freeing underground minerals. For that reason, he thought it would "be extremely unwise of the world to forever end all nuclear explosions."

Teller believed that the uproar over fallout was just a smokescreen. "The real reason against further tests," he claimed, "is connected with our desire for disarmament and for peace." As a refugee from Nazi tyranny, he reminded the American people that the policy of appeasement had not worked in the 1930s. History had shown that disarmament was "the road to war," he asserted; "if we renounce nuclear weapons, we open the door to aggression."

The clinching argument for both Teller and Libby was the

danger in stifling scientific inquiry. "The psychology of banning the discovery of new things is a dangerous road to take," Libby warned the Humphrey subcommittee, while Teller spoke eloquently about the duty of scientists to "explore fearlessly any consequences to which greater knowledge and improved skills can lead us." The most that they would be willing to accept, and then with great reluctance, would be an agreement to restrict fallout sharply. Both men suggested an arrangement whereby most testing would take place underground, with atmospheric experiments limited to a few relatively clean bombs detonated under United Nations supervision. Test limitation, as opposed to suspension, would at least permit the United States to explore the peaceful uses of nuclear explosives, perfect cleaner weapons and allow scientists to continue "the tradition of exploring the unknown."[24]

The test ban advocates within the scientific community rested their case on moral rather than security considerations. Linus Pauling repeatedly charged that American nuclear tests endangered the "lives of hundreds of thousands of people now living and of hundreds of thousands of unborn children." ". . . This sacrifice," he declared, "is unnecessary." Instead, the United States should take the lead in averting nuclear war by "stopping these tests of all nuclear weapons." The Federation of American Scientists, with over 2000 members, agreed. In a statement released on February 1, 1958, the FAS stressed the fallout hazards to mankind in calling for an international agreement to halt all further tests. An Indiana scientist, O. T. Benfey, made the sharpest indictment in a letter to *Science*. Comparing nuclear tests to Nazi experiments on concentration camp inmates, Benfey insisted that they had "no place in the pursuit of science whatsoever." "If the high ideals of democracy can only be defended through the indiscriminate spreading of leukemia," he concluded, "then it may be asked whether democracy is worth the price."

Harrison Brown offered a more realistic assessment. In the Gideon Seymour Memorial Lecture at the University of Minnesota, he warned that unless the arms race stopped soon, nuclear weapons would spread in the next few years to as many as 15 nations, each one poisoning the atmosphere with its tests and increasing the risk of all-out war. A test ban was the only solution. Claiming that Teller's opposition stemmed from "a deeply-rooted hatred of the Soviet Union," Brown charged that the Hungarian-born physicist was "willfully distorting the realities of the situation." In this lecture, as well as in testimony to the Senate disarmament subcommittee, Brown advocated a temporary test ban, lasting from one to three years while the United Nations created an effective control system. Admitting that it would be impossible to identify all underground tests, Brown suggested limiting the ban to those "that could be detected by the established network." Restricting tests to small ones underground would prevent nuclear proliferation, since other nations would find it difficult to conduct such tests, yet would enable American scientists to continue their work on clean bombs and peaceful uses for nuclear explosives.[25]

Brown's proposal attracted little support. Test ban advocates wanted to stop all experiments; opponents insisted on at least a few atmospheric shots. The debate within the scientific community had polarized viewpoints so that compromise appeared to be betrayal. Indeed, the whole discussion revealed the limitations of the scientists' objectivity when debating public policy. Taking positions that went far beyond the scanty evidence on fallout and detection, they tended to cloak their personal opinions in the mantle of science. Hugh Wolfe, chairman of the FAS, noted this tendency when he commented that "the major differences of opinion are political rather than scientific." Clinton Anderson concluded that "science was remarkably like politics, in that the practitioners could usually come up with answers to problems that corresponded to their prejudices or self-interest."

Scientists were no different from other people, Harrison Brown observed, claiming that they "are subject of all the frailties to which the flesh is heir." Scientists had an obligation to speak out on public issues, asserted Chauncey Leake of Ohio State, but they "can't make social or political decisions any better than other groups." Much of the difficulty stemmed from the lack of available data on fallout. Maurice Visscher, a physiologist at the University of Minnesota, warned that it would be at least 20 years before adequate information on the effect of low levels of Sr^{90} on human beings would be available. In the meantime, all that experts could offer would be "educated guesses." Henry Kissinger, at that time a professor of government at Harvard, agreed. Those on both sides of the issue, he noted, use "whatever statistics of effects of radioactive fall-out they can find that fit their political positions." The real problem, according to Visscher, came in mixing science with public policy. "We should all be more careful," he advised his colleagues, "to point out exactly what is fact, what is guess and what is opinion as to public policy."[26]

The failure of scientists to follow this advice meant that the continuing debate about fallout, as well as the new disagreement over detection, served only to confuse the American people. If eminent experts like Teller and Pauling could not agree on the wisdom of a test ban, how could the average American be expected to resolve the conflicting arguments and arrive at a sensible position? Intead of providing the judicious weighing of alternatives, based on an objective analysis, that the nation needed, scientists had intensified the emotional approach of most Americans to the nuclear test ban issue.

VII

The public campaign against nuclear tests continued to grow in the early months of 1958. SANE gave the movement an organizational focus. Reprints of its original advertisement appeared in 32 newspapers by January, and the New York office kept urging correspondents to form additional local committees. "We encourage people to work with fellow members of churches, service clubs, the P.T.A. and other organizations with which they may be affiliated," explained one of SANE's workers. The headquarters did not try to supervise the local activities, preferring to let each committee operate at "its own discretion."

SANE's second major advertisement appeared in the *New York Herald Tribune* on March 24, 1958. Entitled "No Contamination without Representation," the text charged that American tests were poisoning the atmosphere of the entire world. "We do not have the right—nor does any nation—to take risks, large or small, for other peoples without their consent," SANE declared. Some members found this ad too emotional. Playwright Elmer Rice refused to sign, claiming that the copy smacked too much of "commercial advertising" with its "appeal to people's fears and anxieties." But others felt that SANE was still too mild in its approach. Historian Carl Condit wanted the group to launch "a radical attack" on what he termed "this monstrous perversion of scientific and technical ability." Bill Attwood, the editor of *Look,* also favored a frontal assault that would shock the American people into action. "The appeal must be made to the emotions first," he wrote; "the intellectual arguments can come later." [27]

While SANE focused on public education, pacifist groups undertook more direct forms of protest. The American Friend's Service Committee organized a massive petition drive in late 1957. Calling nuclear tests "biologically destructive and morally indefensible," the Quaker petition asked the President to cancel the upcoming HARDTACK series. When Albert Bigelow, a Connecticut architect and peace activist, tried to deliver the first installment of 27,000 signatures in late December, a White House aide, Maxwell Rabb, refused to receive them. "I suspected that, while this group is a well-known and respected agency," Rabb explained to Jim Hagerty, "it was doing pro-Communist work, probably unwittingly." Hagerty finally arranged for the petition to be delivered in mid-January without any publicity. Two months later, a delegation of seven Friends turned over "two big black suitcases filled with 47,000 signatures" to another White House aide who received them politely and joined with the Quakers in a moment of silent prayer.[28]

Another group of pacifists attracted much more attention by staging a "Walk for Peace" on the UN headquarters in New York City. Modeling the event after the British "Ban the Bomb" march on nuclear facilities at Aldermaston, which had attracted worldwide notice, some 50 American marchers set out from New Haven for the 80-mile walk. Smaller groups from Philadelphia and Westbury on Long Island also participated. The three columns converged on the UN buildings on Good Friday, with local New York supporters swelling their ranks to more than 700. Rev. A. J. Muste led the peaceful demonstration which culminated in a call for "an unconditional halt to nuclear testing."[29]

The most dramatic protest came when Albert Bigelow, the Connecticut Quaker, decided to sail a small boat across the Pacific into the American test area during the HARDTACK series. Bigelow, who had commanded a destroyer escort in World War II, and another Quaker architect, William Reed Huntington, chartered a ketch, the *Golden Rule,* for the voyage. On January 8, 1958, Bigelow informed the President of his plan to sail with a crew of three to the forbidden area around Eniwetok. "We intend," he wrote, "come what may, to remain there during the test period, in an effort to halt what we feel is the monstrous delinquency of our government in continuing actions which threaten the well-being of all men. . . ."

Bigelow, Huntington, and two other Quakers sailed the *Golden Rule* out of San Pedro, California, in early February only to return a few days later when the engine on board the 30-foot vessel broke down. After making the repairs, they were forced to turn back again by heavy seas. Finally on March 25, they departed from San Pedro for Hawaii, where they planned to refuel and stock up on provisions for the long voyage to the Marshall Islands. Despite indications that federal agents would detain the *Golden Rule* at Honolulu, Bigelow bravely radioed to the world, "We shall continue . . . come what may."[30]

VIII

The administration ignored the *Golden Rule* as it went ahead with plans for HARDTACK. Throughout February and March, Joint Task Force Seven transported nearly 14,000 military and civilian technicians to the Pacific proving grounds in the Marshall Islands. The AEC planned to detonate more than 20 nuclear explosions. In addition to those designed to achieve cleaner bombs, the experiments included underwater blasts for anti-submarine weapons and at least two high-altitude shots of new anti-missile missiles. New warheads for the developing Polaris and Titan missiles were on the agenda, and the AEC also planned some experiments with smaller warheads for a future generation of still smaller and more sophisticated missiles. Aware that this might be the last series of American tests, the weapons designers were obviously attempting to achieve the maximum amount of technical progress.[31]

While these preparations continued, the Soviets conducted their own test series in Siberia. The first shot came on February 22 and there were two others within a week. Six more, including several in the megaton range, followed in March, with the last occurring on March 22. As usual, the Russian tests were shrouded in secrecy, but American analysts were convinced that like HARDTACK they involved actual missile warheads. Japanese observers reported unusually heavy fallout from the Soviet shots that raised the radiation levels in Tokyo to record levels.[32]

Within the Eisenhower administration, concern began to develop that the Kremlin would announce a unilateral suspension of testing at the end of its current series. Such a move would place the United States in a difficult position. If the administration went ahead with HARDTACK, commented the *New York Times,* the U.S. would "suffer a psychological setback in the eyes of the world," but if we suspended testing immediately, "the United States may be placed at the mercy of the new ballistic missiles developed by the Soviet Union." Dulles now decided that the pressure of world opinion necessitated a shift in American policy. With Stassen gone, he became the administration's leading test ban advocate.

On March 24, President Eisenhower met with his top national security advisers to discuss ways in which the United States could counter the expected Russian move. Secretary Dulles proposed that the President announce immediately that following the HARDTACK series, he would not order any additional tests for the remainder of his term in office. Chairman Strauss of the AEC opposed this idea strongly, as did Pentagon spokesmen, who pointed out the need to test an anti-missile missile and to perfect warheads for "the Polaris and other advanced systems." Eisenhower spoke out forcefully on the need to do something to allay worldwide concern over fallout, but when the hawks continued to insist that additional testing was vital to the nation's security, he permitted Dulles to withdraw his proposal. The President warned his advisers, however, that sooner or later the United States would have to "accept a suspension of testing," and he asked them "to think about what could be done to get rid of the terrible impasse in which we find ourselves with regard to testing." [33]

The President confirmed the plans for HARDTACK at his press conference the next day, saying that he would invite the UN to send representatives to one of the tests. At the same time, he indicated that the United States was aware of a possible unilateral Soviet test suspension. He said that the United States was still willing to negotiate a test ban agreement with the Russians and that he did not want "to take a perfectly rigid position" in respect to such negotiations. In a private note to Dulles the same day, the President expressed his personal commitment to ending the arms race. "To my mind," he told the Secretary of State, "this transcends all other objectives we can have. Security through arms is only a means (and sometimes a poor one) to an end." He was concerned that the Soviets might outmaneuver the United States in the eyes of the world, and he vowed not to stop "searching for ideas to stem and turn the tide of Soviet propaganda success."

Having rejected a preemptive move of its own, the administration tried to take the sting out of the anticipated Soviet test suspension by announcing on March 28 that it expected such a move momentarily. Critics found this a poor substitute for action. On March 29, Senator Humphrey warned that "the Administration's timidity and foot-dragging are costing us a terrible defeat in the propaganda battle." Ironically, he singled out Dulles, the man who had tried so hard to reverse American policy, for special criticism, claiming that the secretary failed to understand "human relations." [34]

Despite the administration's efforts to soften the blow, the Soviet Union scored an impressive triumph on March 31 when Foreign Minister Andrei Gromyko informed the world that Russia was unilaterally halting all further tests of nuclear weapons. The announcement came just four days after Marshall Bulganin resigned as premier to allow Nikita Khrushchev to become the acknowledged leader of the USSR in title as well as in fact. Though Gromyko made the announcement, the new policy was clearly Khrushchev's handiwork, one of his characteristically bold Cold War moves. The statement stressed the Russian desire to liberate mankind from the hazards of radioactive fallout and called upon the United States and Great Britain to stop their own tests. If they did not, the statement continued, "the Soviet Union will, understandably, act freely in the question of testing of atomic and hydrogen weapons."

Khrushchev had displayed great shrewdness. With a Soviet series just completed, he was taking advantage of the normal hiatus in testing to use world opinion to force the United States to cancel HARDTACK. If the administration went ahead with the planned tests in the Pacific, then the Soviets would have a built-in excuse to resume testing without any actual disruption in their nuclear program. Harold Macmillan tried to point out to critics in the House of Commons the cynicism of the Russian position, noting that it meant "three megaton tests in a week—then, no more tests." The *New York Times* labeled it a "spectacular but transparent maneuver," and expressed the hope that the people of the world would not be so easily fooled. But James Reston was impressed. "The Soviet Union," he wrote, "is telling the world what it wants to hear, and the element of wishful thinking is on its side."[35]

The administration's response came on April 1 when Dulles faced reporters in a jammed State Department auditorium. The secretary, who had conferred with Eisenhower in advance about his remarks, spoke even more slowly than usual and looked, according to James Reston, "immensely tired." He attempted to dismiss the Soviet suspension as "propaganda," pointing out that in view of HARDTACK, the Russians could easily justify a resumption of testing at any time in the future. He reiterated the American position on a test ban, arguing that it had to be linked to a cutoff in weapons production in order to achieve genuine disarmament. At the end, he admitted that the Soviets had scored "a certain propaganda victory, or at least a success," but he had no regret over the administration's decision to continue testing.

The President took the same view of the Soviet suspension at his news conference the next day. He referred questioners to Dulles's remarks, and then when pressed, called Gromyko's statement "a gimmick," adding, "I don't think it is to be taken seriously." Eisenhower did express regret, however, that he had not formally announced that the United States had considered and rejected its own unilateral suspension prior to the Soviet statement. Such a step, he said, "might have been a better propaganda move."

Despite his outward calm, the President was seething over the way the Russian suspension had given the United States a black eye in world opinion. He really had no one but himself to blame. For three months, the administration had discussed disarmament policy without arriving at any clear-cut decisions. The President's own inclination was toward a test ban agreement, but he had allowed the AEC and the Pentagon to kill the proposals made by Stassen in January and Dulles in March. On April 4, he decided to try one more time. He ordered the State and Defense Departments, along with AEC and the PSAC, to conduct a final review of American policy. He asked that the study focus on the issue of separating a test ban from other disarmament proposals and he insisted on a report within three weeks. At last, the President was forcing the long overdue showdown within his administration on test ban policy.[36]

IX

The unilateral Soviet test suspension led to widespread demands for similar action by the United States. Liberal journals expressed a grudging admiration for what they termed a "brilliant" and "spectacular" political move on Khrushchev's part. They recognized that the Russians had acted only after completing their own tests, but nevertheless they credited the Kremlin with making an astute estimate of world opinion and displaying "boldness, originality and superb timing." In contrast, they faulted American leaders for failing to respond positively. "If all this is a 'gimmick,' " commented the editors of the *Nation,* "one can only wish to God that our statesmen could concoct such gimmicks once in a while." The only option Eisenhower and Dulles now had was to seek a negotiated test ban agreement. "The nettle has been presented to us with all the world looking on," the *Reporter* stated, "and prickles and all, we must grasp it."

Such prominent Democrats as Eleanor Roosevelt and Estes Kefauver appealed to the administration to enter into test ban negotiations. In late April, Albert Schweitzer issued a second appeal to the world's conscience. Denouncing Teller's concept of a "clean" bomb, the renowned philosopher claimed that the spread of fallout from tests amounted to a crime against the future. "Mankind is imperiled by the tests," he declared. "Mankind insists that they stop, and has every right to do so."

Schweitzer concluded his appeal by asking the United States and Great Britain to follow Russia's example and suspend all future tests.[37]

Test ban advocates in the United States directed their efforts at halting the forthcoming HARDTACK series. Linus Pauling, Norman Thomas, and sixteen other individuals filed suit in federal court on April 4 to enjoin the administration from holding the planned tests, claiming that Congress had never given the government authority to contaminate the atmosphere and threaten future generations with radiation perils. Two weeks later, a group of 140 Protestant clergymen demanded that the AEC cancel HARDTACK, calling the tests "morally indefensible and politically disastrous." Representative Charles Porter of Oregon tried a more direct approach. He flew to Eniwetok on April 28 to dramatize his opposition to HARD-TACK. "I may not be able to stop the tests," Porter admitted, "but I am going to talk to the people conducting them."[38]

The leaders of SANE were outraged by the failure of the United States to follow the Soviet example. They staged a nine-day rally in New York City, holding public meetings and picketing at the United Nations. On April 11, they placed another full-page ad in the *New York Times* frankly designed to frighten the American people. Half the page was taken up with a mushroom cloud with the caption, "Nuclear Tests Are Endangering Our Health Right Now." After calling for an immediate cessation in American testing, the ad closed with the injunction, "We must stop the contamination of the air, the milk children drink, the food we eat." Several signers of earlier SANE ads disagreed with what one called "the frenzied tone" of this statement. "I don't like the confusion of the big issue of world peace," commented Ernest Pollard, a Yale biophysicist, "with the little issue of the contamination of milk."

Norman Cousins, who wrote the copy for SANE, went even further in his *Saturday Review* editorials. In the April 12 issue he called the Soviet suspension "a moral disaster for the United States." A week later he wrote that the people of the world were "worried about the obscene competition in creating weapons that can incinerate millions at a time." This editorial, which Cousins reprinted in an advertisement in the *Times,* stressed his belief that there was "a real threat of contamination to air and food and human tissue." The only solution was for the United States to stop all tests immediately. "No nation," he declared, "has the right to contaminate or jeopardize the air or water or food that belongs to other people." [39]

These emotional outcries brought a cool response from those who favored continued testing. *Time* dismissed the Soviet suspension as simply a cynical move in "the cold-war game," while David Lawrence, the right-wing editor of the *U.S. News and World Report,* denounced it as "a transparently phony scheme." Asserting that the Communists would settle for nothing less than "the unconditional surrender of the Western world," Lawrence rejected test ban negotiations on the grounds that "there can be no compromise with evil." Military spokesmen concurred. Joint Chiefs of Staff Chairman Nathan Twining warned that a test ban would weaken American defensive strength, since we relied on nuclear superiority to offset a Communist manpower advantage. General James Gavin, the former head of the Army's research program, claimed that it was "in the interest of humanity" for America to continue testing. "Whether we like it or not," he argued, "we are living in a nuclear age." [40]

Advocates of testing charged that those who called for suspension were helping the Communist cause. *Time* did a feature story in mid-April in which the editors pointed out that Pauling and several others who had signed the SANE ads had been active in Communist-front groups. Under pictures of the signers, *Time* ran the caption, "Defenders of the unborn . . . or dupes of the enemies of liberty?" The story also cited a *New York Daily News* editorial which said that while the protesters were not "consciously trying to do a job for the Kremlin, . . . they are as nutty as so many fruitcakes." The Reverend Daniel A. Poling of New York's Marble Collegiate Church went further, viewing the call for canceling HARDTACK as part of the "insidious and far-reaching menace of atheist Communism in its world-wide peace drive." Representative Francis Walter of the House Un-American Activities Committee agreed. Behind the respectable façade of the test ban movement, he asserted, "the black hand of the Communist conspiracy remains clearly visible."

Others viewed the protesters as political innocents who unwittingly were repeating the sins of the appeasers of the 1930s. In a letter to the editors of the *New York Times,* Adele Blackman feared "a new Pearl Harbor" if the nation listened to the modern-day counterparts of those "who precipitated Munich." Polly Mills, widow of Mark Mills, a nuclear scientist killed in a helicopter accident while preparing for the HARDTACK series, explained her late husband's views in a letter to President Eisenhower. "Mark thought that the reason so many intelligent and well meaning people want the tests to stop is because emotionally they equate testing with war," she wrote. "Mark thought that this ostrich philosophy was a deadly danger to the country." Her husband, she continued, was a gentle man who wanted peace "with all his being." "Recently, he told me that not once in these last ten years had he known a genuinely carefree moment! Never! He said that he felt as if he were continually looking down the jaws of the monster."[41]

To a surprising degree, the American people agreed with the opponents of a test ban. In mid-April, the Gallup poll asked a group of citizens whether "the United States should stop making tests with nuclear weapons and H-bombs." Sixty per cent said no, while only 29 per cent replied yes, with 11 per cent expressing no opinion. Earlier polls had shown a majority favoring a negotiated test ban; this survey indicated that by a two-to-one margin, the American people rejected a unilateral halt to testing. The same poll revealed that 46 per cent believed that continued testing might harm future generations. Apparently many still felt that national security required that this risk be taken.

Analysis of the poll data shows that fallout anxiety varied inversely with the level of education. Those who had not gone beyond grade school expressed far more concern than the college-educated. On the crucial question of unilateral test cessation, 38 per cent of the grade school sample were in favor, while only 20 per cent of college graduates responded affirmatively. Eugene J. Rosi, in a study published in 1965, reported that the attentive public, those with a college education who voted regularly, were least concerned about fallout and most opposed to unilateral test suspension. Rosi found no evidence that public opinion influenced the Eisenhower administration on test ban policy. Instead he concluded that the public was looking to the administration for leadership on a complex and confusing issue. In this sense, the President and his advisers had great freedom to act in 1958. The American people, worried even more over national security than the humanitarian concerns stressed by test ban advocates, placed their trust in the wisdom and judgment of President Eisenhower.[42]

X

April 1958 was the crucial month in the administration's reconsideration of test ban policy. The panel of experts headed by Hans Bethe completed its report on the feasibility of detecting nuclear tests on March 28, and in early April Bethe presented it personally to the National Security Council. Bethe explained that his group, which included representatives from the military services, the AEC, and the CIA, believed that the United States possessed sufficient nuclear superiority over Russia to justify a test ban agreement. Though no inspection system could be absolutely foolproof, the panel felt that a carefully constructed network of control stations, with at least 25 on Russian soil, backed by mobile teams for on-site inspection, could detect any nuclear blast down to as low as 2 kilotons. This conclusion, which was based on an analysis of the RANIER data, assumed that the detection of first motion by seismographs would be effective in distinguishing between earthquakes and nuclear explosions in 90 per cent of all cases.[43]

On the basis of this study, Dulles decided to renew an earlier offer to the Soviets for technical talks on a possible test ban inspection system. Working at home on Sunday, April 6, with two aides, he drafted a presidential letter to this effect to Soviet Premier Nikita Khrushchev. Without consulting either the AEC or the Pentagon, Dulles telephoned Eisenhower for his approval. The President told the secretary that "we would be quite ready to participate in any study that is technical in character." Eisenhower then added, "Our position is that we want to look on testing as a symptom rather than a disease."

Dulles sent the letter to Khrushchev over the President's signature on April 8. Later that day he met with the press and disclosed in very general terms the recommendations of the Bethe panel. He pointed out that "a fairly complex system is required" to detect underground as well as atmospheric tests, and he repeated Bethe's warning that such a system would not be completely effective. But he pointed out that the system need not be foolproof; a high risk of detection would be enough to deter the Soviets from attempting a covert test. Asked if this meant that the United States was ready to suspend testing after HARDTACK, Dulles equivocated, saying such a step would depend on many factors, including the success of the series in providing the weapons information American scientists were seeking.

The next day at his regular news conference, President Eisenhower was asked the same question. He also hedged, but then said that if the scientists were satisfied, "I should think it would be perfectly proper for us" to consider a ban on further tests. Pressed by a reporter on whether that meant there was a real possibility that testing would end with HARDTACK, Eisenhower replied, "Well, certainly, I would consider it very seriously at that point."[44]

Chairman Strauss, realizing that the President was on the

verge of a major shift in policy, fought hard to block it. While his advice to the President remained confidential, Strauss made clear in public speeches and statements that he had three objections to a test ban. First, he believed that suspension would prevent the United States from developing important new weapons, such as a relatively clean H-bomb, an anti-missile missile, and a new generation of thermonuclear warheads. In order to deter the Soviet Union, he argued, "we must be armed with the most advanced weapons. That is why we conduct our tests—to prove that our advanced weapon designs will work."

Second, when critics suggested that a test ban would preserve American nuclear superiority by freezing technology for both superpowers, Strauss then argued that America's defensive, second-strike strategy required weapons that were "more sophisticated in design, more accurate and more numerous." The Soviets already possessed weapons that would destroy the United States; they could use a test ban to move ahead with improved missiles to deliver existing warheads to American targets more effectively. A test ban, he affirmed, "will result in the improvement of the aggressor's system and a freezing of the defender's system."

Finally, Strauss fell back on the familiar argument that the "real danger" was the threat of nuclear war. As long as the United States maintained its clear superiority in weapons technology, the Soviets would never dare launch a first strike. But if the Russians found a way to cheat on a test ban, they would overcome America's advantage and risk an attack. For that reason, he opposed any step to halt tests that did not include a ban on weapons manufacture as well. In a speech to the National Press Club, he stated this objection most eloquently. "The danger which the world faces is not from nuclear testing but from nuclear war. Those who think otherwise, I submit, mistake the shadow for the substance."[45]

Though the Pentagon supported the AEC chairman, Strauss's arguments failed to persuade the President. Perhaps the fact that he had repeated them so often over the years less-

ened their impact. He had to compete with new advisers, nota-
bly James Killian, and he no longer had the support of John
Foster Dulles. Equally important, Strauss was now a lame duck.
His five-year term as chairman was due to expire on June 31.
Although the President wanted to reappoint him, Strauss had
handed in his resignation in March. In a letter to Eisenhower,
he explained that he had made too many enemies in Congress
and in the press and that a running feud with Senator Clinton
Anderson, who was scheduled to become chairman of the Joint
Committee on Atomic Energy the following January, made his
reappointment unwise. Reluctantly, the President bowed to this
reasoning and accepted his resignation. Eisenhower still valued
Strauss's friendship and advice, but the Admiral no longer determined administration policy on nuclear matters as he had in
the past.[46]

As Strauss's influence waned, that of James Killian began to
prevail. In his role of presidential adviser on science and technology, he was in a key position to shape policy. He had been
responsible for the creation of the Bethe panel, and in early
April he arranged for an unusual three-day meeting of the
science advisory committee at Ramey Air Force Base in Puerto
Rico. On April 8, 9, and 10, the members of PSAC discussed
the implications of the Bethe panel report in detail and concluded that a test ban would "leave the U.S. in a position of
technical superiority for at least several years." On that basis,
they decided to recommend to the President the negotiation of
"a satisfactory agreement for sustained test cessation as soon as
possible after the completion of the Hardtack tests."[47]

Killian presented this recommendation to President Eisenhower in person on April 17. He explained that his committee had agreed that, while adequate inspection would require
an extensive network of control posts, such a system was "feasible." The members of PSAC believed that test cessation
"would leave the United States in a position of technical advantage for a few years," and Killian added that continued testing
would enable the Soviets to close that gap quickly. Therefore,

Killian said, PSAC recommended that the administration "stop testing after the Hardtack series."

Eisenhower listened quietly to Killian's presentation. He agreed with his science adviser that a similar ban on missile testing would not be in America's interest. When Killian observed that many top officials of the Defense Department and the AEC still opposed a test ban, the President reacted by saying that "he had never been too much impressed, or completely convinced by the views expressed by Drs. Teller, Lawrence and Mills that we must continue testing of nuclear weapons." Killian felt reasonably sure that Eisenhower was in agreement with the scientists' recommendation. At the next meeting of PSAC on April 21, Killian told his colleagues that their views would "receive real attention" despite the opposition of the Pentagon and the AEC. When Isador Rabi asked how this conflict would be resolved, Killian responded, "only by the President, perhaps influenced by Sec. of State."[48]

Eisenhower was leaning toward a test ban, but he was still concerned by the continuing opposition of the NATO allies. On April 23, he told his aides that "the thing hinged around our failure to get our principal allies, Britain and France, to agree to cessation of testing." Secretary Dulles, who apparently felt that England and France would have no choice but to go along with a Soviet-American test ban, now pushed hard for a positive decision. On Saturday, April 26, he met at his home with the four distinguished private citizens who served as his disarmament advisers—General Alfred Gruenther, former NATO commander, Robert Lovett, Secretary of Defense under Truman, General Bedell Smith, Ike's wartime chief-of-staff and later CIA director, and John J. McCloy, who had overseen the postwar occupation of Germany. These men, all of whom had close ties to Eisenhower, agreed with Dulles that the United States should take the initiative in seeking a separate test ban agreement.

The secretary felt that a breakthrough on the technical issue of an inspection system was the best way to proceed. Accordingly, over the weekend he prepared a new letter for Eisenhower to send to Khrushchev that repeated the April 8 proposal for a technical conference to work out details of an inspection system for a future test ban. To make sure the Russians understood that this move was to be a prelude to test ban negotiations, Dulles included the following sentence: "Studies of this kind are the necessary preliminaries to putting political decisions into effect." Once again bypassing both the AEC and the Defense Department, on April 28 Dulles sent this letter out under Eisenhower's signature.[49]

Eisenhower's April 28 letter to Khrushchev marked the reversal of the long-standing American policy that test ban negotiations be linked to other disarmament goals. By proposing technical studies of inspection as a preliminary to test ban talks, without any mention of a cutoff in weapons production, Dulles and Eisenhower had taken a decisive step. "We have agreed to separate testing from production," read a presidential briefing paper on April 30. But out of deference to our allies, as well as opponents within the administration, the President would not announce this decision publicly. He was waiting for Khrushchev to respond. Once the Soviet leader agreed to hold the proposed technical talks, then the United States would be publicly committed to a separate test ban negotiation.[50]

XI

Several factors were responsible for the change in American policy. The creation of the President's Scientific Advisory Committee in the wake of Sputnik certainly influenced the outcome. Eisenhower and Dulles were no longer dependent on Lewis Strauss and his tendency to confine scientific consultation to men like Teller and Lawrence. James Killian brought in a wider range of technical opinion, and by exposing the President and Secretary of State to the views of experts such as Rabi and Bethe, he opened up alternatives that had not been considered before at the top levels of government. "The President now listened primarily to men whose information and judgment of fact indicated that a safeguarded arms-control agreement would be to the advantage of the national interest and security of the United States," concluded one scholar, Saville Davis.[51]

The Soviet Union had an equally important impact on the administration's decision. Whatever the Russian motives, their suspension of testing on March 31 focused world pressure on the United States to reverse its stand on testing. Dulles's shift can be traced far more directly to opinion abroad than to Killian's influence. "Wholly apart from the true merits of the argument," the secretary commented later, "the Russians were winning world opinion, and we were losing it." He told one of his aides that unless the United States followed the Russian lead and stopped testing, "public opinion would ascribe aggressive intent to the United States."[52]

President Eisenhower shared Dulles's concern for the respect of mankind. On May 1, he told the secretary that "unless we took some positive action we were in the future going to be in a position of 'moral isolation' as far as [the] rest of the world is concerned." The President had always had strong reservations about the wisdom of unrestricted nuclear testing. He found the views of Killian and the PSAC congenial, and his own military background made him relatively impervious to the dire warnings of the Pentagon. For Eisenhower, the clinching factor was world opinion. Robert Gilpin, after a careful study of the impact of scientists on the test ban decision, concluded that the President's shift was due to his belief "that the political gain to be derived from a nuclear test ban was greater than the possible military advances the future might hold."[53] Eisenhower did not respond to the often frenzied activities of SANE and the pacifist protests; he realized that the American people were more concerned about national security than fallout. Convinced by scientists that a test ban could be properly monitored, he decided that he could safely satisfy both his own desire for a slowing of the arms race and the world's insistence that the fallout danger be ended.

CHAPTER

8

MORATORIUM

The Eisenhower administration's decision to seek a separate test ban negotiation with the Soviets did not interfere with the HARDTACK series. The nuclear tests began secretly on April 28, 1958; the American people did not learn that they had begun until May 7, when Representative Charles Porter of Oregon, who had gone to the Pacific Proving Grounds in a vain effort to halt the explosions, forced the AEC to reveal that they had started nine days earlier. Chairman Strauss claimed that the secrecy was necessary to prevent the Russians from monitoring the tests. The AEC announced ten additional shots over the next two months, though apparently there were at least ten other explosions that were not disclosed. Several tests designed to develop clean bombs failed to meet the scientists' expectation, but the AEC assured President Eisenhower that none of the detonations had produced an excessive amount of fallout.[1]

Protests over HARDTACK continued through May and June. The White House received a steady stream of letters and petitions objecting to the tests from individuals, pacifist organizations, and church groups. Some California Quakers actually sent the President a collection of vegetables from local supermarkets that they claimed had been contaminated from radioactive rainfall. The collection of celery and asparagus, they wrote, "is a symbol of the increasing danger of the whole world of continued nuclear testing." The Los Angeles SANE committee prepared a television cartoon entitled "This is the Bomb that Jack Built." The 40-second animated commercial ended with the lines, "And this is Jack's child that drank the milk that comes from the cow that eats the grass that stores the fallout that falls from the bomb that Jack built."

Political groups also joined in the protest. At its national convention, Americans for Democratic Action adopted a resolution urging an immediate cessation of all American nuclear tests. Adlai Stevenson, who had remained quiet on this issue since his campaign, told reporters on April 30 that he was "gratified" by the renewed interest in a test ban. "At long last," he commented, "the matter has been pushed up to the top of the pyramid." In June, he told a Michigan State University commencement audience that a halt to testing would help "break the disarmament deadlock." [2]

Pacifists continued to rely on more direct types of protest. In early May, a dozen women began a hunger sit-in at the AEC headquarters building in Germantown, Maryland. Instead of trying to remove them forcefully, Lewis Strauss provided the protesters with cots, and they finally left after a week of fasting. A month later, over 100 pacifists staged a "peace walk" on Washington, coming from Winchester, Virginia, Wilmington, Delaware, and such distant cities as New York and Chicago by car and bus. Led by David Dellinger, they arrived in the nation's capital on June 1. Joined by several hundred local participants, they demonstrated for 90 minutes outside the White House and then held a mass meeting beside the Washington monument at which Linus Pauling called for an immediate end to nuclear testing. [3]

Meanwhile, Albert Bigelow continued with his plans to sail the *Golden Rule* into the Pacific Proving Grounds, risking death from fallout as a way to dramatize opposition to the American tests. Federal judge John Wiig issued a restraining order forbidding the voyage, and when the *Golden Rule* sailed on May 1, a Coast Guard cutter halted the yacht only a mile and a half out of Honolulu harbor. Judge Wiig sentenced Bigelow and his three crewmen to 60 days in jail, then suspended the sentence and placed them on probation. After two more attempts to sail from Hawaii, federal marshalls seized the *Golden Rule* and forced Bigelow and his associates to serve their jail terms. Undaunted, the Quakers sent an appeal to President Eisenhower from their cells in the Honolulu City Jail asking him to halt the HARDTACK tests "in the name of humanity."[4]

I

Khrushchev replied on May 9 to Eisenhower's call for a technical conference on detection. After expressing regret over the American insistence on going ahead with HARDTACK, the Soviet leader agreed that the United States and Russia should "designate experts who would immediately begin a study of methods for detecting possible violations of an agreement on the cessation of nuclear tests." In a White House press release two days later, James Hagerty commented that Khrushchev's May 9 letter "seems to constitute recognition" of the American view that technical studies should be the starting point in "progress toward agreement on disarmament."

The President took a much more positive attitude in a letter to the Soviet premier on May 24. He proposed that the two nations send experts to Geneva in an effort to work out an acceptable inspection system for a future test ban agreement. Eisenhower expressed the hope that the scientists could make a preliminary report within 30 days and reach a final statement within 60. To show the Russians how serious he was, the President announced the names of the three American delegates to this proposed Geneva conference on detection. They were James Brown Fisk, executive vice-president of Bell Telephone Laboratories, Professor Robert Bacher of Cal Tech, and Nobel laureate Ernest O. Lawrence of the University of California at Berkeley.[5]

The composition of the American delegation reflected a deliberate attempt at a balanced point of view. Lawrence was well known as an advocate of nuclear testing who would be skeptical of any agreement with the Soviets. Chairman Strauss had wanted Edward Teller to serve, but his extreme views ruled him out. Lawrence was more acceptable to the scientific community; however, ill health forced him to leave the conference early. Both Bacher and Fisk were members of PSAC. Bacher, a distinguished physicist who had opposed Teller during the 1949–50 controversy over the H-bomb, was known to be favorably inclined toward a test ban. Fisk was regarded as neutral in his political views. Known for his patience and tolerance, he had been the AEC's first director of research after World War II, leaving in 1949 to become an executive at the Bell Laboratories. He had impressed the members of PSAC with his objectivity while serving as Killian's deputy; one colleague observed, "I have never seen a more level-headed scientist." [6]

The three men met in Washington in early June to undergo a cram course on the technical issues involved in detection, particularly in regard to underground tests. None of them was a specialist in seismography; they listened intently as experts from the CIA and the PSAC scientific staff briefed them on the intricacies of determining the differences between underground blasts and earthquakes. As *Newsweek* noted, the feasibility of an adequate detection system "hinges in part on the difference between an earthquake squiggle and a A-bomb wiggle on a seismograph." The administration appointed 15 men to serve as advisers to the American delegation. They included scientists Hans Bethe and Harold Brown, the 29-year-old deputy director of Teller's Livermore Laboratory at Berkeley, representatives of the AEC, the military services, and the CIA, as well as three junior State Department officers.

The three American delegates met with Secretary Dulles to receive political guidance before leaving for Geneva. Dulles, who had failed to appoint a high-level diplomat to advise the delegation, told the press later that this omission was deliberate. "I told them to look upon their job as a purely technical scientific job," Dulles explained. "They are to come to their own conclusions as to what is necessary to detect an explosion."[7]

In retrospect, it appears that Dulles was very naive in his advice. The American delegates were undertaking a diplomatic mission. The whole purpose of the Geneva conference on detection was to determine whether it was possible to reach agreement on a system to inspect a future test ban. The technical conclusions would always be subject to political considerations—how many control stations would the Russians accept, how much freedom would an on-site inspection team have, how small an explosion should the monitoring posts be able to detect to prevent cheating. The Soviets understood the political context of the technical talks; their delegation included Semyon K. Tsarapkin. "Old Scratchy," as the press dubbed him, was a veteran diplomat who had served with the Soviet United Nations delegation since 1947. He had no scientific credentials, and he kept silent during the formal conference sessions at Geneva, but observers were quick to note that he set the official line that his scientific colleagues followed.[8]

In mid-June, with the Geneva conference only two weeks away, the Soviets suddenly announced that they would not attend unless the West expanded the agenda to include negotiation of a test ban itself. When the United States insisted that any decision on test suspension would have to await agreement on a workable inspection system, the Soviets finally backed down. The last minute Soviet maneuvering, however, dimmed the outlook for a successful conference. "The Western delegates," *Time* commented, "arrived in Geneva in a mood of no nonsense, no politics, and not much hope."

II

On June 30, 1958, the day before the Geneva conference opened, Lewis Strauss stepped down as chairman of the AEC. In a farewell news conference, he reiterated his opposition to any halt in nuclear testing. He elaborated on his views in an interview two weeks later. The belief that a test ban would not weaken American security, he warned, was a "false and dangerous assumption." Calling the fallout hazard "negligible," he insisted that the real peril for mankind lay "not in the consequences of testing weapons but in the danger of an atomic war." President Eisenhower disagreed with this view, but he acknowledged his high personal regard for the departing chairman by awarding him the Medal of Freedom.[9]

Eisenhower chose John A. McCone, a wealthy California industrialist, to serve as the new head of the AEC. Known as a hard-driving businessman, McCone was an engineering graduate of the University of California at Berkeley who had thrived in the shipping industry during World War II. Owner of a West Coast shipyard as well as a partner in a large construction firm, he had been active in the Republican party, contributing heavily to Eisenhower's presidential campaigns. His friendship with the President went back to the late 1940s, when McCone had served as a deputy to Secretary of Defense James Forrestal and as Under Secretary of the Air Force in the Truman administration.

The press hailed McCone as a welcome successor to the secretive and stubborn Lewis Strauss. McCone, who took pride in his ability to sell himself and his ideas to others, was expected to mend the strained relations between the AEC and the Joint Committee on Atomic Energy. Senator Clinton Anderson, Strauss's bitter enemy, greeted news of the appointment with a noncommital "not bad," while other members of Congress voiced hopes that the new chairman would be more receptive to the growing pressure for a test ban.

In fact, McCone would continue to uphold the same positions that Strauss had taken within the administration. He held hardline views on the Cold War, having served for years as an influential spokesman for the aircraft and other defense-related industries of southern California. He had been a member of the Finletter Air Policy Commission in 1948 and had shared this body's "peace through air power" concepts. In

1956, he had criticized Stevenson's test ban proposal as "a dangerous procedure," and as a member of the Cal Tech board of trustees, he had publicly attacked members of the faculty for supporting Stevenson's call for a halt to testing. The only real change would be in style. In contrast to the prickly Strauss, McCone had an easy, genial manner and considerable charm, which he used to smooth over the troubled relations between the AEC and Congress. As a result, the Senate confirmed his appointment easily, with the Joint Committee on Atomic Energy failing to probe his views on testing in the one brief hearing held on his nomination.[10]

McCone joined the administration just as the President created a new high-level body to formulate policy on nuclear testing. Called the Committee of Principals, this group consisted of Secretary of State Dulles, CIA Director Allen Dulles, Secretary of Defense Neil McElroy, presidential science adviser James Killian, and McCone. Eisenhower wanted this committee to hammer out the issues and arrive at a consensus on the test ban question, but a rift quickly developed between those who advocated a test ban as a first step toward nuclear disarmament, notably the Dulles brothers and Killian, and those who favored continued testing, primarily McElroy, or more often Deputy Secretary of Defense Donald Quarles, and AEC chairman McCone. The rear guard action that Quarles and McCone fought within the Committee of Principals against a test ban blocked the clear-cut agreement that Eisenhower desired. As a result, for the next two years the administration, lacking a unified policy, was forced to make test ban decisions on a day-to-day basis.[11]

III

The HARDTACK series continued in July as the AEC sought to include as many tests as possible in anticipation of a forthcoming ban. Scientists and technicians worked feverishly to try out every conceivable kind of nuclear weapon—small, relatively clean bombs, new ICBM warhead designs, and an experimental anti-missile missile. In addition to the ten shots in May and June, the AEC announced four more in July. Japanese and Australian scientists reported that additional, unannounced explosions had occurred, and in late July the Soviets claimed that they had detected a total of 32 American detonations, some 18 more than the AEC had acknowledged. The administration refused to confirm the Soviet estimate, but it surprised the press in mid-July by canceling the planned "clean bomb" demonstration for foreign observers. The stated reason, that many of those invited were unable to attend, was only partly true. The AEC was opposed, and both Secretary of State Dulles and President Eisenhower had lost their initial enthusiasm for the idea. At the same White House meeting at which the President agreed to the cancellation, he also overrode an astonishing Pentagon proposal—to conduct tests of the experimental anti-missile missile, complete with an atomic warhead, over the Gulf of Mexico. Secretary Dulles reported that both Cuba and Mexico objected strongly to such a nuclear shot in the Gulf, and after Eisenhower expressed his reservations, spokesmen for the Defense Department agreed to transfer this test to the Pacific.[12]

There was one dramatic attempt to penetrate the curtain that the AEC tried to place around the HARDTACK series. Earle Reynolds, an American anthropologist, was on the last leg of a voyage around the world from Hiroshima in his yacht, the *Phoenix*. He had been in Hawaii when the federal government had arrested Bigelow and seized the *Golden Rule*. Impressed by the courage of the Quakers and sharing their pacifist convictions, Reynolds and his wife changed course for the trip back to Hiroshima to enable them to pass through the Pacific Proving Grounds in the Marshall Islands. When they entered the restricted zone on July 1, the coast guard cutter *Planetree* halted the *Phoenix* and escorted it to the U.S. Navy base on Kwajalein. Reynolds was then flown back to Hawaii, where he was tried and found guilty of violating an AEC regulation. Sentenced to a two-year jail term, Reynolds appealed, and in 1960 the Supreme Court finally overturned the verdict. But at the time, the heavy sentence made him an effective martyr for the test ban cause, leading the *New Republic* to claim that his act of defiance had caused the United States to "suffer a moral defeat in the eyes of much of the world." [13]

HARDTACK concluded with two spectacular high altitude tests of anti-missile missiles conducted at Johnston Island, only 540 miles southwest of Hawaii. The first shot, an atomic warhead detonated at an altitude of about 100 miles, came without any advance notice shortly after midnight on August 1. A brilliant flash lit up the sky over the Hawaiian Islands, causing stunned citizens to flood police switchboards with nervous telephone calls. The AEC assured worried Hawaiians there was no danger and notified officials of a second experiment scheduled for August 12. The people of Hawaii took the AEC at its word. They greeted the second high altitude blast in a festive mood, holding bomb parties and crowding the beaches and waterfront streets to watch the dazzling sight.

The second anti-missile missile test high over Johnston Island concluded the HARDTACK series. Officially the AEC admitted to a total of 16 shots, but privately American scientists indicated that the Soviet claim of 18 additional tests was probably correct. Whichever figure one accepts, the AEC assertion of 16 or the Soviet estimate of 34, HARDTACK was by far the most extensive American thermonuclear series ever conducted. In 1954, there had been only 6 shots in the CASTLE series which had included BRAVO; in 1956, REDWING consisted of 6 announced tests and 4 more secret ones. The hectic pace of testing in 1958 confirmed the growing belief that the administration was ready to negotiate a test ban agreement. HARDTACK was thus seen as a final effort to develop every conceivable nuclear weapon that the military might want in the future.[14]

IV

The long-awaited report of the United Nations Committee on the Effects of Atomic Radiation appeared on August 10, 1958.

Its findings confirmed the 1956 report sponsored by the National Academy of Sciences and the consensus reached by scientists testifying at the Holifield subcommittee hearings in 1957. The fifteen scientists from around the world stated that they found it very difficult to analyze the precise effect of bomb fallout on human health. They agreed that the amount of fallout so far was slight, estimating it to be only 5 per cent of the total radiation mankind received from natural sources. The report was especially vague on somatic effects, stating that they "are still largely unknown." The committee assumed that there was no threshold below which radiation was safe, but the members estimated that present levels of fallout would only cause between 400 and 2000 additional deaths from leukemia a year, compared to a worldwide total of 150,000 annually. They were more certain of a harmful genetic effect, yet they admitted that it could not be measured "with any accuracy."

Despite the vagueness of their data, the scientists did stress the danger of fallout for mankind. "Even the smallest amounts of radiation," the report stated, "are likely to cause deleterious genetic, and perhaps also somatic, effects." The committee pointed out the long-run nature of the hazards, cautioning that "even a small rise in the environmental radioactivity in the world . . . might eventually cause appreciable damage to large populations."

The Soviet representative had tried to include a call for the immediate suspension of all nuclear testing. Shields Warren, the American delegate, had opposed this move as a political rather than a scientific judgment, and the committee had voted 9 to 5 to omit such a statement from the final report. The members did agree, however, to include a sentence urging nations to "take all steps designed to minimize the irradiation of human populations," such as excessive medical and dental X-rays, improper disposal of atomic wastes, and "explosions of nuclear weapons."[15]

Both advocates and critics of nuclear testing found the report encouraging. The AEC issued a statement claiming that the UN committee had vindicated its assertions that fallout did not cause a sharp rise in either bone cancer or leukemia. Representative Carl Durham, chairman of the Joint Committee on Atomic Energy, said that he could not find anything in the report "that had not been previously reported by our own committee." The *New York Times* was ambivalent. The editors admitted that the UN document "had intensified the growing psychological pressures" for a ban on testing, but they urged people to weigh the danger from fallout "against the hazards of not testing," which could "deprive the West of its most effective weapons and deterrent to war." On the other hand, test ban advocates rejoiced. Clinton Anderson claimed that the UN committee had destroyed "the pet theories" of the AEC; Hubert Humphrey commented that the report showed that "we are like children playing with dynamite." Though SANE felt that the report had not gone far enough, Norman Cousins was delighted. "Because of this report," he wrote, "the controversy over fallout can now be put to rest." No longer would anyone be able to claim that the resulting radioactivity was harmless to mankind.[16]

Cousins was mistaken. Only a month later, Miriam P. Finkel, a researcher at the AEC-supported Argonne National Laboratory in Illinois, reported on an experiment with mice that suggested the existence of a threshold for radiation effects. Writing in *Science,* Finkel stated that she had exposed groups of 150 mice to both low and high levels of strontium-90. The heavy exposure confirmed the expected results, a shortening of life expectancy and development of both bone cancer and leukemia. But the group given the low dose did not display these effects, leading Finkel to contend that there was a threshold below which radiation was not harmful to mice, nor presumably, to man. She estimated that the threshold for human beings was in the vicinity of 10 millicuries, more than a hundred times as high as the existing maximum permissible concentration and over a thousand times greater than existing levels of Sr^{90} in human bone. On this basis, she concluded that the total fallout to date was "unlikely to induce even one bone tumor or one case of leukemia."

Finkel's study attracted national attention. The *New York Times* summarized it on the front page under the headline, "Cancer Peril Denied in Present Fall-out." Linus Pauling quickly challenged Finkel's findings in a joint study with Cal Tech colleague Barclay Kamb. Subjecting Finkel's data to statistical analysis, they reported in a letter to the editor of the *New York Times* that her conclusions were "completely unjustified." To disprove the linearity concept, Pauling and Kamb argued, one would need to experiment with "at least as many mice as the world's human population, instead of only 150 mice per group." Miriam Finkel sent a rebuttal to the *Times* two weeks later in which she charged that Pauling and Kamb were motivated by political, not scientific, considerations. She defended her calculations and warned the public against accepting "far-fetched, tenuous predictions concerning the health of a certain small proportion of the world population."[17]

Finkel received support from other segments of the scientific community. Austin M. Brues, director of research at Argonne, published an article in *Science* in September 1958 arguing that the theory of linearity remained undocumented. There was no evidence of the effect of radiation below 100r on human beings to sustain the concept that the incidence of leukemia was directly proportional to radiation exposure at any level. Six months later, the committee which had written the section of the National Academy of Science report on somatic effects issued a statement challenging the assumption in the UN Scientific Committee's report that a threshold did not exist. Citing the Finkel study, the panel concluded, "We note that there is a considerable body of experimental evidence favoring nonlinearity in specific instances."

Those who had hoped, like Cousins, that the UN report would end the fallout debate were disappointed to find the controversy still raging. The problem was inherent in the lack of data on the effects of radiation on human beings at the extremely low levels of existing fallout. No one could demonstrate that the bomb tests posed a grave danger to mankind, yet at the same time no conscientious scientist could rule out serious long-term effects if testing continued indefinitely. Dag Hammarskjold, aware of the inconclusive nature of the Scientific Committee's report, suggested that this group be made a permanent body within the UN. After considerable debate, the General Assembly finally voted to extend the life of the committee for another year, authorizing it to continue its investigation in the hope that the scientists would arrive at a more precise definition of the fallout danger.[18]

V

The Geneva conference of experts began on July 1 as scheduled. The Western delegation, which included British and Canadian representatives, found their Soviet counterparts ready to discuss the formidable scientific issues frankly. Reporters who attended the opening session were disappointed; the negotiations would take place behind closed doors. Interpreters spoke of the blackboards filled with mathematical formulas; they commented on how difficult it was "to break down linguistic barriers between Nobel prize-winners in physics." As the press turned its attention elsewhere, the delegates settled down to their technical exchanges in relative obscurity.[19]

The experts continued their deliberations all through July and into August. They gradually reached agreement on the four technical methods for detecting nuclear tests—recording acoustical waves, measuring electromagnetic waves, collecting radioactive debris, and examining seismic signals. The first three methods required little elaboration, but the difficulty in distinguishing between earthquakes and underground nuclear explosions occasioned considerable debate, with the Soviets tending to minimize the problem. They finally accepted the

American concept of first motion, based on the RANIER data, as the best way to tell a man-made blast from a natural movement of the earth.

The real debate came over the size of the proposed inspection system. The Soviet delegation suggested a relatively small network of 110 stations spaced across the world. American scientists quickly calculated that such a system, while reasonably effective in detecting atmospheric explosions, would not be able to distinguish between earthquakes and nuclear explosions as large as 20 kilotons. Harold Brown, with the assistance of Richard Latter of RAND, designed a much more extensive system of 650 stations which had the capability of detecting both atmospheric and subsurface blasts down to a threshold of one kiloton. The Russians, appalled at the idea of as many as 100 control posts on their soil, rejected the American proposal on political grounds. At this point, the British representative offered a compromise—a network of 170 land stations, supplemented by as many as 10 shipboard posts, with a capability of detecting atmospheric blasts down to 1 kiloton and 90 per cent of all underground explosions above 5 kilotons. Delegates from the three nations then accepted this proposal with the idea that mobile teams would conduct on-site inspections of suspicious seismic events, estimated by the Soviets at no more than 20 a year and by the Americans at about 100.

On August 21, the Geneva conference of experts adopted its final report. In careful language, the document stated that the experts concluded that "it was technically feasible" to create "a workable and effective control system to detect violations of an agreement on the worldwide suspension of nuclear weapons tests." The report specified a network of 100 to 110 control posts on the world's continents and 60 stations on islands, supplemented by "about 10" additional shipboard posts. The spacing of the stations would vary from 1000 kilometers on land to 3500 kilometers at sea, with the densest concentration in areas of high earthquake incidence.

The report of the experts was vague on two crucial issues. It did not deal with the question of the make-up of the teams that would man the posts, beyond stating that each would consist of about 30 technicians. The question of the nationality of the controllers was left completely hanging. Nor did the report specify who would determine when an on-site inspection of a suspicious underground event would be made. The document simply said that in such cases, "the international control organ can send an inspection group to the site," without listing any criteria for making this decision. Given the report's assumption that there would be between 20 and 100 such occasions annually, the lack of precise language indicated a serious weakness in the Geneva document.

Indeed, the statement that the experts had determined that it was "technically feasible" to monitor a test ban created the false impression that the problem of detection had been solved. The text of the report itself noted that the network would be unable to identify underground blasts under 5 kilotons, a serious limitation when one recalls that RANIER had only registered 1.7 kilotons. Nor could the Geneva posts detect high altitude shots above 50 kilometers nor those in outer space. The experts did deal with the crucial issue of possible evasive tactics by a violator, noting that it would be difficult to detect "a carefully concealed deep underground explosion." They decided, however, that the risk of detection under the proposed system would be great enough to deter a nation from testing secretly.[20]

Despite these gaps in the report, the American reaction was one of confidence that a test ban was now possible. The *New York Times* called the Geneva conference "one of the most positive steps toward disarmament made in more than a decade of East-West negotiations" and urged the diplomats to take up "where the scientists left off." Norman Cousins agreed, claiming it was now time for the United States to see if the Russians were sincere in calling for a test ban. "We are now in a position to test the Russians instead of the bombs," he wrote. President Eisenhower was a little more cautious when reporters probed for his views. He called the progress at Geneva "encouraging," and added that it "gives grounds to hope that you can go another step." He reiterated his devotion to the cause of disarmament, saying "that is what we have been working on these 5 years."[21]

In fact, at the time that Eisenhower uttered these words on August 20, he had already authorized the State Department to enter into test ban negotiations with the Soviet Union. As early as August 4, when Killian reported on the progress being made at Geneva, the President had expressed his support for a test cessation. He told Killian that "if full technical agreement is reached, the weight of argument for doing so would be very great." Eisenhower then ordered the Committee of Principals to draw up a "plan of action" to implement the expected favorable outcome of the Geneva meeting. Despite strong objections from John McCone and JCS chairman Nathan Twining, the Committee of Principals drafted a statement that embodied the President's wishes.

The NATO allies remained the final obstacle. Charles de Gaulle, who had come back to power in France in the spring of 1958, was committed to acquiring nuclear weapons and therefore opposed any limitation on testing. Dulles and Eisenhower decided to ignore the French objections to test ban negotiations, but they hoped to win British approval. When Prime Minister Macmillan was informed of the probable change in American policy, he protested strongly, pointing out that Britain planned a new series of tests in the early fall. The administration suggested that the suspension could be delayed until the tests were completed, but Macmillan was still not satisfied. "It would be a mistake," he wrote to Eisenhower on August 21, "to concede suspension without securing Russian acceptance of an international control system." The President remained adamant. He impressed Macmillan with his personal commitment to a test ban and his belief that the moment for action was "psychologically correct." The Prime Minister finally decided to defer to the American position.[22]

The President announced the new policy in a statement issued in Washington on the afternoon of August 22; Ambassador Llewellyn Thompson delivered an identical message to the Kremlin at the same time. Eisenhower began by repeating the finding of the Geneva experts that detection of nuclear tests was "technically feasible." Therefore, the United States suggested that the nations possessing nuclear weapons begin negotiations on October 31 in New York for a ban on testing and the creation of an international control system. As a sign of American good faith, the President offered to suspend U.S. tests for one year, provided that Russia did not test during that interval. Furthermore, the United States was prepared to renew the proposed test suspension annually on two conditions—establishment of the inspection network and "satisfactory progress" toward actual nuclear disarmament.

The President made it clear that he did not consider a test ban a panacea. Rather, it was to be a first step toward "more substantial agreements relating to limitation and reduction of fissionable material for weapons." Observers noted how favorable the timing was for the United States. The AEC had just completed the comprehensive HARDTACK series which assured the Pentagon of at least a temporary lead over the Soviets in the development of the latest nuclear weapons. In this sense, the August 22 offer for test ban negotiations accompanied by a moratorium was a belated reply to the March 31 Soviet suspension. Each superpower waited until it completed its current series before offering a halt to testing.[23]

Despite the timing, Nikita Khrushchev responded promptly to the American offer. On August 29, *Pravda* carried an interview with the Russian leader in which he criticized "the reservations and manifestly far-fetched conditions" which Eisenhower had laid down. Nevertheless, he indicated that his government was ready to enter into test ban negotiations on October 31, insisting only that the location be changed from New York to Geneva. The next day, the Soviet government sent a formal reply embodying the points Khrushchev had made. The United States agreed to Geneva as the site for the talks, but

American officials remained puzzled over the Russian position on the 12-month test moratorium. Khrushchev had not agreed to this provision and had instead indicated that the Soviets might resume testing at any time.[24]

The confusion surrounding the forthcoming test ban talks did not stem the rejoicing within SANE. Its leaders sent a telegram to the President on August 22 praising him for his "wise and courageous action." The chairman of the Los Angeles chapter, noting that Edward Teller had recently resigned from the AEC general advisory committee, expressed his delight at the new turn of events: "H-bomb testing is suspended! Teller is out of the AEC! Admiral S. out of the AEC!" Norman Cousins called Eisenhower's statement "historic news indeed," and the national office of SANE claimed that "the stage is now set for important and dramatic moves looking toward agreement for permanent cessation of tests."[25]

Critics of a test ban found the President's action regrettable. Hanson Baldwin, *New York Times* military commentator, saluted those "informed and conscientious officials" within the administration who had fought against suspension. Such a step, Baldwin wrote, "would provide the form of arms limitation without the substance." The most influential dissent came from Henry Kissinger. Writing in *Foreign Affairs,* the Harvard professor feared that a test ban would be a first step in "an increased campaign to outlaw nuclear weapons altogether." Pointing to the substantial Soviet advantage in conventional forces, he warned against any policy that might lead to lessening Western reliance on nuclear deterrence. Instead, the United States needed to continue testing to perfect "nuclear weapons of finer discrimination, less destructive power and greater reduced fallout," Kissinger argued. The world concern over radiation could be alleviated, he concluded, by an agreement to limit the megatonnage of atmospheric tests and to insist on holding future experiments either underground or in outer space.[26]

Test ban opponents blamed the presidents move on world

opinion. They felt that the successful outcome of the conference of experts on detection, coupled with the vague warnings of the UN Scientific Committee's fallout report, led Eisenhower to overrule the AEC and the Pentagon. Yet these critics failed to note the steady shift of administration policy away from the rigid insistence on prior agreement for a cutoff in nuclear weapons production as a condition for a halt to testing. The August 22 statement was the logical culmination of a policy that had been developing through the year, not a sudden change imposed by events in the summer of 1958.

Eisenhower remained the key actor in the drama. In his own characteristically indirect way, he had presided over the change from viewing a test ban as purely a Soviet propaganda ploy to accepting it as a logical first step toward genuine nuclear disarmament. As he explained at his press conference on August 27, the administration had never abandoned its ultimate quest for a halt to the production of fissionable material. The conditions he had laid down on August 22 still meant that "the cesation of tests must be related to the cessation of production of this material for weapons production." The two men who had tried to resist the new policy testified to Eisenhower's intense personal commitment. Harold Macmillan observed in his memoirs that Ike was "unusually excited" about his plans for a test moratorium. And John McCone later recalled the President telling him that his responsibilities compelled him "to take some risk" in order to "do away with atmospheric testing, thus eliminating the health hazard, and at the same time . . . slow down the arms race."[27]

VI

Ironically, the American call for a moratorium beginning October 31 led to a last-minute rash of testing by all three nuclear powers. Great Britain began its series on August 22, the very day Eisenhower made his proposal, with a low yield shot at Christmas Island. Three more followed in September, including two thermonuclear blasts in the megaton range. The United States announced a series of ten small atomic tests at its Nevada Proving Ground on August 29. This series, officially named HARDTACK II but called "Operation Deadline" by the press, had originally been scheduled for the spring of 1959. AEC Chairman McCone and Defense Secretary McElroy stated that the purpose was to try out some small tactical weapons as well as to experiment further with underground explosions.[28]

HARDTACK II began on September 12 at Yucca Flats, 90 miles northwest of Las Vegas. Over the next six weeks, the AEC set off 19 separate explosions, including four subsurface blasts. Eight of the tests were under 100 tons, the smallest ever conducted by the United States, and including a nuclear bazooka shell designed to be fired by two men at a range of less than two miles. There were four underground tests that varied from a fraction of a kiloton up to nearly 20. The last, code-named BLANCA, was so powerful that it burst the surface, allowing a small amount of radioactive dust to escape into the atmosphere. Despite this unforeseen development, the AEC was pleased with the results of the underground tests; McCone indicated that in the future his agency would be content to conduct all its tests below the earth's surface in order to eliminate the fallout hazard.

The pace increased noticeably as the October 31 deadline grew near. On October 23, the AEC tested three weapons in one day. Two more shots came on October 26, and the last three took place on October 30. In the attempt to get in as many tests as possible, the AEC grew careless. A wind shift blew radioactive clouds toward Los Angeles in late October, raising the radiation level in the city's atmosphere to 120 times the normal amount. "FALLOUT RISE HERE SETS OFF PANIC," read the *Los Angeles Mirror-News* headline on October 30; Mayor Norris Poulson called Washington to ask the AEC to cancel the final U.S. tests. Though the Los Angeles readings were the highest ever recorded in the continental United States outside the test grounds, the AEC claimed the level was "harmless" and continued the series. President Eisenhower did cancel a final shot scheduled for the evening of October 30, but he did so for fear of passing the deadline, not out of concern over fallout. The atmospheric readings soon returned to normal in Los Angeles, but as one scientist pointed out: "Radiation is a cumulative thing. What happens today we always have with us."[29]

The Soviet Union broke its own self-imposed moratorium on testing on September 30 with a series that proved far dirtier than HARDTACK II. Over the next 30 days, the Russians detonated 14 nuclear weapons, nearly all in the megaton range, at their proving grounds on the Barents Sea, north of the Arctic Circle. These huge explosions released vast quantities of radioactive material that would cause heavy fallout across the northern hemisphere for the next six months.

The Eisenhower administration contended that the Russian tests proved the hollowness of the March 31 unilateral suspension. Claiming that it took several months to prepare for a test series, State Department spokesmen charged that the Russians had planned to resume testing all along; they simply exploited the normal pause between tests for propaganda purposes. Andrei Gromyko, the Soviet foreign minister, replied that Russia was determined to catch up with the West in nuclear testing, implying that the Kremlin might conduct as many tests as the United States had held since March 31—more than 40 by his count.[30]

It is difficult to make generalizations about Soviet motives, but the slight evidence available suggests that the Russian leaders may well have acted out of fear that HARDTACK I and II were giving the United States an undue advantage. Andrei D. Sakharov, the physicist most responsible for developing the Russian H-bomb, had become convinced by Pauling and Schweitzer's protests that further testing would be dangerous to mankind. When he learned that the Kremlin planned to resume testing, he objected, sending a colleague, I. V. Kurchatov, to plead personally with Khrushchev to cancel the fall series. In his oral memoir, the Soviet leader claims that he rejected the protest purely on grounds of national self-interest. Continued testing by the United States and Great Britain left him no choice, Khrushchev recalls telling Sakharov and Kurchatov. "For me to cancel the tests would be a crime against our state," he told them. Citing the suffering Russia experienced in World War II, Khrushchev remembers saying, "We can't risk the lives of our people again by giving our adversary a free hand to develop new means of destruction." Thus in Russia, as in the United States, the logic of the arms race led to the same conclusion—cram in as many nuclear tests as possible before the moratorium took effect.[31]

VII

The two superpowers engaged in a series of diplomatic exchanges during the last-minute test barrage in the early fall of 1958. The Soviets repeatedly refused to state definitely whether or not they would stop testing by October 31, the date the Geneva Conference was to begin. Instead, the Kremlin pursued a war of nerves.

The first Russian move came at the opening of the UN General Assembly meeting in New York in mid-September. To the astonishment of the American delegation, Valerian Zorin introduced a resolution that called for an immediate suspension of all nuclear tests without any mention of an inspection system. When Henry Cabot Lodge accused the Soviets of "bad faith" in raising the test ban issue at the UN prior to the Geneva conference, Zorin calmly replied that the American conditions for a test suspension were "impossible." After India put forth a resolution proposing a temporary test ban pending the outcome of the Geneva negotiations, Lodge arranged for a 17-nation resolution that linked a test ban to the Geneva talks. The Western proposal stated that all nations should refrain from testing during the forthcoming conference, thus in effect suggesting a UN sanction for Eisenhower's proposed moratorium.

In the debate that ensued, Lodge stressed the American view that a test ban was not an end in itself, but rather only the first step toward genuine disarmament. However, he admitted that it was a vital beginning. "Let us turn the corner toward a relaxation of the present tension and danger," he pleaded. "The survival of civilization is at stake." At the same time, Lodge criticized the Soviets for their failure to state whether or not they would observe the test moratorium on October 31. Accusing the Soviets of being "totally and monumentally silent on this point," Lodge asked, "Will the Soviet Union stop? We would like to have a clear answer to that."

The numerical majority the West enjoyed in the UN proved more decisive than Lodge's rhetoric. The General Assembly voted down both the Soviet and Indian test ban resolutions, and instead adopted the 17-nation call for a moratorium to accompany the Geneva conference, along with a milder resolution which simply expressed hope that the talks would be successful.[32]

Undaunted by this setback, the Soviets continued their diplomatic offensive against the United States. In early October, Gromyko proposed that he and Dulles attend the Geneva conference in person, rather than appointing subordinates. Aware that the Russians were pushing for early agreement on a test ban at the expense of a detailed inspection system, Dulles politely declined the Russian proposal. Claiming that he was "not versed" in the technical subjects to be discussed at Geneva, the secretary added that he would attend, "If I felt my presence was necessary or helpful to assure the success of that conference."

On October 25, the President named a 25-man delegation headed by James Wadsworth, the deputy ambassador to the UN who had succeeded Stassen as America's chief disarmament negotiator earlier in the year. Robert Bacher, who had been a delegate to the conference on detection, was named Wadsworth's deputy. The remaining members of the American delegation included representatives of the State Department, the Pentagon, the AEC, and the PSAC. Senators Albert Gore, Democrat of Tennessee, and Bourke B. Hickenlooper, Republican of Iowa, attended as congressional advisers, with Hubert Humphrey as an alternate. The Soviets appointed Semyon K. Tsarapkin as their chief delegate, making it clear that diplomatic considerations would prevail over scientific ones in this negotiation. David Ormsby-Gore headed the separate British delegation.

When he announced the American contingent on October 25, Eisenhower noted that the Soviets had not yet indicated whether they would stop testing by October 31. Stating that both the United States and Britain had agreed to the moratorium, the President expressed "regret" that the Soviets had not yet done so. When the Russians announced that they might continue testing after October 31, Dulles replied that if they failed to observe the moratorium, then the United States would also feel free to resume testing. The secretary, however, did not make test cessation a condition for the forthcoming Geneva conference. He told the press on October 28 that the American delegation would attend the opening session regardless of Soviet action on testing.[33]

The outlook for a test ban agreement was quite gloomy on the eve of the Geneva conference. The United States and Great Britain both stopped testing, but there was no sign of similar Russian restraint. James Wadsworth expressed the prevailing mood when a reporter asked him how long he expected the conference to last. "It could wind up in a few weeks," he replied, "or it could blow up right away if the Russians get tough. I hope somebody wishes us luck. We'll need it."

SANE obliged by arranging for 19 world leaders, including Albert Schweitzer, Gunnar Myrdal, Bertrand Russell, and Eleanor Roosevelt, to address an appeal to "the men at Geneva." Published as a full-page ad in the *New York Times,* the petition stressed both the fallout danger and the problem of nuclear proliferation and concluded with the statement: "Today is a day that could make a historic beginning in controlling the new power and in safeguarding those fragile conditions on this earth that make human life possible."

The Conference on the Discontinuance of Nuclear Weapons Tests, as it was officially called, opened at 3 P.M. on October 31 at the Palace of Nations in Geneva. The opposing sides immediately deadlocked on the agenda. The Russians insisted that the conference begin by reaching agreement on a ban on all nuclear weapons tests; the United States and Great Britain countered with the demand that the control system be the first order of business. The impasse was familiar; the Soviets focused on disarmament while the West stressed inspection. What Tsarapkin wanted, said one observer, was for the nations "to sign now and negotiate later."[34]

A far more serious development nearly ended the conference in its first week. On November 7, President Eisenhower announced that the United States had detected two Soviet nuclear tests after the moratorium, on November 1 and 3. "This action by the Soviet Union," the President stated, "relieves the United States from any obligation under its offer to suspend nuclear weapons tests." But in hopes that the Kremlin would reconsider, Eisenhower said that the United States would continue to refrain from testing if "the Soviet Union will also do so."

Secretary Dulles elaborated on the Russian action at his press conference later that day. He said the tests were relatively low in yield and had taken place in southern Siberia, not at the usual location north of the Arctic Circle. He conceded that the Russians made no effort to conceal the tests and speculated that they may have simply wanted to try out one last weapon before joining in the moratorium. The secretary was careful to explain that the Soviets had not violated any agreement, pointing out that they had never committed themselves to observe the American moratorium. The Kremlin, he added, would still have to "accept the consequences" which Dulles listed as "worldwide condemnation" and a possible resumption of testing by the United States.

The Soviets did not conduct any tests after the November 3rd shot, at least none detected by the AEC. Observers disagreed on the motives for the final Russian explosions. Some agreed with Dulles that it was a last effort to experiment with a new weapon; one commentator suggested that the lack of concealment indicated that the tests represented a final move in the Soviet war of nerves, intended only for its "psychological impact on the West."

Whatever the explanation, the Soviet Union suddenly ended its intransigent position at Geneva in mid-November by dropping the demand for the immediate signing of a test ban treaty. The Russian, American, and British delegates settled down to the long and laborious task of preparing a draft test ban treaty article-by-article. Implicit in this procedure was the Western insistence that details of a control system must precede a test ban agreement. But at the same time, the Soviets could take comfort in having achieved their long sought goal of unsupervised test suspension. As *Time* pointed out, the Eisenhower administration had done what it had always claimed it would never do, "stopped its own tests primarily on good faith, without any provision for inspection." [35]

VIII

While the negotiations at Geneva continued, the world experienced the first deliberate respite in testing since the nuclear era began in 1945. In the years since Hiroshima, there had been at least 190 atomic and hydrogen bomb tests: 125 by the United States, 44 by the Soviet Union, and 21 by Great Britain. Even though the tests stopped in the fall, 1958 witnessed the largest number ever conducted in one year. The three nuclear powers had admitted to 63 tests since January 1, nearly half as many as in the entire period since 1945. The Soviets detonated more bombs in October than in all of 1957; the American test total, if expanded to include 18 unannounced blasts, was greater in 1958 than the sum of all Russian tests detected by the AEC since 1949. Thus, the moratorium came only after an orgy of testing with each detonation scattering deadly fission products across the world.[36]

The halt in testing did not stop the debate within the administration. John McCone, in a public statement on October 29, declared that the AEC was ready to resume testing at a moment's notice. He openly regretted the moratorium and stated his agency's belief that additional tests were needed to perfect new weapons, especially the desired "clean" bomb. Norman Cousins was incredulous, claiming that every time the administration was ready to stop testing, "some spokesman from the AEC steps forward and holds before us the golden vision of a 'clean' bomb as though this were the ultimate in human refinement." An anonymous member of the PSAC, exhausted by the running debate with testing enthusiasts, put it differently. "These men who don't want a test moratorium are like a kid you are trying to put to bed," he said. "First he wants a drink of water and then he wants to go to the bathroom, but what he really wants is not to go to bed."[37]

The continued resistance to a test ban boded ill for the Geneva negotiations. So did the pessimistic analysis of Eugene Rabinowich. Skeptical of the test ban as a panacea favored by his fellow scientists, Rabinowich warned that cessation, while psychologically helpful, in itself was of "little importance." A test ban would not remove a single weapon from the world's nuclear stockpile, he commented, and the "first step" symbolism seemed misguided to him. "The psychological relief caused by the stopping of tests will wear off," he predicted, "and give place to the realization that the world is still where it was before—a house divided, with nations jealously maintaining their capacity for mutual destruction."[38]

One does not have to accept Rabinowich's belief in world government as the ultimate solution to appreciate his shrewd estimate of the moratorium's significance. The temporary halt in testing spared the world whatever hazard fallout posed for human health; it did not, however, mean that mankind was any closer to ending the nuclear arms race.

CHAPTER

9

DETECTION

Nothing seemed to go right for the Eisenhower administration in 1958. The Cold War became more intense than ever as crises developed in Latin America, the Middle East, Asia, and Europe. The first scare had come in the spring, when Vice President Richard Nixon encountered hostile crowds during a goodwill tour of South America. In Lima, anti-American demonstrators pounded his car with stones; in Caracas two days later, his life was endangered as protesters surrounded and rocked his limousine. Nixon finally escaped unharmed, but the incident served as a grim reminder of the hatred for the United States which flourished within the Western hemisphere. In July, the threat of civil war in Lebanon led Eisenhower to send nearly 15,000 American troops into that country. There was no resistance, and when the competing factions worked out a compromise in the early fall, the President quickly withdrew the U.S. forces.

Two older Cold War battlegrounds suddenly became active again later in 1958, causing even greater concern in Washington. In August, the Communist Chinese began shelling the offshore islands of Quemoy and Matsu, scene of an earlier confrontation in 1955. The United States supplied Chiang Kai-shek's Nationalist garrisons on the beleaguered islands, and after a stiff warning from Eisenhower, Peking gradually eased its harrassment. Then on November 10, Nikita Khrushchev focused attention on Europe by announcing that the Soviet Union planned to sign a peace treaty with East Germany renouncing Russian occupation rights in Berlin. Such a move would threaten the American presence in the city and could well lead to a situation even more dangerous than the 1948 blockade. Despite a strong Western response, Khrushchev declared on November 27 that the future of Berlin must be settled within six months. He proposed high level negotiations with the Western powers to determine the fate of West Berlin, but he warned that if no progress had been made by May, the Soviet Union would reach its own solution with East Germany.

These successive foreign crises were compounded by serious problems at home. A recession that began in late 1957 led to a sharp drop in industrial production and the highest rate of unemployment since the depression of the 1930s. The Democrats exploited this temporary downturn in the economy to win a landslide victory in the fall congressional elections; they picked up 47 seats in the House and 13 more in the Senate to give them commanding majorities in both branches of Congress.

For President Eisenhower, two personal developments hurt even more. In September, he was compelled to accept the resignation of Sherman Adams, who had been his chief White House assistant for six years. Adams had unwisely accepted gifts from Boston businessman Bernard Goldfine, including a vicuña coat, at a time when Goldfine had important matters pending before federal regulatory bodies. The President tried to ignore the storm of protest against Adams, admitting at one time simply, "I need him," but finally the pressure became too intense and Eisenhower let Adams go. Three months later, the other man on whom Ike depended heavily, Secretary of State John Foster Dulles, was suddenly hospitalized. At first, doctors found no further trace of the abdominal cancer they had removed in 1956, attributing the Secretary's intense pain to an inguinal hernia. But an operation in February revealed several malignant growths which indicated that Dulles had only a few more months to live. With remarkable courage, he stayed in office until mid-April, but more and more Ike had to rely on his eventual successor, Under Secretary of State Christian Herter. Despite considerable experience in foreign affairs, Herter lacked Dulles's dominant personality, and he never was able to establish the close rapport with the President that had been the true source of Eisenhower's confidence in Dulles.[1]

The course of the test ban conference in Geneva did little to dispel the gloom in Washington in the fall of 1958. After the initial deadlock over the agenda had been resolved, the delegates began the tedious task of hammering out a draft treaty. A steady stream of disagreements led to a constant struggle between the two negotiators for the Soviet Union and the United States. Both were tall men, but where Tsarapkin was lean and craggy, with what one reporter described as "a broodingly bent walk," Wadsworth was heavy, with a big man's genial and expansive manner disguising a shrewd negotiating style. They came to respect each other, and though they clashed repeatedly, they avoided excessive rhetoric and emotional outbursts.

Two issues quickly blocked rapid progress. The first was the power of the seven-member control commission which would be in charge of the 180-post inspection system. Tsarapkin insisted that the principle of "mutual consent" should govern the commission's actions and that therefore no on-site inspection should take place without the approval of the nation whose territory was involved. Wadsworth objected immediately to what amounted to a veto power, claiming that only the assurance that there could be no obstruction to on-site visits would give the control system the necessary reliability. The other dispute came over the nationality of the technicians at each of the 180 posts. The United States and Great Britain insisted on mixed teams, with equal representation for the Soviets, the West, and neutral members. Tsarapkin, on the other hand, argued for nearly total domination by the host country. Thus he wanted at least 28 of the 30 members of a control team on Russian soil to be Soviet citizens. Such a procedure, which amounted virtually to self-enforcement, was totally unacceptable to the West.[2]

The Soviet bargaining tactics quickly convinced Senator Albert Gore, attending the conference as a representative of Congress, that there was no hope for a comprehensive test ban treaty. Relying on the advice of former AEC member Thomas Murray, who served as a technical expert for the Democratic members of the Joint Committee on Atomic Energy, Gore came forth with a new proposal, which he presented to President Eisenhower on November 17. Claiming that "Russia has been whaling us over the head" with the fallout issue, Gore proposed that the United States unilaterally suspend all atmospheric tests for three years. This would deny the Soviets their propaganda advantage on the radiation issue while permitting the United States to continue vital weapons development underground. Gore was certain that world opinion would force the Soviets to join the U.S. in refraining from testing in the atmosphere; meanwhile, negotiations for a comprehensive test ban, which the senator felt would take several years, could proceed at Geneva.

The President was intrigued by Gore's suggestion, and he asked for a more detailed memorandum on it. The senator repeated the same arguments in a document he sent Eisenhower on November 19. His proposal, he claimed, would permit the United States to blunt "Russia's most powerful propaganda weapon against us" by ending the fallout issue; at the same time the military could perfect the latest nuclear weapons through underground tests. Neither the President nor Secretary of State Dulles would commit himself on the merits of Gore's proposal, but both indicated that it had promise as a fallback position if the Geneva talks failed to achieve progress.[3]

The test ban conference recessed for two weeks over the Christmas holidays. The opposing sides remained as far apart as ever on such issues as the veto and the composition of control teams. Some observers began to see Gore's proposal as an increasingly attractive alternative, but test ban advocates refused to consider such a compromise. A SANE officer described the atmospheric test ban as representing "barbarian outbursts" by Gore and Murray, while the prestigious American Association for the Advancement of Science adopted a resolution expressing the "profound hope" that the Geneva conference would result in a treaty settling a question "which, literally, involves the survival of civilization." Senator Gore was equally adamant against any treaty embodying substantial concessions to the Soviets. "I believe no agreement at all," he wrote, "would be preferable to one which might seriously compromise the security of the United States."

President Eisenhower remained genuinely perplexed. Killian explained to members of the Science Advisory Committee in mid-December the President's deep concern over the disarmament deadlock. In particular, Ike still looked to PSAC for ideas, telling Killian that he would welcome "representative opinions from the scientific community on nuclear testing." But at the same time, Eisenhower insisted that any agreement with the Russians must contain proper safeguards, saying, "you cannot be naive and put the whole safety of the free world in their hands." As he explained to Queen Fredericka of the Netherlands, "he would not want to live, nor would he want his children or grandchildren to live, in a world where we're slaves of a Moscow power." Like Gore, he did not want to reach agreement on nuclear testing at the expense of American security.[4]

I

When the Geneva conference resumed on January 5, Ambassador Wadsworth performed a very unpleasant task. The recent HARDTACK II underground tests, he informed Tsarapkin, had produced evidence that substantially altered the previous American assumptions about detecting subsurface explosions. The new data indicated both that the seismic signal produced by a blast was weaker than first thought on the basis of RANIER and that normal background noise in the earth's crust made it much harder to determine first motion on a seismograph. As a result, the Geneva detection system was no longer adequate; at best, it could only distinguish between earthquakes and nuclear blasts over 20 kilotons. To restore its original capability of discriminating down to 5 kilotons would require either ten times as many on-site inspections, between 200 and 1000 a year, or a control network of at least 500 stations.

The January 5 bombshell was the result of a long series of computations by American scientists. In late November, technicians studying the results of the HARDTACK II underground tests began to realize something was wrong. When the scientific members of the Geneva delegation returned to the United States in mid-December, they met over the Christmas holidays to analyze the new data with a panel of eminent seismologists. On December 30, the full PSAC met with Acting Secretary of State Herter to explain the meaning of the HARDTACK II evidence. The Eisenhower administration decided it had no choice but to inform the Russians of the new scientific information. At the same time, the PSAC released a public statement to accompany Wadsworth's disclosure to the Russians at Geneva.[5]

Eisenhower was furious. He had sided with the scientists against the AEC and the Pentagon in the internal policy debate only to find that his experts had rested their entire case for detection on the single RANIER shot, which now proved to be misleading. He recognized that the new evidence would throw "a pall" over the Geneva conference; the Soviets, suspicious to begin with, were certain to accuse the United States of trickery. And he realized it would undermine the confidence of even the American negotiators. "If such discoveries could bring about drastic changes in the structure of fact upon which we made our calculations," he commented in his memoirs, "what new discoveries were in the offing?"

246

Disturbed as he was, Eisenhower still refused to give up the quest for a test ban. At his suggestion, Killian appointed a special panel on seismic improvement to study the new evidence and report on both its full implications and ways that the Geneva detection system could be restored to its original capability. Headed by Lloyd V. Berkner, the new committee consisted of eight geophysicists, three physicists, including Hans Bethe, who had chaired the earlier panel on detection, one nuclear chemist, one mechanical engineer, and one expert on statistics. At their first meeting, held on January 6 and 7, they identified several promising ways to upgrade the Geneva system, but they informed Killian that it would be at least two months before they could give a formal report.[6]

II

While the Berkner panel conducted its detailed study, a fierce debate broke out in Washington. The AEC and the Pentagon joined with congressional allies to insist that the administration reconsider its position on nuclear testing. A coalition of test ban supporters led by Senator Hubert Humphrey fought a desperate rearguard action in hopes of saving the endangered Geneva negotiations. Before congressional committees, in leaks to the press, and in speeches and magazine articles, the two sides presented their views. The frequent references to first motion, the Richter scale, and the intricacies of seismography left the average American bewildered; even those who followed the discussion closely were often confused. Yet the basic issue was clear: should the United States respond to the new evidence on the difficulty of detecting underground blasts by giving up its quest for a comprehensive test ban treaty, or should it instead concentrate on ways to improve the detection system.

John McCone emerged as the leading spokesman for those who argued for a resumption of testing. Aware of the growing public fear of fallout, McCone followed Senator Gore's example and suggested that the AEC continue to refrain from conducting tests in the atmosphere. At the same time, he and the other AEC commissioners recommended unanimously on January 24 that the administration resume underground tests both to gather more information about detection techniques and to perfect additional nuclear weapons. McCone insisted that he was not opposed to a test ban; he kept saying that his only concern was that it must be "properly" policed. Since it appeared that only a ban on atmospheric testing could be enforced, he believed the United States should restrict its negotiations at Geneva to such a limited measure.[7]

Several members of the Joint Committee on Atomic Energy quickly supported McCone's position. In addition to Gore, who continued to advocate a unilateral suspension of atmospheric tests, Senator Frank Church of Idaho spoke out in favor of a limited test ban. In a resolution he introduced in the Senate in early March, Church suggested that Wadsworth offer the Soviets a proposal calling for a ban on tests in the earth's atmosphere which would specifically permit experiments underground and in outer space. Such a measure, Church argued, would be a "first step" toward a more comprehensive treaty. Unlike Gore's proposal, Church's plan would include an international inspection system, though one more modest than the original Geneva network. The great advantage, the senator claimed, would be to relieve the worldwide fear of fallout. His proposal would "end the further poisoning of the air"; to do anything less, he concluded, would be "an eternal burden on our conscience."

While Church seemed most concerned about fallout, other backers of a limited test ban were motivated by a fear of Soviet duplicity. In a letter to Eisenhower on January 2, Congressman Craig Hosmer of the JCAE warned that signing a test ban without a foolproof detection system would be to "place our neck in a Soviet noose." Pentagon spokesmen agreed. In testimony before the Humphrey disarmament subcommittee, General Thomas D. White, the Air Force Chief of Staff, said he was convinced the Russians would not even discuss a test ban "if they weren't sure they could cheat." General Maxwell Taylor, the Army Chief of Staff, felt that it did not make any difference which nation was presently ahead in the arms race. "If we are ahead and they are behind," he explained, "we lose by a ban because we will obey and they may and probably will cheat. If they are ahead and we are behind, then the agreement freezes us and we still lose." None of the senators listening questioned the assumption that only the Soviets could conduct clandestine nuclear tests. Instead, Senator Wiley summed up the prevailing view by making the inevitable reference to Pearl Harbor in arguing that the United States should never again be caught off guard.[8]

Senator Humphrey led the rebuttal for the advocates of a comprehensive test ban. He held a special hearing of his disarmament subcommittee in early February at which Hans Bethe explained the significance of the HARDTACK II findings. Though Bethe admitted that the new evidence undermined the original detection assumptions which he had helped formulate, the Cornell physicist insisted that there were ways that the Geneva system could be revised to restore its capability to detect underground tests down to 5 kilotons. For the next two hours, Bethe outlined several possible techniques, ranging from the placement of robot seismographs in deep holes to detect first motion without interference from surface noise to the simple idea of increasing the number of seismographs at each control post from 10 to 100. If the details were complicated, the meaning of Bethe's explanations seemed clear enough—a little scientific ingenuity was all that was needed to solve the detection problem. Humphrey expressed his delight at the scientist's testimony by saying, "It is like sitting at the table with Socrates."[9]

The Minnesota senator waged a strenuous campaign to save the Geneva negotiations. He called on Eisenhower to give personal leadership to the quest for a comprehensive test ban, claiming that "his is the only voice" that could convince the world that "we are going to work ceaselessly for an agreement to ban these tests." In March, Humphrey introduced a Senate resolution stating that body's support for the negotiation of "an international agreement for the suspension of nuclear weapons tests." SANE came to Humphrey's side, mounting a campaign for passage of his resolution and sponsoring newspaper advertisements warning that "the price of failure" at Geneva might very well be "the price of human life itself." Both Norman Cousins and Clarence Pickett spoke out against the Church proposal for a limited test ban, and in late April, the Senate finally adopted Humphrey's resolution, with its implicit endorsement of a comprehensive test ban treaty.[10]

Throughout this debate, the opponents of testing revealed that their fear was not of Soviet duplicity, but rather of the danger of nuclear war arising from the unrestrained arms race. Jay Orear, in an article in the *Bulletin of the Atomic Scientists*, claimed that unless a test ban was adopted, within five years a dozen nations would possess nuclear weapons. Such proliferation, he warned, made it likely that there would be "a nuclear war within the next 10 to 20 years." The great fallacy of test ban opponents, he argued, was their "reluctance to take some risks." A statement by 22 national leaders publicized by SANE made the same point. "There are elements of risk in any agreement," they declared, "but the risks of continuing the arms race are even greater."[11]

Humphrey felt that the problem lay in the military's insistence on an "absolutely perfect, absolutely foolproof" inspection system. Such perfection simply was not attainable, he declared. Instead, the United States would have to rely on a control system that would "deter a violator because he can never be sure that he won't be caught." Deterrence, he concluded, was "the same principle" on which the nation's defense had rested since the nuclear age began.

More neutral commentators agreed that the problem turned on the degree of risk involved. "The concept of a hundred percent foolproof system is meaningless," observed James Fisk, the chief negotiator at the Geneva conference of experts, "so the question really is how much is enough." Scientists could not answer that question, pointed out Graham DuShane, the editor of *Science*. The best they could do was to give an estimate of the percentage of underground tests that a given inspection system could detect. "Where that percentage may be safely set is a political decision of great difficulty and great importance," he concluded. As was the case with fallout, scientists could define the problem in broad terms, but they were unable to offer any magic solutions. It would still be up to the nation's political leaders to determine the degree of risk they could safely run on detection in their quest for a test ban agreement.[12]

III

The debate inside the United States had a chilling effect on the Geneva conference. "In view of the deep cleavage of opinion in official Washington," commented the *Bulletin of the Atomic Scientists*, "it is no wonder the Russians are confused and in doubt about our good faith in negotiating a test ban." Tsarapkin rejected the HARDTACK II data out of hand, insisting that the conferees were bound to consider only the report of the earlier conference of experts. When Wadsworth suggested a second technical meeting to assess and evaluate the new evidence, the Soviet delegate accused the United States of deliberately sabotaging the test ban negotiations.

In an effort to end the stalemate and show continued American good faith, Eisenhower instructed Wadsworth to drop the earlier demand that continued progress toward nuclear disarmament be made a condition for a test ban agreement. The Russians had always objected to the American insistence that a test ban be linked to a curb on nuclear weapons production; now the United States formally abandoned this connection. Despite this important concession, the Soviets continued to refuse all Wadsworth's attempts to include the HARDTACK II data in the Geneva negotiations.[13]

Disturbed by the lack of progress at Geneva, President Eisenhower searched for a way to break the deadlock. He gave careful consideration to an idea that British Prime Minister Harold Macmillan favored. Aware of the Soviet reluctance to permit foreigners to move freely within their territory, Macmillan learned from Soviet diplomats that they might agree to on-site inspection more readily if there were a numerical limit on such actions. Accordingly, the British leader proposed to Khrushchev in the course of a visit in late February that the Geneva negotiators set an annual quota for on-site inspections. When Khrushchev showed interest in such a compromise, Macmillan urged the United States to make such an offer at Geneva.

The President was not attracted by the quota idea. His advisers felt that on-site inspections should be determined by scientific evidence of suspicious seismic events, not by a process of political bargaining. When Hubert Humphrey made a similar proposal in a letter to Eisenhower in early March, the President replied coolly, saying only that he would take the suggestion into consideration.

In his discussions with James Killian, Eisenhower showed much more interest in an idea suggested originally by test ban advocate Harrison Brown. Realizing that small underground tests could probably never be detected with certainty, Brown in 1957 had proposed a test ban that would include all explosions that could be monitored easily. In addition to atmospheric tests, this would include large underground blasts above a certain threshold. On February 25, the President told Killian that he and Dulles both felt that on-site inspection, the source of so much of the discord at Geneva, had been overstressed. Mobile teams were unlikely ever to find evidence of small subsurface explosions; a treaty that relied on such uncertain means to detect underground tests would be unfortunate. In such a case, "the tendency for suspicions will be very great," Eisenhower commented, "and our whole nation will become more and more jittery."

A threshold agreement, on the other hand, would be certain to detect all large tests, since a network of control posts had a high reliability for both atmospheric and large underground blasts. The President liked the idea of setting the threshold at 10 kilotons. The advantage in including large underground tests, he commented, was to ensure retention of the Geneva network of 180 control posts. "The President said," according to the official minutes of the February 25th meeting, "that what is essential is the right to inspect." Thus in seeking a compromise, Eisenhower wanted to go one step beyond the Gore-Church plans for an atmospheric test ban—his threshold concept would include large subsurface blasts and require a sophisticated control system.[14]

Two developments in March further complicated the test ban picture and forced the President to abandon his threshold approach. The first was the report of the Berkner panel on seismic improvement. On March 6, this body gave the President a preliminary statement on the concealment of underground nuclear explosions. The full report followed on March 16. Killian distributed copies to other government agencies the next day, but the document was not made public until June.

Berkner and his associates confirmed the earlier analysis of the HARDTACK II evidence. Unsuspected difficulty in identifying first motion as well as the weakness of seismic signals originating from an explosion meant that the original Geneva system was inadequate at its stated capability of detecting nearly all nuclear blasts down to 5 kilotons. The panel claimed that there would be on the order of 1500 suspicious events that would require on-site inspection at the 5 kiloton level; if left unchanged, the proposed network could not identify blasts with reasonable certainty below 20 kilotons. Two feasible modifications in the Geneva system, a ten-fold increase in seismographs at each control post, as Bethe had suggested, and the measurement of surface as well as underground shock waves, would lead to an immediate improvement in the system, according to the Berkner panel. The network would then be able to identify underground tests down to 10 kilotons, and the panel predicted that an intensive program of research and development could probably restore the initial 5 kiloton capability within 2 or 3 years.

The panel, however, also had bad news for advocates of a comprehensive test ban. At the suggestion of Edward Teller, Albert Latter of the RAND Corporation had done a series of theoretical computations to see if it would make any difference if an underground explosion were detonated in a large cavern. His tentative findings, first reported to the PSAC in January, were startling. Latter discovered that an explosion set off in a big hole would be decoupled from the surrounding earth and the resulting seismic signals would be reduced as much as 300 times. Hans Bethe quickly confirmed Latter's decoupling theory, admitting that he had erred in his own earlier assumption that it made no difference how an underground blast was detonated. The Berkner panel treated the new data cautiously, pointing out that a huge cavity would be required, one at least 300 feet in diameter. The members urged that tests with both nuclear and conventional explosives be conducted to verify the theoretical calculations made by Latter and Bethe. But, pending such proof, they did inform the President that they believed that with decoupling it would be possible to "reduce the seismic signal by a factor of ten or more."

The implications of the decoupling phenomenon were devastating. Even if the use of a big hole only reduced the seismic waves tenfold as cited in the Berkner report, rather than the 300 times Latter and Bethe believed possible, such a technique undermined the entire Geneva system. What appeared to be a 5 kiloton blast on the seismographs might well be a 50 kiloton explosion, and conceivably could be as large as 1500 kilotons— the size, in fact, of a 1.5 megaton thermonuclear bomb. At the very least, a nation that muffled its underground nuclear explosions could test weapons ranging up to 10 kilotons with very little chance of being caught. When Killian explained the decoupling effect to Eisenhower on March 13, the President realized immediately that his threshold concept was no longer valid. He and Killian agreed that in view of the latest development, "a system with a low threshold cannot be guaranteed."[15]

While the public would not learn about decoupling until the Berkner report was released in June, the *New York Times* published an equally disturbing story on high altitude testing on March 19. Hanson Baldwin disclosed that in late August and early September of 1958 the Navy had conducted Project Argus, a series of three nuclear explosions some 300 miles above the South Atlantic. Designed to see whether such blasts could be used to prevent missiles from re-entering the earth's atmosphere, the explosions created a weak band of radioactivity that interfered with radio signals but did not have the desired anti-missile effect. The small explosions, in the low kiloton range, did not cause any fallout, and most important, went undetected. The press immediately pointed out the significance of this last fact—nuclear tests could be conducted at high altitudes and in outer space with little chance of detection.

The administration had been aware of the implications of Project Argus for some time. Coupled with the Berkner report, the feasibility of undetected high altitude shots meant that there were now two environments in which a nation could conduct clandestine nuclear tests in violation of a supervised test ban agreement. Edward Teller, who had maintained all along that "in the competition between prohibition and bootlegging, the bootlegger will win," had been vindicated. The outlook for those who favored a comprehensive test ban had suddenly become very dim. All that remained possible, in view of the new scientific knowledge, was a partial test ban—one restricted to tests conducted in the atmosphere.[16]

IV

The Geneva conference recessed on March 19 for the Easter holidays. The next day, Harold Macmillan flew to Washington to consult with Eisenhower on the test ban impasse. The two leaders went to Walter Reed Hospital to visit Dulles, who was

terminally ill with abdominal cancer. Then they adjourned to
Camp David in the nearby Maryland mountains where acting
Secretary of State Christian Herter joined them.

Eisenhower and Macmillan quickly reached agreement. The
President, fearful that Macmillan would press for a test ban
that could not be properly enforced, was pleased to find the
British leader willing to work for the more modest goal of "a
small, enforceable agreement . . . which might generate confidence for more ambitious plans." Macmillan was even more
relieved when the President said that despite the opposition of
some of his advisers, he now favored a ban limited to atmospheric tests "at least for three or four years." The two men
agreed that Eisenhower would make such a proposal to
Khrushchev when the Geneva conference resumed in April.

The President still had to do battle with the AEC and the
Pentagon. McCone in particular fought hard against such a
long-term commitment as he tried to overawe Christian Herter.
Eisenhower refused to back down, telling Herter that he had to
make clear to McCone that McCone "is not making policy of
the United States of America." "He is an operator," Ike added,
"not a foreign policy maker." The President continued to keep
the dying Dulles informed, calling him every day on the telephone. In one of their last conversations, Eisenhower expressed his desire to halt the "terrific" arms race by at least
stopping tests in the atmosphere. ". . . In the long run," the
President concluded, "there is nothing but war—if we give up
all hope of a peaceful solution."[17]

On April 13, Eisenhower sent a letter to Khrushchev proposing a limited test ban as an interim measure. Saying that he still
favored a "lasting agreement" of a more comprehensive nature, the President suggested that the United States, Great Britain, and the Soviet Union agree to halt all tests in the atmosphere up to a height of 50 kilometers. While it was in effect,
the negotiators could continue to work out the details for a
treaty banning underground and space tests as well. "Meanwhile," Eisenhower told Khrushchev, "fears of unrestricted re-

sumption of nuclear weapons testing with attendant additions to levels of radioactivity would be allayed. . . ."

Wadsworth presented the details of the proposal the same day at Geneva. He explained that a much simpler control system would be needed to police an atmospheric ban—one without any provision for on-site inspection and with as few as 8 control posts in Russia. Tsarapkin said he would consult with Moscow on the new American proposal, but he was not very hopeful about Soviet acceptance. "It is nothing," he told reporters. "It would allow underground and high-altitude tests, while we want all tests to be stopped."[18]

The congressional reaction was much more enthusiastic. Senators Church and Gore praised the President for following their advice and concentrating on ending tests in the atmosphere. Gore called the plan "constructive, wise and humane," pointing out that it would solve the urgent fallout problem. Senator Humphrey was more guarded, labeling an atmospheric ban "the irreducible minimum" that he could accept.

Within the administration, attitudes continued to differ. McCone saw the proposal as a way to test Russian sincerity. "If the Soviets refuse our offer," he said, "the motive is clear: Stop the U.S. but let the Soviet Union continue to develop their weapons by tests hidden from view." In that case, he indicated, the United States would have no choice but to resume testing. Ambassador Wadsworth saw the plan in a very different light. It was not meant to foreclose the possibility of a comprehensive agreement, he explained to Norman Cousins. Rather, it was "a negotiating move designed to stimulate some action on the part of the other side."[19]

Khrushchev apparently agreed with Wadsworth's assessment; on April 23, the Soviet leader replied with a counter offer. A partial test ban "would only be misleading the public," he contended, stating that the true goal of the negotiations was that of "preventing the production of new and ever more destructive types of nuclear weapons." He favored a renewed effort at a comprehensive ban, and in order to break the stalemate, suggested adopting Macmillan's proposal for a limited number of on-site inspections each year. Khrushchev shrewdly did not mention a specific figure, simply saying, "Of course, the number of annual trips by inspection teams should not be great."

Eisenhower accepted Khrushchev's reply as a genuine attempt to get the stalled negotiations moving again. He told the Russian leader on May 5 that while he still preferred to sign a limited test ban agreement first, he would instruct the American delegation at Geneva to explore the idea of a "predetermined number of inspections" a year. Both in this letter and in a press conference a week later, the President specified that any annual quota would have to be based on a scientific estimate of the likely number of suspicious seismic events, not on political considerations. In insisting on a number that "conformed to the necessities required by scientific data," Eisenhower clearly had in mind far more than the handful of inspections that Khrushchev apparently wanted.[20]

In early May, the test ban conference adjourned while the Foreign Ministers met in Geneva to deal with other issues, notably the still smoldering Berlin crisis. Khrushchev backed down on his ultimatum to resolve this question separately with East Germany, but most commentators saw little likelihood of a quick settlement of either the Berlin or the test ban problems. The Russians remained adamant in refusing to hold another technical conference on the HARDTACK II data, and the issues of a veto over inspections and the composition of the control teams continued to block agreement on a draft test ban treaty. The negotiations were due to resume in June, but the outlook remained bleak. Harold Macmillan, faced with powerful public and political pressures at home, regretted the increasingly strong American resistance to a comprehensive test ban agreement. "I felt almost in despair," he wrote in his diary, "for if nothing could be achieved in a broader sphere, the end of these tests would be at least a dramatic step forward, and give comfort to millions of people all over the world."[21]

V

What had happened to the bright hopes raised by the conference of experts in 1958? The President's Science Advisory Committee was an obvious scapegoat. James Killian, Hans Bethe, and Isador Rabi had let their desire for a test ban influence their scientific judgment on the detection problem. Relying on the scanty evidence provided by the single case of RANIER, they had argued that it would be possible to identify all but the very smallest clandestine underground blasts. The AEC and the Pentagon spokesmen had fought a stubborn rearguard action, warning that detection might prove much more difficult than the scientists realized, but they were unable to provide any firm data to substantiate their fears of Russian duplicity. The President, who had long sought a break in the arms race, elected to side with his scientific advisers in the belief that a test ban treaty would be a relatively easy first step toward his goal of genuine nuclear disarmament.

The tragic fact was that test detection proved to be far more complex than anyone had realized. Instead of providing an easy way to move into the more significant problems of weapons limitations, it created a whole series of complicated issues that produced a new disarmament stalemate. In fact, the complications surrounding detection may even have set back the cause of general disarmament. The Soviets, suspicious to begin with, began to lose faith in Eisenhower's good intentions when the United States suddenly introduced the HARDTACK II data and tried to change the technical agreement reached by the experts in 1958.

The opponents of a test ban carefully disguised their joy at the scientists' embarrassment, but there could be no mistaking their sense of triumph at the new turn of events. Avoiding public comment, they leaked secret details of the detection controversy to Charles J. V. Murphy, who wrote an article very critical of the PSAC in the March 1959 issue of *Fortune*. Recounting the role of Killian and Bethe in persuading Eisenhower and Dulles to enter into test ban negotiations, Murphy described the episode as "an awkward diplomatic venture" that had embarrassed the United States before the world.[22]

Predictably, calls for a resumption of testing began to be heard again. Thomas Murray, adviser to the Democrats in Congress on nuclear matters, cited the need to perfect new and more "discriminating" weapons in arguing that testing was "not only a military necessity but also a moral imperative." In *U.S. News and World Report,* editor David Lawrence argued that the test ban was part of a Soviet plan to outlaw all nuclear weapons. If that happened, he warned, "the Soviets will rule the world" because of their superiority in conventional forces. The most impassioned plea for renewed testing came from a Virginia resident who wrote to the *Nation* to assert that those who conducted nuclear tests "are fighting the Communist tyranny which seeks to enslave the minds of free men." "Stop tests, stop weapons production," he continued, "and you are, in effect, inviting disaster."[23]

President Eisenhower did not agree. He showed no sign of disillusionment with his scientific advisers. At a meeting on May 19, he reaffirmed his commitment to disarmament and said that "if the scientists can help to show concrete ways to make progress on arms control, he will be most grateful. . . ." He compared scientists to military men, saying that both groups were most successful when "they work themselves out of a job," in this case urging his listeners to find ways to end their role in developing "military weapons systems." Above all, the President was rueful over the slow pace of progress toward a test ban. Saying that he felt "keenly" on this matter, he observed that only a few years ago "we thought about stopping atmospheric tests. Finally, after years of yapping, this has become a fallback position."

Eisenhower made it clear to the American people that while he was discouraged, he had not given up on the test ban. Addressing a press conference on June 17, just after the Berkner report was made public, he admitted that decoupling greatly complicated the task of detection. But then he went on to explain that it would be unrealistic to expect to achieve a completely foolproof system. "There is no system, whether it be defensive or detection or intelligence or planning or anything else, that is 100 percent perfect," he declared. "What we do have to do is to refine the process to the point where we minimize risks and indeed bring them down below the level where they could be truly dangerous to our country."[24]

CHAPTER
10

THE FALLOUT
SCARE

The moratorium on testing in the atmosphere had raised hopes that fallout would no longer be a threat to human health. Neither the United States nor Great Britain had conducted any tests since October 31, 1958; the Russians had apparently stopped after their two tests in early November. Yet the fission products released by the three nuclear nations in the last-minute flurry of testing in the fall of 1958 caused a sharp increase in radioactive fallout during the early months of 1959. The American people, unprepared for this sudden rise in radiation levels, reacted with an alarm that at times bordered on panic.

The first signs of danger came from two isolated incidents. In mid-January, scientists in Sweden reported unusually heavy fallout, presumably from the last Soviet test series. The particles were larger and hotter than any previously recorded, and the resulting radioactivity was five times the normal level for the Scandinavian country. Then a month later, a Pan American 707 jetliner, which had been flying above 30,000 feet, was found to be coated with fallout. The level was low, but the presence of radioactivity on the plane's fuselage and in its engines suggested that there was a heavy concentration of radioactive debris in the earth's upper atmosphere.

Public concern began to mount in February when the Minnesota fallout commission disclosed that samples of wheat in that state contained very high amounts of strontium-90. The AEC confirmed these findings, reporting that readings as high as 155 micromicrocuries per kilogram of Sr^{90} for a small part of the 1958 crop had been made, compared to a permissible level of 100 mmc/kg. Willard Libby quickly pointed out to the Joint Committee on Atomic Energy that this was an isolated case. The average Sr^{90} content for the entire state's wheat crop was only 51 mmc/kg., he claimed. And even the one sample of radioactive Minnesota wheat posed no real danger to human health, Libby contended; a person would have to eat nearly a ton of the contaminated grain before he absorbed enough strontium-90 to harm his body.[1]

New reports of Sr^{90} levels overshadowed Libby's rebuttal. The AEC revealed on March 3 that the deposit of strontium-90 in New York City, where records had been kept since 1954, had more than doubled within four years. The fallout had been particularly heavy across the northern portion of the United States in 1958; the amount in New York City had gone from 40.5 micromicrocuries per square mile to 53.3 mmc/sq. mi. in a year's time; in nearby Westwood, New Jersey, a record 15 mmc/sq.mi. had fallen in 1958.

A sharp rise in the strontium-90 content of milk caused the greatest concern. In July 1958, the Public Health Service had begun monitoring the level of radioactivity in milk supplies at ten stations across the country. The data from the milksheds in 1958 had not been alarming; all the stations averaged less than 10 micromicrocuries of strontium-90 per liter, compared to a maximum permissible dose of 80 mmc, except for St. Louis, with a yearly average of 14.1. In 1959, however, the St. Louis reading jumped to 18.6 mmc in January and to 20.1 in April. An even higher reading was recorded in Mandan, North Dakota—an alarming 32.7 mmc. *Consumer Reports* conducted its own independent study of strontium-90 levels in late 1958; the resulting data confirmed the Public Health Service reports, ranging from a low of 1.9 mmc in Los Angeles to a high of 15.6 in New Orleans. The editors felt that while the national average of 8 mmc was relatively low, there was still "a potential hazard." "The fact is that fresh clean milk, which looks and tastes just as it always did," they concluded, "nevertheless contains . . . an unseen contaminant, a toxic substance known to accumulate in human bone."[2]

Willard Libby, who usually tried to play down the fallout danger, added to the growing furor with a speech at the University of Washington on March 13. In blunt language, he blamed the Soviets for the sudden increase in radioactivity. The 14 Russian tests north of the Arctic Circle in the fall of 1958, Libby charged, had dumped an incredible 20 megatons of fission products into the stratosphere. Explaining that such material passed into the atmosphere much more quickly at northerly latitudes, Libby claimed that there would be a "tremendous" increase in fallout as a result, perhaps as much as ten times the normal amount.[3]

Libby's attempt to blame the Russians for the fallout scare soon backfired. Ten days later Senator Clinton Anderson, the new chairman of the Joint Committee on Atomic Energy, released a letter from General Herbert Loper, special assistant to the Secretary of Defense on atomic energy, with the startling information that the average storage time for strontium-90 in the stratosphere was only two years. This statement directly contradicted the prevailing estimate made by Libby in 1955, that it took on the average of 10 years for strontium-90 from bomb explosions to return to earth. General Loper also asserted that more strontium-90 fell on the United States than on any other nation on earth. The danger, however, was very slight; he claimed it was "much less than other common occurrences such as X-rays, automobiles, chemical contaminants, household cleaners, etc."

Willard Libby replied to General Loper in a letter which Senator Anderson also made public. Admitting that he had overestimated the storage time, Libby reduced his figure to 4 years, but he still held that Loper's assertion of only 2 years was too low. The AEC commissioner also challenged the evidence on the heavy concentration of global fallout in the United States, claiming that local fallout from the Nevada test had skewed the data.

The real debate came over the interpretation to be placed on the new estimate. Senator Clinton Anderson accused Libby and the AEC of deliberately trying to mislead the American people by suppressing the evidence on shorter storage time. "In layman's language," Anderson told the Senate, "it looks like strontium-90 isn't staying up there as long as [the] AEC told us it would, and the fallout is greatest in the United States." At a hearing held by the JCAE, Libby denied that he had been "a party to the suppression or distortion of any information bearing on the safety and health of the American public." He went on to say that in fact he hoped he was wrong about the storage time, pointing out that the faster the fallout came down, the sooner the danger would be over. When Anderson countered by asserting that in his view, the higher the rate of fallout, the greater the danger to mankind, Libby claimed that this issue was irrelevant. Ignoring the issue of testing entirely, he asserted that the "real hazard" was not "stratospheric fallout" but rather the local fallout that would accompany a nuclear war.[4]

Clinton Anderson was not the only member of Congress unhappy with the AEC's handling of the radiation issue. On March 23, Senator Hubert Humphrey released the text of a staff study by his disarmament subcommittee on the fallout problem. Citing the concentration of Sr^{90} in Minnesota wheat and the high levels of fallout recorded in New York City, the study concluded that it would be "foolhardy to ignore blithely potential danger signals in the nuclear age." Humphrey, who earlier had limited his interest in a test ban to the disarmament aspects, now joined Anderson in attacking the AEC for failing to protect the American people against radiation hazards from testing. Claiming that fallout "seems literally to gush down upon us," he suggested that the task of measuring and guarding against excessive radiation be moved from the partisan AEC to the more neutral Public Health Service.

Just three days later, the Surgeon General released a report from the National Advisory Committee on Radiation recommending precisely this transfer of authority. The Committee, composed of twelve distinguished scientists headed by Professor Russell H. Morgan of Johns Hopkins University, felt that there was a clear conflict of interest. The AEC, an agency "with a prime interest in the promotional aspects of the field," should not also be charged with guarding the public against radiation hazards. Instead, the committee favored the creation of a new federal agency with the sole task of radiation protection.[5]

The attack on the AEC continued in April when science writer Walter Schneir charged in the *Nation* that the federal agency was guilty of withholding the latest findings of Laurence Kulp and his Columbia University colleagues on the amount of Sr^{90} in human bone. Schneir claimed that the scientists had given the data to the AEC in January, and he asked why it had not yet been made public.

A week later, the AEC released the third Kulp report, which dealt with strontium-90 in human bone through the end of 1957. The results were disturbing. Kulp and his associates found that while the strontium-90 content of adult bone had not increased greatly, the amount in children up to the age of four had doubled in 1957. They predicted that even without additional atmospheric tests, the average concentration of Sr^{90} in the bones of young children would increase from the present level of 1.33 mmc per gram of calcium to 4 mmc in the mid-1960s. The scientists warned that some children would have as much as five times the average amount, or 20 mmc, still far below the MPC of 80 mmc, but enough to cause concern. Kulp and his colleagues made no attempt to assess the significance of their findings, concluding with the statement, "what hazards these levels present to the human race are still not certain."[6]

By the time the AEC had released the latest Kulp findings,

the American people were in the grip of a full-scale radiation scare. *Newsweek* devoted a special section to the fear of strontium-90, calling it "this insidiously invisible powder" which was so powerful that "a concentrated teaspoonful could kill 30 million people." Manufacturers tried to cash in on the public alarm. One company advertised a "fallout detector" which sold for $5, plugged into a radio or television set and sounded a wailing alarm through the speaker when the fallout was heavy; another entrepreneur offered a FIDO (Fallout Intensity Detector Oscillator) that was no bigger than a pack of cigarettes. Congressmen received thousands of letters from constituents worried about the recent fallout reports; letters to the editors columns were filled with expressions of anxiety over strontium-90. One worried mother spoke of her guilt in feeding "her trusting infant milk contaminated with strontium 90"; another wrote of watching her child "gulp his milk and know that I am witness to possible death." Parents who felt this concern were not satisfied with the argument that the risk of fallout was slight compared to nuclear war. As one mother wrote in a letter to the editors of the *New York Times,* "whereas a nuclear attack is an uncertainty, even an improbability, the peril of increasing fall-out is a dead certainty." [7]

The new concern revived the flagging test ban movement. "The fallout issue has become our 'hottest,' " commented SANE's Washington lobbyist in March, "and we have a real chance to make a significant breakthrough which will affect our drive against testing." In New York City, SANE responded by setting up a storefront information center for two weeks in Times Square. A vivid window display complete with a Geiger counter and a poster asking "Suicide or Sanity?" competed with the shoddy merchandise in nearby stores and the more garish appeals of the neighboring porno movie houses and book stores. A loudspeaker tried to attract the attention of blasé passersby; "Strontium-90 falls to the earth like rain," the spiel began. "It can cause leukemia, cancer, and bone disease. . . ." Inside, there were displays of books and pamphlets, including

267

Nevil Shute's *On the Beach,* and each day speakers addressed the small crowds that gathered at lunch time.

SANE was so pleased with the impact that it kept the information center open for an additional two weeks. An estimated 40,000 people visited the display, taking away some 80,000 pieces of literature and listening to 19 different speakers. Visitors contributed a total of $2200, but not all those who came in were persuaded. One skeptic said, "As an American, I'll take my chances with strontium-90 instead of being unprepared for war with the Russians."[8]

In St. Louis, a group of scientists from Washington University formed the Committee for Nuclear Information. The members prepared bulletins for the news media on fallout hazards, operated a speakers' bureau and held public meetings. To dramatize the danger of strontium-90 to children, they mounted a campaign to collect baby teeth so that they could measure precisely the intake of the deadly silver dust.[9]

The protests mounted in intensity as the spring went on. Linus Pauling, addressing a SANE rally in Brooklyn, warned that the increased level of Sr^{90} would lead to 100,000 deaths in the next generation. "The only safe amount of strontium 90 in the bones of our children," he declared, "is zero." Norman Cousins was equally indignant. "There is no known way of washing the sky" he wrote, "no way to keep the strontium and cesium from falling like rain; no way to keep it from getting into food and milk and thence into the bones of children. . . ." The argument that only a tiny fraction of the world's population would be affected did not impress Cousins. ". . . The heart of the matter is that we have not asked—nor have the Russians nor the English—the permission of other peoples to foul up their air, dust their lands with radioactive poisons, and jeopardize the lives of children in particular."

Members of Congress agreed. Representative Edith Green, Democrat of Oregon, declared that "our Government has no moral right to trifle with the future of the human race by continued tests." The most eloquent appeal came from Hubert

Humphrey, who made the fallout issue a major theme as he began his quest for the 1960 Democratic presidential nomination. "There may still be some of our fellow citizens who doubt that there is one world," he told a group of San Francisco Democrats on April 23. "But no one can deny that we have only one stratosphere, and that we must somehow stop using it as a rubbish dump for radioactive debris."[10]

I

The loud outcry over fallout forced the Eisenhower administration to take steps to reassure the American people. John McCone took the lead. At a hearing of the Joint Committee on Atomic Energy on March 24, the AEC Chairman denied that his agency had ever withheld information on radiation from the public. He claimed that the AEC was spending 18 million dollars annually on radiation protection studies and was cooperating fully with the Public Health Service and the Food and Drug Administration. Then he announced that the administration would conduct a "government-wide" review of the fallout problem. As its contribution, the AEC would hold a special two-day meeting in April of its General Advisory Committee, a group of distinguished scientists, devoted exclusively to the hazards of radiation.

Later that same day, Dr. Detlev Bronk, president of the National Academy of Sciences, announced that he had asked the six committees that had written the 1956 report on radiation hazards to reconvene and prepare a new study of the problem. The timing was not accidental. Presidential science adviser James Killian had conferred with Bronk about the new NAS studies in early March and pointed out the "timeliness of such a review and updating."[11]

President Eisenhower spoke out on the radiation issue at his press conference on March 25. Like McCone, he rebutted Senator Anderson's charges by stating, "To my knowledge, there has been no suppression of information on fallout." He cited both the forthcoming meeting of the AEC's General Advisory Committee and the new National Academy of Science study as proof of his administration's concern. "Every effort is being made by this Government," he declared, "to develop the facts about fallout and to disclose these facts fully to the public."

Two weeks later, the President announced that he had created a new committee to study the desirability of transferring the responsibility for radiation safety from the AEC to the Public Health Service. Maurice Stans, director of the Bureau of the Budget, headed this study group, which included both John McCone and Arthur S. Flemming, Secretary of Health, Education and Welfare. Anticipating an affirmative finding, Senator Lister Hill of Alabama introduced legislation in Congress on April 10 authorizing the transfer of all radiation protection programs to the Public Health Service.[12]

Despite these efforts to ease public concern, a development in late April once again placed the administration on the defensive. The National Committee on Radiation Protection, a quasi-official body composed of 42 representatives of government agencies and private scientific and medical organizations, authorized a change in the existing safety standards for strontium-90. Apparently without consulting the administration, the NCRP doubled the maximum permissible dose of Sr^{90} for workers in atomic industries, raising it from 1000 to 2000 mmc, and increasing the maximum permissible concentration of Sr^{90} in milk by 25 percent, from 80 to 100 mmc/liter.

The higher MPC for milk troubled those already concerned about fallout, but the occupational increase had even broader implications. The NCRP set the safety level for the general population at one-tenth of the industrial standard; suddenly the American people were told that up to 200 mmc exposure from Sr^{90}, rather than 100, would not harm them. Critics quickly pointed out that the International Commission on Radiological Protection recommended that the population standard be set at one-thirtieth of the occupational level instead of one-tenth. The American MPD for strontium-90 was now far out of line with the worldwide limit—200 mmc compared to 67. This discrepancy did not seem to bother the NCRP, which was chaired by Lauriston Taylor, head of the National Bureau of Standards, and dominated by the AEC. One member told a reporter that "the nation's security may demand the exposure of people to higher levels of radiation than those just established by the International Commission."

The *Nation* condemned the action of the National Committee on Radiation Protection as "bad science and bad ethics." Whatever the committee's motives, its cavalier attitude toward the public's fear of radiation exposure proved embarrassing to the Eisenhower administration. At a time when the President and his aides were trying desperately to reassure the people about fallout, raising the safety levels seemed like a cynical attempt to evade the issue.[13]

II

The most significant effort to relieve public anxieties over fallout in 1959 came from Congress. Representative Chet Holifield held a four-day hearing before his radiation subcommittee in early May. The proceedings were very different from the ones held by the same group in 1957. Instead of a broad approach designed to explore all aspects of radiation hazards, Holifield confined the 1959 hearing to the specific issues raised by the spring scare—the nature and distribution of Sr^{90} fallout, the proper safety levels for the nation's soil and milk supplies, and the outlook for future human intake of strontium-90.

The greatest contrast with the 1957 hearings lay in the tone of the hearings. Holifield made it clear from the outset that he believed the fallout fears were unfounded. In a nationally televised interview two days before the hearings opened, he said that nuclear tests created such an "infinitesimal amount" of danger to human life that they could not be considered "detrimental, in a global way, to the people of the world." Identifying completely with the AEC's position, he told a reporter, "We feel that the national defense is important enough that if there is some risk involved, we must take that risk." Accordingly, he confined the list of witnesses largely to government spokesmen. Men like Linus Pauling and Edward Lewis were not invited to testify but instead were asked only to submit written statements for the record. As the hearings progressed, Holifield repeatedly cut off testimony that dealt with unknown radiation dangers. At one point he said, "The committee does not intend to be swayed by emotional arguments on the relative dangers or lack of dangers from fallout." Like the popular television program of the time, "Dragnet," all Holifield was interested in was "the facts, just the facts." [14]

Despite the chairman's attempts to restrict the hearings, the four days of testimony did reveal that there was a substantial basis for concern over fallout. AEC witnesses, notably Dr. Charles Dunham, director of the division of biology and medicine, stated frankly that the American, British, and Soviet tests in 1958 had led to a substantial increase in radioactive fallout. Dunham said that in the past year an average of 30 microcuries of strontium-90 per square mile fell on the United States, twice the amount of any previous 12-month period. He and one of his assistants also confirmed that the deposit of Sr^{90} was heaviest in a band along the 40th degree of latitude in the northern hemisphere, the area of greatest population concentration in the United States. Dunham, however, discounted the importance of high readings for milk in Mandan, North Dakota, and wheat in Minnesota. These "hot spots" were isolated phenomena owing to unusually heavy rains which temporarily affected local crops but had no lasting impact.

The most revealing testimony came from Dr. Frank H. Shelton, technical director of the Armed Forces Special Weapons Project. He had supervised a Pentagon program which used U-2 aircraft to sample the Sr^{90} content of the stratosphere and which had been the basis for General Loper's revelation to Senator Anderson that the stratospheric storage time was far less than the ten years Willard Libby had estimated. Shelton reported that this program had revealed that the 1958 testing had increased the inventory of Sr^{90} in the stratosphere from 12 to 30 megatons, a rise that would double the amount of strontium-90 in the soil by 1960. The U-2 sampling had also made clear that the fission products from testing fell back to earth in only one year's time and concentrated heavily in the north temperate zone.[15]

A major controversy developed among the government witnesses about the reasons for the rapid nature of Sr^{90} fallout. Lester Machta of the Weather Bureau contended that there was a break in the tropopause, the boundary between the troposphere surrounding the earth up to 35–40,000 feet, and the stratosphere. This break, located near the 40th parallel, was where the exchange of air between the stratosphere and the troposphere took place, and consequently where fallout debris entered into the cloud level and fell to earth with rain and snow. This process was most active in the spring, and therefore, according to Machta, most of the earth's fallout was recorded in March, April, and May. Because the exchange between the two parts of the atmosphere took place near the 40th parallel, the fallout was heaviest around that latitude.

Dr. E. A. Martell of the Air Force's Cambridge Research Center had a different explanation. He claimed that fission products injected into the stratosphere in northerly latitudes returned to earth much more rapidly than those that originated near the Equator. He thus explained the early and heavy Sr^{90} spring fallout as being the result of Russian tests north of the Arctic Circle. Fallout from American tests held in the Marshall Islands stayed in the stratosphere far longer and fell back more evenly on the earth. Willard Libby, who found support for his estimate of a relatively long storage time in Martell's theory, endorsed the Air Force scientist's explanation. Holifield, intent on justifying American tests, liked this approach. He voiced his belief that "the Russian tests are depositing faster and hotter fissionable material on the people of the world than the U.S. tests."

273

Whatever the explanation, all the experts agreed that fallout was coming down much more quickly than they had anticipated and that it tended to concentrate along the 40th parallel. Senator Anderson, attending the hearings as a guest, asked about the significance of these findings. The shorter storage time, he suggested, meant greater radioactivity, since very little decay took place when the Sr^{90} fell back to earth quickly. An AEC representative reluctantly agreed, admitting that the reduced storage time meant that the resulting Sr^{90} radioactivity would be about 10 to 15 per cent stronger than if the same material stayed in the stratosphere for up to ten years. More importantly, everyone agreed that the level of Sr^{90} in the United States had doubled since 1957, and was likely to double again even if no further tests were conducted in the atmosphere.[16]

The hearings also dealt with the threshold issue for somatic effects, the genetic hazards of fallout and question of where to set population safety standards. Just as in 1957, the scientists could not agree on whether or not there was a threshold below which radiation did not cause cancer or leukemia. Government witnesses doubted that low-level radiation was dangerous, but they admitted that they could offer no conclusive proof that a threshold existed. In a written statement, Dr. Edward Lewis, the chief proponent of linearity, warned of a new fallout hazard—iodine-131. Scientists previously had ignored this fission product since it had a half-life of only 8 days. But Lewis pointed out that during its brief period of radioactivity, it became concentrated in cow's milk and that when children drank this milk the radioactive iodine settled in the thyroid gland. He estimated that existing fallout could easily lead to a doubling of the rate of cancer of the thyroid in children under 10. A Public Health Service physician confirmed Lewis's findings and said his agency was now monitoring the iodine-131 levels in the nation's milk supply.[17]

Geneticists reported only one change from the 1957 consensus that all radiation caused mutations and therefore was undesirable from a hereditary standpoint. Experiments with mice at the Oak Ridge National Laboratory had shown that low-level radiation over a long period caused fewer mutations than the same total exposure received at one time. While there was no threshold below which mutations did not occur, the new data suggested that chronic radiation at fallout levels did less genetic damage than previously thought. Professor James Crow of the University of Wisconsin reminded the subcommittee, however, that although the fraction of the world's population affected by fallout-induced mutations was minute, "it is likely that tens or hundreds of thousands or more persons will be diseased or deformed, or die prematurely."

The experts who testified had a difficult time arriving at a recommendation on the proper level for radiation safety. They tended to feel that the international standard for the population as a whole, one-thirtieth of the occupational MPC, or 67 mmc for strontium-90, was better than the American recommendation of one-tenth, or 200 mmc. Professor Crow suggested that it would be more appropriate to set the population standard in terms of the natural background radiation rather than as a proportion of an aribitrary industrial level. "This is the level of radiation to which the human population has been exposed throughout its history," he argued. "The further we get from this level, the less confidence we have that any effects will be similar in kind and quantity to those that the population has experienced in the past and has been able to tolerate."[18]

III

On the last day of the hearings, a panel of 23 experts, who had been conferring privately on the likely future levels of Sr^{90} in human beings, gave their prediction. They estimated that of the 90 megatons of fission products released by all nuclear explosions since 1945, some 30 megatons were still circulating in the stratosphere. The resulting fallout of Sr^{90} was likely to double the amount of that substance on the earth's surface and lead ultimately, provided that tests did not resume, to an average body burden of 7 mmc for every person in the world. This figure, as Chairman Holifield was quick to point out, was only about one-tenth of the MPC set by the International Commission on Radiological Protection; another witness calculated that it amounted to about 5 per cent of the natural background radiation that Crow suggested as the proper standard. But the experts went on to warn that additional nuclear tests would lead to a doubling of this figure every five years. Future testing in the atmosphere, in other words, would soon lead to dangerous burdens of strontium-90 in the body of everyone on earth.

Professor William Neumann of Rochester University, who presented the panel's predictions, spelled out their meaning in somber terms. The group, he explained, "felt that no single or simple relation between radiation dosage and biological effect has as yet been established." Therefore, they did not believe that fallout from past tests constituted a significant hazard to human health. But future tests were a different matter. "We are playing with cosmic forces," Neumann warned; "some of us think that we are lifting the lid on Pandora's box." If we open the box by resuming tests in the atmosphere, he prophesied, "we can very easily get in serious trouble." [19]

IV

Unlike the 1957 hearings, the press gave relatively little coverage to the new Holifield subcommittee hearings. The *New York Times* carried brief stories each day on inside pages. The *Times* gave the hearings front-page treatment only when Holifield released the report of the AEC's General Advisory Committee, which had met for two days in April to study the radiation issue. "STUDY MINIMIZES FALL-OUT DANGER," the *Times* headline proclaimed. The report amounted to little more than a rehash of earlier AEC statements. The distinguished scientists on the panel concluded that the hazard from Sr^{90} was slight, amounting to less than 5 per cent of the radiation exposure the average American received from natural background sources and medical and dental X-rays. This small risk was well worth running, the panel concluded, pointing out that "weapons tests have been an essential part of our effort to prevent the occurrence of nuclear war."[20]

The only extensive comment came from test ban advocates, who were outraged by both the restricted nature of the Holifield hearings and the defensive nature of the General Advisory Committee's report. Ralph Lapp accused the AEC of using the GAC report to divert attention from the congressional hearings; Walter Schneir focused his criticism on Holifield, accusing the subcommittee chairman of conducting a whitewash. The *New Republic* called the hearings "a complete farce," and demanded that they be reopened to allow critics of testing to present their case to the American people. SANE made the same point in a full-page advertisement in the *New York Times*. It claimed that the hearings had ignored the high level of radioactivity in the American food supply. Calling for a new congressional inquiry, SANE stressed its belief "that humanity has a common right and a common will to survive."[21]

The very shrillness of this criticism suggested that the hearings had succeeded in easing the fallout scare. The testimony that existing fallout amounted to only a tiny fraction of natural background radiation helped the American people put the fear of strontium-90 in perspective. Yet the Holifield hearings had been more than just a clever public relations manuever. The witnesses who appeared before the subcommittee had made clear that, however small the present danger from fallout, renewed testing in the atmosphere would pose a serious threat to all mankind. The subcommittee's final report, released by Holifield in August, stated unequivocally that future tests would increase the human intake of strontium-90 to the point where it would become "a hazard to the world's population."[22]

V

The fallout scare gradually eased in the summer and fall of 1959. Government agencies began issuing frequent reports on the level of strontium-90 which showed a sharp decline from the highs reached in March and April. In September, the Public Health Service reported that the Sr^{90} content of the nation's milk supplies had returned to normal by June. The AEC confirmed this trend, noting that areas with very high readings in the spring were now experiencing far lower levels—the Sr^{90} content of milk at Mandan dropped from 47.4 mmc/liter to 22.2, while the St. Louis average fell from 37.3 in April to 11.2 in June. These government figures, which supported the testimony at the Holifield subcommittee hearings on the temporary nature of the spring fallout rise, relieved the anxiety of the American people.[23]

President Eisenhower aided the process of reassuring the public with an executive order on August 14 which stripped the AEC of its radiation safety responsibilities. Instead of transferring them to the Public Health Service, Ike compromised by creating a new Federal Radiation Council, headed by HEW Secretary Arthur Flemming, to determine safety standards and to oversee the actual protective measures, which would be carried out by the states and by other federal agencies, such as the Food and Drug Administration and the Public Health Service. Congress confirmed the new arrangements in September, and under Flemming's leadership, the new Federal Radiation Council moved quickly to convince the American people that the government was now genuinely concerned about the fallout hazard.[24]

Although the declining strontium-90 readings and the creation of the Radiation Council helped restore public confidence, the spring scare left behind a lasting fear of fallout. The scientists may not have been able to decide on the exact nature and extent of radiation peril from bomb tests, but the public was convinced that atmospheric testing created risks for their health and safety which they no longer wished to endure.

The new resistance to nuclear testing became apparent in the nation's magazines. The *New Yorker* began a new column in May entitled, "These Precious Days." "Because the slaughter of the innocents continues, here and abroad, and the contamination of air, sea and soil proceeds apace," the editors explained, they planned to print regular bulletins "tracing Man's progress in making the planet uninhabitable." The first column included figures on the high radioactivity in St. Louis milk, predictions of increased bone cancer and leukemia rates from fallout, and the statement by Dr. Lauriston S. Taylor, the chairman of the committee that set radiation standards, "There is a lot we do not know."[25]

The *Saturday Evening Post,* which reflected conservative, middle-class values, published a two-part article in the early fall entitled "Fallout: The Silent Killer." The author began his account by describing the "pervasive by-product of weapons testing" that now "blankets the entire planet." He went on to point out that "every living creature, man included, has in its body a few particles of radioactive strontium 90, some of which will remain for life." He described the conflicting views of scientists, giving great weight to the alarmist views of A. H. Sturtevant and Linus Pauling. He called fallout "a silent killer which hides its poisons among the more familiar causes of human illness and death." The long-term consequences might take a half-century or more to show up, he concluded, "but there will be a cost, a heavy cost in disease, deformity and early death for many yet unborn."[26]

Readers received a more balanced analysis of the fallout problem in the September issue of *Scientific American,* which was devoted entirely to the subject of "Ionizing Radiation." Eleven contributors described the known and suspected effects from fallout. There were approximately 140 pounds of Sr^{90} that had been released into the atmosphere, they pointed out, but this seemingly small quantity had a total radioactivity of more than 9 million curies. George Beadle, a Nobel Prize winning biologist from Cal Tech, summed up the problem which fallout posed for the concerned citizen. He explained that scientists were unsure about somatic effects from low-level radiation but pointed out that there was no disagreement about the genetic damage caused by even the slightest amount of radioactivity.

He admitted that the scanty evidence let experts with strong views on war and peace take "extreme positions with regard to genetic and other hazards." Each citizen, he argued, must make his own estimate of the risk in the awareness that a genuine moral dilemma was involved. For himself, he felt that there was no escaping the fact that fallout "contributes in a small way to world-wide levels of radiation. For this reason alone the tests should be discontinued, or conducted in such a way as not to lead to atmospheric contamination."[27]

Beadle expressed what had become the emerging public consensus by mid-1959. The fallout scare had convinced the American people that nuclear testing in the atmosphere was too dangerous to tolerate any longer. The presence of strontium-90 in their milk, even in minute quantities, had brought home to them a sense of peril which far transcended the earlier warnings of men like Albert Schweitzer and Linus Pauling about the effect of testing on all human life. John McCone, the foremost advocate of nuclear testing within the government, realized the significance of the changed public mood. "We should give serious consideration to curtailing atmospheric tests," he told the Joint Committee on Atomic Energy in June, "for the simple reason of eliminating this fear, whether the fear is warranted or not, because it is there."[28]

CHAPTER

11

THRESHOLD

The emerging public consensus that fallout was dangerous focused attention once again on the question of underground nuclear tests. Despite the continued stalemate at Geneva, it became increasingly apparent by mid-1959 that the temporary moratorium on atmospheric testing would continue indefinitely. President Eisenhower avoided any public statement on the testing issue, but during a National Security Council meeting in July, an aide noted, "The President grew heated about atmospheric tests," indicating that "he would not approve them." Consequently the military shifted its emphasis to subsurface blasts, urging the President to resume underground testing as a way to perfect new weapons without endangering public health.[1]

In the course of the ensuing debate, detection became the focus of scientific controversy. Scientists like Hans Bethe who believed that a comprehensive test ban would be a vital first step toward nuclear disarmament argued that an all-out research effort would enable them to find ways to identify virtually all underground explosions. The opposition, led by Edward Teller, contended that there was no foolproof way to detect concealed blasts and warned that the Soviets would use a test ban treaty to overtake and surpass the United States in nuclear technology. Moreover, test ban foes saw outer space shots as yet another way for the Russians to conduct secret nuclear tests.

At Geneva, James Wadsworth and Semyon Tsarapkin, guided by their technical advisers, kept searching for a formula that would fulfill the earlier promise of the 1958 conference of experts. Despite their efforts, the deadlock continued on two fundamental points, seismic detection of underground blasts and on-site inspections.

The American position on detection stemmed from the data resulting from the HARDTACK II underground tests conducted in the fall of 1958. Realizing that the new evidence contradicted the conclusions reached by the conference of experts as the basis for the Geneva detection system, Wadsworth asked Tsarapkin for another technical conference which could use the HARDTACK findings to design a more complex and sophisticated detection network. When Wadsworth finally transmitted the report of the Berkner panel, with its specific suggestions for such an improved system, the Soviet spokesman rejected it out of hand. Given this intransigent Russian attitude, American scientists realized that they had little chance of convincing their Soviet counterparts that decoupling presented an even greater obstacle to agreement on detection. The so-called "big hole" theory advanced by Albert Latter, with the notion that seismic signals could be reduced up to 300 times, was certain to provoke an incredulous response from Tsarapkin and his advisers.

On-site inspection seemed to offer the only hope of solving the detection problem. In May, Eisenhower had agreed to permit Wadsworth to explore the possibility of setting an annual quota for on-site inspections of suspicious seismic events. The outlook for agreement was not promising. The Soviets refused to state how many observations they would permit on their territory, but they were apparently thinking in very low terms, on the order of three each year. The United States, on the other hand, insisted that instead of reaching a political compromise, the number of inspections be based on scientific evidence. AEC Chairman McCone, claiming that there were as many as 3500 earthquakes a year in the Soviet Union, wanted at least 350 such inspections annually. It was unlikely that the Soviets would ever permit neutral teams to carry on such regular activity on Russian soil. Moreover, a panel of the President's Science Advisory Committee reported by July that even such on-site inspection would not be a foolproof way to determine whether an underground blast had actually occurred.

The only bright spot in the gloom at Geneva came in June when the Russians agreed to hold a meeting of experts to study ways to monitor nuclear tests in space. An American delegation headed by Stanford University physicist Wolfgang Panofsky met with a group of Soviet scientists for three weeks. On July 10, Technical Working Group I issued its report, in the form of agreed recommendations. The scientists suggested the use of elaborate satellite systems to detect nuclear blasts above the earth's atmosphere, outlining three possible systems. The report made no firm assessment on how effective such systems would be, nor did it estimate the huge costs that would be involved. Privately, the American members admitted that there were "holes" in the proposed system, both at low altitudes and in the far reaches of outer space. The prompt agreement reached by the scientists, however, obscured the tentative and incomplete nature of their report and restored public faith in the ability of technical experts to succeed where diplomats failed.[2]

I

While the negotiations continued at Geneva, the policy split within the Eisenhower administration deepened. John Mc-Cone, a far more adroit bureaucrat than Lewis Strauss, led the opposition to a test ban treaty. In June, after a brief trip to Geneva, the AEC chairman told a congressional committee that he favored breaking off the talks and resuming underground testing. Later in the month, he took a five-member congressional delegation to the test ban talks to convince them of the futility of further negotiation. Senator Albert Gore, discouraged by the lack of progress, renewed his 1958 proposal for a ban limited solely to tests in the atmosphere. The new Secretary of State, Christian Herter, treated this proposal carefully, telling his first press conference that the administration might decide to pursue a partial test ban agreement as a "more expedient and more practical" way to proceed.

McCone kept up steady pressure within the administration for a resumption of underground testing. The AEC built a series of tunnels in the Nevada desert for subsurface blasts and pushed hard for non-military shots designed to provide new data on the crucial issue of seismic detection. The President firmly ruled out such experiments, telling McCone that the United States would not be the first nation to resume nuclear tests. The military, however, backed McCone strongly, insisting that they needed to try out new warheads for the solid-state Minuteman ICBM, perfect an anti-missile missile system and develop a tactical H-bomb that could be used at a range of only 1000 yards. Teller became the champion of this last item, the so-called neutron bomb, which he envisioned as the final culmination of the clean bomb crusade, a "pure radiation" weapon which would enable the American forces in Europe to balance off the numerically stronger Soviet army.[3]

A new member of the administration, George B. Kistiakowsky, who replaced James Killian as the President's science adviser in July 1959, soon became the chief defender of the test ban cause. A distinguished Harvard University chemistry professor who had served on the PSAC since its founding, Kistiakowsky was a 58-year-old Ukrainian who had fought the Bolsheviks in Russia, come to the United States in the 1920s, and played a key role in the wartime Manhattan Project. Fiercely anti-Soviet, the new science adviser was also convinced that a comprehensive test ban offered mankind the best chance to regain control over the dangerous nuclear arms race. A shy, quiet man, he had originally thought that he would confine his advice to technical matters, but he quickly developed a strong antipathy to John McCone that caused him to take the lead in arguing against the resumption of nuclear testing.

Kistiakowsky was dismayed to find that the State Department offered little resistance to McCone's bullying tactics. Secretary of State Herter and his chief deputy, Douglas Dillon, believed that Edward Teller would use the decoupling theory to persuade the Senate to vote against a comprehensive test ban treaty on the grounds that the Russians would use underground caverns in Siberia to cheat. On July 23, the State Department suggested that the administration abandon a comprehensive treaty and try instead to secure Russian agreement to a ban limited to atmospheric tests. Eisenhower indicated that he was now willing to follow this course, but first he asked Kistiakowsky to have the PSAC evaluate the Pentagon's claims that renewed testing was vital for weapons development.

The new science adviser appointed a panel to carry out the weapons study. While waiting for its results, Kistiakowsky began lobbying with the State Department for a renewed effort at Geneva for an all-inclusive test ban treaty based on between 100 and 200 on-site inspections each year. To his surprise, Herter and Dillon accepted this approach. On August 13, they informed McCone and Deputy Secretary of Defense Thomas Gates at the meeting of the Committee of Principals that the President had agreed to extend the test moratorium from its October 31 expiration date until the year's end. This move provoked a "wild reaction" by McCone and Gates, who insisted that the Joint Chiefs of Staff would have to be consulted.[4]

The report of the PSAC weapons panel on August 18 undercut the military's insistence that testing had to be resumed immediately. Weighing the various weapons programs, the panel saw no urgent need for tests before early 1960. Kistiakowsky then received valuable support on August 18 when Hubert Humphrey, aware of the debate within the administration, delivered an impassioned speech on the Senate floor on behalf of continued test ban negotiations. Claiming that the Geneva conference had reached "a critical stage," Humphrey declared, "Nuclear weapons tests should not be resumed on the part of the United States unless the nuclear test ban negotiations collapse."[5]

The President decided to override the military's objections. On August 26, the State Department announced that Eisenhower had directed that the one year moratorium on nuclear tests which had begun on October 31, 1958, "be extended throughout this calendar year." Noting that the Geneva talks were in recess, the administration expressed a desire "to allow a reasonable period of time for the negotiations to proceed following their resumption on October 12, 1959." The next day the British announced their intention of honoring the moratorium's extension and on August 28 the Kremlin stated that the Soviet Union would not conduct any tests unless the Western nations did so first.

The decision to extend the moratorium on testing through the end of 1959 failed to resolve the fundamental issue facing the Eisenhower administration. Neither McCone nor the Pentagon leaders were pleased; the moratorium meant a continuation of a condition they had always opposed, a de facto suspension of testing without any supervision. Kistiakowsky and the State Department officials were also uneasy since they were aware that the stalemate over detection and on-site inspection at Geneva was unlikely to be broken before the end of the year. And President Eisenhower, although genuinely desirous of signing a test ban treaty as a first step toward moderating the Cold War, was under no illusions about the danger of relying on Soviet good faith. Under steady pressure from Harold Macmillan to sign a test ban treaty based on "the mere exchange of unsecured promises," Eisenhower refused to give in. "To the making of such 'agreements,' " he wrote in his memoirs, "I was opposed."[6]

II

With the Geneva conference in recess, the United Nations became the scene of diplomatic maneuvering on the test ban issue in the fall of 1959. On September 17, Secretary of State Christian Herter described the impasse on detection and on-site inspection in a speech to the General Assembly. The United States still hoped to negotiate a comprehensive test ban treaty, he affirmed, but President Eisenhower was prepared to accept an atmospheric ban immediately as "a first step toward the ultimate objective." Two days later, Nikita Khrushchev delivered the Russian response in person. The Soviet leader startled the General Assembly by calling for a total abolition of all weapons, nuclear and conventional, over the next four years, without any provision for inspection or supervision. If such general disarmament was too radical for the Western nations, Khrushchev added, then he was willing to pursue the stalled test ban issue, which he described as "acute and eminently ripe for solution." Two weeks later, UN ambassador Henry Cabot Lodge gave the American reply. Taking a soft line, he praised Khrushchev's desire for total disarmament and asked him to reduce his proposal to a series of specific measures which would include the all-important concept of supervision. "There cannot be 100 percent disarmament," Lodge concluded, "with only 10 percent inspection."

After his speech to the UN, Khrushchev undertook a whirlwind tour of the United States and then climaxed his American visit with a two-day meeting with Eisenhower at Camp David. The two leaders discussed disarmament matters only in broadest terms, leaving more detailed negotiations to Herter and Foreign Minister Andrei Gromyko. They failed to make any progress, with the inspection issue once again the sticking point. Khrushchev later admitted that his intransigence was based on an awareness that the Soviet Union trailed the United States in both missile development and nuclear technology; a test ban at that time would have frozen the Russians in second place. Moreover, Khrushchev feared that on-site inspections would enable the West to learn how far behind the Soviets actually were in strategic striking power. ". . . Inspectors criss-crossing around the Soviet Union," Khrushchev observed in his memoirs, "would have discovered that we were in a relatively weak position." [7]

After Khrushchev's return to Russia, the Americans and Soviets agreed at the United Nations to create a 10-member disarmament committee to replace the defunct five-nation subcommittee. The new body, with equal representation from the East and the West, would deal with all phases of disarmament, not just the test ban issue. At the same time, the smaller nations, led by Austria, Sweden, and Japan, introduced two resolutions urging the nuclear powers to conclude a test ban as soon as possible and to refrain from testing in the interim. The United States voted for the first resolution, but opposed a second which included language aimed at France, which was planning to detonate its first atomic bomb in the Sahara in early 1960. Ambassador Lodge spoke out against a third resolution aimed specifically at the forthcoming French test series, claiming that small nuclear explosions like those the United States conducted in Nevada did not endanger human health. Despite this plea, the General Assembly voted 51 to 16 to express its "grave concern" over the French test and urge President Charles de Gaulle to cancel it.

The discussion at the United Nations had virtually no effect on the test ban issue. Russian and American leaders used the General Assembly to score debating points, not to open up new avenues toward agreement. The passage of the resolutions favoring a test ban and opposing the French series served as a useful reminder that world opinion still strongly desired an end to testing. But de Gaulle went ahead with plans for the Sahara explosion and the nuclear powers remained deadlocked on the inspection issue. The only hopeful sign was the announcement in late 1959 that the Big Four leaders would meet in a summit conference at Paris the following spring. If the

Geneva negotiators could find a way to resolve their differences within six months, then perhaps Paris could become the scene for the signing of the long-awaited test ban treaty.[8]

III

Although the 1960 presidential election was still a year away, the test ban became a political issue in the fall of 1959. New York Governor Nelson Rockefeller, Richard Nixon's main challenger for the Republican nomination, began the process on October 25 when he advocated the resumption of nuclear testing, saying that the United States "cannot afford to fall behind in the advanced techniques of the use of nuclear materials." He discounted the fallout problem, but said that to avoid public alarm, he would favor only underground tests.

The presidential aspirants in both parties quickly came out against Rockefeller's position. In a speech at U.C.L.A. on November 2, Senator John Kennedy urged that the United States continue its moratorium "indefinitely," provided that the Russians did not resume testing. A week later, Vice President Nixon voiced a similar view, saying that those who called for test resumption were "ignorant of the facts." Praising Eisenhower for the moratorium, Nixon said the U.S. should refrain from testing as long as the negotiations continued at Geneva.

Hubert Humphrey, who was emerging as Kennedy's leading opponent for the Democratic nomination, made the most significant statement on the test ban issue. Speaking to a political gathering in Pontiac, Michigan, on October 30, the Minnesota Senator outlined a three-point proposal designed to break the deadlock in the test ban negotiations. First, Humphrey urged Eisenhower to extend the existing cessation for a full year beyond the December 31, 1959, expiration date. Second, during that time, the United States should negotiate with Russia for a ban on all tests in the atmosphere and those conducted underground above 5 kilotons, the present threshold for detection. Third, Humphrey suggested that Eisenhower propose a two-year moratorium on tests below the 5 kiloton limit while undertaking a joint research effort with the Soviets that would eventually permit the ban to cover all underground tests. In addition, Humphrey recommended that the United States lower its demand for several hundred on-site inspections annually to the more reasonable range of 25 to 50. To make sure that this comprehensive proposal came to Eisenhower's attention, the senator sent a copy to presidential science adviser Kistiakowsky.[9]

Despite the views expressed by Kennedy and Humphrey, several prominent Democrats endorsed Rockefeller's position. Former President Truman came out in favor of renewed underground testing in a syndicated newspaper column. "You can never freeze any discovery," he argued. "You must go on experimenting." Senator Henry Jackson of the Joint Committee on Atomic Energy agreed, warning that the Russians were probably already conducting secret tests underground and in outer space. Paul Nitze, a protégé of Dean Acheson and defense expert on the Democratic Advisory Council, voiced the defense establishment's desire for tests to perfect new weapons. Claiming that there was "still much work to be done . . . [on] small weapons with minimum radiation hazard," Nitze told a Washington audience, "We could not accept a complete ban on atomic weapons."

The debate over test resumption spread beyond political circles. SANE issued a statement denouncing Rockefeller's statement as "unstatesmanlike and unwise," and raised funds to place another full-page advertisement against testing in the *New York Times*. Military leaders leaked stories to friendly reporters stressing the need to perfect nuclear warheads for both the Navy's improved Polaris missile and the Air Force's new, untried Minuteman ICBM. "Without further tests," an anonymous general told a *Time* reporter, "the development of our next generation of weapons is stopped cold." John McCone was the only official to speak out publicly, telling a "Meet the Press" panel that he felt the moratorium should be continued only on a week-to-week basis and be made contingent on Soviet willingness to stop stalling at Geneva.[10]

Rockefeller's initiative failed to persuade the American people that the time had come to resume testing. A Gallup poll taken in mid-November showed that an overwhelming 77 per cent of those asked wanted to see "the agreement to stop testing H-bombs" extended for another year. There was no significant political variation; 78 per cent of the Republicans favored the moratorium compared to 77 per cent of the Democrats polled. The Democratic Advisory Council quickly closed ranks behind Kennedy and Humphrey, issuing a statement on December 19 that advocated continued test suspension as "a first step toward disarmament and the relaxation of tensions." Most observers agreed that Rockefeller's trial balloon had shown that the American people, relieved by the respite from fallout, were reluctant to see the tests resume, even underground. The most notable outcome of this brief debate was the universal conviction that, as *Science* noted, "if tests are resumed they should not take place in the atmosphere." The editors of the *Bulletin of the Atomic Scientists* rejoiced that the "good old days when the AEC felt free to test as it pleased" were over. "This general agreement that the air we breathe is the common property of mankind and not to be polluted at the will of sovereign nations," the *Bulletin* concluded, "is a step forward in the education of the human race."[11]

IV

The public debate in the fall of 1959 was accompanied by hopeful signs of progress toward a test ban treaty in both Washington and Geneva. Surprisingly, it was John McCone who broke the deadlock between the State Department, which still favored a comprehensive treaty, and the Pentagon, which preferred to limit the ban to atmospheric tests and resume underground experiments as soon as possible. In October, Mc-

Cone suggested to the Committee of Principals that the United States insist that the Russians agree to a new technical conference to consider both the HARDTACK II data and the concept of decoupling. If the Soviets refused to hold such a meeting, or if the experts met and failed to agree on a more elaborate detection system, McCone proposed that the United States should continue the moratorium on a day-to-day basis after January 1, 1960, but not resume underground tests until the Soviets did so. Kistiakowsky immediately backed McCone's plan, terming it "a surprisingly sensible proposal which really represents his complete about-face from last summer."[12]

Secretary of State Herter concurred and when the Geneva Conference reconvened on October 27, Ambassador Wadsworth made the proposal for a new technical conference on detection. Only a week later, Tsarapkin startled the American delegation by agreeing to send a team of Russian experts to discuss the American seismic evidence. The press in the United States reacted favorably, calling the Russian action a "major concession" and predicting a breakthrough in the long-stalled test ban conference. President Eisenhower was more cautious in his comments, telling reporters that the experts would deal with "a very tricky question," and then he added, "if we can get to a really intelligent discussion of the matter, we may make progress."

An air of optimism swept over the Eisenhower administration. Kistiakowsky commented on the "tremendous change" that had taken place among the President's advisors. He prevailed upon James Brown Fisk, the man who headed up the 1958 delegation of experts, to chair the new technical team, and he was especially pleased when Hans Bethe agreed to serve as a member. Secretary Herter was a little more restrained, warning the press on November 24, the day before the experts met in Geneva, that the discussion would be "highly technical." "It will have a very important bearing on what kind of an agreement might be made," he added, but Herter did not disclose that future American policy on the moratorium depended on the outcome of the experts' deliberations. President

Eisenhower expressed his feeling of hopefulness when he replied to Senator Humphrey about the three-point threshold plan, declaring that he was willing to take some risk in negotiating a test ban treaty in order to avoid "the enormous risks entailed if reasonable steps are not taken to curb the international competition in armaments."[13]

The two delegations of experts met at Geneva on November 25, and for the next three weeks they pursued the intricate and complex issue of differentiating between the seismic signals from earthquakes and underground nuclear blasts. The goal was to reach agreement on "objective criteria" which the proposed control commission could use to determine whether an on-site inspection was necessary to identify suspicious seismic events. From the outset, the Soviets rejected the data from the HARDTACK II experiments, complaining that the instruments used by the AEC were not as sensititve as those proposed in the original Geneva system. As James Fisk explained, "The Soviets agreed on all things that make the control system look better and on nothing that makes the system look worse." Yet viewed from the Russian perspective, the American delegation could be charged with seeking only to show how easy it would be to evade detection as they concentrated on loopholes in the 1958 Geneva system.

Hans Bethe had the most difficult assignment of all. In early December, with the conference already going badly, he presented the decoupling theory developed originally by Albert Latter. As he explained how detonations set off in deep underground holes might be muffled so that the resulting seismic signals were reduced as much as 300-fold, the Russians appeared to be stunned. They finally admitted that Latter's calculations were technically correct, but they insisted that decoupling was a purely theoretical concept that had never been proven in practice. In essence, they viewed it as one more American effort to go to fantastic extremes in devising objections to the detection network agreed upon by eminent scientists from both countries at Geneva in 1958.

The failure to reach agreement at the technical level ended

tragically. While the Russians wanted simply to adjourn for the Christmas holidays, the American delegation insisted on issuing a separate report detailing the inability to arrive at agreed recommendations. The Soviet scientists responded with a biting attack on their American colleagues, accusing them of the "tendentious use of one-sidedly developed material" and claiming that their arguments were "on the brink of absurdity." Thus, instead of providing the hoped-for breakthrough at Geneva, the meeting of the experts had intensified the sense of deadlock and frustration. Worse yet, the recriminations threatened to end the sense of kinship that had grown up between Russian and American scientists at Geneva and had led men like Hans Bethe and George Kistiakowsky to believe that they could succeed where the diplomats had failed.[14]

The breakup of the experts' conference brought renewed demands for test resumption. On December 11, when it became clear that no agreement was forthcoming from Geneva, Thomas Gates, the new Secretary of Defense, urged the Committee of Principals to recommend underground testing when the moratorium expired on December 31. Herter strongly opposed this move, as did Vice President Nixon, and the discussion became, in Kistiakowsky's words, "utterly inconclusive." Fearful that the advocates of testing would win out, the science adviser outlined a compromise to McCone when the two men had lunch at the White House on December 16. Echoing Humphrey's three-point proposal of October 30, Kistiakowsky suggested a ban on both atmospheric tests and underground experiments above a specified kiloton level. The threshold for testing under this proposal would depend on how many on-site inspections the Soviets would permit. McCone found the new plan attractive, and by the time the technical conference ended on December 19, the Committee of Principals had given it tentative approval.

The bitterness at the Soviet verbal attack on the American experts nearly undid Kistiakowsky's compromise. McCone began to have second thoughts, feeling that the situation called for "a drastic response on the highest level." Both Gates and JCS Chairman Nathan Twining renewed the demands for underground tests, but Herter and Kistiakowsky finally prevailed. On December 28, the Committee of Principals agreed to proceed quietly with studies on the threshold plan. Meanwhile, they prepared a presidential statement announcing that the United States would end the formal moratorium on December 31 but would not resume testing without giving advance notice to the world.[15]

The next day, the members of the Committee flew to Georgia to present their recommendations to the vacationing President. The meeting, which took place in a second floor room at the Augusta National Golf Club, lasted less than an hour. Angry at the Russian attack on American scientists, Eisenhower quickly approved the public statement ending the moratorium and authorized the State Department to develop the threshold plan. "He was obviously tired and impatient with the whole subject," Kistiakowsky noted in his diary.

James Hagerty released the presidential statement ending the moratorium late on December 29. Asserting that "no satisfactory agreement is yet in sight" at Geneva, Eisenhower nevertheless promised that "we shall not resume nuclear weapons tests without announcing our intention in advance of any resumption." The new policy, in essence the day-by-day approach advocated by John McCone, was clearly designed to put pressure on the Russians to negotiate in good faith. Ambassador Wadsworth, who had favored continuing the formal moratorium, assured peace groups that the administration would not resume testing as long as the negotiations continued at Geneva.[16]

The public reaction was mixed. The *New York Times* praised Ike's new policy as a "reasonable one," while Senator Clinton Anderson wanted to go one step further and inform the Russians that if there was no progress at Geneva by a specified date, the U.S. would resume testing. Hubert Humphrey, on the other hand, unaware of the administration's decision to pursue his threshold plan, accused the President of engaging in "nuclear brinksmanship." The *New Republic* blamed Edward Teller, claiming that he was behind the decoupling theory which had led to the fiasco at Geneva. Eugene Rabinowich agreed that "scientists who have searched for difficulties of underground test detection have won out," but he refused to single out one man or nation for the responsibility. "The lesson we have to learn from this disappointment," he wrote, "is that the first need is for imaginative policies on both sides which would increase mutual trust."[17]

The failure at Geneva and the expiration of the moratorium marked the effective end of the quest for a comprehensive test ban. For fourteen months, diplomats had tried to exploit the scientific agreement reached in the summer of 1958 to achieve a complete halt to nuclear testing. The inadequacy of the technical data combined with the mutual Cold War suspicions had ultimately blocked what had appeared to be a promising first step toward nuclear disarmament. Now the best that could be hoped for would be some kind of partial test ban treaty, one that limited atmospheric tests and possibly large underground ones. Such an achievement would spare the world additional fallout, but it would not secure the second goal of test ban advocates—a halt to the spread of nuclear weapons. With France about to explode its first atomic bomb, that disappointment weighed heavily on those who sought to bring the nuclear arms race under control.

V

When the Geneva test ban conference reconvened on January 12, the outlook was bleak. Though President Eisenhower expressed hope for progress in the talks, Ambassador Wadsworth had no new proposals to offer to Tsarapkin. The Soviets had responded cautiously to Eisenhower's statement ending the formal moratorium. On January 3, 1960, Khrushchev pledged to the world that the Soviet Union would not resume testing unless the Western nations did so first. But in a speech to the Supreme Soviet on January 14, the Russian leader boasted that his scientists had a new and "fantastic" weapon in "the hatching stage." At the same time, Khrushchev admitted that it was possible to conceal underground nuclear tests, the first such admission by the Russians, while he repeated his promise not to do so.

In Washington, Eisenhower's advisers continued to work on the details of the threshold test ban offer. A PSAC panel completed a study which recommended that the limit for underground tests be placed at 4.75 on the Richter scale, a figure which the experts felt would enable the United States to detect all tests above 20 kilotons. The Pentagon resisted both the 4.75 figure and the idea of a threshold ban, but by late January, the Defense Department officials reluctantly gave way. The British were "violently opposed" to the new plan, according to Kistiakowsky, and insisted that it be coupled with a two-year moratorium on tests below the threshold that could not be monitored. Both the Pentagon and the AEC strongly objected to this new concept, which was similar to the third step in Senator Humphrey's October proposal. State Department Soviet expert Chip Bohlen advised that such a moratorium was essential to secure Russian approval, but the military's objections to an unsupervised ban finally prevailed.[18]

The President announced the new proposal at his press conference on February 11. Ambassador Wadsworth, he stated, was presenting a plan in Geneva "for the ending of nuclear weapons test in all the environments that can now be effectively controlled." If adopted, this proposal would mean the end of testing in the atmosphere, in the oceans and in space up to altitudes, "where effective controls can now be agreed to." Setting the threshold of the proposed ban at explosions registering 4.75 on the Richter scale, Eisenhower called for a coordinated research effort to improve detection so that eventually all underground tests could be included. The President pointed out that the new proposal would "prevent increases of radioactivity in the atmosphere and so allay worldwide concern," but he refused to say whether or not the United States would resume underground tests below the 4.75 threshold.

In his presentation at Geneva, Wadsworth explained that the 4.75 limit would cover all tests above 20 kilotons by American criteria. At the same time, he announced that the United States was prepared to accept a fixed quota for on-site inspections to determine if seismic signals below 4.75 came from earthquakes or from nuclear blasts. Tsarapkin replied disdainfully, calling the new plan "a step backward." He promised to send it to Moscow for a formal appraisal, but he gave little hope for a successful outcome. "We will try to convince our partners in the talks," he told American reporters, "that the only plan is a plan to end all tests."[19]

The reaction in the United States was more positive. Ernest Lindley praised Eisenhower for proposing an end to fallout and said Ike had gone "as far as any informed and thoughtful leader in the free world should want us to go." Senator Humphrey was delighted that the administration had adopted a major part of his October 30 proposal, calling the step "a sound, constructive endeavor." The only dissent came from David Inglis, who pointed out that only a comprehensive test ban could prevent other nations from developing nuclear weapons. "The atomic age is inherently dangerous," he commented. "The best we can do is to choose the least dangerous course."

As if to underscore this objection, France exploded its first atomic bomb on February 13, just two days after Eisenhower unveiled the threshold plan. The 60-kiloton blast rocked the remote Sahara oasis some 750 miles southwest of Algiers and produced a strange, cauliflower-shaped cloud. The French government reported that the fallout had been contained within the nearby unpopulated desert area, but the world trembled at the first atmospheric nuclear explosion since early November 1958. The Soviet Union issued a statement saying that the French test "cannot but be deplored," while the State Department said simply that the shot was "not unexpected." Despite these mild official reactions, the first French atomic bomb helped create a new sense of urgency in both Moscow and Washington.[20]

The first sign of a new breakthrough at Geneva came on February 16, when the Soviets responded favorably to Wadsworth's suggestion for a quota on inspections. Although Tsarapkin refused to cite a definite number, for the first time he indicated that the Russians would be willing to base the number of inspections on seismic criteria rather than seek a purely political compromise. The Soviet action raised hopes in Washington, but Eisenhower quickly pointed out that the problem was far from solved. ". . . You get into the old numbers racket that everybody seems to love so much," he told reporters; "just exactly what is adequate would be a very difficult thing."[21]

For the next few weeks, the negotiations moved along slowly. Suddenly, on March 19, Tsarapkin called for a special Saturday meeting. Timing his announcement to catch the front pages of American Sunday newspapers, the Soviet negotiator said that his government was willing to accept the American threshold plan with one proviso—that the United States agree to a moratorium on tests below the 4.75 limit for an indefinite time. In essence, the Russians were agreeing to accept a supervised test ban for all atmospheric, underwater, and large underground tests in exchange for a voluntary cessation of all small underground tests based solely on good faith. If the United states would agree to this proposal, Tsarapkin promised, a test ban treaty could be signed within a month.[22]

The initial reaction in the United States was hostile. Senator Clinton Anderson branded the Russian move as "phony." According to the chairman of the Joint Committee on Atomic Energy, the offer was only "a tactical shift on their part merely to accomplish what they have been striving for all along," a test ban without inspection. The *New York Times* agreed. A self-enforcing moratorium, the editors argued, "would leave the Soviets free to continue experiments behind the Iron Curtain to develop Premier Khrushchev's 'fantastic weapons.' . . ."

British Prime Minister Harold Macmillan was very upset by the American hostility. He had long been urging the United States to agree to accept the idea of a moratorium on small underground tests. Convinced that the AEC and the Pentagon were the true source of difficulty, Macmillan confided in his diary, on March 20, "We must now bring tremendous pressure on the Americans to agree." The next day he telephoned Eisenhower, who "seemed rather vague about it," but asked for time to discuss the issue with his advisers. On March 23, to Macmillan's relief, Eisenhower called back and invited the British leader to Washington for a personal conference on the test ban impasse. Macmillan readily agreed to make the trip, but he was not optimistic. "The Americans are divided, and with an administration on the way out," he commented, "the Pentagon and the Atomic groups are gaining strength."[23]

Unknown to Macmillan, the long-standing split within the administration was finally coming to an end. In a two-day meeting of the Committee of Principals, Secretary Herter argued strongly for a positive response to the Soviet offer. Predictably, John McCone and John Irwin, assistant secretary of defense for international affairs, objected violently, claiming that the Russians would use a moratorium to conduct secret tests and surpass the United States in nuclear technology. However, James Douglas, deputy secretary of defense who spoke for the Pentagon in the absence of Secretary of Defense Gates, in Europe, took a different line. "To my surprise and pleasure," recorded George Kistiakowsky, "Jim Douglas rather sided with the State Department." A former secretary of the Air Force, Douglas saw an advantage for the United States in opening up Russia to limited international inspection. When CIA Director Allen Dulles observed that a test ban would freeze the nuclear weapons race with the United States still in the lead, McCone found himself completely alone.

The next day, March 24, the Committee met with Eisenhower to present its recommendation for a positive reply to the Soviet offer. McCone voiced his objections to any unsupervised moratorium, "whereupon the President in a sharp voice rejected McCone's point of view," according to Kistiakowsky, "and got obviously angry when McCone suggested that the State [Department] proposal was a surrender of our basic policy." Eisenhower then told the group that he had decided to offer the Russians a moratorium on tests below the threshold limited to one or two years. He added that he did not think the Russians would agree, "but felt that this was in the interests of the country, as otherwise all hope of relaxing the cold war would be gone." [24]

Neither the American press nor Macmillan was aware of Eisenhower's decision. On March 27, the day the British leader arrived in the United States, James Reston wrote in the *New York Times* that the President was "confronted with the most serious decision he has had to make since he ordered the Allied troops to cross the English Channel for the invasion of Europe in 1945 [*sic*]." When the discussions began at Camp David on March 28, Macmillan found the American proposal "surprisingly good." "It obviously represents a triumph for the State Department over the Pentagon and the Atomic Energy Commission," he noted in his diary. The two leaders quickly agreed to accept the Russian proposal for a voluntary moratorium on tests below the 4.75 threshold in return for Soviet agreement to sign a treaty banning all tests above that level.

Two issues remained to be settled. One was the duration of the moratorium. Eisenhower wanted it brief, no more than a year, while Tsarapkin had indicated at Geneva that Russia would insist on a four- to five-year period. Macmillan suggested moving to two, and possible three years, during the final negotiations with the Soviets. The other question was the number of on-site inspections for suspicious seismic events above 4.75 on the Richter scale. They failed to settle on an acceptable number, but on Herter's advice, decided to let Eisenhower and Khrushchev set the actual annual quota at the forthcoming Paris summit conference.

Despite these unresolved problems, Macmillan was pleased with the outcome of his visit to the United States. "All the omens were good," he commented in his diary. He was especially pleased that the President had confided in him of "his hopes for a Nuclear Test Agreement." "He is *really* keen on this and—although he has not said much about it yet—would accept further concessions in the course of negotiation to get it. . . ."[25]

Eisenhower seemed equally optimistic in his comments to the press on his conference with Macmillan. He explained that the Western nations had agreed on a twofold approach, a formal treaty banning all tests in the atmosphere, underwater, and underground above the 4.75 threshold and a "voluntary moratorium of agreed duration" for subsurface tests below that level. When reporters asked about the gamble involved in such a course, Ike replied, "you have to make some concessions as to stopping this whole business." He replied to a follow-up question by stating his personal belief that halting the spread of nuclear weapons was worth the risk entailed. "There are already four nations into it, and it's an expensive business," he added. "And it could be finally more dangerous than ever. . . ."

Critics quickly questioned the moratorium. Some objected to the President binding the nation to a unilateral policy that would extend beyond his term in office. Eisenhower admitted that he could not commit the United States past January 1961, and said it would be up to his successor to continue or suspend the test cessation. Senator John Kennedy, the leading Democratic challenger, soon made this point moot by sending Eisenhower a letter promising "to carry out in good faith any moratorium extending beyond your term of office which you now decide to be in the best interests of the nation." Within a week, all the other announced presidential candidates made a similar pledge, thereby removing the constitutional obstacle.[26]

Others attacked the idea of a moratorium on its merits. Members of the Joint Committee informed the administration that they had "serious concern" about relying on Russian good faith after a private briefing by State and AEC representatives. In the press, military commentators such as Hanson Baldwin and conservative columnists such as Arthur Krock warned that the Pentagon needed to test warheads for such new weapons as the Minuteman ICBM and the proposed anti-missile missile. The editors of *Life* stressed the fact that the moratorium marked "a retreat from the previous U.S. stand on disarmament." The Russians, they commented, were "getting the result they wanted anyway—a total ban on all tests—by the moratorium route."[27]

Despite these comments, most observers agreed that Eisenhower had finally resolved the issue that had deadlocked test ban negotiations for nearly two years. By accepting the Soviet moratorium proposal, commented *Newsweek,* "the President made clear his determination to do everything he could to achieve nuclear peace." *Time* was equally impressed with Ike's role: "The word in Washington was that the U.S. will test no more nuclear deterrent weapons while Dwight Eisenhower is still in the White House." The *New Republic,* which had long called for a test ban, praised the President for protecting "this and coming generations from further poisoning by radioactive fallout."

Yet even the most enthusiastic test ban advocates realized that the struggle was not yet over. Thorny issues still had to be resolved on the duration of the moratorium and the number of on-site inspections. Most observers felt that if Eisenhower and Khrushchev could reach agreement on these two critical points at the summit meeting in May, then a test ban treaty could be a reality within 90 days. There would still be a final hurdle—the foes of a test ban were certain to wage an all-out campaign against ratification in the Senate. Secretary Herter gave the most sensible forecast. He doubted that the treaty could be achieved in two or three months, but with the new breakthrough, he was "reasonably optimistic" that there would be eventual agreement to end all nuclear tests.[28]

VI

Opponents of a test ban, worried by the administration's reaction to the Soviet moratorium offer, launched a spirited counterattack. A group of distinguished scientists led by Edward Teller, whom Isidore Rabi described as "brilliant in inventing excuses and ways" that a test ban "could be circumvented," stressed the difficulty in identifying concealed underground blasts and the danger in relying on Soviet good faith. At the very least, they hoped to convince enough senators of the grave risk involved in the pending test ban treaty to block its ratification. Antoher group of equally prominent scientists, headed by Hans Bethe, tried desperately to blunt this assault and state the case for a threshold test ban as the best way to achieve the long-sought goal of nuclear disarmament.[29]

The first clash came over the neutron bomb. In the April issue of *Foreign Affairs,* Freeman Dyson, a British-born physicist at the Institute for Advanced Study in Princeton, published an article advocating development of a tactical nuclear weapon that he described as "a fission-free bomb." Such a device, he argued, would be the logical outgrowth of the AEC's quest for a "clean" bomb, a weapon that would release a devastating shower of neutrons with very little blast effect and virtually no lingering radioactivity. The advantages of such bombs, Dyson argued, would lie in their low cost and their adaptability for battlefield use in limited wars. Dyson claimed that the Russians had been working on such a weapon since the early 1950s and he warned that the United States could not afford to lag behind on its development. "Any country which renounces for itself the development of nuclear weapons," he concluded, "without certain knowledge that its adversaries have done the same, is likely to find itself in the position of the Polish Army in 1939, fighting tanks with horses."

Though Dyson never specifically called for the resumption of testing, the whole thrust of his article was in this direction. He challenged the prevailing assumption of test ban advocates that nuclear technology had reached a dead end. Comparing the idea for the neutron bomb to the decisions in the past to build both the atomic and hydrogen bombs, Dyson claimed that you either went ahead and tested such a weapon, "or you leave it to chance to decide who makes it." Ominously, he pointed out that given the small size of the proposed neutron bomb, it could easily be tested secretly, below the threshold of 4.75 on the Richter scale.[30]

Test ban advocates quickly challenged Dyson's article. Hans Bethe claimed that the weapon would take at least ten years to develop, since it would mean finding a way to detonate a fusion explosion without using an atomic bomb as the trigger. David Inglis pointed out that Dyson had offered no evidence that such a weapon was feasible beyond the assertion that there was no law of nature forbidding its construction. At best, Inglis continued, a neutron bomb was "a bare possibility," and he thought it would be "a great mistake" to forsake a test ban treaty in pursuit of such a "technical dream." It was hard enough, he continued, for the average citizen to understand the technical aspects of the test ban debate; the American people "should be spared the confusion of nuclear phantasmagoria and trivia."

Despite these objections, opponents of the test ban found Dyson's article irresistible. In a May speech Senator Thomas Dodd of Connecticut demanded that President Eisenhower inform the American people about this new weapon. Stating his understanding that such a bomb would wipe out all human life in the target area while leaving buildings and structures intact, Dodd declared, "It would, in short, operate as a kind of death ray." How would the administration's plan for a test ban treaty,

Dodd wanted to know, affect America's chances of developing this dread weapon ahead of the Russians? The *U.S. News and World Report* echoes Dodd's concern over the possible "death ray." "Scientists see the Russians as moving ahead with research and possibly even with secret tests of the components of a neutron bomb," the editors commented. In view of this possibility, they concluded, there was "increasing opposition in this country to a test ban agreement of any kind with the Russians."[31]

The furor over the neutron bomb died away quickly; a far more serious threat to a test ban treaty came out of hearings held by the Joint Committee on Atomic Energy in April. Under the chairmanship of Representative Chet Holifield, the sub-committees on radiation and on research and development heard witnesses who testified on the problem of detecting and identifying underground nuclear tests. The information presented during the four-day hearing was familiar to the committee members, who had been briefed on the detection issue by the AEC. The real purpose of the hearing was to bring home to the American people the degree of risk involved in both the threshold treaty and the voluntary moratorium on small tests. To achieve this purpose, Chairman Holifield narrowly restricted testimony to the detection issue, preventing witnesses like Hans Bethe from describing the political and diplomatic advantages that might be gained from a test ban agreement.[32]

The first two witnesses, Harold Brown and Wolfgang Panofsky, stressed the inherent difficulty in distinguishing between small earthquakes and underground nuclear tests. Both men had attended the recent technical meeting in Geneva and both were dubious about the chances of perfecting a seismic system that would be foolproof. Panofsky pointed out that any inspection system would entail "an element of risk," while Brown stated that even on-site inspection could not rule out the possibility that a suspicious seismic event was in fact a concealed underground test. A violator could hide the evidence so carefully, Brown argued, that "it would only be an accident. . . . if it were detected." When pressed by the subcommittee on the degree of risk involved in the proposed threshold treaty, Panofsky estimated that there was one chance in ten that a concealed nuclear shot registering 4.75 on the Richter scale could be positively identified. Brown quickly added that the odds of detecting a test below the threshold were "close to zero."

Albert Latter of the RAND Corporation then explained his theory of decoupling to show how the use of large holes for nuclear explosions would make detection even less reliable. He explained that the original data from the RAINIER shot was based on an explosion in volcanic tuff, which proved to be a sensitive conductor of seismic waves. Underground blasts set off in granite or in a salt formation would produce much smaller signals, and the greatest reduction would occur in hollow chambers, which could reduce the seismic waves by a factor of 300. Recent chemical explosive tests conducted in Louisiana salt mines had confirmed the decoupling theory, Latter explained, indicating that it would be possible to detonate 100 kiloton bombs without any chance of their being detected.

Another witness, L. P. Meade of Phillips Petroleum, explained how easy it would be to convert existing salt domes into huge underground test chambers. The oil industry had already developed the technology to flush the salt out of the ground as brine and use the resulting caverns for petroleum storage reservoirs. He estimated that a salt dome 516 feet in diameter, large enough to muffle a 30 kiloton blast, could be excavated in less than two years at a cost of $11 million. Similar salt domes existed in the Soviet Union, he continued, and the same techniques were available to the Russians through their petroleum industry.[33]

Edward Teller capped off the testimony; he endorsed Latter's decoupling studies and suggested that "this wonderful science of seismology will reveal still more ways to conceal nuclear explosions underground." He admitted that better detection systems could be developed, but they would cost millions and take several years to perfect. And then they might be easily outmoded by such techniques as firing several underground blasts simultaneously in a circular pattern, which would create seismic signals identical to those produced by earthquakes. There was no such thing as a perfect system, Teller concluded; "the question is only one of the threshold." Seismologists might be able to reduce that threshold to lower and lower levels, he asserted, but physicists could use even the smallest nuclear blasts to gain the knowledge they needed to perfect newer and more deadly weapons.

Hans Bethe tried hard to rebut this pessimistic testimony. Admitting the validity of Latter's decoupling concept, the Cornell physicist maintained that the detection system could be upgraded to overcome this new obstacle. He outlined a plan to revise the 1958 Geneva system, with the control posts located 1000 kilometers apart, to one in which there were seismograph stations only 200 kilometers from each other. Such a network would have the capability of detecting the seismic signals from all explosions above 20 kilotons, even decoupled ones. Unfortunately, he admitted, such a system would require 600 control posts in Russia alone, but he added that such an elaborate network was no more impractical than his opponents' idea of digging huge holes in the earth to achieve decoupling. "I only want to leave with you the impression that these further decoupling schemes are by no means as simple as appears on the surface and by no means as sure," Bethe concluded. "It is my opinion that the next round ought to go to the detection rather than the concealment." [34]

Other witnesses supported Bethe's remarks. A veteran oil prospector pointed out how slight changes in the earth's crust were readily apparent from the air. The very techniques used to discover promising underground petroleum formations could be exploited to detect the site of subsurface explosions. Harold Urey, a distinguished physicist, argued that traditional intelligence gathering methods could be used to supplement seismic detection to provide reliable clues to secret underground tests. Jay Orear supported Bethe's proposal for a

600-station network in Russia and contended that any tests it could not detect would be too small to be militarily useful.

These counterarguments were not very persuasive. Test ban opponents were quick to cite the political difficulty posed by 600 control stations on Soviet territory. A nation that objected to any form of international supervision was unlikely to agree to such a massive invasion of its privacy. The closed nature of the Russian regime cast doubt on reliance on both espionage and aerial overflights as supplements to a seismic detection system. And Harold Brown, who had worked on bomb design as Teller's assistant at Livermore Laboratory, pointed out to Orear that a one kiloton test "could develop almost any tactical weapon that one had in mind." [35]

The hearings had precisely the impact that the Joint Committee apparently desired. After the first day of testimony, the *New York Times* commented that the net effect "was to present a far more pessimistic appraisal than has generally been given by Administration spokesmen." The chances for Senate support for the threshold test ban treaty, commented *Newsweek,* "seemed more remote than ever." Chairman Holifield's closing statement left little doubt of his position. The hearings revealed, he stated, that it would be impossible to detect and identify unmuffled nuclear blasts under 20 kilotons. "Further," Holifield continued, "it appears that . . . it will not be possible to detect muffled tests of 100 kilotons or more set off deep underground in large cavities." [36]

Hans Bethe registered his dissent with the Joint Committee's findings in a speech to the Washington Philosophical Society on April 25. Accusing Teller of raising "most unlikely technical difficulties," Bethe declared, "I think we are all behaving like a bunch of lunatics to take any such thing as the big hole seriously." He denied that he wanted to impose a 600-station system on Russia; all he was trying to do was to show that there were ways to upgrade the 1958 Geneva system. Above all, Bethe called for a weighing of the risks in the continuing arms race against the possible danger from a threshold treaty. "We have lost our sense of balance in pursuing complicated technical problems," he concluded, pleading for consideration of "the political objectives of a test-ban agreement."[37]

John McCone denounced Bethe to Kistiakowsky for going back on the testimony he gave at the Joint Committee hearings. Growing emotional, McCone declared that the proposed test ban was "a national peril" that might force him "to resign his job" if it went into effect. Other sources within the government informed Kistiakowsky that McCone was the prime mover behind the Joint Committee hearings. The AEC chairman, Kistiakowsky recorded in his diary, was "maneuvering public opinion, including the Senate, so that the President will have a very difficult time getting a treaty ratified."

Arthur Krock had a different explanation for the hearings. Although he shared McCone's doubts about the wisdom of such an agreement, the *New York Times* columnist saw the Democratic members of the Joint Committee as the prime movers. Krock believed they feared the political consequences of Eisenhower negotiating a test ban treaty at Paris which would enable the Republican party to monopolize the peace issue in the coming presidential election. By stirring up doubts about the validity of such a treaty in advance, he felt the congressional Democrats were engaging in subtle but effective partisan infighting.[38]

Whatever the motivation, the hearings served their purpose. They effectively undercut the optimism building up after Macmillan's visit and cast a long shadow over the forthcoming Paris summit. Eisenhower would not only have to wring important concessions from Khrushchev on the number of on-site inspections and the length of the moratorium, but he would have to persuade the Russian leader that he could carry the Senate with him on any treaty they signed at Paris.

VII

Despite the reemergence of the detection issue, the President and his advisers still hoped to break the test ban deadlock at the Paris summit. After a meeting with the British and French foreign ministers in Washington in mid-April, Secretary of State Herter announced that they had decided to give disarmament priority over a negotiated settlement of the Berlin crisis. Ambassador Wadsworth, at home during a recess in the Geneva talks, expressed his confidence that the heads of government would reach agreement on the length of the moratorium and the number of on-site inspections in their meeting. The President was more guarded in his remarks at a press conference on April 27. He refused to comment specifically on the test ban issue, but he told reporters that at Paris he hoped to achieve an "ease of tension, some evidence that we are coming closer together . . . so that people have a right to feel a little bit more confident in the world in which they are living and in its stability." [39]

Speeches by two key Democratic senators in late April encouraged the administration. Hubert Humphrey, reaffirming his support for a test ban treaty, urged the President to seek a minimum of 20 on-site inspections a year in his talks with Khrushchev. If the administration could secure Russian agreement to that number, Humphrey asserted, then the Senate was likely to ratify the proposed threshold treaty. Even more significant, Senator Albert Gore, who had opposed a comprehensive treaty in favor of a ban limited to atmospheric tests, announced a change in his position. He now felt that a treaty based on the February 11 threshold plan "would merit sympathetic and favorable consideration by the United States Senate." This last-minute support from leading Democrats brightened the outlook for Senate ratification of a threshold treaty and gave Eisenhower a much stronger bargaining position in his talks with Khrushchev. [40]

The U-2 affair suddenly altered the situation. On May 1, high above Sverdlovsk, a Soviet ground-to-air missile disabled an American U-2 spy plane and forced the pilot to parachute to safety. When President Eisenhower learned that the plane was missing, though not that the Russians had captured the pilot alive, he authorized his aides to issue a prepared statement to the effect that the U-2 was a NASA weather plane that had strayed accidentally into Soviet air space. The administration stuck to its cover story even after Khrushchev announced on May 5 that the Soviets had shot down an American reconnaissance aircraft, but when the Russian leader produced both the pilot, Francis Gary Powers, and the wreckage of his U-2 in Moscow the next day, the President directed Secretary of State Herter to acknowledge that the United States had been overflying the Soviet Union. The State Department spokesman insisted that Soviet refusal to agree to aerial inspection justified the U-2 flights; there was no escaping the fact, however, that the United States had been caught lying before the world.

President Eisenhower's main concern was to prevent the U-2 incident from sabotaging the forthcoming Paris summit. Disregarding advisers who wanted him to place the blame for the May 1 overflight on subordinates, the President issued a statement on May 11 in which he took personal responsibility for the U-2 mission. Declaring that "no one wants another Pearl Harbor," he described the valuable intelligence information the flights had provided since 1956 and seemed to imply that they would continue for the indefinite future. Then Ike, aware of the furor his words would invoke, smiled glumly and told his aides, "We will now just have to endure the storm."[41]

Eisenhower's decision to take full responsibility for the Powers mission put the Paris summit in jeopardy. Khrushchev arrived in Paris on May 14 and in meetings with Harold Macmillan and Charles de Gaulle, he made clear that he expected Eisenhower to give him both a personal apology for the overflights and an assurance that the United States would never again send a U-2 over Russian soil. The President, who reached Paris on May 15, had already ordered the suspension of further U-2 flights, but he was unwilling to make the public commitments that Khrushchev demanded as the price for holding the conference. "I hope that no one is under the illusion," he told de Gaulle, "that I am going to crawl on my knees to Khrushchev."

When the French President convened the summit conference on May 16, the outlook was bleak. Khrushchev immediately demanded the right to speak first, and after receiving a nod of approval from Eisenhower, de Gaulle recognized the Soviet leader. Khrushchev proceeded to denounce Eisenhower in vitriolic language, ungraciously withdrew an earlier invitation to Ike to visit the Soviet Union, and suggested that the conference be rescheduled after Eisenhower's term in office had ended.

The President spoke next, and belatedly he tried to mollify the angry Khrushchev. Although Ike continued to justify past U-2 flights, he announced that he had suspended the program and promised that there would be no future U-2 missions over Russian territory. Then he made his final plea for peaceful negotiations. "I have come to Paris to seek agreements with the Soviet Union which would eliminate the necessity for all forms of espionage, including overflights," Eisenhower declared. "I see no reason to use this incident to disrupt the conference."

Khrushchev refused to respond to the President's efforts at conciliation. Instead he stormed out of the conference chamber and the next day excoriated Eisenhower at a press conference attended by over 3,000 journalists from around the world. Ike left Paris the following day, saddened by the realization that the unfortunate U-2 incident had destroyed the promising Paris conference and with it his fond hopes for agreement on at least the essentials of a test ban treaty. ". . . The chances for agreement on disarmament or the ending of nuclear tests had been blown to bits," commented the *New York Times*, "and it would take considerable time to paste together again."[42]

For a while, it appeared possible that the U-2 crisis could even lead to a resumption in nuclear testing. Both Secretary of Defense Gates and AEC Chairman McCone advised the President at Paris to break off the Geneva talks and authorize new underground tests. At home, Edward Teller issued a public call for immediate tests of new weapons. Kistiakowsky strongly opposed what he termed such "saber-rattling moves," and at a National Security Council meeting on May 24, Secretary of

State Herter urged that the administration continue both the Geneva conference and the moratorium on testing. When Mc-Cone objected, the President, who had remained silent, spoke up to say that there would be no change—the United States would refrain from testing and continue to seek a test ban treaty at Geneva.[43]

But Eisenhower knew that the U-2 crisis had ended any possibility for a threshold treaty during his term in office. The "dreary exercise" at Geneva would continue, he wrote in his memoirs, but the issue had obviously reached "a blind alley." A few weeks later, a despondent Eisenhower commented to Kistiakowsky on the repercussions of the Powers flight. As the science adviser recalled later, "the President began to talk with much feeling about how he had concentrated his efforts the last few years on ending the cold war, how he felt that he was making big progress, and how the stupid U-2 mess had ruined all his efforts. He ended very sadly that he saw nothing worthwhile left for him to do now until the end of his Presidency."

It was natural for Eisenhower to blame the U-2 incident. Yet in the long run the failure to negotiate a test ban treaty was due primarily to his own lack of leadership. For two years, he had permitted a difference of opinion between his diplomatic and scientific advisers and his military and national security experts to paralyze the negotiations at Geneva. One may well question the sincerity of the Soviet advocacy of a comprehensive test ban treaty, but American indecision meant that Russian intentions were never fully probed. By the time the President finally came down on the side of Herter and Kistiakowsky, it was too late. As the editors of the *Nation* commented, the man who all his life had been the beneficiary of amazing good luck had finally met his nemesis. "It was as if the gods finally had enough of the President's faults," they wrote; "at the end they punished him for all he had done, all he had left undone, and for all their gifts of the past."[44]

EPILOGUE

The Geneva negotiations resumed after the break-up of the Paris summit. For three months, Wadsworth and Tsarapkin went through the motions of seeking agreement on the outstanding issues. But it was apparent to observers that no further progress was possible. Both sides were simply marking time until a new administration took office in the United States.

President Eisenhower was fully aware of the futility of the Geneva exercise, but he was determined not to jeopardize the chances of the next president to succeed where he had failed. He steadily resisted pressure from John McCone to order the resumption of underground testing, saying that he would not act "until we could exhaust every possibility of reaching some worthwhile agreement." In particular, he made clear his refusal even to consider atmospheric tests. "I will adhere, as long as I am here, to the one promise I made," he told reporters in August: "I will not allow anything to be exploded in the atmosphere that would add anything to the apprehensions of people about their health."

Yet the President became disenchanted with the moratorium he had begun in 1958. By the fall of 1960, he realized that it was hurting the nuclear weapons program. Worried that cessa-

315

tion had placed the United States in a "disadvantageous position," he wrote in his memoirs that "prudence demanded a resumption of testing." He felt he could not act during the fall campaign, but after Kennedy's victory, he told the President-elect "that our nation should resume needed tests without delay."[1]

During his first year in office, Kennedy tried to continue the moratorium. He appointed Arthur H. Dean, a former law partner of John Foster Dulles, to head the American negotiating team at Geneva, where the test ban talks resumed in March, 1961. Early hopes for agreement ended in late August, however, when Tsarapkin rejected both a modified version of Eisenhower's threshold test ban with a three-year moratorium on low-level underground shots and a comprehensive test ban which included a strengthened inspection system. On August 31, the Kremlin announced its plans to resume nuclear testing in the atmosphere, and the next day the AEC reported a nuclear explosion in Siberia of "a substantial yield in the intermediate range." Over the next three months, the Soviets detonated at least 31 atmospheric tests, including several multi-megaton blasts and one enormous shot which the AEC estimated to be 58 megatons in explosive energy. Fallout once again rained down on the northern hemisphere, causing such respected leaders as Jawaharlal Nehru, Adlai Stevenson, and Bertrand Russell to denounce the Soviet Union for endangering the health of all mankind.

President Kennedy, sensitive to world opinion, restricted the American response to underground shots in 1961, but pressures from testing advocates, headed once more by Edward Teller, as well as from the Pentagon, forced him to announce the resumption of American tests in the atmosphere in a televised speech to the nation on March 2, 1962. The AEC detonated the first American atmospheric shot at Christmas Island on April 25, and during the remainder of the year, the United States set off an additional 32 blasts in the Pacific, nearly all below one megaton in size. The relatively low yield of these tests produced far less fallout than the Soviet explosions, but nevertheless concerned people in the United States and throughout the world voiced their resentment against the additional risk of cancer and birth defects that they feared would result.

The Geneva talks went on while the testing resumed, but the continued refusal of the Soviet Union to expand the inspection network proposed by the conference of experts in 1958 blocked all progress. The peaceful resolution of the Cuban missile crisis led to renewed efforts to break the inspection deadlock, and in early 1963 a compromise involving an annual quota of on-site inspections to differentiate between earthquakes and suspected underground tests seemed feasible. Kennedy insisted on seven such inspections a year, however, and Khrushchev would not go beyond three. Finally, the two leaders decided to abandon the fruitless quest for a comprehensive test ban and to settle instead for the more limited measure Eisenhower had proposed in April, 1959—an atmospheric test ban. Kennedy sent Averell Harriman to Moscow, and in only ten days he reached agreement with Khrushchev and a British representative for an end to testing underwater, in the atmosphere, and in outer space. Since tests in such environments could be detected at great distances, the limited test ban treaty did not require on-site inspection.

The treaty signed in Moscow in the summer of 1963 ended the era of extensive atmospheric testing. Since that agreement, the world has been spared the danger of further fallout except for sporadic tests by France, China, and India. Nuclear tests, however, did not end in 1963; they simply went underground. The United States and the Soviet Union have engaged in extensive subsurface testing designed to perfect the warheads for a variety of new delivery systems, ranging from the MIRV to the cruise missile. Far more nuclear tests have been conducted since the signing of the limited test ban treaty than in the period from 1945 to 1963. The unresolvable problem of inspection, together with the continuing tension of the cold war, frustrated the best efforts of test ban advocates to bring the arms race under control.

Despite this ultimate failure, Dwight D. Eisenhower must be credited with making a sincere effort to use the test ban as a first step toward genuine nuclear disarmament. He was willing to take a chance with national security by initiating the first moratorium on testing in 1958. For three years, he spared the world the danger of fallout, and in the long run it was his April 1959 proposal for a test ban limited to the atmosphere that finally became the basis for the two superpowers agreeing in 1963 to stop poisoning the earth. Eisenhower took great pride in his contribution, writing in his memoirs that his administration "did everything possible to encourage the Soviets to act with us and to remove this cloud that so darkened the skies at mid-century."[2]

I

The nationwide concern over fallout continued to recede in 1960. A series of developments contributed to the growing sense of reassurance. The Public Health Service reports on the amount of strontium-90 in the nation's milk supply showed that the 1959 rise had leveled off well below the danger level set by the National Committee on Radiation Protection. In April, HEW Secretary Flemming, who chaired the government's new Federal Radiation Council, announced the "heartening" news that Sr^{90} levels in all forms of food had declined during the last three months of 1959 and no longer posed a threat to human health. The fourth report on the level of strontium-90 in human bones by Laurence Kulp and his Columbia University associates was even more encouraging. The average uptake of Sr^{90} for adults in 1959 was just 0.3 mmc, and even infants were only absorbing 2.1 mmc, far below the danger level. Moreover, Kulp reported, earlier forecasts of eventual human absorption had been too high. "Thus, the peak in the diet passed in 1959," the report stated; "the peak in growing bones will pass this year; and the equilibrium level will be lower than had been predicted by a factor of 5 to 10."[3]

At the same time, the government tacitly admitted that the problem was more serious than it had previously acknowledged. In February 1960, the Federal Radiation Council suddenly lowered the maximum permissible level for Sr^{90} in milk from 80 micromicrocuries per liter to 33 mmc/l. Though the national average of 8.8 mmc/l was still far below the new standard, the margin of safety was sharply reduced. In May, the Council issued new standards for radiation safety. Accepting the argument that there was no threshold below which radiation was safe to human health, the new guidelines no longer used the terminology "maximum permissible exposure." Instead the report set forth general guides for both occupational and general population purposes. For the population as a whole, the guide was set at an annual whole body dose of 0.5r, a figure which would limit the 30-year exposure to reproductive organs to a maximum of 5r. Several months later, the AEC followed the Council's example, lowering the radiation limit for employees in atomic energy industries from 15r to 5r annually, with a maximum exposure of 3r in any three month period.[4]

Despite these more conservative guidelines, the government refused to concede that there was a serious radiation safety problem. A National Academy of Sciences review of its 1956 report released in May 1960 sustained this position. The updated study, which incorporated all scientific evidence that had come to light since the original report, concluded that "these new findings have not changed the evaluations presented in 1956." The genetic committee found that the possible harmful effect of heavier fallout since 1956 had been more than offset by the discovery that low-level radiation caused fewer mutations than had been thought likely. Therefore, the geneticists felt that their earlier recommendation that the exposure of the reproductive organs be held to 10r over the first 30 years of an individual's life still offered a reasonable standard. The somatic committee discounted the earlier concern that radiation would shorten life expectancy, expressed doubt that leukemia could be induced by low-level radiation, and concluded that the present levels "remain well below those that need to be considered cause for concern."

The National Academy of Sciences 1960 report contained the warning that there were "many questions about radiation hazards which are unanswerable with present data." Twelve years later, a new NAS study stated that while the scientific evidence was still too scanty to answer these questions conclusively, the 1956 standard of a maximum exposure of 10r over 30 years remained reasonable. In 1972, the geneticists concluded that their predecessors had been too conservative in their findings—they had overstated the rate of mutations from low-level radiation. On the other hand, the 1972 study found that the somatic effects were a little more serious. Though there was still no conclusive evidence on the threshold issue, the committee accepted the premise that the risk of cancer was directly proportional to the total radiation exposure. On that basis, they estimated that each additional .1r exposure a year would cause between 1350 and 3300 additional cancer deaths, or an increase of less than 1 per cent in the total cancer death rate. Since the fallout rate had never approached the level of 0.1r, which was approximately the natural background radiation, the 1972 findings suggested that the concern expressed by test ban advocates in the 1950s was exaggerated.[5]

The scientific issues raised by fallout in the 1950s still remain unanswered two decades later. On balance, however, the 1956 National Academy of Sciences report which became the basis for government policy stood the test of time remarkably well. Attacked by critics as too conservative in its estimate of the danger, it proved a reliable guide in an area where evidence was scanty. Radiation was indeed dangerous, as the NAS study pointed out, but the fallout hazard was small compared to radiation from other sources, such as medical and dental X-rays. By creating a marginally higher exposure, the nuclear tests of the 1950s increased mankind's risk of cancer by only a small amount. Testing did not create a serious threat to human health, but it did raise a profound moral issue—whether or not the United States and the Soviet Union should expose the world's population to even a slight health hazard in the name of national security. The realization by the two superpowers that neither had the right to do so finally brought about the end of atmospheric testing.

II

How responsible were the scientists who participated in the fallout debate? In one sense, they failed to give the calm, objective advice that both the people and political leaders expected them to provide. Swept away by their emotions, they entered the controversy as advocates, using their scholarly reputations to advance their chosen causes. Though Linus Pauling eventually won the Nobel prize for peace on the basis of his test ban activities, he was guilty of making exaggerated and dubious claims about the potential danger of fallout to human health. And Edward Teller was equally culpable. His ceaseless lobbying for continued testing and the extreme arguments he developed on the detection issue stemmed from his distrust of the Soviet Union, not from his scientific knowledge. These scientists, as citizens in a democracy, had the right to express their views and engage in the normal excesses of political rhetoric. But by failing to make clear that their judgments on fallout stemmed from deep-seated feelings and not from their professional expertise, they served only to confuse and mislead the American people.

Yet it would be wrong to condemn all scientists for the actions of a few. Many eminent researchers sought to serve the nation by providing the data and judgment needed by the political leaders who were wrestling with such complex and technical issues as radioactive fallout and the detection of underground nuclear blasts. The linearity studies by Edward Lewis, the thoughtful contributions of Hermann Muller to the genetic issue, the careful analysis of the strontium-90 content of human bone by Laurence Kulp and his associates—these are but a few examples of the constructive contributions many scientists made to an understanding of the issues involved in the fallout debate. Equally important, men such as James Killian, Hans Bethe, and George Kistiakowsky abandoned their own research and teaching activities to devote themselves full time to advising the Eisenhower administration in the late 1950s. They proved as fallible as the politicians in their judgments, often letting their desire for a breakthrough in the arms race influence their decisions, but at least they raised the level of scientific advice the government received to a new high standard.

In the long run, the scientists failed because the problem defied scientific analysis. The questions that had to be answered went far beyond evidence that could be subjected to critical study and made to yield universally accepted conclusions. How could one measure objectively the amount of radiation it was permissible to shower on the world against the presumed danger of falling behind in the arms race? Just what degree of risk did the United States run from secret underground Soviet tests if the original 1958 Geneva detection system became the basis for a test ban treaty? And even more fundamentally, on what basis could one be sure that a test ban would be an effective first step toward control of the arms race when it did not involve any actual disarmament? Scientists could help identify the issues involved in these political questions, but they could not provide definitive answers. The belief that they could, shared by some scientists as well as by many laymen, testifies only to a misplaced faith in science in an age of great uncertainty.

III

The test ban issue was bound to lead to frustration because it raised false expectations. "What happened, in effect," wrote Thomas Murray in 1960, "was that all the bewilderments of the unfolding Nuclear Age . . . came to focus in a mounting emotional resentment against nuclear tests, regardless of type."[6] The horror of the hydrogen bomb was so great that most people could not face it directly. Yet try as they might, they could not ignore it. The testing issue gave them a way to deal with it obliquely. Instead of coping with the danger of all-out nuclear war, in which the blast and heat and fallout might destroy most of the American population, they focused on the less drastic but still insidious threat of poisoned milk and contaminated air. The test ban became a kind of magic talisman, a way that the nation could confront a real and present danger without coming to grips with the true reality of the 1950s—the possibility of total destruction.

The failure to resolve the test ban controversy in the 1950s was not completely unfortunate. A successful treaty might have led to the assumption that the nuclear evil had been overcome, permitting the nation to relax once more. Instead, both scientists and politicians found that the problem of testing could not be easily separated from the far graver question of nuclear disarmament. The cold war tensions that led to the deadlock on all arms control efforts prevented Eisenhower and Khrushchev from reaching an agreement and finally made them aware that as long as the two superpowers distrusted each other, there was no real possibility for nuclear disarmament. Only after going to the brink of nuclear holocaust during the Cuban missile crisis would the two nations finally accept a limited test ban as a tentative first step toward the détente that both so stubbornly resisted.

APPENDIX

Chronology of the Nuclear Test Ban Debate,
1950–1963

1950
January 31   President Truman orders development
                              of hydrogen bomb

1951
April–May   Operation GREENHOUSE in Pacific
                              demonstrates feasibility of fusion explo-
                              sion
June 19–20   Edward Teller reveals his breakthrough
                              on H-bomb to panel of scientists at In-
                              stitute for Advanced Study in Princeton

1952
October 13   Great Britain tests its first atomic bomb
November 1   MIKE hydrogen device tested at Eniwe-
                              tok

APPENDIX

1953
August 12 — First Soviet H-bomb test detected by AEC

1954
March 1 — AEC fires BRAVO shot at Bikini

March 31 — Admiral Strauss reveals destructive nature of H-bomb at presidential press conference

April 19 — United Nations establishes five-nation disarmament subcommittee

September 24 — Death of *Lucky Dragon* crew member Aikichi Kuboyama

September–October — Soviets conduct H-bomb test series

1955
February 15 — AEC releases report on BRAVO fallout

February 18–May 15 — Operation TEACUP atomic tests held in Nevada

March 19 — Harold Stassen appointed special assistant to the President for disarmament

August 4 — Soviet Union begins new H-bomb test series

December 3 — United Nations General Assembly creates scientific committee to study radiation hazards

1956
January 25 — Senate Foreign Relations Subcommittee on Disarmament begins hearings

April 21 — Adlai Stevenson proposes test ban in speech to American Society of Newspaper Editors

May 21–July 21 — Operation REDWING nuclear tests conducted in Marshall Islands

June 12 — National Academy of Sciences releases report on radiation hazards

| August 24–September 2 | Soviet Union conducts nuclear tests in Siberia |
| November 6 | President Eisenhower re-elected |

1957

January 14	Ambassador Lodge presents five-point disarmament proposal to United Nations
January 19–April 26	Soviet Union conducts nuclear tests in Siberia
March 18	United Nations disarmament subcommittee talks resume in London
April 24	Albert Schweitzer issues appeal for a test ban
May 15	Great Britain conducts its first H-bomb test at Christmas Island
May 25	Eisenhower approves temporary test ban proposal
May 27–June 7	Holifield's subcommittee on radiation of the Joint Committee on Atomic Energy holds fallout hearings
May 28–October 7	Operation PLUMBOB atomic tests conducted in Nevada
June 3	Linus Pauling submits scientists' test ban petition to White House
June 24	Teller, Lawrence, and Mills inform Eisenhower of quest for "clean" bomb
August 22	Soviet Union begins series of 6 H-bomb tests in Pacific
August 29	United States proposes a two-year suspension of testing, conditioned on a cutoff in nuclear weapons production
September 19	AEC detonates RANIER, the first underground nuclear test, in Nevada
October 4	Soviet Union launches Sputnik

November 7	Eisenhower appoints James Killian to new post of special assistant for science and technology

1958

January 13	Pauling presents scientists' test ban petition to the United Nations
February 15	Stassen resigns as special assistant to the President for disarmament
February 22– March 27	Soviet Union conducts series of nine H-bomb tests in Siberia
March 31	Khrushchev announces unilateral Soviet test suspension
April 17	Killian presents Scientific Advisory Committee recommendation for a comprehensive test ban to Eisenhower
April 28	Eisenhower separates test ban from other disarmament proposals in message to Khrushchev calling for technical conference on inspection and detection
April 28–August 12	HARDTACK I H-bomb tests held in Pacific
June 30	Lewis Strauss retires as chairman of the AEC; Eisenhower appoints John McCone as Strauss's successor
July 1	Soviet and American scientists meet at Geneva to discuss inspection and detection
August 10	United Nations scientific committee releases report on radiation hazards
August 21	Geneva conference of experts reaches agreement on extensive inspection system
August 22	Eisenhower proposes that test ban negotiations begin on October 31 and

	pledges a one-year moratorium on American tests after the talks begin
August 30	Soviet Union conditionally accepts Eisenhower's August 22 proposals
September 12	HARDTACK II atomic tests begin in Nevada
September 30	Soviet Union begins H-bomb test series in Siberia
October 30	AEC fires last shot in HARDTACK II series
October 31	Conference on the Discontinuance of Nuclear Weapons Tests opens at Geneva
November 3	AEC detects final Soviet nuclear test in fall series
November 17	Senator Gore proposes an atmospheric test ban

1959
January 5	Ambassador Wadsworth informs Tsarapkin of HARDTACK II data casting doubt on ability of Geneva network to detect all underground tests
March 15	Senator Anderson touches off fallout scare by releasing letter from General Loper indicating that strontium-90 fallout returns to earth much more rapidly than predicted
March 16	Berkner panel confirms HARDTACK II findings on detection in report to Eisenhower administration
March 19–24	Prime Minister Macmillan visits Washington to discuss test ban impasse with Eisenhower
April 13	Eisenhower proposes interim atmospheric test ban in letter to Khrushchev

April 23	Khrushchev proposes an annual quota of on-site inspections in letter to Eisenhower
May 5–8	Holifield's subcommittee on radiation holds second series of fallout hearings
May 7	AEC's General Advisory Committee releases report minimizing the fallout hazard
June 12	Berkner panel findings made public
June 22–July 10	Technical Working Group I discusses problem of detecting high altitude and space explosions
August 14	Eisenhower transfers supervision over radiation safety from AEC to new Federal Radiation Council
August 26	Eisenhower extends moratorium on testing through the end of the year
November 25–December 18	Technical Working Group II meets at Geneva and fails to reach agreement on detection issue
December 29	Eisenhower ends moratorium but pledges that the United States will not resume tests without prior notice

1960

February 11	Eisenhower proposes a ban on all atmospheric tests and those underground ones above a threshold of 4.75 on the Richter scale
February 13	First French atomic test conducted in the Sahara
March 19	Soviet Union agrees to Eisenhower's February 11 test ban proposal, provided the United States agrees to an unsupervised moratorium on tests below the 4.75 threshold

March 29	Eisenhower and Macmillan issue communiqué after Camp David meeting accepting in principle the Soviet proposal for a moratorium below the 4.75 threshold
April 19–22	Joint Committee on Atomic Energy holds subcommittee hearings on difficulties of detecting underground nuclear explosions
May 1	Soviet missile downs U-2 plane piloted by Gary Powers
May 4	National Academy of Sciences updates report on radiation hazards and concludes that danger from fallout is still slight
May 16	Khrushchev breaks up Paris summit conference over U-2 incident
1961	
September 1	Soviet Union resumes nuclear testing in atmosphere
September 15	United States resumes testing underground
October 30	Soviet Union detonates 58 megaton explosion
1962	
April 25	United States resumes atmospheric nuclear testing in Pacific
1963	
August 5	Limited nuclear test ban treaty signed in Moscow

NOTES

List of Abbreviations Used in Notes

AEC   Atomic Energy Commission
BAS   *Bulletin of the Atomic Scientists*
DDE   Dwight D. Eisenhower
NYT   *New York Times*
PPP   *Public Papers of the Presidents*
PSAC   President's Scientific Advisory Committee
SANE   National Committee for a Sane Nuclear Policy

CHAPTER ONE

1. "Unclassified History of Operation Castle, 1952–1954," compiled by Lt. H. Gordon Bechanan and 2nd Lt. Charles O. Jones, pp. 53, 120–21; and "Summary of Weather Situation for Bravo Shot," compiled by Col. H. K. Gilbert, May 12, 1954, Atomic Energy Commission Files, Germantown, Maryland.

2. "Operation Castle," pp. 122–29; Edward Teller and Albert L. Latter, *Our Nuclear Future* (New York, 1958), pp. 88–92; *New York Times,* July 8, 1954 (hereafter cited as *NYT*); *Newsweek* 43 (March

29, 1954), 20; Daniel Lang, *From Hiroshima to the Moon* (New York, 1959), pp. 370–72.

3. *Ibid.*, p. 372; Ralph E. Lapp, *The Voyage of the Lucky Dragon* (New York, 1958), pp. 27–44.

4. *Bulletin of the Atomic Scientists* (hereafter *BAS*) 10 (Feb. 1954), 61; *Newsweek* 43 (Mar. 8, 1954), 29.

5. *Ibid.*, 19–20; "Operation Castle," pp. 6–8, 10, 53; Thomas Murray to Dwight Eisenhower, Jan. 4, 1954, and Lewis Strauss to Eisenhower, Jan. 26, 1954, Dwight D. Eisenhower Papers (hereafter DDE Papers), Administration File, Dwight D. Eisenhower Library, Abilene, Kansas.

6. *NYT*, March 2, 7, and 12, 1954; "Operation Castle," p. 109.

7. *NYT*, Mar. 12 and 18, 1954; *BAS* 10 (Apr. 1954), 141; *Newsweek* 43 (March 29, 1954), 19–20.

8. Lang, *Hiroshima*, p. 372; Lapp, *Lucky Dragon*, pp. 55–112; *NYT*, Mar. 17 and 18, 1954; Department of State, *Bulletin* 30 (March 29, 1954), 466; *Newsweek* 43 (March 29, 1954), 23.

9. *NYT*, Mar. 16, 20, 21, and 27, 1954; *Life* 36 (Mar. 29, 1954), 17–21.

10. *Public Papers of the Presidents of the United States: Dwight D. Eisenhower, 1954* (Washington, 1960), pp. 342, 346 (hereafter *PPP*); James Hagerty diary, Mar. 23 and 24, 1954, James Hagerty Papers, Eisenhower Library; *NYT*, Mar. 16, 25, and 31, 1954.

11. Strauss to Eisenhower, Mar. 26, 1954, DDE Papers, Admin. File; *NYT*, Mar. 28, 30, and 31, 1954; *Newsweek* 43 (April 5, 1954), 23; Hagerty diary, Mar. 30 and 31, 1954.

12. Lewis L. Strauss, *Men and Decisions* (Garden City, N.Y., 1962), *passim;* Duncan Norton-Taylor, "The Controversial Mr. Strauss," *Fortune* 51 (Jan. 1955), 110–12, 164–70.

13. Hagerty diary, April 2 and 6, 1954; Carl Van Doren, *Benjamin Franklin* (New York, 1938), p. 694.

14. State Dept., *Bulletin* 30 (April 12, 1954), 548–49; *PPP: Eisenhower, 1954,* p. 370n.

15. "Excerpts from President Eisenhower's Press Conference, Wednesday, March 31, 1954," AEC Files; Hagerty diary, Mar. 31, 1954.

16. *NYT*, Apr. 1, 1954; *Time* 63 (Apr. 12, 1954), 21; *Newsweek* 43 (Apr. 12, 1954), 39; Strauss, *Men and Decisions*, p. 410.

17. Roland Sawyer, "The H-Bomb Chronology," *BAS* 10 (Sept. 1954),

287–88; Stanley A. Blumberg and Gwinn Owens, *Energy and Conflict: The Life and Times of Edward Teller* (New York, 1976), p. 382; *Newsweek* 44 (Aug. 2, 1954), 23–25.

18. Sawyer, "H-Bomb Chronology," pp. 288–90; *NYT*, Apr. 2, 1954.

19. Sawyer, "H-Bomb Chronology," pp. 290, 300; Edward Teller, "The Work of Many People," *Science* 121 (Feb. 25, 1955), 272–73; *NYT*, July 4, 1954; Herbert F. York, *The Advisors: Oppenheimer, Teller, and the Superbomb* (San Francisco, 1976), pp. 78–80.

20. Earl H. Voss, *Nuclear Ambush: The Test-Ban Trap* (Chicago, 1963), pp. 31–33; Thomas W. Wilson, Jr., *The Great Weapons Heresy* (Boston, 1970), pp. 142–43; Bernard C. Bechhoefer, *Postwar Negotiations for Arms Control* (Washington, 1961), pp. 170–71; Harry S Truman, *Memoirs*, 2 vols. (Garden City, N.Y., 1956), 2: 313–14.

21. Blumberg and Owens, *Energy and Conflict*, pp. 292–95; York, *The Advisors*, pp. 82–83; *Time* 60 (Nov. 24, 1952), 23.

22. Strauss, *Men and Decisions*, pp. 345–46; Nat S. Finney, "Atomic Dilemma," *BAS* 10 (Apr. 1954), 117; York, "The Advisors," pp. 89–91.

23. *NYT*, Apr. 2 and 3, 1954; "The Making of the H-Bomb," *BAS* 10 (June 1954), 228.

24. *BAS* 10 (June 1954), 198; Ralph Lapp, "Does the Superbomb Add to Our Security?" *Reporter* 10 (May 11, 1954), 10–11.

25. *Newsweek* 43 (Apr. 12, 1954), 6; *New Republic* 130 (Apr. 5, 1954); *Nation* 178 (Mar. 27, 1954), 249; *Scientific American* 190 (May 1954), 46.

26. *NYT*, Mar. 25 and 28, 1954; *Time* 63 (Apr. 12, 1954), 21; *Nation* 178 (Apr. 17, 1954), 320; William J. Hopkins to Ann Whitman, Apr. 28, 1954, and Brennan to C. D. Jackson, Mar. 26, 1954, DDE papers, GF 155-B; Compton to Eisenhower, Mar. 30, 1954, DDE Papers, OF 108-A.

27. *NYT*, Mar. 28 and Apr. 7, 1954; *Newsweek* 43 (Apr. 12, 1954), 46; *Reporter* 10 (Apr. 27, 1954), 2; *Time* 63 (Apr. 12, 1954), 22.

28. *NYT*, Mar. 29, Apr. 1 and 3, 1954; Department of State, *Documents on Disarmament, 1954–1959*, 2 vols. (Washington, 1960), 1: 409, 411.

29. David E. Lilienthal, *Venturesome Years, 1950–1955* (New York, 1966), p. 497; C. L. Sulzberger, *The Last of the Giants* (New York, 1970), p. 133; *NYT*, Apr. 2, 1954; State Dept., *Bulletin* 30 (May 3, 1954), 687.

30. *BAS* 10 (Nov. 1954), 339; *NYT,* Apr. 15 and 19, 1954.

31. *Ibid.,* Mar. 26, 28, 31, and Apr. 6, 1954; *Nation* 178 (Apr. 10, 1954), 293.

32. *NYT,* Mar. 27, 1954; William Beale to Hagerty, Mar. 25, 1954, DDE Papers, GF 155B; Hagerty diary, Apr. 1, 1954.

33. *Newsweek* 43 (Apr. 12, 1954), 41; *Time* 63 (Apr. 12, 1954), 25; *Life* 36 (Apr. 12, 1954), 25; *ibid.* (Apr. 19, 1954), 21–24; *NYT,* Apr. 4, 1954.

34. Cole to Eisenhower, Apr. 5, 1954, DDE Papers, Name Series; Hagerty diary, March 30, 1954; memorandum of telephone conversation between Eisenhower and Strauss, DDE Papers, Eisenhower Diary Series; Strauss to Eisenhower, Apr. 5, 1954, DDE Papers, OF 108.

35. *PPP: Eisenhower, 1954,* pp. 375, 381–82; Hagerty diary, Apr. 6, 1954.

36. Hughes to Dulles, April 15, 1954, text of Dulles statement, Apr. 23, 1954, and Livingston Merchant to Bedell Smith, Apr. 23, 1954, in *Declassified Documents* (Washington, 1975), 1975 Series, 198-A and 198-D.

37. Murray to Eisenhower, Feb. 5, 1954, and Eisenhower to Murray, Feb. 10, 1954, DDE Papers, Admin. File; Thomas E. Murray, *Nuclear Policy for War and Peace* (Cleveland, 1960), pp. 76–78; State Dept., *Bulletin* 35 (Nov. 5, 1956), 711.

38. *NYT,* May 14, 1954; *BAS* 10 (June 1954), 234; York, *The Advisors,* pp. 86–87.

39. *NYT,* Apr. 4, 1954; George Gallup, ed., *The Gallup Poll: Public Opinion, 1935–1971,* 3 vols. (New York, 1972), 2: 1229–30; *Newsweek* 43 (Apr. 5, 1954), 28.

40. *Time* 63 (Apr. 26, 1954), 32; *ibid.* (May 24, 1954), 31; *Newsweek* 43 (Apr. 26, 1954), 28–29.

41. *NYT,* May 15, 1954; State Dept., *Bulletin* 30 (June 7, 1954), 887–89; *BAS* 10 (June 1954), 234; *Time* 63 (May 24, 1954), 22.

42. *NYT,* May 15 and July 8, 10, 13, and 15, 1954; State Dept., *Bulletin* 31 (July 26, 1954), 137–40.

43. *NYT,* July 16 and 17, 1954; State Dept., *Bulletin* 31 (July 26, 1954), 139; *New Republic* 131 (July 26, 1954), 5; Emanuel Margolis, "Legality of Bomb Tests," reprinted from *Yale Law Journal* in *Nation* 181 (Dec. 31, 1955), 570–72.

44. State Dept., *Bulletin,* 30 (June 7, 1954), 887; *ibid.,* 31 (July 26, 1954), 140; *Sixteenth Semiannual Report of the Atomic Energy Commis-*

sion (Washington, 1954), p. 52; *Time* 65 (June 20, 1955), 66; *Newsweek* 45 (June 20, 1955), 82; *Science* 122 (Dec. 16, 1955), 1178–79.

45. State Dept., *Bulletin* 30 (Apr. 19, 1954), 598–99; *Newsweek* 43 (Apr. 19, 1954), 47; *BAS* 10 (June 1954), 234; *NYT*, Apr. 17, May 29, July 5 and 7, 1954.

46. *Ibid.*, Mar. 26, Aug. 23, and Sept. 24, 1954; *Newsweek* 44 (Aug. 23, 1954), 74; *ibid.* (Sept. 13, 1954), 52–54; State Dept., *Bulletin* 31 (Oct. 4, 1954), 492.

47. *NYT*, Sept. 24, 25, and Oct. 4, 1954; *ibid.*, Apr. 3 and Aug. 23, 1955; *Newsweek* 46 (Sept. 5, 1954), 65–66.

48. *Ibid.* 44 (Oct. 4, 1954), 40; *NYT*, Nov. 9, 1954; *PPP: Eisenhower, 1954*, p. 1043; State Dept., *Bulletin* 32 (Jan. 17, 1955), 90; John M. Allison, *Ambassador from the Prairie or Allison Wonderland* (Boston, 1973), p. 263.

49. *NYT*, Sept. 23, 1954; *Time* 64 (Oct. 11, 1954), 77; State Dept., *Bulletin* 31 (Nov. 8, 1954), 700.

50. *NYT*, Nov. 3, 7 and Dec. 25, 1954; Sulzberger, *Last of the Giants*, p. 89; *Time* 64 (Dec. 20, 1954), 66–67.

51. Ralph E. Lapp, "Civil Defense Faces New Peril," *BAS* 10 (Nov. 1954), 349–50; *New Republic* 131 (Nov. 8, 1954), 3.

52. *Science* 120 (Sept. 10, 1954), 406–9; *Newsweek* 45 (Jan. 17, 1955), 52–53.

53. "Civil Defense Program," *Hearings* before the Subcommittee on Civil Defense of the Senate Armed Services Committee, 84th Congress, 1st Session (Washington, 1955), pp. 240–44, 311–17.

54. *Newsweek* 44 (Oct. 11, 1954), 21; *ibid.* 45 (Jan. 17, 1955), 54; *Time* 64 (Nov. 22, 1954), 81; Eugene Rabinowich, "People Must Know," *BAS* 10 (Dec. 1954), 398.

55. *Newsweek* 45 (Jan. 17, 1955), 53; Lapp, "New Peril," p. 350; *New Yorker* 30 (Jan. 15, 1955), 19; *New Republic* 131 (Dec. 27, 1954), 4.

CHAPTER TWO

1. "AEC-FCDA Relationship," *Hearing* before the Subcommittee on Security of the Joint Committee on Atomic Energy, 84th Congress, 1st Session (Washington, 1955), pp. 9–10; *NYT*, Feb. 22, 1955; Strauss to Eisenhower, Dec. 10, 1954, DDE Papers, Admin. File.

2. *BAS* 11 (May 1955), 198–99; "AEC-FCDA Relationship,"

pp. 35–36; *Nation* 180 (Feb. 5, 1955), 116–18; "Civil Defense Program," *Hearings* before the Subcommittee on Civil Defense of the Senate Armed Services Committee, 84th Congress, 1st Session (Washington, 1955), pp. 480–83.

3. Strauss to Eisenhower, Feb. 7 and 9, 1955, DDE Papers, Admin. File; Percival Brundage to Andrew Goodpaster, Feb. 3, 1955, DDE Papers, OF 108-A; *PPP: Eisenhower,* 1955, pp. 255–56.

4. *New Republic,* 132 (Feb. 14, 1955), 8–12; *BAS* 11 (Feb. 1955), 45–51; *NYT,* Feb. 11, 1955; *Newsweek* 45 (Feb. 21, 1955), 55; *ibid.* (March 14, 1955), 8; *New Republic* 132 (Mar. 7, 1955), 9–11.

5. *U.S. News and World Report* 38 (Feb. 25, 1955), 130–32; *NYT,* Feb. 16, 1955; *Newsweek* 45 (Feb. 28, 1955), 19–20; *Time* 65 (Feb. 28, 1955), 10.

6. *U.S. News and World Report* 38 (Feb. 25, 1955), 132–34.

7. *Ibid.,* pp. 35–38, 134; *NYT,* Feb. 17, 1955; "Civil Defense," p. 231.

8. *Ibid.,* pp. 48–52; Ralph Lapp, "Fallout and Candor," *BAS* 11 (May 1955), 170, 200; *Newsweek,* 45 (Mar. 7, 1955), 23; *Time* 65 (Feb. 28, 1955), 10.

9. *NYT,* Feb. 20 and 21, 1955; *Newsweek* 45 (Apr. 4, 1955), 53; *New Republic* 132 (Feb. 28, 1955), 3; *PPP: Eisenhower, 1955,* p. 332.

10. *NYT,* Feb. 14 and 19, 1955; memorandum of telephone conversation between Strauss and Eisenhower, Feb. 23, 1955, DDE Papers, Diary Series.

11. *NYT,* Mar. 6, 11, and 13, 1955; *Newsweek* 45 (Mar. 21, 1955), 30; Carey McWilliams, "Perils Unknown," *Nation* 180 (Apr. 9, 1955), 302.

12. *Newsweek* 45 (Mar. 21, 1955), 30–31; Gallup, *Gallup Poll* 2, 1322.

13. *U.S. New and World Report* 38 (Mar. 25, 1958), 21–26.

14. "Health and Safety Problems and Weather Effects Associated with Atomic Explosions," *Hearing* before the Joint Committee on Atomic Energy, 84th Congress, 1st Session (Washington, 1955), pp. 1–8, 10, 14, 26–27, 32, 35–37; Merril Eisenbud and John Harley, "Radioactive Fallout in the United States," *Science* 121 (May 13, 1955), 667–79; L. Machta and D. L. Harris, "Effects of Atomic Explosions on Weather," *ibid.* (Jan. 21, 1955), 75–81.

15. *NYT,* Mar. 30 and May 16, 1955; *Newsweek* 45 (May 16, 1955), 31; *Time* 65 (May 9, 1955), 20; *ibid.* (May 16, 1955), 24–25.

16. *NYT,* June 7, 1955; typescript of Strauss speech, June 6, 1955, AEC Files.

17. Lapp, *Lucky Dragon,* pp. 154–55; Gene Marine, "The Delayed U-Bomb and the *N.Y. Times,*" *Nation* 182 (Jan. 28, 1956), 67–68; *PPP: Eisenhower, 1955,* pp. 337–38; *Newsweek* 45 (Mar. 21, 1955), 62; *Time* 65 (Mar. 28, 1955), 66–67.

18. "Civil Defense," p. 692; Ralph Lapp, "Radioactive Fallout III," *BAS* 11 (June 1955), 206–8; J. Rotblat, "The Hydrogen-Uranium Bomb," *ibid.* (May 1955), 171–72, 177.

19. Willard Libby, "Radioactive Fallout," *ibid.* (Sept. 1955), 256–60; *NYT,* June 4 and 12, Oct. 1, 1955; *New Republic* 132 (June 27, 1955), 2; *Reporter* 12 (June 30, 1955), 2.

20. William C. Maloney and Marvin A. Kastenbaum, "Leukemogenic Effects of Ionizing Radiation on Atomic Bomb Survivors in Hiroshima City," *Science* 121 (Feb. 25, 1955), 308–9; *Time* 65 (Mar. 7, 1955), 89; *U.S. News and World Report* 38 (April 8, 1955), 46; *NYT,* Mar. 30, 1955.

21. C. H. Waddington, "Peril from A-Dust," *Nation* 180 (Feb. 19, 1955), 155–57; *NYT,* Mar. 27 and May 30, 1955; Norman J. Birrell, "How Much Can We Stand?" *Nation* 181 (July 23, 1955), 69.

22. *NYT,* June 14, 1955; "Civil Defense," pp. 797–98; Herman M. Slatis, "Current Status of Information on the Induction of Mutations by Irradiation," *Science* 121 (June 10, 1955), 820–21.

23. "The Nature of Radioactive Fallout and Its Effect on Man," *Hearings* before the Special Subcommittee on Radiation of the Joint Committee on Atomic Energy, 85th Congress, 1st Session (Washington, 1957), p. 1049; *NYT,* Sept. 18, 1955; *New Republic* 132 (May 9, 1955); *U.S. News and World Report* 38 (May 13, 1955), 72, 74, 76; H. J. Muller, "The Genetic Damage Produced by Radiation," *BAS* 11 (June 1955), 210–12, 230.

24. *NYT,* Sept. 18 and Oct. 4, 1955; *Newsweek* 46 (Oct. 3, 1955), 77; Eugene Rabinowich, "Genetics in Geneva," *BAS* 11 (Nov. 1955), 314–16; H. J. Muller, "How Radiation Changes the Genetic Constitution," *ibid.,* 329–37.

25. *Ibid.,* 337; Mogens Westergaard, "Man's Responsibility to His Genetic Hertitage," *ibid.,* 352.

26. *Science* 122 (Aug. 5, 1955), 234; A. H. Rosenfeld, E. J. Story, and S. D. Warshaw, "Fall-Out: Some Measurements and Damage Estimates," *BAS* 11 (June 1955), 213–16.

27. L. W. Nordheim, "Tests of Nuclear Weapons," *ibid.* (Sept. 1955), 253, 272; Howard L. Andres, "Radioactive Fallout from Bomb

Clouds," *Science* 122 (Sept. 9, 1955), 456; Lapp, "Radioactive Fallout III," p. 230.

28. *NYT*, Mar. 7, 1955; *BAS* 11 (May 1955), 185–86.
29. *Science* 121 (Apr. 15, 1955), 543; *ibid.* 122 (Aug. 19, 1955), 311; Rusk to Eisenhower, Feb. 23, 1955, and Eisenhower to Rusk, Feb. 28, 1955, DDE Papers, OF 108-A; *NYT*, Apr. 8, 1955; *Newsweek* 45 (Apr. 18, 1955), 58.
30. *NYT*, Apr. 9 and May 31, 1955.

CHAPTER THREE

1. *Time* 65 (Mar. 14, 1955), 32–33; *New Republic* 132 (Mar. 14, 1955), 9–11; *Newsweek* 45 (Feb. 28, 1955), 40; *ibid.* (Mar. 14, 1955), 42; *NYT*, Mar. 23, Apr. 29, and June 17, 1955.
2. Earl H. Voss, *Nuclear Ambush: The Test-Ban Trap* (Chicago, 1963), pp. 53–56; *NYT*, Apr. 11, 18, and 25, 1955.
3. Bernard G. Bechhoefer, *Postwar Negotiations for Arms Control* (Washington, 1961), pp. 208–9, 211, 230–34.
4. *PPP: Eisenhower, 1955*, pp. 343–44, 362; *Newsweek* 45 (Mar. 28, 1955), 22; Department of State, *Disarmament: The Intensified Effort, 1955–1958* (Washington, 1960), pp. 8–13; Voss, *Nuclear Ambush*, pp. 60–62.
5. David R. Inglis, "H-Bomb Control," *Nation* 179 (July 24, 1954), 67–70; David R. Inglis, "Ban H-Bomb Tests and Favor the Defense," *BAS* 10 (Nov. 1954), 353–56; David R. Inglis, "We Haven't Really Tried," *BAS* 11 (Jan. 1955), 3–4; I. F. Stone, *The Haunted Fifties* (New York, 1963), 90–91.
6. *PPF: Eisenhower, 1955*, pp. 286–87; State Dept., *Bulletin*, 35 (Nov. 5, 1956), 712; Voss, *Nuclear Ambush*, p. 63; State Dept., *Disarmament*, pp. 15–18.
7. Payne to Nelson Rockefeller, June 21, 1955, DDE Papers, OF 108; State Dept., *Bulletin* 33 (July 11, 1955), 54; *ibid.* (Aug. 29, 1955), 365–66; *ibid.* (Oct. 3, 1955), 528.
8. *NYT*, Oct. 14 and 29, Nov. 1, 3, and 8, Dec. 4, 1955; State Dept., *Bulletin* 33 (Nov. 21, 1955), 852, 853–56; *BAS* 11 (Dec. 1955), 379.
9. State Dept., *Bulletin* 33 (Nov. 21, 1955), 855–56; *ibid.* (Dec. 19, 1955), 1031; *NYT*, Dec. 10, 1955.

10. *Ibid.,* Aug. 5, Sept. 25, Nov. 24 and 27, Dec. 13, 1955; *Time* 66 (Dec. 5, 1955), 29; *ibid.* (Dec. 12, 1955), 50; York, *The Advisors,* p. 92.

11. State Dept., *Bulletin* 35 (Nov. 5, 1956), 712; Voss, *Nuclear Ambush,* p. 63; *NYT,* Nov. 30, 1955.

12. Voss, *Nuclear Ambush,* p. 71; *NYT,* Dec. 14 and 30, 1955; *Vital Speeches,* 22 (Jan. 15, 1956), 198; William R. Frye, "The Disarmament Dilemma," *BAS* 12 (Mar. 1956), 83.

13. State Dept., *Bulletin* 34 (Jan. 23, 1956), 122; *NYT,* Jan. 12, 1956.

14. "Control and Reduction of Armaments," *Hearings* before a Subcommittee of the Senate Committee on Foreign Relations, 84th Congress, 2nd Session (Washington, 1957), pp. 1–2, 15–16, 21–22, 49, 54, 77–78, 124, 126; *Nation* 182 (Mar. 17, 1956), 209–10.

15. *New Republic* 134 (Apr. 2, 1956), 5; *BAS* 12 (May 1956), 181; William R. Frye, "The Disarmament Turning Point," *ibid.,* 166–68; *Time* 67 (Apr. 9, 1956), 29.

16. "Control of Armaments," pp. 401, 415; L. K. Truscott, Jr., to Bedell Smith, June 7, 1956, in *Declassified Documents* (Washington, 1975), 1975 Series, 6A.

17. State Dept., *Bulletin* 35 (July 30, 1956), 204, 207.

18. *NYT,* Nov. 18, 1955; typescript of Murray speech, Nov. 17, 1955, AEC Files; *Time* 66 (Nov. 28, 1955), 17; *Newsweek* 46 (Nov. 28, 1955), 30; Murray, *Nuclear Policy,* pp. 80, 86–87.

19. "Control of Armaments," pp. 335–40, 354; *NYT,* Apr. 13, 1956.

20. Walter Johnson, ed., *The Papers of Adlai E. Stevenson: Toward a New America, 1955–1957* (Boston, 1976), pp. 115–18.

21. *NYT,* April 22, 1956; *Time* 67 (Apr. 30, 1956), 20; Johnson, *New America,* p. 127.

22. *NYT,* Apr. 25, 1956; *Time* 67 (May 7, 1956), 34; *PPP: Eisenhower, 1956,* p. 434.

23. Johnson, *New America,* pp. 129, 133.

24. "Control of Armaments," pp. 438–39, 480, 529, 567.

25. David Inglis, "National Security with the Arms Race, Limited," *BAS* 12 (June 1956), 198–99; Eugene Rabinowich, "A Last Chance?" *ibid.,* p. 187.

26. *New Republic* 134 (June 4, 1956), 3; Stone, *Haunted Fifties,* p. 123.

27. *NYT,* Feb. 23 and 27, 1956.

28. *Ibid.*, Mar. 18, 28, 30, and Apr. 21, 1956; Hobart Mitchell to Eisenhower, Feb. 24, 1956, DDE Papers, GE 155-B; *BAS* 12 (May 1956), 182.

29. State Dept., *Bulletin* 34 (Apr. 2, 1956), 566–67; *NYT*, Mar. 2, 24, and 28, 1955; Maxwell Rabb to Hobart Mitchell, Feb. 28, 1956, DDE Papers, GF 155-B.

30. *NYT*, Mar. 22 and Apr. 5, 1956; Strauss to Eisenhower, Mar. 28, 1956, DDE Papers, Admin. File; memorandum of meeting by Andrew Goodpaster, Mar. 22, 1956, DDE Papers, Diary Series; *PPP: Eisenhower, 1956*, pp. 377–79.

31. *NYT*, Apr. 22 and 30, 1956; Pickett to Eisenhower, May 4, 1956, DDE Papers, GF 155-B; Sherman Adams to Paul James, May 2, 1956, DDE Papers, GF 155.

32. *NYT*, May 21, 22, 27, and June 16, 1956; *Newsweek* 47 (May 14, 1956), 39; *ibid.* (May 28, 1956), 27–29; *Time* 67 (May 28, 1956), 21; *PPP: Eisenhower, 1956*, pp. 523–24.

33. *NYT*, June 13, 1956; *Science* 123 (June 22, 1956), 1110; *ibid.* (June 29, 1956), 1157–64; *ibid.* 124 (July 13, 1956), 60–63.

34. *NYT*, June 13, 1956; *Science* 124 (July 20, 1956), 112–13.

35. Strauss to Eisenhower, June 13, 1956, DDE Papers, Admin. File; *U.S. News and World Report* 40 (June 22, 1956), 60–61, 70; *Science* 124 (July 20, 1956), 101; *Time* 67 (June 25, 1956), 64.

36. *NYT*, Jan. 20 and Apr. 21, 1956; Willard F. Libby, "Radioactive Fallout and Radioactive Strontium," *Science* 123 (Apr. 20, 1956), 657–60.

37. *NYT*, June 21, 1956; *New Republic* 135 (July 9, 1956), 4–5; Ralph Lapp, "Strontium Limits in Peace and War," *BAS* 12 (Oct. 1956), 287–88; *Science* 124 (Nov. 2, 1956), 882–83.

38. *NYT*, June 29, 1956; *Newsweek* 48 (July 9, 1956), 26–27.

39. *NYT*, July 11, 20, and 23, Aug. 3, 1956; *New Republic* 135 (July 30, 1956), 4; *BAS* 12 (Sept. 1956), 263.

40. *NYT*, July 29, 1956; Murray, *Nuclear Policy*, p. 86; *New Republic* 135 (July 30, 1956), 3; *BAS* 12 (Sept. 1956), 234; Ralph Lapp, "The 'Humanitarian' H-Bomb," *ibid.*, 264.

CHAPTER FOUR

1. Robert A. Divine, *Foreign Policy and U.S. Presidential Elections, 1952–1960* (New York, 1974), pp. 121–24, 131–32.

2. *PPP: Eisenhower, 1956,* pp. 715–16; State Dept., *Bulletin* 35 (Sept. 10, 1956), 424–25; *NYT,* Sept. 3 and 4, 1956.

3. *Ibid.,* Sept. 1, 14, and 15, 1956.

4. Eisenhower to Strauss, Aug. 30, 1956, DDE Papers, Admin. File; Chalmers Roberts, "The Case for Harold Stassen," *New Republic* 138 (Mar. 10, 1956), 16; *NYT,* Oct. 8, 1956.

5. *Ibid.,* Sept. 6 and 7, 1956; *Time* 68 (Sept. 17, 1956), 28–29; *Newsweek* 48 (Sept. 28, 1956), 41.

6. *New Republic* 135 (Oct. 8, 1956), 5–6; *NYT,* Sept. 22, 1956; *BAS* 12 (Nov. 1956), 350.

7. *PPP: Eisenhower, 1956,* p. 786; *Newsweek* 48 (Oct. 1, 1956), 22–23; Voss, *Nuclear Ambush,* p. 84.

8. Emmet J. Hughes, *The Ordeal of Power: A Political Memoir of the Eisenhower Years* (New York, 1963), p. 186; Kenneth S. Davis, *The Politics of Honor: A Biography of Adlai E. Stevenson* (New York, 1967), p. 341; Stuart G. Brown, *Conscience in Politics: Adlai E. Stevenson in the 1950s* (Syracuse, N.Y., 1961), pp. 199–200; Adlai E. Stevenson, "Why I Raised the H-Bomb Question," *Look* 21 (Feb. 5, 1957), 23–25.

9. Johnson, *Papers of Stevenson,* 6: 248–49.

10. *NYT,* Sept. 27, Oct. 3, 4, and 11, 1956.

11. *Ibid.,* Sept. 30 and Oct. 4, 1956.

12. *Ibid.,* Oct. 7 and 9, 1956; *Newsweek* 48 (Oct. 15, 1956), 42–43.

13. *PPP: Eisenhower, 1956,* pp. 858, 863–66.

14. *NYT,* Oct. 8 and 14, 1956; *Newsweek* 48 (Nov. 12, 1956), 24; *PPP: Eisenhower, 1956,* pp. 881–82.

15. Dwight D. Eisenhower, *Waging Peace, 1956–1961* (Garden City, N.Y., 1965), pp. 17–18; Hughes, *Ordeal of Power,* p. 203; *NYT,* Oct. 11 and 14, 1956.

16. *NYT,* Oct. 8 and 14, 1956; Newton H. Minow, "Marching to the Beat of Mankind," in Edward P. Doyle, ed., *As We Knew Adlai* (New York, 1966), p. 185.

17. *NYT,* Oct. 10, 13, 15, and 16, 1956.

18. *Ibid.,* Oct. 12, 1956; *Time* 68 (Oct. 29, 1956), 16; Johnson, *Papers of Stevenson,* 6: 277–78; Clinton P. Anderson and Milton Viorst, *Outsider in the Senate* (New York, 1970), pp. 141–42.

19. Adlai E. Stevenson, *The New America* (New York, 1957), pp. 44–49.

20. *NYT,* Oct. 16, 1956; *U.S. News and World Report,* 41 (Oct. 26, 1956), 128.

21. *NYT*, Oct. 17, 1956; *Nation* 183 (Oct. 27, 1956), 337; *Reporter* 15 (Nov. 1, 1956), 1, 8.

22. *NYT*, Oct. 17 and 18, 1956; *Newsweek* 48 (Oct. 29, 1956), 40; *Time* 68 (Oct. 22, 1956), 19; Anderson and Viorst, *Outsider in the Senate*, p. 143.

23. Flanders to Adams, Oct. 16, 1956, DDE Papers, GF 155-B; Sherman Adams, *Firsthand Report: The Story of the Eisenhower Administration* (New York, 1961), pp. 317, 325; *Newsweek* 48 (Oct. 29, 1956), 29; Murray Snyder to Adams, Oct. 16, 1956, White House memorandum, Oct. 16, 1956, and Dulles memorandum, Oct. 17, 1956, DDE Papers, OF 108-A.

24. *NYT*, Oct. 18 and 19, 1956; *PPP: Eisenhower, 1956*, pp. 938–39, 944, 959, 962, 976.

25. State Dept., *Bulletin* 35 (Oct. 29, 1956), 662–64; *NYT*, Oct. 21 and 22, 1956; *Newsweek* 48 (Oct. 29, 1956), 27.

26. *PPP: Eisenhower, 1956*, pp. 983–84; Eisenhower, *Waging Peace*, pp. 60–61; *NYT*, Oct. 22, 1956.

27. *Time* 68 (Oct. 29, 1956), 15; *NYT*, Oct. 23, 1956; *Newsweek* 48 (Oct. 29, 1956), 27.

28. *NYT*, Oct. 22, 23, 24, and 25, Nov. 4, 1956; mimeographed copy of Nixon speech excerpts, Estes Kefauver Papers, Presidential Campaign Issues File, University of Tennessee Library, Knoxville, Tennessee.

29. Memorandum of telephone conversation between Dulles and Eisenhower, Oct. 23, 1956, DDE Papers, Diary Series; *PPP: Eisenhower, 1956*, pp. 997–1002.

30. State Dept., *Bulletin* 35 (Nov. 5, 1956), 705–15; *PPP: Eisenhower, 1956*, p. 1022.

31. *NYT*, Oct. 13, 1956; mimeographed summary of Libby speech, Oct. 12, 1956, AEC Files.

32. *BAS* 12 (Nov. 1956), 379; *NYT*, Oct. 26, Nov. 1 and 3, 1956; *Newsweek* 48 (Nov. 12, 1956), 88; *Science* 124 (Nov. 2, 1956), 894; *New Yorker* 32 (Nov. 3, 1956), 200.

33. *Science* 124 (Nov. 9, 1956), 925–26; *ibid.* (Nov. 23, 1956), 1020; *NYT*, Oct. Oct. 15, 22, 25, and Nov. 4, 1956.

34. *U.S. News and World Report* 41 (Oct. 26, 1956), 127; *NYT*, Oct. 20, 1956; mimeographed text of Strauss speech, Oct. 19, 1956, AEC Files.

35. Robert Cutler, *No Time for Rest* (Boston, 1966), p. 345; *NYT*, Oct. 21 and Nov. 6, 1956.

36. Eugene Rabinowich, "The Lessons of a Fateful Month," *BAS* 12 (Nov. 1956), 354.

37. *NYT*, Oct. 24 and 27, 1956; *Time* 68 (Nov. 5, 1956), 24; Stevenson, *New America*, pp. 49–58.

38. Roland Nachman to Stevenson, Oct. 19, 24, and 25, 1956, Kefauver Papers, Presidential Campaign Issues File; Susan Fillips to Eisenhower, Oct. 22, 1956; Adeline Nelson to Eisenhower, Oct. 23, 1956; Mrs. James Bristah to Eisenhower, Oct. 22, 1956; William Cary to Eisenhower, Oct. 22, 1956; and Mrs. R. D. Franklin to Eisenhower, Oct. 23, 1956, DDE Papers, GF 155-B.

39. Gallup, *Gallup Poll*, 2: 1452; *Newsweek* 48 (Oct. 29, 1956), 31; *Nation* 183 (Nov. 24, 1956), 447–48.

40. Divine, *Foreign Policy and Presidential Elections, 1952–1960*, pp. 166–76; *NYT*, Nov. 2 and 6, 1956.

41. *Nation* 183 (Nov. 24, 1956), 446–47; *Newsweek* 48 (Nov. 5, 1956), 25; ibid. (Nov. 12, 1956), 61; Herbert J. Muller, *Adlai Stevenson: A Study in Values* (New York, 1967), p. 193; John B. Oakes, "Visit with Private Citizen Stevenson," *New York Times Magazine* (Nov. 25, 1956), p. 12; Johnson, *Papers of Stevenson*, 6: 335, 344.

42. Eugene Rabinowich, "The Bomb Test Controversy," *BAS* 12 (Nov. 1956), 322; David R. Inglis, "Prospects for Stopping Nuclear Tests," *ibid.*, 13 (Jan. 1957), 19–20.

43. Senators Anderson, Fulbright, Mansfield, and Monroney to Eisenhower, Oct. 31, 1956, and I. Jack Martin to Anderson, Fulbright, Mansfield, and Monroney, Nov. 2, 1956, DDE Papers, OF 108-A; *NYT*, Nov. 1 and 2, 1956.

44. Stevenson, "The H-Bomb Question," p. 24; *PPP: Eisenhower, 1957*, p. 74; memorandum of meeting of the President's Science Advisory Committee, May 19, 1959, DDE Papers, Diary Series.

CHAPTER FIVE

1. State Dept., *Bulletin* 36 (Feb. 11, 1957), 225–28; *BAS*, 13 (Jan. 1957), 37; William Frye, "A New Chapter," *ibid.* (Mar. 1957), 91–93; *ibid.* (Mar. 1957), 110.

2. State Dept., *Bulletin* 36 (Apr. 8, 1957), 561–62; *ibid.* (Apr. 15, 1957), 601; Dulles memorandum, Mar. 25, 1957, DDE Papers, Diary Series.

3. Memorandum of telephone conversation between Dulles and Eisenhower, Dec. 21, 1956, DDE Papers, Diary Series; *Newsweek* 49

(Mar. 11, 1957), 25; *Nation* 184 (Mar. 16, 1957), 225–26; *BAS* 13 (May 1957), 174–75.

4. State Dept., *Bulletin* 36 (Apr. 1, 1957), 538; *ibid.* (May 13, 1957), 770, 772.

5. "Control and Reduction of Armaments," pp. 902, 952, 1066, 1142–45.

6. *NYT*, Nov. 16, 1956, and Feb. 1, 1957; *BAS* 13 (Jan. 1957), 37; *Newsweek* 48 (Nov. 26, 1956), 65.

7. J. Laurence Kulp, Walter R. Eckelman, Arthur R. Schulert, "Strontium-90 in Man," *Science* 125 (Feb. 8, 1957), 219–25; *BAS* 13 (Apr. 1957), 148; *NYT*, Feb. 8 and 10, 1957; Ralph Lapp, "Strontium-90 in Man," *Science* 125 (May 10, 1957), 933–34.

8. *BAS* 12 (Nov. 1956), 379; *Science* 124 (Nov. 23, 1956), 1019; *ibid.* 125 (May 10, 1957), 924–25.

9. *NYT*, Jan. 22 and 30, 1957; *BAS* 13 (Mar. 1957), 111; Strauss to Eisenhower, Dec. 21, 1956, and Eisenhower to Strauss, Dec. 28, 1956, DDE Papers, Admin. File; memorandum of conference with Dulles by Andrew Goodpaster, Dec. 27, 1956, DDE Papers, Diary Series.

10. State Dept., *Bulletin* 36 (June 3, 1957), 901–4; *NYT*, May 14 and 29, June 3, 6, 19, and 25, July 6, 1957.

11. *Ibid.*, Nov. 18, 1956, Jan. 21, Mar. 10, Apr. 6, 9, 11, 14, and 19, May 31, 1957; *New Republic* 136 (Apr. 29, 1957), 3.

12. John A. Burns to Eisenhower, Mar. 6, 1957, DDE Papers, GF 155-B; State Dept., *Bulletin* 36 (Mar. 25, 1957), 484; *NYT*, Mar. 2, 5, and 14, Apr. 2, 1957; *BAS* 13 (May, 1957), 182; *Newsweek* 49 (May 6, 1957), 51–58.

13. Norman Cousins, *Dr. Schweitzer of Lambaréné* (New York, 1960), pp. 18, 130, 165, 173; *Saturday Review* 40 (May 18, 1957), 13.

14. *NYT*, Apr. 24, 1957; *BAS* 13 (June 1957), 204–5; *Science* 125 (May 10, 1957), 923; *Nation* 184 (May 4, 1957), 382.

15. *NYT*, Apr. 26 and 28, 1957; *Time* 69 (May 6, 1957), 24; *Saturday Review* 40 (May 25, 1957), 9–10; *BAS* 13 (June 1957), 201, 206–7.

16. *NYT*, Apr. 4 and 17, May 1 and 9, 1957; *Science* 125 (May 17, 1957),˙; Harold Macmillan, *Riding the Storm* (New York, 1971), p. 297; *Time* 69 (Apr. 29, 1957), 26; *ibid.* (May 20, 1957), 32; *BAS* 13 (June 1957), 202–3, 230.

17. *NYT*, Apr. 30, May 8, 9, 11, 16, and 17; June 1 and 20, 1957; *Time* 69 (Apr. 29, 1957), 26; *ibid.* (May 20, 1957), 32; *ibid.* (May 27,

1957), 28; *Newsweek* 49 (May 27, 1957), 49–50; *BAS* 13 (June 1957), 230; Macmillan, *Storm*, pp. 298–99.

18. *Newsweek* 49 (June 17, 1957), 38; Helen C. Allison, "Outspoken Scientist," *BAS* 16 (Dec. 1960), 382, 390.

19. Linus Pauling, *No More War!* (New York, 1958), pp. 160–62, 169–71; "Testimony of Dr. Linus Pauling," *Hearing* before the Senate Judiciary Subcommittee on Internal Security, 86th Congress, 2nd Session (Washington, 1960), p. 16; *NYT*, June 4, 1957; Pauling to Eisenhower, June 4, 1957, DDE Papers, OF 108-A.

20. *BAS*, 13 (Sept. 1957), 264; James L. McCamy, *Science and Public Administration* (University, Ala., 1960), pp. 194–95; *U.S. News and World Report* 42 (June 21, 1957), 52; *Science* 125 (June 14, 1957), 1190.

21. *NYT*, June 3 and 12, 1957; *New Republic* 136 (May 20, 1957), 8.

22. *NYT*, May 28, 1957; *New Republic* 136 (June 10, 1957), 3–4; "The Nature of Radioactive Fallout and Its Effect on Man," *Hearings* before the Special Subcommittee on Radiation of the Joint Committee on Atomic Energy, 85th Congress, 1st Session (Washington, 1957), pp. iii, 1.

23. *Ibid.*, pp. 14, 16, 53, 66, 71, 74.

24. *Ibid.*, pp. 496, 1198–202; Ralph E. Lapp, "Sunshine and Darkness," *BAS* 15 (Jan. 1959), 27.

25. "Nature of Fallout," pp. 148–61, 1211–18, 1331–35.

26. *Ibid.*, pp. 577–83, 676–91, 710–19, 750, 769–73.

27. E. B. Lewis, "Leukemia and Ionizing Radiation," *Science* 125 (May 17, 1957), 965–72; "Nature of Fallout," pp. 59–61, 1092–93, 1114–16, 1307–08, 1313; *Newsweek* 49 (May 6, 1957), 98.

28. "Nature of Fallout," pp. 897, 901–4, 978–87, 1002–7, 1159, 1193.

29. *Ibid.*, pp. 1009–24, 1028–37, 1045–47, 1057–59.

30. *Ibid.*, pp. 691, 1222, 1258, 1374–74, 1418–19.

31. *NYT*, June 8, 1957; *New Republic* 137 (July 1, 1957), 13–15; *Scientific American* 196 (Aug. 1957), 56; *Congressional Record*, June 28, 1957, p. 10573.

32. "Nature of Fallout," pp. 1264–65, 1452–53; *NYT*, June 7, 1957; Ernest C. Pollard, "Fall-out Fever," *Atlantic Monthly* 200 (Aug. 1957), 31; *Reporter* 16 (June 27, 1957), 26.

33. Gallup, *Gallup Poll*, 2: 1487–88; Eugene J. Rosi, "Mass and Attentive Opinion on Nuclear Weapons Tests and Fallout, 1954–1963," *Public Opinion Quarterly* 29 (Summer 1965), 283, 286–87, 290;

Newsweek 50 (July 1, 1957), 2; Mrs. Barbara Scott to Norman Cousins, July 23, 1957, Papers of the National Committee for a SANE Nuclear Policy, Swarthmore College Peace Collection, Swarthmore, Pa., Series B, Box 6 (hereafter cited as SANE Papers).

34. Strauss to Eisenhower, July 23, 1957, DDE Papers, Admin. File; Clayton Wallace to Sherman Adams, July 3, 1957, and R. M. Tildesley to Eisenhower, June 29, 1957, DDE Papers, GF 155-B.

35. *Saturday Review* 40 (June 15, 1957), 24; *Reporter* 16 (May 16, 1957), 8–9; *Congressional Record,* June 17, 1957, pp. 9311, 9939; *ibid.,* June 20, 1957, p. 9857.

36. *NYT,* June 6 and 22, Aug. 19, 1957; *U.S. News and World Report* 42 (May 17, 1957), 70.

37. *NYT,* Apr. 21 and May 28, 1957; *U.S. News and World Report* 42 (June 7, 1957), 28; draft letter by Strauss, June 21, 1957, DDE Papers, OF 108-A.

38. *PPP: Eisenhower, 1957,* pp. 429, 431–32; *U.S. News and World Report* 42 (June 7, 1957), 25; *ibid.* (June 14, 1957), 75–79; *Congressional Record,* June 4, 1957, pp. 8315–16, 8319.

39. *Reporter* 16 (May 16, 1957), 13; Jack Shubert and Ralph Lapp, "Radiation Dangers," *New Republic* 136 (May 20, 1957), 13; ibid., 9; *Science* 125 (May 17, 1957), 963.

40. *BAS* 13 (Jan. 1957), 7; *Time* 69 (June 3, 1957), 65; *New Republic* 136 (June 10, 1957), 3.

CHAPTER SIX

1. Saville R. Davis, "Recent Policy Making in the United States Government," *Daedalus* 89 (Fall 1960), 954–55; Chalmers M. Roberts, "The Hopes and Obstinacy of Harold Stassen," *Reporter* 17 (Sept. 5, 1957), 25–26; Bechhoefer, *Arms Control,* pp. 350–53; *Time* 69 (June 3, 1957), 13–14.

2. *PPP: Eisenhower, 1957,* p. 405; Eisenhower to Cole, May 27, 1957, DDE Papers, Diary Series; Adams, *Firsthand Report,* p. 326.

3. *NYT,* May 25 and 26, June 1 and 6, 1957; *Newsweek* 48 (June 3, 1957), 25–26; *New Republic* 136 (June 24, 1957), 3–4; *Time* 69 (June 3, 1957), 14; *PPP: Eisenhower, 1957,* pp. 435, 439–40.

4. *Newsweek* 49 (June 24, 1957), 42; *Time* 69 (June 24, 1957), 23; Eisenhower, *Waging Peace,* pp. 472–73; Macmillan, *Riding the Storm,* pp. 300–3.

5. *Newsweek* 49 (June 24, 1957), 27; *ibid.* 50 (July 1, 1957), 30; *PPP: Eisenhower, 1957,* pp. 476–79; *NYT,* June 20, 1957.

6. *Ibid.,* June 27, 1957; Edward Teller, "The Nature of Nuclear Warfare," *BAS* 13 (May 1957), 162; *Time* 70 (Nov. 18, 1957), 21–22; *U.S. News and World Report* 43 (July 12, 1957), 86–88.

7. *Newsweek* 50 (July 1, 1957), 48; *NYT,* June 21. 1957; *PPP: Eisenhower, 1957,* p. 430; Strauss, *Men and Decisions,* pp. 418–19; Blumberg and Owens, *Energy and Conflict,* p. 397.

8. *NYT,* June 25, 1957; memorandum of conference with the President by Andrew J. Goodpaster, June 24, 1957, DDE Papers, Diary Series.

9. Memorandum of telephone conversation between Eisenhower and Dulles, June 25, 1957, DDE Papers, Diary Series; Dulles to Eisenhower, June 26, 1957, Hagerty Papers.

10. *PPP: Eisenhower, 1957,* pp. 498–99; *Newsweek* 50 (July 8, 1957), 58; *NYT,* June 23, 27, and 30, 1957.

11. *Ibid.,* June 28 and 30, July 2, 1957; *U.S. News and World Report* 43 (July 5, 1957), 23; Norman Cousins, "Clean Bombs and Dirty Wars," *Saturday Review* 40 (July 13, 1957), 20; *New Republic* 137 (July 15, 1957), 3; State Dept., *Bulletin* 37 (July 29, 1957), 185; *Newsweek* 50 (July 22, 1957), 22.

12. *PPP: Eisenhower, 1957,* p. 520; *Newsweek* 50 (July 22, 1957), 31, *NYT,* June 30, 1957.

13. Davis, "Recent Policy Making, p. 955; Bechhoefer, *Arms Control,* pp. 354–55; *NYT,* June 26 and July 3, 1957; State Dept., *Bulletin* 37 (July 15, 1957), 99; *Time* 70 (July 15, 1957), 15.

14. *NYT,* July 9, 1957; *Newsweek* 50 (July 22, 1957), 34–35; Macmillan, *Riding the Storm,* pp. 306–7.

15. *NYT,* July 23, 1957; State Dept., *Bulletin* 37 (Aug. 12, 1957, 267–72.

16. *PPP: Eisenhower, 1957,* p. 627; Eisenhower, *Waging Peace,* p. 475; *NYT,* July 28 and Aug. 22, 1957.

17. *NYT,* Aug. 28 and Sept. 7, 1957; memorandum of telephone conversation between Dulles and Stassen, Aug. 27, 1957, DDE Papers, Diary Series; *PPP: Eisenhower, 1957,* p. 635; State Dept., *Bulletin* 37 (Sept. 16, 1957), 451–55; *BAS* 13 (Oct. 1957), 310.

18. State Dept., *Bulletin* 37 (Oct. 7, 1957), 556; *ibid.* (Oct. 21, 1957), 633; *PPP: Eisenhower, 1957,* p. 716.

19. Minutes of SANE organizing committee, Oct. 1, 1957, SANE Papers.

20. *NYT*, Aug. 24, Sept. 10, 15, and 25; Oct. 8, 10, and 13, Nov. 9 and Dec. 29, 1957; *Newsweek* 50 (Oct. 21, 1957), 96; *BAS* 13 (Nov. 1957), 343.
21. *Science* 126 (Aug. 2, 1957), 200; *NYT*, Sept. 4, 19, 20, and 21, Dec. 3, 1957; "Control of Armaments," pp. 1367–68; *Newsweek* 50 (Sept. 30, 1957), 86.
22. Strauss to Eisenhower, Aug. 2, and Sept. 12, 1957, DDE Papers, Admin. File; *NYT*, Sept. 16, 1957; *Science* 126 (Oct. 4, 1957), 647.
23. *NYT*, Oct. 14, 1957.
24. Ethyl Taylor to James Hagerty, Nov. 20, 1957, DDE Papers, GF 155-B; *NYT*, July 28, Aug. 6 and 7, Dec. 2, 1957; *BAS* 13 (Oct. 1957), 311; *Newsweek* 50 (Sept. 2, 1957), 51.
25. *NYT*, July 12, 1957; *BAS* 13 (Sept. 1957), 244–45, 249–53; Eugene Rabinowich, "About Disarmament," *ibid.* (Oct. 1957), 281; Hans Thirring, "Perils from War vs. Those from Tests," *ibid.* 14 (Mar. 1958), 121.
26. Nevil Shute, *On the Beach* (New York, 1957), pp. 46–47, 94; *New Republic* 137 (Sept. 1957), 9; *ibid.* (Aug. 12, 1957), 20; *Reporter* 17 (Aug. 8, 1957), 50; *BAS* 14 (Feb. 1958), 93.
27. Strauss to Annalee Stewart, undated, DDE Papers, GR 155-B; *NYT*, Oct. 20, Dec. 22 and 23, 1957; *BAS* 13 (Dec. 1957), 374.
28. *NYT*, Feb. 24, 1957; *Science* 126 (Dec. 27, 1957), 1335; *BAS* 14 (Jan. 1958), 62.
29. *NYT*, Nov. 8 and 9, 1957.
30. Norma J. Thickstun to Homer Jack, Sept. 10, 1957, and memorandum by Homer Jack, Sept. 1957, SANE Papers, Ser. B; Lawrence Scott to Homer Jack, May 13, 1957; Scott to organizing committee, May 27, 1957, "History of SANE, 1957–1963," and minutes of meeting of June 21, 1957, SANE Papers, Ser. A.
31. Cousins to Ed Snyder, June 22, 1957, Trevor Thomas to Coleman Blease, Nov. 9, 1957, Erich Fromm to Pickett, July 18, 1957, and Cory to Cousins and Pickett, Sept. 20, 1957, SANE Papers, Ser. B; minutes of meeting of Sept. 24, 1957, SANE Papers, Ser. A; Nathan Glazer, "The Peace Movement in America, 1961," *Commentary* 31 (April 1961), 290–91.
32. *NYT*, Nov. 15, 1957.
33. List of individuals refusing to sign first SANE ad, Nov. 1957 and Rabinowich to Cousins, Nov. 13, 1957, SANE Papers, Ser. A; Bullis to Pickett, Nov. 19, 1957, Alfred Kohlberg to SANE, Nov.

22, 1957, Carl Landauer to SANE, Dec. 17, 1957, and Dichter to John St. John, Dec. 10, 1957, SANE Papers, Ser. B.

34. Minutes of executive council meeting, Dec. 10, 1957, SANE Papers, Ser. A; Arno G. Huth, "Response to the First Statement . . . ," Jan. 1958 and Lewis Lincoln to SANE, Nov. 22, 1957, SANE Papers, Ser. B; Lawrence S. Wittner, *Rebels against War: The American Peace Movement, 1941–1960* (New York, 1969), pp. 243–45.

35. *Newsweek* 50 (Oct. 14, 1957), 37–38; *Time* 70 (Oct. 14, 1957), 27; *Nation* 185 (Oct. 19, 1957), 253; *BAS* 13 (Dec. 1957), 346.

36. *NYT*, Aug. 27, 1957; *Newsweek* 50 (Sept. 9, 1957), 43; *ibid.* (Oct. 7, 1957), 42; *BAS* 13 (Oct. 1957), 311; *ibid.* (Dec. 1957), 357; *PPP: Eisenhower, 1957*, pp. 791–92; memorandum of telephone conversation between Eisenhower and Strauss, Nov. 25, 1957, DDE Papers Diary Series.

37. Eisenhower, *Waging Peace*, p. 212; memorandum of conference with the President by Andrew Goodpaster, Oct. 16, 1957, DDE Papers, Diary Series; Cutler, *No Time for Rest*, p. 352; *PPP: Eisenhower, 1957*, pp. 796–97; *NYT*, Nov. 8, 1957; *Time* 70 (Nov. 18, 1957), 20; *Newsweek* 50 (Nov. 18, 1957), 42.

38. Cutler, *No Time for Rest*, p. 352; Robert Gilpin, *American Scientists and Nuclear Weapons Policy* (Princeton, 1962), pp. 176–77; Ralph E. Lapp, *The New Priesthood: The Scientific Elite and the Uses of Power* (New York, 1965), pp. 194–95.

39. *Newsweek* 50 (Nov. 11, 1957), 35–36; *ibid.* (Nov. 18, 1957), 37; *ibid.* (Dec. 30, 1957), 14; *BAS* 14 (April 1958), 131; George B. Kistiakowsky, with introduction by Charles S. Maier, *A Scientist at the White House: The Private Diary of President Eisenhower's Special Assistant for Science and Technology* (Cambridge, Mass., 1976), p. xxvi.

40. Eugene Rabinowich, "New Year's Thoughts," *BAS* 14 (Jan. 1958), 2–4.

CHAPTER SEVEN

1. *NYT*, Oct. 29, Nov. 7, 10, and 20, Dec. 28, 1957; State Dept., *Bulletin* 37 (Dec. 16, 1957), 961–66.

2. *Ibid.* 38 (Jan. 27, 1958), 130; *NYT*, Dec. 1 and 19, 1957; *Time* 70 (Dec. 9, 1957), 29; *Newsweek* 51 (Jan. 20, 1958), 34.

3. *NYT*, Dec. 11, 1957; *PPP: Eisenhower, 1957*, pp. 832–33; *ibid.*,

1958, pp. 79–82; State Dept., *Bulletin* 38 (Mar. 10, 1958), 377; *ibid.* (Mar. 24, 1958), 459, 460.

4. *NYT*, Dec. 25 and 27, 1957, Jan. 6 and 7, 1958; minutes of PSAC meeting, Jan. 2 and 3, 1958, DDE Papers, Records of the President's Science Advisory Committee (hereafter cited as PSAC Records); Dillon Anderson oral history, Dec. 30, 1969, DDE Papers; *Newsweek* 51 (Jan. 13, 1958), 16; *ibid.* (Jan. 20, 1958), 17; *Time* 71 (Jan. 20, 1958), 16.

5. *NYT*, Feb. 8 and 16, 1958; Chalmers M. Roberts, "The Case for Harold Stassen," *New Republic* 138 (Mar. 10, 1958), 13–15; State Dept., *Bulletin* 38 (Mar. 24, 1958), 491; *Newsweek* 51 (Feb. 10, 1958), 44.

6. "Control and Reduction of Armaments," p. 1345; memorandum of conference with Humphrey, Jan. 11, 1958, and memorandum of telephone conversation between Trevor Thomas and Thomas Hughes, Jan. 30, 1958, SANE Papers, Ser. B.

7. *Congressional Record,* Feb. 4, 1958, pp. 1607–24; telegram to SANE chapters, Feb. 4, 1958, and Thomas to Robert Garrett, Feb. 5, 1958, SANE Papers, Ser. B; *NYT*, Feb. 5 and 19, 1958.

8. "Control and Reduction of Armaments," pp. 1337, 1343, 1351, 1355, 1358.

9. Memorandum of telephone conversation between Eisenhower and Dulles, Feb. 5, 1958, DDE Papers, Diary Series; *PPP: Eisenhower, 1958*, p. 190; *NYT*, Feb. 25, 1958.

10. *Ibid.*, Jan. 14, 1958; *Science* 127 (Feb. 7, 1958), 277; *Life* 44 (Feb. 10, 1958), 64–66.

11. *Newsweek* 51 (Mar. 3, 1958), 40; *Time* 71 (Apr. 7, 1958), 16; *NYT*, Mar. 30, 1958.

12. Edward Teller and Albert L. Latter, *Our Nuclear Future* (New York, 1958); Linus Pauling, *No More War!* (New York, 1958); *Science* 128 (Aug. 15, 1958), 352; Peter Charlton to Donald Keys, Aug. 23, 1958, SANE Papers, Ser. B.

13. Walter R. Eckelmann, J. Laurence Kulp, and Arthur P. Schulert, "Strontium-90 in Man, II," *Science* 127 (Feb. 7, 1958), 267–73; *NYT*, Feb. 16, 1958.

14. *Ibid.*, Mar. 17, Apr. 4 and 7, 1958; *Newsweek* 51 (Apr. 21, 1958), 89; *ibid.* (June 30, 1958), 48.

15. *BAS* 14 (Jan. 1958), 7, 17–18, 21.

16. Pauling, *No More War!*, pp. 72, 74–76, 92, 102, 104, 108; *NYT*, Apr. 29 and May 16, 1958.

17. Teller and Latter, *Our Nuclear Future*, pp. 95, 119–20, 123, 124, 129–30; "Control and Reduction of Armaments," p. 1477.

18. *NYT*, Apr. 30 and May 2, 1958; Lapp to Cousins, May 23, 1958, SANE Papers, Ser. B.

19. Actions taken as PSAC meeting, Dec. 9 and 10, 1957 and summary of PSAC actions, May 8, 1959, DDE Papers, PSAC Records; *NYT*, Mar. 13, 1958.

20. *Ibid.*, Mar. 12 and 16, 1958; *Newsweek* 51 (Mar. 24, 1958), 37; *Science* 127 (Apr. 18, 1958), 866; *BAS* 14 (May 1958), 197.

21. "Control and Reduction of Armaments," pp. 1495–1513, 1525–46; *NYT*, Apr. 3, 1958; Jay Orear, "Detection of Nuclear Weapons Testing," *BAS* 14 (Mar. 1958), 98–101.

22. "Control and Reduction of Armaments," pp. 1454–58, 1478–80, 1367–70, 1372–75, 1607–10; Edward Teller, "Alternatives for Security," *Foreign Affairs* 36 (Jan. 1958), 204; *NYT*, Mar. 3, 1958.

23. "Control and Reduction of Armaments," pp. 1376–77.

24. *Ibid.*, pp. 1375, 1378, 1382, 1460–63, 1493; Teller and Latter, *Our Nuclear Future*, p. 145; Edward Teller, "Alternatives for Security," 204; *Life* 44 (Feb. 10, 1958), 69–70.

25. Pauling, *No More War!*, pp. 108–11; *BAS* 14 (Mar. 1958), 125; *Science* 127 (Mar. 14, 1958), 608; Harrison Brown, "A Scientist's Proposal for Limiting Atomic Tests," *Reporter* 18 (Apr. 3, 1958), 12–14; "Control and Reduction of Armaments," pp. 1428–30.

26. *BAS* 14 (Mar. 1958), 128; Anderson and Viorst, *Outsider in the Senate*, p. 203; "Control and Reduction of Armaments," p. 1448; *NYT*, Mar. 4, 19, and April 20, 1958.

27. Trevor Thomas to Robert Hoagland, Jan. 28, 1958, Alfred Williams to James Hamilton, June 26, 1958, Williams to Curtis Crawford, Apr. 5, 1958, and Carl Condit to SANE, Mar. 13, 1958, SANE Papers, Ser. B; copy of SANE ad. Mar. 24, 1958, Elmer Rice to SANE, Mar. 17, 1958, and Bill Attwood to Norman Cousins, Apr. 4, 1958, SANE Papers, Ser. A.

28. *Nation*, 186 (Feb. 8, 1958), 109; *NYT*, Jan. 1, 1958; Rabb to Hagerty, Jan. 14, 1958, and memorandum by Frederick Fox, Mar. 27, 1958, DDE Papers, GF 155-B.

29. *Reporter* 18 (May 15, 1958), 32; *NYT*, Mar. 6, 30, and Apr. 4, 1958.

30. Albert Bigelow, *The Voyage of the Golden Rule* (New York, 1959); *NYT*, Feb. 7, 11, 20, 27, and Mar. 26, 1958; *Newsweek* 51 (Feb. 10, 1958), 74; *ibid.* (Apr. 21, 1958), 89.

31. *Ibid.* (Feb. 24, 1958), 60; *ibid.* (Apr. 14, 1958), 82; *NYT,* Mar. 27, 30, and Apr. 6, 1958.

32. *Newsweek* 51 (Mar. 10, 1958), 25; *NYT,* Feb. 24 and 25, Mar. 15, 16, 22, 23, and 24, 1958; *BAS* 14 (May 1958), 197.

33. *Newsweek* 51 (Mar. 31, 1958), 19; *ibid.* (Apr. 14, 1958), 41; *NYT,* Mar. 9, 10, 22, and 23, 1958; Charles J. V. Murphy, "Nuclear Inspection: A Near Miss," *Fortune* 59 (Mar. 1959), 160; memorandum of presidential conference by Andrew Goodpaster, March 24, 1958, DDE Papers, Diary Series.

34. *PPP: Eisenhower, 1958,* pp. 232–35; Eisenhower to Dulles, Mar. 26, 1958, DDE Papers, Diary Series; *NYT,* Mar. 29 and 30, 1958.

35. State Dept., *Bulletin* 38 (Apr. 21, 1958), 647–48; *Newsweek* 51 (Apr. 7, 1958), 31; Macmillan, *Riding the Storm,* p. 482; *NYT,* Apr. 1, 1958.

36. Memorandum of telephone conversation between Eisenhower and Dulles, Apr. 1, 1958, DDE Papers, Diary Series; State Dept., *Bulletin* 38 (Apr. 21, 1958), 639–40, 642; *PPP: Eisenhower, 1958,* pp. 261–62, 265; *Newsweek* 51 (Apr. 14, 1958), 32; *NYT,* Apr. 2 and 4, 1958.

37. *New Republic* 138 (Apr. 7, 1958), 4; *Nation* 186 (Apr. 12, 1958), 305; *Reporter* 18 (Apr. 17, 1958), 2; *ibid.* (May 1, 1958), 22; *NYT,* Apr. 8, 13, and 28, 1958; *Saturday Review* 41 (May 24, 1958), 21–23.

38. *BAS* 14 (June 1958), 239; *NYT,* Apr. 19 and 21, 1958; *Congressional Record,* April 21, 1958, p. 6824; *ibid.,* April 28, 1958, p. 7557.

39. *NYT,* Apr. 11, 15, and 18, 1958; Ernest C. Pollard to Clarence Pickett, Apr. 15, 1958, SANE Papers, Ser. B; *Saturday Review* 41 (Apr. 12, 1958), 26; *ibid.* (Apr. 19, 1958), 26, 58.

40. *Time* 71 (Apr. 7, 1958), 15; *U.S. News and World Report* 44 (Apr. 11, 1958), 112; *ibid.* (Apr. 18, 1958), 66–67; *NYT,* Apr. 1, 1958.

41. *Time* 71 (Apr. 21, 1958), 13–14; *NYT,* Apr. 9, 24, and May 26, 1956; Polly Mills to Eisenhower, Apr. 20, 1958, DDE Papers, OF 108-A.

42. Gallup, *Gallup Poll,* 2: 1541, 1552–53; Eugene J. Rosi, "Mass and Attentive Opinion on Nuclear Weapons Tests and Fallout,

1954–1963," *Public Opinion Quarterly* 29 (Summer 1965), 280–97.

43. Gilpin, *American Scientists,* pp. 179–80; Murphy, "Near Miss," pp. 124, 160; memorandum of PSAC actions, May 8, 1959, DDE Papers, PSAC Records; *Newsweek* 51 (May 19, 1958), 72.

44. Davis, "Recent American Policy Making," p. 961; memorandum of telephone conversation between Eisenhower and Dulles, Apr. 8, 1958, DDE Papers, Diary Series; *PPP: Eisenhower, 1958,* pp. 291–92, 298–99; State Dept., *Bulletin* 38 (Apr. 28, 1958), 582–83; 688; *NYT,* Apr. 9, 1958.

45. "Control and Reduction of Armaments," pp. 1550–51, 1552, 1558; *U.S. News and World Report,* 44 (May 2, 1958), 66; text of Strauss speech, May 8, 1958, AEC Files.

46. Memorandum of presidential conference by Andrew Goodpaster, Jan. 22, 1958, DDE Papers, Diary Series; Strauss to Eisenhower, Mar. 31, 1958, DDE Papers, Admin. Series; Anderson and Viorst, *Outsider in the Senate,* p. 205.

47. Memorandum of PSAC actions, May 8, 1959, DDE Papers, PSAC Records.

48. Memorandum of meeting between Eisenhower and Killian by Andrew Goodpaster, Apr. 17, 1958, DDE Papers, Diary Series; notes of PSAC meeting, Apr. 21, 1958, DDE Papers, PSAC Records.

49. Pre-press conference notes, Apr. 23, 1958, DDE Papers, Diary Series; *NYT,* Apr. 27, 1958; *PPP: Eisenhower,* 1958, pp. 350–51; Harold Koran Jacobsen and Eric Stein, *Diplomats, Scientists and Politicians: The United States and the Nuclear Test Ban Negotiations* (Ann Arbor, 1966), pp. 49–50.

50. Pre-press conference notes, Apr. 30, 1958, DDE Papers, Diary Series; State Dept., *Bulletin* 38 (May 19, 1958), 806–7, 809.

51. *Saturday Review* 41 (Sept. 6, 1958), 46; Davis, "Recent Policy Making," p. 958.

52. Murphy, "Near Miss," p. 123; Andrew H. Berding, *Dulles on Diplomacy* (Princeton, 1965), p. 144.

53. Memorandum of telephone conversation between Eisenhower and Dulles, May 1, 1958, DDE Papers, Diary Series; Gilpin, *American Scientists,* p. 197.

CHAPTER EIGHT

1. *Congressional Record,* May 7, 1958, pp. 8263–65; *NYT,* May 8, 12, 26, June 11, 15, and 29, 1958; *BAS* 14 (Sept. 1958), 279; memo-

randum of PSAC meeting with Eisenhower, June 17, 1958, DDE
Papers, PSAC Records.
2. Robert Randolph to Eisenhower, June 17, 1958, John Allen to
Bryce Harlow, June 18, 1958, and Clarence Cunningham to Eisenhower, Apr. 15, 1958, DDE Papers, GF 155-B; Ed Elias to
Trevor Thomas, May 16, 1958, SANE Papers, Ser. B; *NYT,* May 1
and 18, June 9, 1958.
3. Strauss, *Men and Decisions,* p. 413; *NYT,* May 9, 19, and 31, June 2,
1958.
4. *Ibid.,* Apr. 25, May 2, and June 5, 1958; *Newsweek* 51 (May 12,
1958), 27; Bigelow, *Golden Rule,* pp. 104–24, 181–98; Bigelow and
others to Eisenhower, June 23, 1958, DDE Papers, GF 155-B.
5. State Dept., *Bulletin* 38 (June 9, 1958), 939–40; *PPP: Eisenhower,
1958,* pp. 422–23; *NYT,* May 25, 1958; *Newsweek* 51 (June 2,
1958), 17–18.
6. *NYT,* July 4, 1958; I. F. Stone, *The Haunted Fifties* (New York,
1963), p. 228; Jacobson and Stein, *Diplomats, Scientists and Politicians,* p. 54.
7. *NYT,* June 24, 1958; State Dept., *Bulletin* 38 (June 30, 1958), p.
1085; *ibid.* 39 (July 14, 1958), 48; *Newsweek* 51 (June 23, 1958),
68.
8. Jacobson and Stein, *Diplomats, Scientists and Politicians,* pp. 57–58;
Gilpin, *American Scientists,* pp. 221–22.
9. *NYT,* June 6, July 1, 13, and 15, 1958.
10. *Ibid.,* June 7 and 15, 1958; *Newsweek* 51 (June 16, 1958), 27; Gene
Marine, "McCone of the AEC," *Nation* 188 (April 1, 1959),
307–10; *BAS* 14 (Sept. 1958), 279; "Nomination of John A. Mc-
Cone . . . ," *Hearing* before the Senate Section of the Joint
Committee on Atomic Energy, 85th Congress, 2nd Session (Washington, 1958), pp. 12–13, 21–22.
11. Jacobson and Stein, *Diplomats, Scientists and Politicians,* pp. 85–89.
12. Edward Teller, with Allen Brown, *The Legacy of Hiroshima* (Garden
City, N.Y., 1962), pp. 70–71; *NYT,* July 3, 6, 13, 14, 27, and 29,
1958; State Dept., *Bulletin* 39 (Aug. 11, 1958), 237; memorandum
of conference between Eisenhower and Strauss by Andrew Goodpaster, Jan. 22, 1958, DDE Papers, Diary Series; memorandum of
White House conference by Andrew Goodpaster, July 24, 1958,
DDE Papers, Diary Series.
13. *NYT,* July 2 and 6, Aug. 29, and Sept. 27, 1958, Dec. 30, 1960;

Earle Reynolds, *The Forbidden Voyage* (New York, 1961), pp. 13–15, 36–37, 57–60; *New Republic* 141 (Sept. 14, 1959), 5.

14. *Time* 72 (Aug. 11, 1958), 38; *NYT*, Aug. 2, 9, 13, and 24, Sept. 9, and Oct. 10, 1958.

15. *Science* 128 (Aug. 22, 1958), 403–5; *Time* 72 (Aug. 25, 1958), 37; *NYT*, Aug. 11, 1958; *BAS* 14 (Oct. 1958), 331.

16. *NYT*, Aug. 11 and 12, 1958; *Saturday Review* 41 (Sept. 6, 1958), 24.

17. Miriam P. Finkel, "Mice, Men and Fallout," *Science* 128 (Sept. 19, 1958), 637–41; *NYT*, Sept. 19, Nov. 16 and 30, 1958.

18. Austin M. Brues, "Critique of the Linear Theory of Carcinogenesis," *Science* 128 (Sept. 26, 1958), 693–98; *ibid.* 129 (Feb. 13, 1959), 377–78; *NYT*, Aug. 15 and Dec. 9, 1958.

19. State Dept., *Bulletin* 39 (July 14, 1958), 47; *NYT*, July 1, 2, and 3, 1958; *Time* 72 (July 14, 1958), 27.

20. Jacobson and Stein, *Diplomats, Scientists and Politicians*, pp. 67–81; State Dept., *Bulletin* 39 (Sept. 22, 1958), 453–62; Gilpin, *American Scientists*, pp. 186–93, 202–14.

21. *NYT*, Aug. 20, 1958; *Saturday Review* 41 (Sept. 6, 1958), 25; *PPP: Eisenhower, 1958*, pp. 622, 628.

22. Memorandum of conference between Eisenhower and Killian by Andrew Goodpaster, Aug. 4, 1958, and memorandum of telephone conversation between Eisenhower and Dulles, Aug. 21, 1958, DDE Papers, Diary Series; *NYT*, Aug. 22, 1958; Macmillan, *Riding the Storm*, pp. 560–63; Eisenhower, *Waging Peace*, p. 477.

23. *PPP: Eisenhower, 1958*, pp. 635–36; *Newsweek* 52 (Sept. 1, 1958), 13; *U.S. News and World Report* 45 (Aug. 29, 1958), 27–29.

24. State Dept., *Bulletin* 39 (Sept. 29, 1958), 503–4; *NYT*, Aug. 30, 1958; Jacobson and Stein, *Diplomats, Scientists and Politicians*, pp. 97–99.

25. Telegram from Clarence Pickett and Norman Cousins to Eisenhower, Aug. 22, 1958, DDE Papers, GF 155-B; Peter Charlton to Donald Keys, Aug. 23, 1958, SANE Papers, Ser. B; *NYT*, Aug. 23, 1958; *Saturday Review* 41 (Sept. 6, 1958), 25.

26. *NYT*, Aug. 24, 1958; Henry A. Kissinger, "Nuclear Testing and the Problems of Peace," *Foreign Affairs* 37 (Oct. 1958), 1–18.

27. *NYT*, Aug. 31, 1958; *PPP: Eisenhower, 1958*, pp. 645–46; Macmillan, *Riding the Storm*, p. 562; John A. McCone oral history, January 1971, DDE Papers.

28. *NYT*, Aug. 23, 30, and Sept. 3, 12 and 24, 1958.

29. *Ibid.*, Sept. 19, 20, and 30, Oct. 23, 27, and 29, Nov. 1, 2, and 4, 1958, Mar. 11, 1959; *Newsweek* 52 (Oct. 6, 1958), 63; *Reporter* 19 (Nov. 13, 1958), 2–3; *Time* 72 (Nov. 10, 1958), 30; Voss, *Nuclear Ambush*, pp. 247, 249–51.

30. *NYT*, Oct. 1, 3, 16, 21, 23, 25, and 26, 1958; *Time* 72 (Oct. 13, 1958), 18; *Newsweek* 52 (Oct. 20, 1958), 48; State Dept., *Bulletin* 39 (Oct. 20, 1958), 617.

31. Andrei D. Sakharov, *Sakharov Speaks* (New York, 1974), pp. 10, 32; Nikita S. Khrushchev, *Khrushchev Remembers: The Last Testament,* translated and edited by Strobe Talbott (Boston, 1974), pp. 69–70.

32. *NYT*, Sept. 17, Oct. 4, 6, 10, 12, Nov. 2, 4, and 5, 1958; State Dept., *Bulletin* 39 (Nov. 10, 1958), 747–53; *ibid.* (Nov. 17, 1958), 787–92; Jacobson and Stein, *Diplomats, Scientists and Politicians,* pp. 100–9.

33. *NYT*, Oct. 2, 21, 26, and 28, 1958; *PPP: Eisenhower, 1958,* pp. 796–97; State Dept., *Bulletin* 39 (Nov. 3, 1958), 686; *ibid.* (Nov. 10, 1958), 723–25; *ibid.* (Nov. 17, 1958), 768–73.

34. *NYT*, Oct. 31 and Nov. 1, 1958; *Newsweek* 52 (Nov. 3, 1958), 71; *Time* 72 (Nov. 10, 1958), 30.

35. *PPP: Eisenhower, 1958,* pp. 838–39; State Dept., *Bulletin* 39 (Nov. 24, 1958), 809–13; *ibid.* (Dec. 15, 1958), 952; *NYT*, Nov. 8 and 17, 1958; *Time* 72 (Nov. 10, 1958), 30.

36. *U.S. News and World Report* 45 (Nov. 7, 1958), 57.

37. *NYT*, Oct. 30, 1958; *Saturday Review* 41 (Nov. 15, 1958), 24; *Time* 72 (Dec. 1, 1958), 14.

38. *BAS* 14 (Oct. 1958), 282–87.

CHAPTER NINE

1. Herbert S. Parmet, *Eisenhower and the American Crusades* (New York, 1972), pp. 519–23, 528–35, 539–41.

2. *NYT*, Nov. 9, Dec. 10, 13, 16, and 18, 1958, Feb. 12, 1960.

3. *Ibid.*, Nov. 18, 1958; Murray, *Nuclear Policy,* p. 96; memorandum of conversation between Eisenhower and Gore by Bryce Harlow, Nov. 17, 1958, memorandum by Gore, Nov. 19, 1958, and Harlow to Gore, Jan. 15, 1959, DDE Papers, OF 108-A; State Dept., *Bulletin* 39 (Dec. 15, 1958), 951.

4. *NYT*, Nov. 19 and Dec. 31, 1958; Donald Keys to A. K. Mutra,

Dec. 1, 1958, and Gore to Keys, Jan. 13, 1959, SANE Papers, Ser. B; minutes of PSAC meeting, Dec. 15 and 16, 1958, DDE Papers, PSAC Records; memorandum of conversation between Eisenhower and Queen Fredericka, Dec. 9, 1958, DDE Papers, Diary Series.

5. *Newsweek* 53 (Jan. 26, 1959), 91; *BAS* 15 (Feb. 1959), 96; *ibid.* (Mar. 1959), 109; "Technical Aspects of Detection and Inspection of a Nuclear Weapons Test Ban," *Hearings* before the Special Subcommittee on Radiation and the Subcommittee on Research and Development of the Joint Committee on Atomic Energy, 86th Congress, 2nd Session (Washington, 1960), p. 630.

6. Murphy, "Near Miss," pp. 155, 162; Eisenhower, *Waging Peace*, p. 479; memorandum by Killian on Berkner panel, Jan. 12, 1959, DDE Papers, Project Clean-Up Records; Jacobson and Stein, *Diplomats, Scientists and Politicians*, p. 151n.

7. Davis, "Recent American Policy," p. 963; *NYT*, Jan. 22 and 25, 1959; *Time* 73 (Feb. 2, 1959), 17.

8. *Congressional Record*, Mar. 2, 1959, pp. 3128–32; *ibid.*, Mar. 5, 1959, p. 3396; *ibid.*, April 7, 1959, p. 5415; *Reporter* 20 (April 16, 1959), 18–19; Hosmer to Eisenhower, Jan. 2, 1959, DDE Papers, GF 155-B; "Disarmament and Foreign Policy," *Hearings* before the Senate Subcommittee on Disarmament, 86th Congress, 1st Session (Washington, 1959), pp. 132, 135, 186.

9. *Ibid.*, pp. 166–85.

10. *Ibid.*, p. 449; *Congressional Record*, Mar. 26, 1959, p. 5347; *ibid.*, Apr. 30, 1959, p. 7196; *BAS* 15 (May 1959), 186; *NYT*, Feb. 13, 1959; Cousins and Pickett to Eisenhower, Mar. 3, 1959, DDE Papers, GF 155-B.

11. Jay Orear, "How Feasible Is a Test Ban?" *BAS* 15 (Mar. 1959), 99; *NYT*, Feb. 2, 1959.

12. *BAS*, 15 (Mar. 1959), 110; "Disarmament and Foreign Policy," p. 24; *Science* 129 (Jan. 20, 1959), 241.

13. *BAS* 15 (Mar. 1959), 137–38; State Dept., *Bulletin* 40 (Feb. 9, 1959), 188–89; Jacobson and Stein, *Diplomats, Scientists and Politicians*, pp. 136–41.

14. Memoranda of conferences between Eisenhower and Killian by Andrew Goodpaster, Jan. 14, Feb. 25, and Feb. 28, 1959, DDE Papers, Diary Series; *NYT*, Mar. 13, 1959; Jacobson and Stein, *Diplomats, Scientists and Politicians*, pp. 167–68.

15. *Ibid.*, pp. 147–54; *BAS* 15 (May 1959), 224; State Dept., *Bulletin* 41 (July 6, 1959), 17–18; memorandum of PSAC actions, May 8, 1959, DDE Papers, PSAC Records; McCone to Killian, Mar. 24, 1959, DDE Papers, Protect Clean-Up Records; memorandum of conference between Eisenhower and Killian on Mar. 13, 1959, by Andrew Goodpaster, Mar. 17, 1959, DDE Papers, Diary Series.

16. *NYT*, Mar. 19 and 20, 1959; *BAS* 15 (May 1959), 223; *Time* 73 (Mar. 30, 1959), 70; Teller and Latter, *Our Nuclear Future*, p. 141.

17. *NYT*, Mar. 21 and 22, 1959; Eisenhower, *Waging Peace*, pp. 352–53; Macmillan, *Riding the Storm*, pp. 647–48; *Nation* 188 (Apr. 4, 1959), 285–86; memorandum of telephone conversation between Eisenhower and Herter, undated, and between Eisenhower and Dulles, Apr. 7, 1959, DDE Papers, Diary Series.

18. Eisenhower, *Waging Peace*, p. 479; *PPP: Eisenhower, 1959*, pp. 331–32; *Time* 73 (April 27, 1959), 16; *NYT*, Apr. 14, 1959.

19. *Congressional Record*, Apr. 13, 1959, p. 5735; *ibid.*, Apr. 17, 1959, p. 6201; *Newsweek* 53 (Apr. 27, 1959), 52; Wadsworth to Cousins, May 18, 1959, SANE Papers, Ser. B.

20. State Dept., *Bulletin* 40 (May 18, 1959), 705; *NYT*, Apr. 26, 1969; *PPP: Eisenhower, 1959*, pp. 390–91, 418–10.

21. *NYT*, May 27 and June 8, 1959; *BAS* 15 (June 1959), 269; Macmillan, *Pointing the Way*, p. 74.

22. Murphy, "Near Miss," pp. 122, 162; *Nation* 188 (Mar. 14, 1959), 219.

23. *NYT*, May 16, 1959; *U.S. News and World Report* 46 (May 25, 1959), 128; *Nation* 188 (May 9, 1959), inside front cover.

24. Memorandum of meeting between Eisenhower and PSAC on May 19, 1959, by Andrew Goodpaster, May 20, 1959, DDE Papers, Diary Series; minutes of PSAC meeting with President, May 19, 1959, DDE Papers, PSAC Records; *PPP: Eisenhower, 1959*, pp. 462–63.

CHAPTER TEN

1. *NYT*, Jan. 12, Feb. 18, 25, and 28, 1959; "AEC Authorizing Legislation for Fiscal Year 1960," *Hearings* before the Subcommittee on Legislation of the Joint Committee on Atomic Energy, 86th Congress, 1st Session (Washington, 1959), pp. 193–96.

2. *Scientific American* 200 (May 1959), 68; *BAS* 15 (April 1959), 174; *ibid.* (May 1959), 223; *NYT*, Jan. 5, Apr. 13, and June 13, 1959; *Consumer Reports* 24 (Feb. 1959), 102–11.

3. *NYT*, Mar. 18, 1959; *BAS* 15 (May 1959), 223.

4. *NYT*, Mar. 20 and 22, 1959; *Science* 129 (Apr. 3, 1959), 884–85; *U.S. News and World Report* 46 (Apr. 6, 1959), 48; *Congressional Record*, Mar. 23, 1959, pp. 4876–80; "AEC Authorizing Legislation," pp. 313–14, 320–22, 326.

5. *Congressional Record*, Mar. 23, 1959, pp. 4881–82; *Science* 129 (Apr. 17, 1959), 1014–16.

6. *Nation* 188 (Apr. 25, 1959), 355–57; J. Laurence Kulp, Arthur R. Schulert, and Elizabeth J. Hodges, "Strontium-90 in Man III," *Science* 129 (May 8, 1959), 1249–55.

7. *Newsweek* 53 (Apr. 6, 1959), 34–36; *ibid.* (May 11, 1959), 20; *Time* 73 (Jan. 26, 1959), 88; *New Yorker* 35 (Aug. 22, 1959), 95; *NYT*, Mar. 28, 1959.

8. Sanford Gottlieb to Don Keys, Mar. 24, 1959, SANE Papers, Ser. B; executive committee minutes, Apr. 15, 1959, SANE Papers, Ser. A; Dan Wakefield, "Beachhead on 42nd Street," *Nation* 188 (Apr. 25, 1959), 357–59.

9. *BAS* 15 (Sept. 1959), 318–19; *Nation* 188 (Jan. 3, 1959), inside back cover; *NYT*, Mar. 19, 1959.

10. *Ibid.*, Apr. 28, 1959; *Saturday Review* 42 (Apr. 4, 1959), 26; *ibid.* (May 2, 1959), 28; *Congressional Record*, May 11, 1959, p. 7926; *ibid.*, May 14, 1959, p. 8222.

11. "AEC Authorizing Legislation," pp. 311–13; *NYT*, Mar. 25, 1959; Killian to Bronk, Mar. 13, 1959, DDE Papers, PSAC Records.

12. *PPP: Eisenhower, 1959*, pp. 302–3; *NYT*, Mar. 26, Apr. 4 and 11, 1959; *Science* 129 (May 1, 1959), 1210–12.

13. *Ibid.* (May 29, 1959), 1473; *NYT*, Apr. 23 and May 5, 1959; *New Republic* 140 (May 4, 1959), 4–5; *Nation* 188 (May 2, 1959), 397–98.

14. Ralph Lapp, "Fallout Hearings; Second Round," *BAS* 15 (Sept. 1959), 302; "Fallout from Nuclear Weapons Tests," *Hearings* before the Special Subcommittee on Radiation of the Joint Committee on Atomic Energy, 86th Congress, 1st Session (Washington, 1959), pp. 1, 1786.

15. *Ibid.*, pp. 10–40, 262–64, 763–66.

16. *Ibid.*, pp. 779–86, 807, 882–98, 929–37; E. A. Martell, "Atmospheric Aspects of Strontium-90 Fallout," *Science* 129 (May 1, 1959), 1197–205.

17. "Fallout from Nuclear Weapons Tests," pp. 1282, 1305, 1392–94, 1414–20, 1550–52; *NYT*, June 21, 1959.

18. "Fallout from Nuclear Weapons Tests," pp. 30, 1563–64, 1565, 1588–92, 1596, 1607.

19. *Ibid.*, pp. 1061–66; 1785–94, 1802–03.

20. *NYT*, May 6, 7, 8, and 9, 1959; *Time* 73 (May 18, 1959), 59; *Newsweek* 53 (May 18, 1959), 75; *BAS* 15 (June 1959), 258.

21. Ralph E. Lapp, "A Criticism of the GAC Report," *BAS* 15 (Sept. 1959), 311; Walter Schneir, "A Primer on Fallout," *Reporter* 21 (July 9, 1959), 17–23; *New Republic* 140 (May 18, 1959), 4; *ibid.* (June 1, 1959), 4; *NYT*, Aug. 13, 1959.

22. *Science* 130 (Sept. 11, 1959), 612–14; *NYT*, Aug. 24, 1959.

23. *Ibid.*, Sept. 9 and Oct. 10, 1959; *BAS* 15 (Dec. 1959), 429.

24. *NYT*, Aug. 15, 1959; *BAS* 15 (Oct. 1959), 351; *ibid.* (Nov. 1959), 398–99; *Scientific American* 201 (Oct. 1959), 80.

25. *New Yorker* 35 (May 16, 1959), 180–81.

26. Steven M. Spencer, "Fallout: The Silent Killer," *Saturday Evening Post* 232 (Aug. 29, 1959), 26, 89; *ibid.* (Sept. 5, 1959), 86.

27. *Scientific American* 201 (Sept. 1959), 73, 89, 224, 229–30, 232.

28. "Testimony of John A. McCone on the Geneva Test Ban Negotiations," *Hearing* before the Senate Foreign Relations Subcommittee on Disarmament, 86th Congress, 1st. Session (Washington, 1959), p. 24.

CHAPTER ELEVEN

1. George B. Kistiakowsky, *A Scientist at the White House: The Private Diary of President Eisenhower's Special Assistant for Science and Technology* (Cambridge, Mass., 1976), p. 17.

2. *Newsweek* 53 (June 22, 1959), 28, 55; *NYT*, July 11, 1959; *Science* 130 (July 24, 1959), 208–9; *BAS* 15 (Dec. 1959), 422; Jacobson and Stein, *Diplomats, Scientists, and Politicians*, pp. 188–94.

3. *NYT*, June 28, July 2 and 20, 1959; *Time* 74 (July 20, 1959), 18; State Dept., *Bulletin* 41 (July 27, 1959), 111; Kistiakowsky, *Scientist*, pp. 45–46.

NOTES

4. *Newsweek* 53 (July 8, 1959), 32; Kistiakowsky, *Scientist,* pp. 17–18, 22, 23–24, 33, 36.

5. *Ibid.,* p. 43; *Congressional Record,* August 18, 1959, pp. 16135–44; *Science* 130 (Sept. 11, 1959), 611.

6. *State Dept., Bulletin* 41 (Sept. 14, 1959), 374; *NYT,* Aug. 26, 28, and 29, 1959; *Time* 74 (Sept. 7, 1959), 12; Macmillan, *Pointing the Way,* p. 86; Eisenhower, *Waging Peace,* p. 422.

7. State Dept., *Bulletin* 41 (Oct. 5, 1959), 471; *ibid.* (Oct. 12, 1959), 499; *ibid.* (Oct. 26, 1959), 578; *ibid.* (Nov. 2, 1959), 615; *NYT,* Sept. 19, Oct. 15 and 28, 1959; Khrushchev, *Last Testament,* pp. 410–11, 536.

8. Jacobson and Stein, *Diplomats, Scientists and Politicians,* pp. 204–9; *NYT,* Nov. 5, 13, 21, and 22, 1959; State Dept., *Bulletin* 41 (Nov. 30, 1959), 806; *ibid.* (Dec. 21, 1959), 918–19; *Newsweek* 54 (Nov. 2, 1959), 42.

9. *NYT,* Oct. 26 and 31, Nov. 1, 3, and 13, 1959; *Time* 74 (Nov. 9, 1959), 22; *BAS* 15 (Dec. 1959), 423; Humphrey to Kistiakowsky, Nov. 4, 1959, DDE Papers, OF 108-A.

10. *NYT,* Nov. 8, 15, and 23, 1959; *New Republic* 141 (Nov. 2, 1959), 3–4; press release by Norman Cousins, Oct. 26, 1959, SANE Papers, Ser. A; Donald Keys to Steve Allen, Nov. 23, 1959, SANE Papers, Ser. B; *Time* 74 (Nov. 30, 1959), 15.

11. Gallup, *Gallup Poll,* 3: 1643; *NYT,* Dec. 20, 1959; *Science* 130 (Nov. 20, 1959), 1381; *BAS* 15 (Dec. 1959), 424.

12. Kistiakowsky, *Scientist,* pp. 106, 108–9.

13. *BAS* 15 (Dec. 1959), 428; *PPP: Eisenhower, 1959,* p. 770; Kistiakowsky, *Scientist,* pp. 150, 152; State Dept., *Bulletin* 41 (Dec. 14, 1959), 863; *NYT,* Nov. 27, 1959.

14. Jacobson and Stein, *Scientists, Diplomats, and Politicians,* pp. 218–30; *BAS* 16 (Feb. 1960), 78; *Science* 131 (Jan. 1, 1960), 23; *ibid.* (Jan. 15, 1960), 129; *NYT,* Dec. 20, 1959; Edward Gamarekian, "Quarrels over Underground Testing," *Nation* 190 (Feb. 27, 1960), 179–82.

15. Kistiakowsky, *Scientist,* pp. 195, 197–98, 204, 211–12.

16. *Ibid.,* p. 213; *NYT,* Dec. 29 and 30, 1959; *Time* 75 (Jan. 11, 1960), 12; *Newsweek* 55 (Jan. 11, 1960), 34; *PPP: Eisenhower, 1959,* p. 883; notes on remarks by Wadsworth, undated, SANE Papers, Ser. B.

NOTES

17. *NYT*, Dec. 31, 1959, and Jan. 2, 1960; *New Republic* 142 (Jan. 11, 1960), 5; *BAS* 16 (Feb. 1960), 35.
18. *PPP: Eisenhower, 1960–61*, p. 4; *NYT*, Jan. 4, 12, 15, and 27, Feb. 7 and 8, 1960; Kistiakowsky, *Scientist*, pp. 222, 232, 250, 252.
19. *PPP: Eisenhower, 1960–61*, pp. 166–67, 170; State Department, *Bulletin* 42 (Feb. 29, 1960), 327–28.
20. *Newsweek* 55 (Feb. 22, 1960), 37; *NYT*, Feb. 12, 13, and 14, 1960; *New Republic* 142 (Mar. 7, 1960), 11–13; *Time* 75 (Feb. 22, 1960), 22; *BAS* 16 (Apr. 1960), 142.
21. *NYT*, Feb. 17, 1960; *Science* 131 (Feb. 26, 1960), 595; *PPP: Eisenhower, 1960–61*, p. 194.
22. State Dept., *Bulletin* 42 (Mar. 28, 1960), 493; *Science* 131 (Apr. 1, 1960), 975; *NYT*, Mar. 19 and 20, 1960.
23. *NYT*, Mar. 22 and 23, 1960; *Newsweek* 55 (Apr. 4, 1960), 29; Macmillan, *Pointing the Way*, pp. 185–86.
24. *Time* 75 (Apr. 11, 1960), 25; Chalmers M. Roberts, "The Hopes and Fears of an Atomic Test Ban," *Reporter* 22 (Apr. 28, 1960), 20–23; Kistiakowsky, *Scientist*, pp. 279, 281, 282.
25. *NYT*, Mar. 27, 1960; *BAS* 16 (May 1960), 190; Kistiakowsky, *Scientist*, pp. 285–88; Macmillan, *Pointing the Way*, pp. 188–91.
26. *PPP: Eisenhower, 1960–61*, pp. 317, 319, 321, 326–27, 329; Kennedy to Eisenhower, Mar. 30, 1960, DDE Papers, OF 108-A; *NYT*, Apr. 4 and 5, 1960.
27. Special legislative note, Mar. 31, 1960, DDE Papers, Diary Series; *NYT*, Mar. 27, 30, and 31, 1960; *Life* 48 (Apr. 4, 1960), 33.
28. *Newsweek* 55 (Apr. 11, 1960), 34; *Time* 75 (Apr. 11, 1960), 10; *New Republic* 142 (Apr. 4, 1960), 3; *NYT*, Mar. 30, 1960; State Dept., *Bulletin* 42 (Apr. 25, 1960), 647.
29. Blumberg and Owens, *Energy and Conflict*, p. 407.
30. Freeman J. Dyson, "The Future Development of Nuclear Weapons," *Foreign Affairs* 38 (Apr. 1960), 457–64.
31. *Newsweek* 55 (Apr. 4, 1960), 66; *New Republic* 142 (Apr. 25, 1960), 9; *BAS* 16 (May 1960), 168–72; *NYT*, May 13, 1960; *U.S. News and World Report* 48 (May 30, 1960), 56, 59.
32. *Science* 131 (Apr. 29, 1960), 1298–99; "Technical Aspects of Detection and Inspection Controls of a Nuclear Weapons Test Ban," *Hearings* before the Special Subcommittee on Radiation and the Subcommittee on Research and Development of the Joint Com-

mittee on Atomic Energy, 86th Congress, 2nd Session (Washington, 1960), pp. 1–2.

33. *Ibid.,* pp. 8–9, 21–23, 78–80, 124–29, 138–42.

34. *Ibid.,* pp. 158–59, 164, 171–72, 177, 197.

35. *Ibid.,* pp. 201–3, 204, 208, 214–15.

36. *NYT,* Apr. 20 and 23, 1960; *Newsweek* 55 (May 2, 1960), 60; "Technical Aspects of Detection," pp. 417–18.

37. *NYT,* Apr. 26, 1960; *Scientific American* 202 (June 1960), 81.

38. Kistiakowsky, *Scientist,* pp. 307–8; *NYT,* Apr. 24, 1960; *Nation* 190 (May 7, 1960), 394.

39. *NYT,* Apr. 13 and 21, 1960; *PPP: Eisenhower, 1960–61,* pp. 364–65.

40. *NYT,* Apr. 28, 1960; *BAS* 16 (June 1960), 223.

41. Herbert S. Parmet, *Eisenhower and the American Crusades* (New York, 1972), pp. 555–58; Eisenhower, *Waging Peace,* pp. 543–52.

42. Peter Lyon, *Eisenhower: Portrait of the Hero* (Boston, 1974), pp. 811–14; David Wise and Thomas B. Ross, *The U-2 Affair* (New York, 1962), pp. 149–58; Eisenhower, *Waging Peace,* pp. 553–56; *NYT,* May 18, 1960.

43. *Science* 131 (May 27, 1960), 1594; Kistiakowsky, *Scientist,* p. 335.

44. Eisenhower, *Waging Peace,* p. 480; Kistiakowsky, *Scientist,* p. 375; *Nation* 190 (June 11, 1960), 501.

EPILOGUE

1. *U.S. News and World Report* 48 (June 6, 1960), 57; Kistiakowsky, *Scientist,* pp. 364, 383; *PPP: Eisenhower, 1960–61,* pp. 559–60, 620; Eisenhower, *Waging Peace,* p. 481.

2. Arthur M. Schlesinger, Jr., *A Thousand Days: John F. Kennedy in the White House* (Boston, 1965), pp. 454–61, 495–97, 893–98; Facts on File, *Disarmament and Nuclear Tests, 1960–63* (New York, 1964), pp. 46–53, 66–67, 74–75, 91–94; Eisenhower, *Waging Peace,* p. 482.

3. *NYT,* Feb. 4 and Apr. 28, 1960; *Consumer Reports* 25 (Feb. 1960), 68; J. Laurence Kulp, Arthur P. Schulert, Elizabeth J. Hodges, "Strontium-90 in Man, IV," *Science* 132 (Aug. 19, 1960), 449–54.

4. *NYT,* Feb. 26 and May 17, 1960; special staff note, April 25, 1960, DDE Papers, Diary Series; "Radiation Protection Criteria and Standards: Their Basis and Use," *Hearings* before the Special Sub-

committee on Radiation of the Joint Committee on Atomic Energy, 86th Congress, 2nd Session (Washington, 1960), pp. 93, 122; *Science* 132 (Sept. 16, 1960), 724.

5. "Selected Materials on Radiation Protection Criteria," *Print* of the Joint Committee on Atomic Energy, 86th Congress, 2nd Session (Washington, 1960), pp. 1192–93, 1204–10; *Science* 131 (May 13, 1960), 1428; "The Effects on Populations of Exposures to Low Levels of Ionizing Radiation," *Report* of the Advisory Committee on the Biological Effects of Ionizing Radiation, National Academy of Sciences—National Research Council (Washington, 1972), pp. 1, 44–46, 89, 168.

6. Thomas E. Murray, *Nuclear Policy for War and Peace* (Cleveland, 1960), p. 75.

ESSAY ON THE SOURCES

Because the debate over nuclear fallout took place publicly, this study is based primarily on newspapers, periodicals, and government documents. A limited number of archival sources, however, proved helpful in piecing together the controversy within the Eisenhower administration over test ban policy. The recently opened Ann Whitman files at the Dwight D. Eisenhower Library in Abilene, Kansas, especially the Eisenhower Diary Series, contain a great deal of important material. Summaries of the President's telephone conversations, notably those with Secretary of State Dulles, and memoranda of White House meetings prepared by Andrew Goodpaster, staff secretary to the President who sat in on all conferences dealing with national security matters, give a revealing insight into Eisenhower's thinking. The records of the President's Science Advisory Committee and the papers of James Hagerty, particularly a diary that the press secretary kept in 1954, also provide useful information.

The records of the Atomic Energy Commission, maintained by its successor agency, the Energy Research and Development Administration, at its Germantown, Maryland, headquarters, proved disappointing. Nearly all the pertinent documents are classified; only a few scattered items are open to researchers.

The files of the National Committee for a Sane Nuclear Policy are open to scholars at the Swarthmore College Peace Collection. The SANE papers, well-preserved and arranged, provide a full and candid picture of the test ban movement in the late 1950s.

Government documents offer the fullest range of information on the fallout issue. The two hearings held by the Holifield subcommittee, "The Nature of Radioactive Fallout and Its Effect on Man," *Hearings* before the Special Subcommittee on Radiation of the Joint Committee on Atomic Energy, 85th Cong., 1st Sess. (1955) and "Fallout from Nuclear Weapons Tests," *ibid.*, 86th Cong., 1st Sess. (1959), give a comprehensive picture of the conflicting scientific views on radiation hazards. The hearings held by the Humphrey subcommittee, "Control and Reduction of Armaments," *Hearings* before a Subcommittee of the Senate Foreign Relations Committee, 84th Cong., 2nd Sess. and 85th Cong., 1st and 2nd Sess. (1955–1958), reveal the growing congressional pressure for a test ban agreement. On the question of detecting underground nuclear tests, the most important source is "Technical Aspects of Detection and Inspection Controls of a Nuclear Weapons Test Ban," *Hearings* before the Special Subcommittee on Radiation and the Subcommittee on Research and Development of the Joint Committee on Atomic Energy, 86th Cong., 2nd Sess. (1960).

The annual volumes of the *Public Papers of the Presidents of the United States: Dwight D. Eisenhower* contain the full transcript of all the President's statements on fallout and testing, including complete texts of White House press conferences. The *Bulletin* of the State Department prints all relevant public diplomatic exchanges with the Soviet Union as well as speeches by departmental officials and transcripts of the Secretary's news conferences. The two-volume collection published by the Department of State, *Documents on Disarmament, 1945–1959,* contains the pertinent documents on the test ban negotiations.

The *New York Times* is the single most important source for reconstructing the course of the public debate over fallout and test ban proposals. The *Times* covered all aspects of the controversy, ranging from statements by scientists to analyses of administration policy. *Time* and *Newsweek* provided more selective coverage, while the *U.S. News and World* concentrated on presenting the AEC point of view. Liberal journals of opinion, especially the *Nation, New Republic,* and *Reporter,* offer insight into the test ban movement and its rationale, as do Norman Cousin's editorials in the *Saturday Review.*

The *Bulletin of the Atomic Scientists* was indispensable. Nearly every issue included articles on the test ban question, with particularly important contributions by David Inglis, Ralph Lapp, and Eugene Rabinowich. *Science,* the weekly journal of the American Association for the Advancement of Science, printed major articles on radiation dangers, most notably the four on strontium-90 in man by Laurence Kulp and his associates at Columbia University. The *Scientific American* proved less helpful, except for an important symposium on radiation in the September 1959 issue.

A diary kept by George Kistiakowsky, *A Scientist at the White House,* gives a candid account of the Eisenhower administration's decision-making process in 1959 and 1960. Two memoirs, Dwight D. Eisenhower, *Waging Peace, 1956–1961* and Lewis L. Strauss, *Men and Decisions,* are much more fragmentary in their coverage of the testing issue. Harold Macmillan provides a useful British insight into the test ban negotiations in his memoirs, *Riding the Storm, 1956–1959* and *Pointing the Way, 1959–1961*. On the Russian side, Nikita Khrushchev, *Khrushchev Remembers: The Last Testament,* and Andrei D. Sakharov, *Sakharov Speaks,* give a few glimpses into the tensions between Soviet policy-makers and dissident scientists.

Although there are no satisfactory studies of the fallout debate within the United States, two scholarly books deal with important aspects of the test ban negotiations. Harold Koran Jacobson and Eric Stein, *Diplomats, Scientists, and Politicians: The United States and the Nuclear Test Ban Negotiations,* traces the course of diplomacy from the Geneva Conference of Experts in

1958 through the limited test ban treaty of 1963; Robert Gilpin perceptively analyzes the debate among scientists over the wisdom of a test ban in *American Scientists and Nuclear Weapons Policy.* For the story of disarmament efforts from the end of World War II through 1960, Bernard G. Bechhoefer, *Postwar Negotiations for Arms Control* is reliable and judicious. Two articles, Saville R. Davis, "Recent Policy Making in the United States Government," *Daedalus* 89 (Fall 1960) and Charles J. V. Murphy, "Nuclear Inspection: A Near Miss," *Fortune* 59 (March 1959), discuss the reversal of administration policy in 1958 with the help of leaks from policy makers. Earl H. Voss gives a comprehensive but frankly hostile account of the test ban issue in *Nuclear Ambush: The Test-Ban Trap.*

Ralph E. Lapp has recounted the fate of the 23 Japanese fishermen exposed to BRAVO's radiation in *The Voyage of the Lucky Dragon.* The most helpful accounts of the development of the H-bomb are Herbert F. York, *The Advisors: Oppenheimer, Teller, and the Superbomb,* and Roland Sawyer, "The H-Bomb Chronology," *Bulletin of the Atomic Scientists* 10 (September 1954).

The major participants in the fallout debate presented their views in books published as part of the controversy. Linus Pauling argues passionately for a test ban in *No More War!,* while Edward Teller offers a defense of testing with Albert L. Latter in *Our Nuclear Future.* For additional information on Teller's role, see Edward Teller, with Allen Brown, *The Legacy of Hiroshima,* and Stanley A. Blumberg and Gwinn Owens, *Energy and Conflict: The Life and Times of Edward Teller,* an uncritical biography. Thomas Murray gives his maverick views in *Nuclear Policy for War and Peace.*

The best account of the peace movement in the 1950s is Lawrence S. Wittner, *Rebels against War: The American Peace Movement, 1941–1960,* which includes a penetrating analysis of the role of SANE. Nathan Glazer probes the weaknesses of SANE in "The Peace Movement in America, 1961," *Commentary* 31 (April 1961). For personal accounts of two quixotic protests against testing, see Albert Bigelow, *The Voyage of the Golden Rule,* and Earle Reynolds, *The Forbidden Voyage.* Norman Cousins describes his efforts to enlist Albert Schweitzer in the test ban crusade in *Dr. Schweitzer of Lambaréné.* Nevil Shute's novel, *On the Beach,* helped make the American people aware of the danger of fallout from nuclear war.

The second volume of George H. Gallup, *The Gallup Poll: Public Opinion, 1935–1971,* provides the basic data on public attitudes toward testing in the 1950s. Eugene J. Rosi plays down the influence of public opinion on the Eisenhower administration's decision to seek a test ban in "Mass and Attentive Opinion on Nuclear Weapons Tests and Fallout, 1954–1963," *Public Opinion Quarterly* 29 (Summer 1965).

BIBLIOGRAPHY

MANUSCRIPT COLLECTIONS

Atomic Energy Commission Papers, Energy Research and Development Administration, Germantown, Maryland

Dwight D. Eisenhower Papers, Eisenhower Library, Abilene, Kansas

James C. Hagerty Papers, Eisenhower Library, Abilene, Kansas

C. D. Jackson Papers, Eisenhower Library, Abilene, Kansas

Estes Kefauver Papers, University of Tennessee Library, Knoxville, Tennessee

National Committee for a Sane Nuclear Policy Papers, Swarthmore College Peace Collection, Swarthmore, Pennsylvania

President's Science Advisory Committee Records, Eisenhower Library, Abilene, Kansas

Project Clean-up Records, Eisenhower Library, Abilene, Kansas

ORAL HISTORY

Dillon Anderson Memoir, Eisenhower Library, Abilene, Kansas

Andrew J. Goodpaster Memoir, Eisenhower Library, Abilene, Kansas

John A. McCone Memoir, Eisenhower Library, Abilene, Kansas

Jmes J. Wadsworth Memoir, Eisenhower Library, Abilene, Kansas

GOVERNMENT DOCUMENTS

Declassified Documents, 1975 Series. Washington, 1975

Public Papers of the Presidents of the United States: Dwight D. Eisenhower, 1954–61. 8 vols., Washington, 1960–61

U.S. Congress, *Congressional Record*

———, "AEC Authorizing Legislation for Fiscal Year 1960," *Hearings* before the Subcommittee on Legislation of the Joint Committee on Atomic Energy, 86th Cong., 1st Sess., 1959

———, "AEC-FCDA Relationship," *Hearing* before the Subcommittee on Security of the Joint Committee on Atomic Energy, 84th Cong., 1st Sess., 1955

———, "Civil Defense Program," *Hearings* before the Subcommittee on Civil Defense of the Senate Armed Services Committee, 84th Cong., 1st Sess., 1955

———, "Communist Infiltration in the Nuclear Test Ban Movement," *Hearing* before a Subcommittee of the Senate Committee on the Judiciary, 86th Cong., 2nd Sess., 1960

———, "Control and Reduction of Armaments," *Hearings* before a Subcommittee of the Senate Committee on Foreign Relations, 84th Cong., 2nd Sess. and 85th Cong., 1st and 2nd Sess., 1956–58

———, "Disarmament and Foreign Policy," *Hearings* before a Subcommittee of the Senate Committee on Foreign Relations, 86th Cong., 1st Sess., 1959

———, "Disarmament Developments, Spring, 1960," *Hearing* before a Subcommittee of the Senate Committee on Foreign Relations, 86th Cong., 2nd Sess., 1960

———, "Fallout from Nuclear Weapons Tests," *Hearings* before the Special Subcommittee on Radiation of the Joint Committee on Atomic Energy," 86th Cong., 1st Sess., 1959

———, "Heath and Safety Problems and Weather Effects Associated with Atomic Explosions," *Hearing* before the Joint Committee on Atomic Energy, 84th Cong., 1st Sess., 1955

———, "The Nature of Radioactive Fallout and Its Effect on Man," *Hearings* before the Special Subcommittee on Radiation of the Joint Committee on Atomic Energy," 85th Cong., 1st Sess., 1957

———, "Nomination of John A. McCone to be a Member of the Atomic Energy Commission," *Hearing* before the Senate Section of the Joint Committee on Atomic Energy, 85th Cong., 2nd Sess., 1958

———, "Radiation Protection Criteria and Standards: Their Basis and Use," *Hearings* before the Special Subcommittee on Radiation of the Joint Committee on Atomic Energy, 86th Cong., 2nd Sess., 1960

———, "Review of Foreign Policy, 1958," *Hearings* before the Senate Foreign Relations Committee, 85th Cong., 2nd Sess., 1958

———, "Technical Aspects of Detection and Inspection Controls of a Nuclear Weapons Test Ban," *Hearings* before the Special Subcommittee on Radiation and the Subcommittee on Research and Development of the Joint Committee on Atomic Energy, 86th Cong., 2nd Sess., 1960

———, "Technical Problems and the Geneva Test Ban Negotiations," Hearing before the Senate Foreign Relations Subcommittee on Disarmament, 86th Cong., 2nd Sess., 1960

———, "Testimony of Dr. Linus Pauling," *Hearing* before the Subcommittee on Internal Security of the Senate Committee on the Judiciary, 86th Cong., 2nd Sess., 1960

———, "Testimony of John A. McCone on the Geneva Test Ban Negotiations," *Hearing* before the Senate Foreign Relations Subcommittee on Disarmament, 86th Cong., 1st Sess., 1959

———, "Control and Reduction of Armaments," *Staff Study No. 10,* Senate Foreign Relations Subcommittee on Disarmament, 85th Cong., 2nd Sess., 1958

———, "Fallout from Nuclear Weapons Tests," *Summary-Analysis* of Hearings before the Special Subcommittee on Radiation of the Joint Committee on Atomic Energy, 86th Cong., 1st Sess., 1959

———, "Technical Aspects of Detection and Inspection Controls of a Nuclear Weapons Test Ban," *Summary-Analysis* of Hearings before the Special Subcommittee on Radiation and the Subcommittee on Research and Development of the Joint Committee on Atomic Energy, 86th Cong., 2nd Sess., 1960

U.S. Department of State, *Bulletin*

———, *Disarmament: The Intensified Effort, 1955–1958.* Washington, 1960

———, *Documents on Disarmament, 1945–1959.* 2 vols., Washington, 1960

PERIODICALS AND NEWSPAPERS

Bulletin of the Atomic Scientists
Consumer Reports

Foreign Affairs
Fortune
Life
Nation
New Republic
New York Times
New Yorker
Newsweek
Reporter
Saturday Review
Science
Scientific American
Time
United States News and World Report

DIARIES, MEMOIRS, AUTOBIOGRAPHIES AND COLLECTED LETTERS

Adams, Sherman. *Firsthand Report.* New York, 1961
Allison, John M. *Ambassador from the Prairie or Allison Wonderland.* Boston, 1973
Anderson, Clinton P., and Viorst, Milton. *Outsider in the Senate.* New York 1970
Cutler, Robert. *No Time for Rest.* Boston, 1966
Eisenhower, Dwight D. *Waging Peace, 1956–1961.* Garden City, N.Y. 1965
Johnson, Walter, ed. *Toward a New America, 1955–1957.* Vol. 6 of *The Papers of Adlai E. Stevenson.* Boston, 1976
Khrushchev, Nikita, A. *Khrushchev Remembers: The Last Testament.* Translated and edited by Strobe Talbott. Boston, 1974
Kistiakowsky, George B. *A Scientist at the White House: The Private Diary of President Eisenhower's Special Assistant for Science and Technology.* Introduction by Charles S. Maier. Cambridge, Mass., 1976
Lilienthal, David E. *Venturesome Years, 1950–1955.* Vol. 3 of *The Journals of David E. Lilienthal.* New York, 1966
Macmillan, Harold. *Pointing the Way, 1959–1961.* London, 1972
———. *Riding the Storm, 1956–1961.* London, 1971
Sakharov, Andrei D. *Sakharov Speaks.* New York, 1974
Strauss, Lewis L. *Men and Decisions.* Garden City, N.Y., 1962
Sulzberger, C. L. *The Last of the Giants.* New York, 1970

BIBLIOGRAPHY

Truman, Harry S. *Memoirs.* 2 vols., Garden City, N.Y., 1956
Wadsworth, James J. *The Price of Peace.* New York, 1962

BOOKS

Bechhoefer, Bernard G. *Postwar Negotiations for Arms Control.* Washington, 1961

Berding, Andrew H. *Dulles on Diplomacy.* Princeton, N.J., 1965

Bigelow, Albert. *The Voyage of the Golden Rule.* New York, 1959

Bloomfield, Lincoln P., Clemens, Walter C., Jr., and Griffiths, Franklyn. *Khrushchev and the Arms Race: Soviet Interests in Arms Control and Disarmament, 1954–1964.* Cambridge, Mass., 1966

Blumberg, Stanley A., and Owens, Gwinn. *Energy and Conflict: The Life and Times of Edward Teller.* New York, 1976

Brown, Stuart G. *Conscience in Politics: Adlai E. Stevenson in the 1950s.* Syracuse, N.Y. 1961

Cousins, Norman. *Dr. Schweitzer of Lambaréné.* New York, 1960

Davis, Kenneth S. *The Politics of Honor: A Biography of Adlai E. Stevenson.* New York, 1967

Divine, Robert A. *Foreign Policy and U.S. Presidential Elections, 1952–1960.* New York, 1974

Doyle, Edward P., ed. *As We Knew Adlai.* New York, 1966

Fowler, John M., ed. *Fallout: A Study of Superbombs, Strontium 90 and Survival.* New York, 1960

Gallup, George H., ed. *The Gallup Poll: Public Opinion, 1935–1971.* 3 vols., New York, 1972

Gilpin, Robert. *American Scientists and Nuclear Weapons Policy.* Princeton, N.J., 1962

Hoopes, Townsend. *The Devil and John Foster Dulles.* Boston, 1973

Hughes, Emmet J. *The Ordeal of Power: A Political Memoir of the Eisenhower Years.* New York, 1963

Jacobson, Harold Karan, and Stein, Eric. *Diplomats, Scientists, and Politicians: The United States and the Nuclear Test Ban Negotiations.* Ann Arbor, Mich., 1966

Lang, Daniel. *From Hiroshima to the Moon: Chronicles of Life in the Atomic Age.* New York, 1959

Lapp, Ralph E. *The New Priesthood: The Scientific Elite and the Uses of Power.* New York, 1965

———. *The Voyage of the Lucky Dragon.* New York, 1958

376

BIBLIOGRAPHY

Lyon, Peter. *Eisenhower: Portrait of the Hero.* Boston, 1974

McCamy, James L. *Science and Public Administration.* University, Ala., 1960

Muller, Herbert J. *Adlai Stevenson: A Study in Values.* New York, 1967

Murray, Thomas E. *Nuclear Policy for War and Peace.* Cleveland, 1960

Parmet, Herbert S. *Eisenhower and the American Crusades.* New York, 1972

Pauling, Linus. *No More War!* New York, 1958

Reynolds, Earle. *The Foribdden Voyage.* New York, 1961

Schubert, Jack and Lapp, Ralph E. *Radiation: What It Is and How It Affects You.* New York, 1957

Shute, Nevil. *On the Beach.* New York, 1957

Stevenson, Adlai E. *The New America.* New York, 1957

Stone, I. F. *The Haunted Fifties.* New York, 1963

Teller, Edward, with Brown, Allen, *The Legacy of Hiroshima.* Garden City, N.Y. 1962

—————— and Latter, Albert L. *Our Nuclear Future.* New York, 1958

York, Herbert F. *The Advisors: Oppenheimer, Teller, and the Superbomb.* San Francisco, 1976

Voss, Earl H. *Nuclear Ambush: The Test-Ban Trap.* Chicago, 1963

Wilson, Thomas W., Jr. *The Great Weapons Heresy.* Boston, 1970

Wise, David, and Ross, Thomas B. *The U-2 Affair.* New York, 1962

Wittner, Lawrence S. *Rebels against War: The American Peace Movement, 1941–1960.* New York, 1969

ARTICLES

Allison, Helen C. "Outspoken Scientist," *Bulletin of the Atomic Scientists* 16 (December 1960), 382–90

Bethe, Hans, and Teller, Edward. "The Future of Nuclear Tests," Foreign Policy Association *Headline Series,* No. 145 (January–February, 1961)

Brown, Harrison, "A Scientist's Proposal for Limiting Atomic Tests," *Reporter* 18 (April 3, 1958), 12–14

Davis, Saville R. "Recent Policy Making in the United States Government," *Daedalus* 89 (Fall 1960), 951–66

Dyson, Freeman J. "The Future Development of Nuclear Weapons," *Foreign Affairs* 38 (April 1960), 457–64

BIBLIOGRAPHY

Glazer, Nathan. "The Peace Movement in America, 1961," *Commentary* 31 (April 1961), 288–96

Kissinger, Henry A. "Nuclear Testing and the Problems of Peace," *Foreign Affairs* 37 (October 1958), 1–18

Kulp, J. Laurence, *et al.* "Strontium-90 in Man," *Science* 125 (February 8, 1957), 219–25

———. "Strontium-90 in Man, II," *Science* 127 (February 7, 1958), 267–73

———. "Strontium-90 in Man, III," *Science* 129 (May 8, 1959), 1249–55

Marine, Gene. "McCone of the AEC," *Nation* 188 (April 1, 1959), 307–10

Murphy, Charles J. V. "Nuclear Inspection: A Near Miss," *Fortune* 59 (March 1959), 122–25, 155–63

Norton-Taylor, Duncan. "The Controversial Mr. Strauss," *Fortune* 51 (January 1955), 110–12, 164–70

Orear, Jay. "Detection of Nuclear Weapons Testing," *Bulletin of the Atomic Scientists* 14 (March 1958), 98–101

Roberts, Chalmers M. "The Hopes and Fears of an Atomic Test Ban," *Reporter* 22 (April 28, 1960), 20–23

Rosi, Eugene J. "Mass and Attentive Opinion on Nuclear Weapons Tests and Fallout, 1954–1963," *Public Opinion Quarterly* 29 (Summer 1965), 280–97

Sawyer, Roland. "The H-Bomb Chronology," *Bulletin of the Atomic Scientists* 10 (September 1954), 287–90

Spencer, Steven M. "Fallout: The Silent Killer," *Saturday Evening Post,* 232 (August 29, 1959), 28, 87–90 and (September 5, 1959), 25, 84–86

Stevenson, Adlai E. "Why I Raised the H-Bomb Question," *Look* 21 (February 5, 1957), 23–25

INDEX

Acheson, Dean, 290

Adams, Sherman, 97, 144, 170, 242

Allison, John M., 29-31

American Friends Service Committee, 74, 77, 165, 196; and test ban petitions, 160, 196-97

Americans for Democratic Action, 214

Amory, Cleveland, 167

Anderson, Carl D., 104

Anderson, Clinton, 96, 110, 130, 194, 209, 218, 223, 295, 299; on testing and national security, 44, 136-37; and Adlai Stevenson, 94, 97; on strontium-90, 132, 264, 265, 274

Anderson, Robert, 177

Andrews, Howard L., 55

Anti-missile missile, 91, 105, 119, 159, 173, 220, 221, 255, 284, 303

Argonne National Laboratory, 61, 104, 223

Arms control. *See* Disarmament

Ascoli, Max, 19, 96, 140; and SANE, 167

Association for the Advancement of Science, 245

Atomic Energy Commission (AEC), 1, 6, 53, 61, 81, 120, 148, 160, 181, 191, 203, 206, 207, 210, 211, 216, 217, 218, 219, 221, 239, 256, 269, 271, 300, 306, 316; conducts nuclear tests, 1, 5, 9, 25, 75, 118-19, 158, 164, 198, 219, 232, 316; contends fallout hazards minimal, 8, 30, 31, 36-40, 43, 65, 116-17, 163, 222-23, 276-77; and test secrecy, 6, 22, 71, 213, 220; on strontium-90, 39, 131, 184-85, 263, 265, 272; and radiation safety responsibilities, 137-38, 164, 265-66, 270, 278, 319; and test ban proposals, 188, 202, 247, 284, 297. *See also* Libby, Willard; Nuclear testing—U.S.; Project Sunshine; Strauss, Lewis

Attwood, Bill, 196

Bacher, Robert, 215, 216, 235-36

Baldwin, Hanson, 230, 255, 303

Bandung Conference, 59

"Ban the Bomb" march (Britain), 197

Baruch, Bernard, 59

379

Baruch plan, 60, 101

Beadle, George, 128, 279-80

Benfy, O. T., 193

Berkner, Lloyd V., 247, 253

Berkner panel on underground test detection, 253, 282

Bethe, Hans, 15, 167, 170, 171, 211, 259, 294, 306, 322; favors test ban, 184, 206, 304, 305, 309-10; and underground test detection problem, 188, 189, 190, 247, 249, 281; as Geneva technical conference delegate, 216, 292, 293; on decoupling theory, 254, 293, 308

Bigelow, Albert, 196, 197, 214-15. See also *Golden Rule*

Birrell, Norman J., 51

Blackman, Adele, 205

Bohlen, Chip, 297

Bowles, Chester, 167

BRAVO test, 1, 17, 25, 47-48, 131, 133; fallout effects, 2, 3, 5-8, 27, 38, 185; and public reaction, 13, 18, 35. *See also* Nuclear testing—U.S.

Brennan, Hank, 19

Britain: nuclear testing program, 58-59, 120, 157, 231; and disarmament, 69, 155; and test ban proposals, 145, 146, 153, 175, 226, 228, 243, 286, 297

British Atomic Scientists Association, 123

British Medical Research Council, 79

Bronk, Detlev, 57, 269

Brown, Harold, 216, 226, 306-7, 309

Brown, Harrison, 94, 123, 184, 193-94, 252

Brownell, Herbert, 89

Brucker, Wilbur M., 85

Brues, Austin M., 224

Bugher, John C., 34

Bulganin, Nikolai, 62, 65, 66, 175, 176; proposes test ban, 85-86, 98; accused

of interfering in American politics, 99-100; resigns as premier, 200

Bulletin of Atomic Scientists, 37, 40, 49, 53, 162, 185, 250, 251; favors test ban, 74, 291; on Sputnik, 169

Bullis, Harry H., 167

Bush, Vannevar, 16

Cahan, William G., 104

Campbell, Charles, 103

Canada, 69

Casanova, Margaret, 18

Carbon-14, 186, 187

Cesium-137, 131

Chiang Kai-Shek, 242

Christian Science Monitor, 50

Christmas Island, 120, 123, 124, 125, 157, 231, 316

Church, Frank, 248, 257

Churchill, Winston, 21, 32, 58

Civil Defense, 172

Civil Defense Advisory Council, 37

"Clean bomb," 82, 130, 148-52, 159, 170, 183, 192, 194, 198, 202, 208, 213, 219-20, 239, 284, 290, 304-6. *See also* Neutron bomb

Cockroft, John, 54

Cohen, Benjamin, 73

Cole, W. Sterling, 8, 23, 130, 144, 148, 151

Committee for Nuclear Information, 268

Committee for 10,000 Babies, 165

Committee of Principals, 219, 228, 294-95, 300-301

Commoner, Barry, 127

Compton, Arthur, 19

Compton, Karl, 171

Condit, Carl, 196

Condon, Edward U., 127

Conference on the Discontinuance of Nuclear Weapons Tests. *See* Geneva Test Ban Conference

Consumer Reports, 263-64
Cory, Catherine, 166-67
Council of Churches, 160
Cousins, Norman, 121, 139, 187, 257; favors test ban, 140, 157, 203-4, 227, 230, 250; called communist dupe, 141; denounces "clean bomb" concept, 151, 239; and SANE, 165, 166, 168; on strontium-90, 223, 268
Crow, James F., 135, 185, 275
Cuban missile crisis, 317
Cutler, Robert, 105, 144, 170

Dean, Arthur, 316
Dean, Gordon, 165, 167
"Death ray." See Neutron bomb
Decoupling theory, 254, 261, 282, 293, 307, 308; criticized, 296
De Gaulle, Charles, 228, 288, 312, 313
Dellinger, David, 214
Democratic Advisory Council, 290, 291
Dewey, Thomas, 89, 100, 108
Dien Bien Phu, 26
Dillon, Douglas, 285
Disarmament, 56-60, 287, 288; and inspection issue, 59, 61, 62, 66, 69, 113, 287; and test ban, 62, 88, 96, 113-16, 143-46, 153-56, 161, 230, 235, 251
Disarmament subcommittee, Senate, 67, 71, 74, 116-17, 265
Dodd, Thomas, 305-6
Douglas, James, 300
Dulles, Allen, 16, 219, 300
Dulles, John Foster, 24, 36, 85, 100, 120, 155, 176, 177, 178, 181, 201, 202, 216-17, 219, 235, 236, 237-38, 244; and Harold Stassen, 60, 86, 146-47, 153; on radiation hazards, 63, 67; and inspection issue, 66, 67, 154; defends nuclear testing, 68, 119, 156; favors advance notice for

all tests, 114-15; on disarmament, 115-16, 144, 145, 152-53, 154; becomes test ban advocate, 143, 199, 207, 209, 210, 211, 212, 228; criticizes "clean bomb" concept, 150, 220; test ban views criticized, 200; terminal illness, 242-43, 255-56
Durham, Carl, 7, 223
Durham, Charles, 130, 272
Du Shane, Graham, 142, 165, 167, 251
Dyson, Freeman, 304-5

Eaton, Cyrus, 161
Eden, Anthony, 59
Einstein, Albert, 107
Eisenbud, Merril, 44-45, 116-17, 133
Eisenhower, Dwight, 6, 24, 84, 111, 156, 161, 206, 218, 233, 242, 247, 303, 310, 318; declines to view nuclear tests, 6, 42, 77; on BRAVO test, 8, 9, 48; and Lewis Strauss, 10, 11, 13, 23, 37, 209, 218; on test hazards, 23, 37, 41, 101, 144; orders studies of test ban concept, 24, 86, 177, 202; defends testing on national security grounds, 25, 90-91, 101, 118, 156, 159; and Harold Stassen, 60, 76, 115, 145, 178; presents "open skies" plan, 62; and summit conferences, 62, 114, 176, 287, 300, 311, 313; on disarmament, 62, 156, 175, 176; criticizes Adlai Stevenson's test ban proposals, 73, 87-88, 91, 92, 97, 98; on allowing observers at U.S. nuclear tests, 76, 151-52; announces Soviet tests, 85, 237; on inspection issue, 99, 101, 102, 245, 252, 258, 299; denounces Soviet test ban proposals, 99, 201; cautions John Foster Dulles against rigid rejection of test ban concept, 100-101; re-elected, 109; and test ban activists, 141, 167, 181, 213-14; concern about global anti-

Eisenhower, Dwight (*continued*)
testing opinion, 143, 149; on test moratorium proposals, 146, 155, 199-200, 229, 231, 236, 285, 286, 301; on "clean bomb," 150, 151, 220; on Sputnik, 170-71; suffers stroke, 175; concern about NATO allies' test ban views, 181-82, 210; and test ban negotiations, 207, 211, 215, 227, 228, 235, 251, 293, 296; and Committee of Principals, 219, 228; and Christian Herter, 243; considers atmospheric test ban, 244, 252-53, 256-57, 285, 287; on underground test detection problem, 246, 254-55, 260-61, 292, 297-98; and Atomic Energy Commission's radiation safety responsibilities, 269, 270, 278; refuses to resume nuclear tests, 281, 284, 295, 315; approves end to formal test moratorium, 295; on dangers of nuclear proliferation, 302; and U-2 incident, 311-12, 313, 314; advises John Kennedy to resume underground tests, 315-16
England. *See* Britain
Estabrook, Robert, 162

Fallout, 23, 37-41, 101, 144, 195; and weather effects, 78; patterns, 4, 38, 131-32, 238-39; and storage time issue, 264-65, 272-74. *See also* Radiation; Strontium-90
Fallout Intensity Detector Oscillator (FIDO), 267
Federal Radiation Council, 278, 318, 319
Federation of American Scientists: advocates United Nation's study on nuclear testing hazards, 55-56, 63; urges test ban, 74, 104, 140, 193; on radiation hazards, 103, 134
Fermi, Enrico, 10, 15, 147

Finkel, Miriam, 223-24
Finletter Air Policy Commission, 218
Fisk, James Brown, 215, 216, 250, 292, 293
Fission-fusion-fission bomb, 47-50
Flanders, Ralph, 97
Flemming, Arthur S., 270, 318
Foreign Affairs, 230, 304
Forrestal, James V., 10, 218
Fosdick, Harry Emerson, 160-61, 167
France, 69, 155; opposes test ban proposals, 145, 146, 175, 228; conducts nuclear tests, 288, 298
Frenchman's Flat, Nevada, 41, 119, 158, 160
Fromm, Erich, 166, 180
Fukuryo Maru. *See Lucky Dragon*
Furth, Jacob, 134

Gaither, H. Rowan, Jr., 172
Gaither report, 172
Gallup poll: on H-bomb and deterrence, 25-26; reveals public opposes unilateral test suspension, 26, 108, 205-6; reveals public ignorance about fallout, 43; on test ban, 139, 291
Gates, Thomas, 285, 294, 295, 313
Gavin, James M., 81, 204
Geneva conference on detection, 215, 217, 225-27, 293-94
Geneva summit conference, 62
Geneva test ban conference, 237, 243-44, 282-83, 296, 315, 316-17; and underground test detection problem, 245-46, 251; and on-site inspection issue, 298-99
Glass, Bentley, 104, 135, 167
Golden Rule, 197, 198, 215, 220; attempts to sail into Pacific test area, 214-15
Gore, Albert, 96, 236, 311; advocates

atmospheric test ban, 244, 245, 248, 257, 284
Graham, Evarts, 103-4
Graves, Alvin C., 130
Green, E. L., 45
Green, Edith, 268
Griggs, David T., 158
Gromyko, Andrei, 200, 233, 235, 287
Gruenther, Alfred, 210

H-bomb. *See* Hydrogen bomb
Hagerty, James, 8, 11, 22, 23, 40, 90, 97, 98-99, 111, 146, 151, 196, 215, 295
Hammarskjold, Dag, 182, 225
Harriman, W. Averell, 99, 317
Hersey, John, 167
Herter, Christian, 243, 256, 284, 287, 292, 302, 303-4, 311; and underground test detection problem, 246, 285; advocates continuing test moratorium, 294, 295, 300, 314
Hickenlooper, Bourke B., 236
Hill, Lister, 270
Hinshaw, Carl, 44
Hiroshima, 133
Hoffman, Frederic, 15
Holifield, Chet, 7, 8, 138, 273, 306, 309; contends radiation hazards minimal, 7, 271-72, 276; and committee hearings on radiation, 129, 130, 271-73; accused of conducting "whitewash," 277
Hoover, Herbert, 10
Hoover, Herbert, Jr., 76
Hosmer, Craig, 248
Humphrey, Hubert, 67, 68, 180, 236, 293, 298; on radiation hazards, 116, 223, 268-69; proposes test moratorium, 178-79; advocates comprehensive test ban, 178, 179, 247, 249-50; attacks Atomic Energy Commission, 188, 265-66; condemns

John Foster Dulles' test ban views, 200; on inspection issue, 252, 290, 311; on atmospheric test ban proposals, 257, 289-90; urges continued test moratorium, 285-86, accuses Eisenhower of nuclear brinkmanship, 295-96
Huntington, William Reed, 197
Hydrogen bomb, 5, 25, 26, 70, 75, 77, 80, 82, 83, 90, 92, 96, 100, 108, 109, 114, 119, 123, 125, 130, 147, 157, 159, 205, 216, 232, 233, 238, 316; destructive capacity discussed, 13, 22, 38, 39, 65, 70, 120-21, 151; early development of, 14-17; and deterrence, 58; production moratorium suggested, 66, 71; test ban proposed, 66, 71-74, 86, 88, 94, 160; proliferation of feared, 95; and "clean bomb" goal, 130, 137, 151, 170, 208. *See also* Fallout; Nuclear testing; Radiation; Strontium-90

ICBM, 17, 74, 169-70, 220, 284, 290, 303
India: objects to American nuclear tests, 27, 75; on proposed United Nations radiation study, 63, 64; proposes test moratorium, 234
Inglis, David: advocates nuclear test ban, 61, 62; advocates ICBM test ban, 74; criticizes Adlai Stevenson, 74, 110; on dangers of nuclear proliferation, 74, 298; on "clean bomb" concept, 151, 305
International Commission on Radiological Protection, 270-71, 276
Iodine-131: somatic effects cited, 274
Irwin, John, 300

Jack, Homer, 166
Jackson, Henry, 130; defends nuclear testing, 137, 148; urges resumption of underground tests, 290

Japan: public reaction to BRAVO test, 7; urges U.S. to cancel new tests, 75, 119; criticizes Soviet tests, 120; criticizes British tests, 120, 124; sponsors U.N. test ban resolution, 288

John, Uunar, 121, 122

Johnson, Ed C., 42

Johnson, Lyndon, 170, 172

Joint Committee on Atomic Energy (JCAE), 6-7, 148, 209, 218, 223, 248, 269, 280, 290, 303; endorses Edward Teller on H-bomb research, 15; conducts hearings on fallout effects, 44-46; subcommittee hearings on radiation hazards, 129-37; subcommittee hearings on test detection problems, 188-92, 306-9; fails to probe John McCone's test ban views, 219; on strontium-90 hazards, 263, 265

Jones, Hardin, 134

Jones, James, 167

Kamb, Barclay, 224

Kefauver, Estes, 40, 72, 84; advocates test ban, 99, 202

Kennedy, John F., 84, 316, 317; on nuclear test moratorium, 289, 302; announces resumption of American atmospheric tests, 316

Khrushchev, Nikita, 65, 202, 207, 242, 302, 303, 310, 311; meets with Eisenhower, 62, 287, 313; advocates disarmament, 66, 287; claims Russia has H-bomb too big to test, 120; criticizes Eisenhower for "clean bomb" enthusiasm, 151; and Nikolai Bulganin, 174-75, 200; becomes premier, 200; and proposed conference on test detection, 211, 215; agrees to test ban negotiations, 229; rejects American test moratorium offer, 231; rejects scientists' plea for

end to Soviet tests, 234; on inspection issue, 252, 258, 287, 288, 297, 317; and atmospheric test ban proposal, 256, 257; promises Russia will not resume testing first, 296-97; meets with Macmillan and de Gaulle, 312; and U-2 incident, 312-13

Killian, James, 170, 211, 212, 228, 245, 259, 322; becomes head of President's Science Advisory Council, 170, 171; influence on Eisenhower, 209; advocates test ban negotiations, 209-10; member of Committee of Principals, 219; appoints Berkner panel, 247; on inspection issue, 252, 254; advocates new radiation hazard study, 269; replaced as presidential science advisor, 284

King, Martin Luther, Jr., 160-61

Kishi, Nobusuke, 120, 156

Kissinger, Henry, 195; criticizes nuclear test moratorium, 230

Kistiakowsky, George B., 297, 300, 314, 322; replaces James Killian as presidential science advisor, 284; opposes John McCone's test ban views, 285, 310; and underground test detection problem, 286, 292; suggests atmospheric test ban, 294; notes Eisenhower's impatience with test ban issue, 295; opposes American test resumption, 313

Knowland, William, 89, 100

Krock, Arthur, 96, 303, 310

Kuboyama, Aikichi, 30

Kulp, Laurence, 322; on strontium-90 hazards, 117, 132, 133, 184, 266, 318; criticizes Linus Pauling, 187

Kurchatov, I. V., 233-34

Labor Party (British), 21, 58, 59, 123

Lapp, Ralph, 17, 35, 55, 136, 142; on

fallout hazards, 32-33, 37-38; criticizes Atomic Energy Commission, 38, 40, 138, 277; on BRAVO test, 47, 49; on strontium-90 hazards, 80-81, 118; rejects "clean bomb" concept, 83; endorses Adlai Stevenson's test ban proposal, 93; criticizes Linus Pauling, 187

Latter, Albert, 183; and decoupling theory, 254, 282, 293, 307

Latter, Richard, 226

Laurence, William, 118

Lawrence, David, 204, 260

Lawrence, Ernest O., 10, 150, 152, 210, 211; advocates H-bomb development, 11; and Edward Teller, 15, 147, 148; opposes test ban negotiations, 69; contends fallout hazards minimal, 105, 124; defends testing on national security grounds, 106; on "clean bomb" concept, 148; member of Geneva conference on detection, 215-16

Leake, Chauncey, 195

Leviero, Anthony, 50

Lewis, E. B., 165-66

Lewis, Edward, 272, 321; rejects radiation threshold concept, 133-35, 274

Libby, Willard, 38, 44, 158, 264; contends fallout hazards minimal, 33, 102-3, 122, 140, 183, 263; comments on fission-fusion-fission bomb, 49; on strontium-90 hazards, 80, 102-3, 163, 263; advocates nuclear testing, 122, 136, 137, 184, 192-93; views on radiation hazards challenged, 123; heads Project Sunshine, 131; on fallout patterns and storage time issue, 132, 264-65, 273; criticizes Linus Pauling, 187; on underground test detection problem, 188, 191

Life, 8; features color photos of H-bomb test, 22; criticizes proposed moratorium on small underground tests, 303

Lilienthal, David, 10, 15

Lindley, Ernest, 19; criticizes Adlai Stevenson's test ban proposal, 96; on "clean bomb" concept, 152; on proposed partial test ban, 298

Lippmann, Walter, 72

Livermore Laboratory, 148, 216

Lodge, Henry Cabot: rejects Indian call for testing halt, 20-21; expresses regret for BRAVO test effects, 27, 29; suggests UN conduct radiation study, 63; on disarmament proposals, 113, 235, 287; defends nuclear testing, 156; opposes Soviet effort to expand UN disarmament commission, 174; supports Harold Stassen's test ban proposal, 177; accuses Soviet Union of bad faith, 234; opposes UN resolution criticizing French nuclear test, 288

London Times, 21

Loper, Herbert, 264

Los Angeles Mirror-News, 232

Lovett, Robert, 210

Lucky Dragon (Fukuryo Maru): crew affected by BRAVO test fallout, 4, 5, 7, 29; crew's fate covered in *Life*, 8; suspected by Lewis Strauss of being a spy ship, 11

Lutheran World Federation, 160

Machta, Lester, 131-32, 273

Macmillan, Harold, 124, 125, 231, 258, 312; confers with Eisenhower, 114, 255, 313; and test ban proposals, 153, 228, 256, 286; criticizes Soviet test suspension, 200-201; on inspection issue, 252; and underground test moratorium, 300-302

Manhattan Project, 14, 284

Mansfield, Mike, 96, 140

Margolis, Emanuel, 28-29
Marshall islands, 4; residents complain to UN about BRAVO test fallout, 27; BRAVO test's effects on residents, 27-29
Marshall, S. L. A., 162
Martell, E. A., 273
Martin, Charles Noel, 32
McCarthy, Joseph, 126
McCloy, John, 210
McCone, John A., 219, 231, 232, 257, 270, 280; appointed chairman of Atomic Energy Commission, 218; cold war views discussed, 218-19; confirmed by Senate, 219; opposes test ban proposals, 219, 228, 256, 283, 294, 300; opposes test moratorium, 239, 285, 286, 290-91, 300; advocates test resumption, 247, 248, 313; denies AEC has withheld radiation hazard information, 269; on inspection issue, 283; advocates termination of Geneva test ban conference, 283-84, 313-14; on underground test detection problem, 292; threatens to resign if test ban treaty goes into effect, 310
McElroy, Neil, 172, 219, 232; opposes Harold Stassen's test ban proposal, 177
Mead, L. P., 69, 307
Menon, Krishna, 28
Mills, Mark, 148, 149, 150, 205, 210
Mills, Polly, 205
Misaki, Yoshio, 4
Morgan, Russell, 266
Muller, Hermann, 78, 321; on radiation hazards, 52-53, 135-36; defends testing on national security grounds, 53; blacklisted by AEC, 53; advocates test ban, 104, 127; and SANE, 167
Mumford, Lewis, 18; and SANE, 167

Mundt, Karl, 89
Murphy, Charles, 259-60
Murray, Thomas, 72, 244, 322; advocates test moratorium, 24, 87; on radiation hazards, 71-72; prefers tactical atomic weapons to H-bomb, 71; advocates test resumption, 260
Murrow, Edward R., 183
Muste, A. J., 160-61, 197
Myrdal, Gunnar, 236

Nagasaki, 133
Nasser, Gamal, 85
Nation, 260, 266, 314; advocates test moratorium, 18; praises Adlai Stevenson's test ban proposal, 96; on Sputnik and cold war tensions, 169; on Soviet test suspension, 202; on strontium-90 hazards, 271
National Academy of Sciences, 56, 164, 222, 224, 269; reports on radiation hazards, 78-79, 319-20
National Advisory Committee on Radiation, 266
National Committee for a Sane Nuclear Policy. See SANE
National Committee on Radiation Protection (NCRP), 270, 271, 318
National Science Foundation, 138
National Security Council, 22, 110, 111, 206, 281, 313; considers publicizing AEC fallout report, 37; authorized to study test ban concept, 86; rumored to have recommended test ban negotiations, 91; receives Gaither report, 172; discusses Stassen's test ban proposal, 177
Nehru, Jawaharlal: advocates immediate test suspension, 20, 59; urges disarmament, 66; praises Bulganin's test suspension proposal, 175; denounces Soviet test resumption, 316

Neumann, William F.: cites radiation hazards, 103, 132-33, 185, 276; and SANE, 166

Neutron bomb, 284, 304-6; described as "death ray," 305, 306. *See also* "Clean bomb"

New Republic, 18, 35, 37, 162, 221, 277; praises Krishna Menton's test ban proposals, 28; on testing hazards, 41, 142; on public apathy regarding Adlai Stevenson's test ban proposal, 75; denounces "clean bomb" concept, 82, 151; praises Adlai Stevenson's test ban proposal, 87; criticizes polemics in test ban debate, 128-29; blames Edward Teller for end to test moratorium, 296; praises Eisenhower for proposing underground test moratorium, 303

New York Daily News, 204

New York Times, 13, 19, 50, 99, 122, 167, 182, 198-99, 203, 204, 205, 236, 277, 290, 301; on radiation hazards, 6, 117-18, 122-23, 137, 223, 276; reports AEC has established radiation monitoring stations, 8; calls for study of fallout effects, 41; defends testing on national security grounds, 57, 108-9, 140; criticizes Adlai Stevenson's test ban proposal, 96; on "clean bomb" concept, 151; criticizes Soviet test suspension, 201; on test detection problem, 224, 227, 255, 309; praises end to formal test moratorium, 295; condemns Soviet proposal for unsupervised underground test ban, 299-300; on U-2 incident, 313

New Yorker, 278-79

Newsweek, 8, 100, 121; on fallout hazards, 34, 38, 39, 43, 267; on "U-bomb," 48; contends public opposes Adlai Stevenson's test ban proposal, 108; on "clean bomb" concept, 151; on Sputnik, 169, 172; on underground test detection problem, 216, 309; praises Eisenhower's test ban stance, 303

Newton, Quigg, 42

Nitze, Paul, 290

Nixon, Richard, 84, 241; denounces Adlai Stevenson's test ban proposal, 87, 89-90, 100; opposes test resumption, 289, 294

No More War! and Linus Pauling's test ban views, 183

Nordheim, L. W., 54-55

Nuclear proliferation, 62, 74, 95, 193-94, 250, 298, 302

Nuclear testing: and fallout patterns, 3-4, 38, 131-32, 238-39, 264-65; number of tests, 238-39

—opposition to: in Japan, 7, 30, 75, 120, 124, 142, 156; in the United States, 18-19, 33, 43, 62, 71-77, 87, 88-89, 93-96, 99, 104, 106-8, 126-27, 128, 136, 137, 139-40, 142, 151, 160-62, 165-68, 179, 180-81, 182, 183, 185-86, 193-94, 195-97, 202-4, 213-15, 220-21, 227, 230, 236-37, 239, 245, 248, 249-50, 267-69, 277, 285, 286, 289-90, 291, 311, 316; in India, 20, 59, 69, 175, 234, 316; by Albert Schweitzer, 21, 121-22; in Britain, 21, 32, 59, 123, 124, 153, 300, 316; in the United Nations, 27-28, 222, 234-35, 288; by Pope Pius, 59, 66; in West Germany, 124-25; in the Soviet Union, 233-34

—British, 120, 157, 231-37

—Soviet, 16-17, 119, 157, 233, 234; and secrecy, 31, 76, 85, 198

—United States: CASTLE series, 1, 5, 6, 25, 221; CROSSROADS series, 4; and secrecy, 5, 6, 18, 25, 70, 71, 76,

Nuclear testing (*continued*)
81-82, 114, 115, 149, 152, 213, 220, 221; MIKE test, 5, 16, 21, 22; Operation GREENHOUSE, 15; and national security justification, 39-42, 44, 46, 47, 53, 54-55, 57, 67-68, 75, 76, 87, 89, 90-91, 101, 105, 108-9, 122, 128, 136-37, 140-41, 145, 156, 159, 159, 163, 192, 204, 208; Operation TEACUP, 41, 42, 46; REDWING series, 75, 76, 77, 78, 81, 82, 97, 221; and clean bomb goal, 82, 130, 148-52, 159, 170, 183, 192, 194, 198, 202, 208, 213, 219-20, 239, 284, 290, 304-6; and anti-missile missile development, 91, 105, 119, 159, 173, 220, 221, 255, 284, 303; PLUMBOB series, 119, 157-58; RANIER test, 157, 158, 180, 188, 190, 191, 206, 226, 227, 246, 259, 307; HARDTACK series, 159, 165, 196-201, 203, 205, 207, 209, 210, 213, 215, 219-21, 229; HARDTACK II series, 232, 233, 245-47, 249, 251, 253, 258, 259, 282, 292, 293; Project Argus, 255. *See also* Atomic Energy Commission; BRAVO test; Fallout; Radiation; Test Ban

Okazaki, Katsuo, 20
On the Beach, 161-63; SANE distributes copies, 268
Open skies plan, 62-63, 101; variations of, 113, 154, 155
"Operation Deadline." *See* Nuclear testing—U.S.: HARDTACK II series
Oppenheimer, Robert, 14, 57; and H-bomb development, 15, 16; stripped of security clearance, 26; warns of radiation hazards, 35
Orear, Jay, 191; advocates test ban, 184, 250; on underground test detection problem, 188-89, 190, 308-9
Ormsby-Gore, David, 236
Our Nuclear Future, 183

Panofsky, Wolfgang, 283; on underground test detection problem, 306, 307
Paris summit conference: plans for, 310, 311; ruined by U-2 incident, 312-13
Pastore, John, 7, 68
Pauling, Linus, 126, 184, 195, 272, 279, 280; cites radiation hazards, 41, 123-24, 128, 183, 185-86, 193, 278; advocates immediate test halt, 125-27, 214; alleged communist activities cited, 126, 141, 204; circulates test ban petitions, 127, 128, 182; publishes *No More War!*, 183; radiation claims criticized, 187; files suit to prevent HARDTACK II tests, 203; on radiation threshold issue, 224; wins Nobel Peace Prize, 321
Payne, Frederick C., 63
Pearson, Drew, 22
Peterson, Val, 37, 41
Phoenix, 220
Pickett, Clarence, 77, 250; and SANE, 165, 168
Polaris missile, 198, 199, 290
Poling, Daniel A., 204-5
Pollard, Ernest, 135, 203
Pope Pius XII, 21, 59, 66
Porter, Charles, 140, 203, 213
Poulson, Norris, 233
Powers, Francis Gary, 312
Pravda, 229
President's Science Advisory Committee (PSAC), 211, 216, 239, 245, 254, 284; created, 171; studies Harold Stassen's test ban proposal, 177; and underground test detection prob-

lem, 188, 246, 283, 297; ordered by Eisenhower to review American nuclear policy, 202; recommends test ban negotiations, 209; recommends test suspension, 210; evaluates weapons testing need, 285. *See also* Killian, James; Kistiakowsky, George B.

Price, Charles, 74, 93

Project Sunshine, 131, 132

Public Health Service, 266, 269, 270; monitors strontium-90 levels in milk, 263, 278, 318

Pugwash statement, 161

Quarles, Donald, 144, 219

Rabb, Maxwell, 196

Rabi, Isidor, 86, 170, 171, 211, 259; criticizes Edward Teller, 304

Rabinowich, Eugene: criticizes AEC secrecy, 34; advocates test ban, 74; criticizes "clean bomb" concept, 82-83; on science corrupted by politics, 106; criticizes Adlai Stevenson's test ban rhetoric, 110; cites radiation hazards, 123, 143; on importance of disarmament, 161; objects to SANE's emotionalism, 167-68; on Sputnik and test ban hopes, 173; contends test ban not a panacea, 239; on end of formal testing moratorium, 296

Radford, Arthur, 144

Radiation, 33, 34, 50-52, 54, 76, 78-81, 89, 103-4, 116, 133, 164, 184-85, 222, 265, 266, 269, 274-75; somatic effects termed minimal, 44, 45, 122, 123, 132, 163, 186-87, 319-20; genetic effects termed minimal, 44, 45, 105, 122, 163, 164, 319; genetic hazards cited, 49, 128, 131, 135-36, 183, 185-86, 279; somatic hazards

cited, 50, 51, 121, 123, 128, 130-31, 166, 183, 186, 268, 279; and threshold issue, 78, 133-35, 185, 223-24, 274-75

RAND Corporation, 131, 254

Randall, Clarence, 170

Rayburn, Sam, 172

Reporter, 96, 202

Reston, James, 100, 152, 201, 301

Reynolds, Earle, 220-21

Rice, Elmer, 196

Robinson, William, 37

Rockefeller, Nelson, 62, 291; advocates test resumption, 289; criticized by SANE, 290

Roosevelt, Eleanor, 167, 202, 236

Rotblat, J., 49

Rusk, Dean, 56

Russell, Bertrand: advocates nuclear disarmament, 124; and Pugwash conference, 161; and SANE, 236; denounces Soviet test resumption, 316

Russell, W. L., 134

Russia. *See* Soviet Union

Sakharov, Andrei, 233, 234

Salisbury, Harrison, 93

SANE, 165, 169, 173, 195; internal divisions concerning tactics, 166-67, 196, 203; publicity efforts of, 167, 168, 196, 203, 214, 236, 277; promotes Hubert Humphrey's test ban proposals, 179-80, 250; lack of influence on Eisenhower, 212; praises Eisenhower for halting tests, 230; opposes limited, atmospheric test ban, 245; exploits fallout scare, 267-68; condemns Nelson Rockefeller's call for test resumption, 290

Saturday Evening Post, 279

Saturday Review, 122, 203

Schlesinger, Arthur, Jr., 73
Schneir, Walter, 266, 277
Schubert, Jack, 142
Schweitzer, Albert, 280; advocates test ban, 21, 121-22, 202-3; radiation views challenged by Willard Libby, 122; denounces "clean bomb" concept, 202; and SANE, 236
Science, 142, 193, 223, 224; on radiation hazards, 80; opposes resumption of atmospheric testing, 291
Science Advisory Committee, 171. See also President's Science Advisory Committee
Scientific American, 18, 279
Sears, Mason, 28, 29
Selove, Walter, 134
Sevareid, Eric, 138, 141
Sheil, Bernard, 76
Shelton, Frank A., 272-73
Short, Dewey, 7
Shotwell, James, 167
Shute, Nevil, 161-63, 268
Singh, J. J., 20
Slatis, Herman M., 52
Smith, Bedell, 210
Smith, Lawrence H., 141
Smyth, Henry, 96
Snyder, Lawrence, 93
Society to Abolish Nuclear Explosions, 165
Sorokin, Pitirim A., 167
Soviet Union, 64, 108, 120, 174, 199-202, 212, 236, 288, 296-97; condemns American nuclear testing, 27, 75; conducts tests, 31, 65, 76, 85, 119, 157; and inspection issue, 59, 60, 98, 125, 146, 226, 243-44, 282-83, 299, 317; advocates test ban, 63-64, 66, 69, 85, 98, 114, 125, 144, 146, 153, 175, 217, 222, 234, 237, 238; rejects U.S. test ban proposals, 154-55, 156; proposes summit conference, 176; announces unilateral testing halt, 200; agrees to test ban negotiations, 229; on test detection problem, 251, 258, 283, 292, 293; pledges not to resume testing first, 286; accuses U.S. of frustrating test ban negotiations, 294; deplores French nuclear test, 298; resumes atmospheric testing, 316; criticized for resuming testing, 316
Sputnik, 169, 174, 176, 211; and U.S. public's reaction, 169-70, 172, 173; adverse effect on test ban prospects, 169, 172, 173; significance minimized by Eisenhower administration, 170
Stans, Maurice, 270
Stassen, Harold, 60, 61, 76, 84, 182, 202; appointed special assistant to the President for disarmament, 60; considers test ban, 61, 62; and "open skies" proposal, 62, 68-69; defends testing on national security grounds, 67, 69; on test detection problem, 68; advocates test ban negotiations, 86, 144, 177, 180, 181; criticizes Adlai Stevenson's test ban proposal, 90, 97; made subordinate to John Foster Dulles, 115; conducts test ban negotiations, 143, 145, 153, 155; reprimanded by John Foster Dulles, 146; on "clean bomb" concept, 152; resigns, 178
State Department, 76, 98, 286; ordered to review U.S. testing policy, 202; criticizes Soviet tests, 233; comments on French nuclear test, 298-99. See also Dulles, John Foster
Steele, Harold, 124, 125
Stevenson, Adlai, 74, 84, 214; advocates test ban, 72, 73, 86-88, 93-95, 99, 106-7; on need for ICBM development, 73; test ban views criti-

cized, 74, 87-90, 97-100; on radiation hazards, 89; on dangers of nuclear proliferation, 95; pleased with public reaction to test ban speeches, 96; claims National Security Council had recommended test ban negotiations, 111; condemns Soviet test resumption, 316

Stone, I. F., 62, 75, 188

Straight, Michael, 38

Strauss, Lewis, 6, 9-11, 12, 23, 36, 37, 41, 56, 97, 118, 144, 151, 159, 170, 199, 209, 214, 216; appointed chairman of AEC, 10; hatred of Communism noted, 10; reveals H-bomb could destroy entire cities, 13; contends testing hazards minimal, 40, 44, 46, 75, 79-80, 105, 140, 163, 218; maintains testing vital to national security, 42, 46, 47, 68, 75, 105, 141, 163, 207-8; accuses test ban proponents of irresponsible claims, 46-47, 77; apologizes for AEC blacklisting of Hermann Muller, 53; and U.S. test secrecy, 76, 149, 213; on "clean bomb" goal, 82; criticizes Soviet test secrecy, 85; policy influence wanes, 143, 208, 209; opposes Stassen's test ban proposal, 177; endorses Edward Teller's call for continued testing, 184; resigns as AEC chairman, 217; awarded Medal of Freedom, 218

Strontium-90, 30, 95, 125, 163, 168, 263, 266, 271, 279, 319; characteristics discussed, 39, 80-81, 103-4, 105, 117, 130-31, 132, 135; hazards termed minimal, 44, 45, 50, 103, 117, 122, 132, 184-85; somatic hazards cited, 70, 118, 121, 186, 268; and National Academy of Sciences report on, 78, 79; and Project Sunshine, 131, 132; and increasing content in bones, 184-85; lack of reliable data on, 195; and threshold issue, 223; and storage time issue, 264, 265, 272-74; and fallout scare, 267, 277-78; levels no longer increase, 318

Sturtevant, A. H., 279; on radiation's genetic hazards, 33, 51, 136

Suez crisis, 108

Symington, Stuart, 40, 94, 96, 192

Szilard, Leo, 10

Taketani, Mituo, 48, 142

Taylor, Lauriston, 271

Taylor, Maxwell, 249

Teller, Edward, 14, 69, 147, 152, 158, 184, 195, 202, 210, 216, 230, 254, 255, 285, 321; and early H-bomb development, 14-16; hatred of the Soviet Union, 14, 194; contends testing hazards minimal, 105, 183, 186-87; on testing and national security, 106, 182-83, 192; on "clean bomb" goal, 148-50, 192, 284; contends Russia would evade test ban, 149, 190-91; compares Sputnik to Pearl Harbor, 170; publishes *Our Nuclear Future*, 183; on testing and the right of scientific inquiry, 192-93; on underground test detection problem, 281, 304, 307-8; views criticized by Hans Bethe, 309; advocates immediate test resumption, 313

Test ban: and disarmament, 88, 95, 96, 113-15, 116, 143-46, 153-56, 161, 175-76; and inspection issue, 61, 66-68, 69, 86, 95, 96, 98-101, 125, 143, 146, 154, 175, 176, 180, 189-91, 206, 207, 209-11, 215, 226, 227, 237, 243-44, 250-51, 252, 258, 282-83, 285, 287, 288, 290, 298-302, 306, 308, 309-11, 316, 317; and preven-

Test ban (*continued*)

tion of nuclear proliferation, 74, 95, 250, 298; advocates accused of aiding communist cause, 126, 141, 196, 204-5; and fear of Soviet cheating, 149, 190-91, 245, 248-49, 285, 300, 303, 304; and underground test detection problem, 158, 180, 188-91, 206, 207, 216, 225-26, 245-47, 249, 251-55, 261, 281-23, 292, 293, 297, 304, 305, 306-7; and high altitude detection problem, 255; and underground test threshold issue, 294, 295, 297, 299, 301, 307, 308; treaty signed, 317. *See also* Geneva conference on detection; Geneva test ban conference; Nuclear testing—opposition to

Thomas, Norman, 165, 167, 180, 203

Thomas, Trevor, 180

Thompson, Llewellyn, 229

Tillich, Paul, 167

Time, 22, 46, 48, 145, 217, 238; opposes calls for testing halt, 19; on radiation hazards, 34, 38, 39, 80, 122-23; on testing and national security, 40-41; criticizes Adlai Stevenson's test ban proposal, 72, 96; on Sputnik, 169; criticizes Soviet test suspension, 204; cites communist front activities of SANE leaders, 204; predicts no further tests during Eisenhower's presidency, 303

Truman, Harry S, 10, 16; approves development of H-bomb, 15; opposes Adlai Stevenson's test ban proposal, 90; defends testing on national security grounds, 140-41; advocates underground testing resumption, 290

Tsarapkin, Semyon, 245, 296, 301, 315; appointed to Soviet delegation at Geneva test ban negotiations, 217,

236; on inspection issue, 243-44; on underground test detection problem, 251, 282, 292, 299; considers atmospheric test ban proposal, 257; criticizes U.S. test ban proposals, 298, 316

Tsutsui, Hisakichi, 4

Twining, Nathan, 177, 204, 228, 295

U-2 incident, 311-14

"U-bomb." *See* Fission-fusion-fission bomb

Ulam, Stanislaus, 15

United Nations, 174, 194, 197, 203; debates reglutions criticizing U.S. tests, 27, 28, 75; and study of radiation hazards, 63-64, 164-65, 221, 222-23, 224-25; and test ban resolutions, 113, 114, 234-35, 287; and disarmament, 113, 114, 143, 153, 156, 287; invited to send observers to U.S. tests, 159; supervision of atmospheric tests proposed, 193; urges France to cancel nuclear test, 288

U.S. News and World Report: on fallout hazards, 43-44, 80; analyzes Linus Pauling's test ban petitions, 127-28; calls test ban proposals "Communist-inspired," 141; on "clean bomb" concept, 151; criticizes Soviet test suspension, 204; contends test ban would serve Soviet aims, 260; fears Russia will develop neutron bomb first, 306

Urey, Harold, 308

Van Zandt, James, 7

Visscher, Maurice, 195

Von Neumann, John, 45

Waddington, C. H., 51, 52

Wadsworth, James, 178, 299, 311; opposes Soviet and Indian test ban resolutions, 64; on testing hazards, 69-70; on testing and national security, 164; and Geneva test ban negotiations, 235, 236, 251, 296, 311, 315; and inspection issue, 243, 298; and underground test detection problem, 245, 282, 292; opposes ending formal test moratorium, 295

Walters, Francis, 141, 205

Warren, Shields, 65, 78, 222; on radiation hazards, 52; on testing and national security, 105, 136; on radiation threshold issue, 134-35

Washington Post, 50, 138

Weaver, Warren, 78, 116

Westergaard, Mogens, 54

West Germany, 124-25

Wexler, Harry, 45

White, E. B., 35, 104

White, Thomas D., 248-49

Wiig, John, 214, 215

Wiley, Alexander, 191-92, 249

Wilson, Charles E. (General Electric chairman), 165, 167

Wilson, Charles E. (Secretary of Defense), 8, 97, 172; on fallout hazards, 140; on Sputnik, 170

Wolfe, Hugh, 194

Women's International League for Peace and Freedom, 74, 77, 160

Zorin, Valerin, 143, 146, 153, 234